TWENTIETH-CENTURY
ROOTS OF
RHETORICAL STUDIES

TWENTIETH-CENTURY ROOTS OF RHETORICAL STUDIES

Edited by Jim A. Kuypers
and Andrew King

Westport, Connecticut
London

Library of Congress Cataloging-in-Publication Data

Twentieth-century roots of rhetorical studies / edited by Jim A. Kuypers and Andrew King.
    p. cm.
    Includes bibliographical references and index.
    ISBN 0–275–96420–5 (alk. paper)
    1. Rhetoric. 2. Oral communication. I. Kuypers, Jim A. II. King, Andrew, 1947–
PN4121.T94   2001
  808—dc21   00–058018

British Library Cataloguing in Publication Data is available.

Library of Congress Catalog Card Number: 00–058018
ISBN: 0–275–96420–5

First published in 2001

Praeger Publishers, 88 Post Road West, Westport, CT 06881
An imprint of Greenwood Publishing Group, Inc.
www.praeger.com

Printed in the United States of America

The paper used in this book complies with the
Permanent Paper Standard issued by the National
Information Standards Organization (Z39.48–1984).

10 9 8 7 6 5 4 3 2

To the Founders and the Builders

Contents

Introduction: Our Roots Are Strong and Deep

ANDREW KING AND JIM A. KUYPERS

Misunderstanding of the term "rhetoric" is common among the American public, yet our communication discipline graduated 689,917 students with bachelor degrees, 67,099 students with master's degrees, and 4,126 students with Ph.D. degrees in the years between 1973 and 1992.[1] If one were to add the other eight decades of the twentieth century, the total could well reach 2 million bachelor degrees, perhaps 200,000 M.A. degrees, and more than 10,000 doctoral degrees. Many of these students move into journalism, government, business, publishing, and politics, as well as the bustling academy. Given these huge numbers of enlightened communicators, one might expect that rhetoric would become an honored disciplinary and professional term. Why it is not an honored term remains mysterious. Despite our professed best efforts the derogatory definition of rhetoric as insincere words and inflated style remains the predominant usage both inside and beyond the academy. Moreover, even in communication classrooms students often exhibit a sketchy knowledge of the discipline. Few undergraduates can name more than a handful of the major figures of our discipline's history. Too often our survey courses teach Aristotle and Bacon, Burke and Baudrillard but ignore our own founders. Professors themselves propagate an incomplete and inaccurate picture of our discipline.

UNTANGLING THE ROOTS OF OUR PAST PRACTICES

Goaded by this confusion, we offer this book as yet another attempt to set the record straight about the theory and practice of rhetoric. We offer a collection of chapters, each of which is dedicated to assessing the work of a twentieth-century rhetorical scholar. Our mission is to convey each scholar's particular understanding of rhetorical studies. We do not attempt an historical or biblio-graphic journey through each scholar's life. Every chapter, rather, attempts a distillation of a particular scholar's life work. The communication discipline often features the work of others whose background and training have little to do with our discipline; in what some may well consider a radical turn, we intend to acclaim the work of our own thinkers. In this book we honor and explore the individual visions of eleven rhetorical scholars. In so doing, we hope to expand our disciplinary understanding of the term "rhetoric" and to simultane-ously share with our readers the rich complexity of our early discipline's un-derstanding of the nature of rhetoric. In this manner we also hope to accomplish several objectives.

To Dispel a Myth

Our first objective is to dispel the myth that the discipline of speech com-munication was spawned from a monolithic center, a method unhappily named neo-Aristotelianism. Edwin Black's *Rhetorical Criticism: A Study in Method* is often cited as a definitive proof for the monolithic view, and this book's chapter on Black neatly sums this orthodox point of view. His book is regularly used to justify the departure from so-called confining neo-Aristotelian standards. It is well known that Black attacked, at times scathingly, the tradition of rhetorical scholarship prior to 1965. He believed that "neo-Aristotelians ignore the impact of the discourse on rhetorical conventions, its capacity of disposing an audience to expect certain ways of arguing and certain kinds of justifications in later discourses that they encounter, even on different subjects."[2] As Thomas Benson has written: "For many younger academics, suspicious that neo-Aristotelian crit-icism had become ideologically conservative, Black's book took on a force he had perhaps not intended it to have."[3] It is unfortunate, however, that so many others since Black have continued to overstate the case. Take, for instance, these lines penned by Martin Medhurst, who, writing of the Brigance volumes of *A History and Criticism of American Public Address*, stated:

[V]irtually no progress in critical methodology had been made from the publication of Wichelns's essay in 1925. Brigance admits as much in his preface when, concerning critical methodology, he notes: "Some prefer the pure Aristotelian pattern. Some prefer their Aristotelianism diluted. Others abjure it altogether." However, even a casual reading reveals that Aristotelianism or neo-Aristotelianism dominates both volumes. Worse yet, it is a bastardized form of Aristotelianism that Aristotle, himself, probably would not recognize. In general the contributors reduced Aristotle's Rhetoric to commentary on the three types of oratory (deliberative, forensic, and epideictic), the five canons of rhetoric (invention, disposition, style, memory, and delivery) and the three modes of proof (ethos, pathos, and logos), with some historical background on speech training and preparation added for good measure.[4]

We feel that if Medhurst, along with scores of others, engaged in more than "a casual reading," he would discover that a close reading of the Brigance volumes yields a different conclusion. Less than half are orthodox neo-Aristotelian; several are rather daring. Given this reality, the Brigance quotation chosen by Medhurst actually belies his assertion.

The words of Hoyt Hopewell Hudson provide a cautionary warning to Black, Medhurst, and others who decry the critical work of an earlier day: "Probably we ever protest too much about the elocutionists and this over-emphatic protest may be partly due to a bad conscience caused by our never having taken the trouble to examine their system to see what was in it."[5] We may easily substitute "neo-Aristotelians" for "elocutionists" without doing damage to Hudson's intent, for, as in our day, when simplistic attacks on neo-Aristotelianism go unchallenged, simplistic attacks on the elocutionists abounded in Hudson's day. The problem with Black's charges is that they were so utterly commonplace. Similar accusations were being made by others throughout the humanities and social sciences during the decade of the 1960s. Viewing the enterprise as a whole, Black's indictment seems more like a cultural twitch than the outrage of a single, intellectually awakened scholar. It was an historical moment when attacks upon established procedures became the soup dujour. In one angry book, Black cut us off from our past and made us ashamed of our progenitors.

Reclaim Our Past

Our second objective is to help reclaim a usable past. The disciplinary criticism of the past three decades, though often well intended, has turned our founders to stone. It has been asserted that many of our early critics were elitists, victims of a Great Books education, and that their objects of study were over-produced literary speeches created by Protestant males who were predominantly Anglo-Saxon and North European in background. It has been charged that most early critics were united in their practice of a narrow and highly elaborated critical method; furthermore, it is said that these critics shared a narrow conception of text, culture, social order, economics, politics, and scholarship. When our disciplinary founders were not being abused collectively, individual scholars were exhumed and beaten across the soles of their bare feet with the rattan whips of postmodern theory. To ensure future identification, they were branded on the tongue with a Gothic letter "M" for modernist. In a reversal of oppressor and oppressed, the fathers were silenced. Many of their students of the second and third—nay, even to the fourth—generation feared the wrath of the stridently vocal, yet new, radical minority who, like Cacús, sought to take the heads of the elders as trophies. This must cease. We cannot also devour our young through a caricature of the past.

This book provides in-depth examination of some of the early scholars. We think that any fair-minded reader will conclude that our founders are not the stone golems that they have been made out to be. Rather, they are unique, many-sided people, each with a special angle of vision.

Setting the Record Straight

Our third objective is to set the record straight. Most of the writers in this volume were not narrow but pluralistic, not provincial but cosmopolitan, not methodologically impoverished but inventive and subtle. They were broadly educated with catholic views of life and the world. Finally, they were remarkably free of the brittle jargon that settled upon us in the late decades of the last century. Moreover, if one delves deeply into the beginnings of the discipline, one finds ample evidence of a multiplicity of views on how good criticism is performed. For an extended example, one need go no further than the much maligned 1943 Brigance editions of *A History and Criticism of American Public Address*. These volumes represent a wide array of scholarly platforms upon which to engage in criticism. Although Brigance stated early in his introduction to the volumes that the primary judgments used by the authors were underpinned by "effect" and "influence," he also stated quite clearly that the various authors did "not follow one standard of critique." When one engages in a close, as opposed to casual, reading, one finds Brigance's assertion validated by the scope and variety of the individual essays. Whereas Orville Hitchcock's "Jonathan Edwards" most certainly represents neo-Aristotelian criticism in full cry, one also finds that the other authors do not readily follow Hitchcock's prescription for success. One need go no further than Wichelns's "Ralph Waldo Emerson" essay to find that he who is described as the progenitor of neo-Aristotelianism by no means follows a rigid neo-Aristotelian pattern. So it is with the majority of the authors. Although this may be surprising to some, it may be said that only 40 percent of the essays even follow loosely the formula described by Black.[6]

Neo-Aristotelianism was one method among several. From the earliest days our journals contained varied suggestions for engaging in the study of rhetoric. The collected works of Hoyt Hopewell Hudson and James A. Winans come to mind, as does the work of Carroll C. Arnold and Robert Gray Gunderson. Also consider Brigance's 1935 book, *Jeremiah Sullivan Black: A Defender of the Constitution and the Ten Commandments*. In 1936 Bower Aly published the "Scientist's Debt to Rhetoric." This work opened another path for the discipline to pursue and may well have presaged what is currently thought of as the rhetoric of science. Also in 1936 Ross Scanlan published "Rhetoric and Drama." In 1943 he published the "History of American Public Address as a Research Field," in which he listed numerous areas of analysis other than the single orator and which would necessitate a means of analysis other than neo-Aristotelianism. In 1944 Loren Reid published "The Perils of Rhetorical Criticism," in which he clearly stated, "Aristotelian rhetoric cannot be made to cover every aspect of all types of speaking. Some modern treatises are more helpful. . . . As these developments lead the critic away from Aristotle at many points, it is folly to think that the Rhetoric is the only book on the shelf."[7] Alternatives to the predominant method were widely practiced. The tyranny of "effect" was not as absolute as Black and his followers have made it seem.

Black was certainly hyperbolic in asserting—and others take their case too far by insisting—that those following the neo-Aristotelian pilot believed effects to be only "immediate effects." As seen in the Hochmuth and Hudson chapters, effects were not limited to those upon the immediate audience but rather involved past, present, and future generations and orators as well. Indeed, Hochmuth was well aware of the inherited nature of rhetoric. She believed that manifested perfection "in any age is a response to ideals insistently proclaimed, recalled, or restated." This is a rather blatant reminder that what we study now as discourse has its roots in past discourse. Effect, then, is much larger than just immediate effects; it is rather the impact of past discursive practices up to the present day. By "cherry picking" his examples, Black grossly mischaracterized the practice of his time. He largely ignored the methodological innovation of four decades.

We are inclined to believe it unfortunate that so many students of rhetoric today uncritically accept the folklore of neo-Aristotelianism birthed by Black, who stated that neo-Aristotelian criticism comprehends "rhetorical discourse as tactically designed to achieve certain results with a specific audience on a specific occasion."[8] Black and later critics of neo-Aristotelianism charged neo-Aristotelian critics with the crime of focusing too heavily on intended persuasive effects upon the immediate audience and following too closely the rhetorical grammar set out in Aristotle's *Rhetoric*. In the words of Black, "the evaluation of rhetorical discourse in terms of its effects on its immediate audience" was too heavily emphasized by those employing this method.[9] The text preceding this Black assertion is interesting, especially in light of the words of Medhurst that were quoted earlier (in block form), for Black stated: "The primary and identifying ideas of neo-Aristotelianism that we can find recurring in the critical essays of this school are the classification of rhetorical discourses into forensic, deliberative, and epideictic; the classification of 'proofs' or 'means of persuasion' into logical, apathetic, and ethical; the assessment of discourse in the categories of invention, arrangement, delivery, and style; and the evaluation of rhetorical discourse in terms of its effects on its immediate audience."[10] Medhurst's muse may well be Echo, who most certainly read Black's book with admiration in her eyes. When one looks at the citations used by Black in his book, it seems that he and, by extension, many of those who follow him looked primarily at the first volume of A *History and Criticism of American Public Address* when making their assessment. Black and followers seem also to forget that the 1943 volumes were an attempt to build a rhetorical bank of sorts: a history of significant practitioners. Also, the product reflected the thinking of the late 1930s. Certainly, by the time Black's book came out, neo-Aristotelianism had been expanded beyond his formalistic characterization of it.

Some evidence of this change lies within the covers of the book that you now hold in your hands. The chapter on Everett Lee Hunt most certainly belies the assertions that those practicing rhetorical criticism before Black's book were theoretically retarded in their range of thought. We urge you to read what Hudson was writing and to look closely at Arnold, Braden, Gunderson, or Nichols' conception of rhetoric. Moreover, the second volume of the Brigance volumes is hardly an example of orthodoxy. Wilbur Samuel Howell and Hoyt Hopewell Hudson's essay retails a collage of various perspectives, with neo-Aristotelianism playing only a minor role.

Throughout the 1950s and the early 1960s the methodological possibilities were gradually being expanded; today the complexity of the work of these scholars seems surprising in a day when rhetoric is too often reduced by cultural critics to discourses of domination. At mid-decade Black rode on the winds of our social discontent, and the entire corpus of scholarly work prior to 1965 was dismissed as anachronistic and wrongheaded. Furthermore, it is said that Black's attack created a void partially filled by Kenneth Burke. But other writers embraced the assault with a whoop of delight, riding out of the foothills to shoot the corpse long after neo-Aristotelianism was dead. In some cases these writers were long on diatribe and short on evidence. In others a germ of truth became the basis for vituperative overstatement. Most of our founders were emphatically people of their own time, not seers or gifted revolutionaries. Ewbank and others cannot be blamed for not being superior to their own era. They are what they are. So are the scholars of the 1990s who pride themselves on being so eloquently superior in their own era. They, too, will be judged by revisionists. These post-1965 scholars are now our only surviving tradition. Will they, too, be rushed to the guillotine by their own children in another great twitch of the societal pendulum? We hope not, and with that hope we highlight the work of three: Lloyd Bitzer, Ed Black, and Ernest Bormann, all of whom we believe to be much misunderstood, but all for very different reasons made clear in their respective chapters.

RECONSTITUTION THROUGH THE STUDY OF OUR ROOTS

It is with a reconstitutive purpose that we offer this present volume. Our broad purpose, then, is to reeducate our discipline concerning the development of our understanding of the term "rhetoric" as we move into the twenty-first century. In setting the record straight, we hope to dispel the current myth of a suffocating and all-embracing neo-Aristotelianism and thereby reclaim a usable and honorable past for our discipline. We believe that the chapters in the book will help to do this. Some of the chapters in this book treat authors who penned essays contained in the watershed Brigance volumes and others who predate them. In addition, this book includes critics whose strongest contributions came after the publication of the Brigance volumes. The work of the earliest scholars included in this book involved the creation of a discipline and the genesis of twentieth-century disciplinary knowledge; later scholars built upon these foundations and advanced the scope and influence of our discipline. In tracing the great and varied influences upon our roots, we proudly highlight the contributions of four scholars from the early part of the century: Everett Lee Hunt, Henry Lee Ewbank, Sr., Hoyt Hopewell Hudson, and Wilbur Samuel Howell. Four are from the middle part: Marie Hochmuth Nichols, Waldo Braden, Carroll C. Arnold, and Robert Gray Gunderson. Three fall into the last third of the century: Ernest G. Bormann, Edwin Black, and Lloyd F. Bitzer.

Who is included and why? Some may ask, Where is Brigance? Where is Bower Aly? Others may well lament the omission of Ernest Wrage, Leland Griffen, Barnett Baskerville, Wayland Maxfield Parrish, Loren Reid, or Donald Cross Bryant. What of Herbert Wichelns and James A. Winans? In any project decisions must be made. We would like to stress that as a discipline we are fortunate, indeed, to have so many estimable scholars from whom to choose. To include all of our finest scholars would necessitate a multiple-volume effort. Decisions had to be made, and we had several guiding principles when making ours. We wanted a primary focus on those scholars interested in rhetorical studies; thus, we did not include scholars whose primary interest was speech science, for example, James O'Neill, Charles Henry Woolbert, V. E. Simrell, or William E. Utterback. We also focused on those whose contributions have been overlooked or pushed to the side for more continental or Francophallic thinkers. For example, Bryant, Winans, and Wichelns are well known today, with the later two even being honored with a National Communication Association award in their honor. Concerning the first two time periods that we cover, we desired to highlight scholars whose work belies the stereotype of neo-Aristotelianism imposed today upon them. Finally, we considered who would be of interest to our readers as well as to our contributing authors.

Another important reason for this project is that there is a paucity of information about the founders of the communication discipline. Although there exists a great deal of commentary on the effect that the work of critics from other fields has had upon communication scholars, there are but scant offerings that detail the priceless contributions of the early speech scholars. This book corrects that deficiency. During the earliest years of our discipline the vast majority of our scholars were concerned with pedagogy, not research or criticism. The focus was on the pedagogy of public speaking, oral interpretation, argumentation, and debate, to name a few. Recall that teaching, not research, was the primary mission of universities until the middle of this century. The focus was on students and the locale. Early models were classics and literature; in the mid-1930s the shift was to history; however, some, Hudson and Hunt, for example, planted seed, employing multiple perspectives to illustrate a unifying idea. These genesic contributions began their growth into a sustained interest in criticism and theory by the late 1930s. Not at all bad considering that the discipline was establishing a history and trying to discover whence it came and was to go. Nevertheless, more than cursory study of these early roots is needed.

Perhaps other barriers keep us from fully appreciating the work of the scholars contained in this book and, by extension, the work of the scholars whom we could have included but did not. This conventional wisdom affirms that five changes separate the first three quarters of the twentieth century from the last quarter: (1) different norms of productivity; (2) the relevance issue; (3) the politicizing of scholarship; (4) new norms of discourse from the media and the street; and (5) epistemological relativism. While these changes are real, we believe that they involve issues that were foreshadowed in our early scholarship. The common belief about each of these changes will be detailed briefly.

Norms of Productivity

The great "author" in *Confederacy of Dunces* executed his master works with a number 2 pencil on a Big Chief tablet. The writing tools possessed by the scholars in this volume were hardly more formidable. They wrote with pencils, ballpoint pens, and huge, clunky cast-iron, annual typewriters. In a spoofing mood, the late Wilbur Samuel Howell told a gathering at the annual convention of the Eastern Communication Association in 1980, held in honor of Everett Lee Hunt, that he (Howell) had produced his books with a quill pen using soot and lampblack on foolscap. Those who were still working in the 1970s experienced the dying days of the academic steam age. They began each morning by switching on massive IBM electric typewriters that took fully twelve minutes to warm up. But at the beginning of the 1980s the new, one-eyed god arrived, an electronic cyclops that soon dominated every desk and cubicle. The "younger" scholars of this book embraced the new computers eagerly, and even now writers such as Bormann and Black are still doing computer-assisted research, hewing from the stubborn textual granite further works to justify their intellectual lives. But even in the case of younger titans such as Bormann and Black, it is well worth noting that these new machines did not arrive until their reputations had been long established.

Those who would diminish the contribution of early writers say that they worked with different norms of creativity. Even if this is true, it is only part of the story. Recently, at the retirement of one of our field's greatest scholars (a person whose work does not appear in this volume) one of his young eagles averred: "The master has a terrific mind but I have to say that he would never have made *it* today with that slender output. Of course they expected less publishing in the old days. We have raised the bar and today we have new norms of productivity." This new lament is the obverse of the oldster's wail that "the younger generation is weak and soft. By God, I delivered milk cans on days when the snow was up over the mule's shoulders." Younger scholars forget that as late as 1970 there was no release "research time" in most major institutions outside of the so-called hard sciences. Professors often taught four courses a semester with three different preparations and still served on as many committees as they do at present. Not until the mid-1970s did one hear distinguished professors ask that they be insulated from undergraduates. Until 1990, at least two Big Ten universities required that full professors teach at least one basic course every two years to keep them in contact with the undergraduate mind.

There were many fewer research outlets in those decades when ink, chemical, and glue dominated the journal publishing process. We had few journals before 1970, and we had not yet cracked the scholarly book market. Again, Howell claimed that the very act of writing was different before 1975. He believed that there was more "fore-writing." Writers spent time staring at blank sheets while they ruminated, and as a result the printed words were produced with a different cadence and resonance. In this sense, then, earlier texts are more formal and literary but less jargon-bound than much of our present research. Our predecessors were usually humbler in their conclusions, less obsessed with Grand Theory, and more alive to the nuances of individual texts. Finally, we should acknowledge that they were strongly attached to rather elite norms of civic discourse; their work was permeated by a genteel quality, even at the largest northern schools. Their smaller voices have posed problems for those of us who revere them and continue to teach their work. Fewer of the founders knew how to "merchandise" themselves beyond the boundaries of their institutions than we do now. Our graduate students find their work lacking in irony, innocent of the role of coercion, and all too often theory-blind.

The Relevance Issue

We live in the age of chasm. The older humanism and individualism represented by so many of our early scholars are wounded, but not dead. Humanism lingers old and holy and nearly paralytic, but like "Banquo's Ghost it will not down." Yet postmodernism's Pyrrhic victories have only deepened our sense of spiritual isolation from our heritage. No discipline can thrive that does not have what J. D. Plumb named "a useable past," but even some among us who desire assimilation of the old and the new have begun to fear that we are shackled to a corpse. The old world will not die, and the new world is not yet born.

All this creates a special burden for those of us who want to keep the tradition of the great foundational scholars alive. What do we say when our young student eagles ask us: "What do these ancients and graybeards have to teach us? Why should we be so mindful of their work?" Behind this salvo is more than the traditional haste of the young to devour the old and occupy their high seats in the citadel. It is more akin to the sort of feeling that Marie Hochmuth Nichols identified in the early 1970s: we all suffer from a deep fear of being labeled irrelevant.

The irrelevance of classical studies has been the spectre haunting American universities since the 1850s, when the pitched battles with modern languages and the sciences (a little later) began for curricular dominance. The classics suffered defeat and displacement. To read Bromley Smith or James Winans is to have dialogue with them, and one of our brightest recent students at Lousiana State University wryly compared his experience with that of a philosopher transported back in time to discuss religious belief with Carlyle or civic politics with St. Augustine. "Most of what they would say would sound obvious or pompous or just plain irrelevant," said the student in a tone almost devoid of affect. Never mind that these students have barely skimmed the masters. Their assumption is based on a fixed idea of our age. A door has been closed. We have crossed the final frontiers of the secular society, and now many fear that there is no going back.

The Frontier of Raised Consciousness

Long ago Sartre foretold that this hypersensitivity was to be our fate. Not only would intellectuals and ruling elites suffer from too much reflection, but eventually all people would suffer the nausea and vertigo of heightened self-consciousness. In 1983 Philip Wander exposed the ideological perspective of our founding scholars. The tether has been cut, the leases and covenants are broken, the house is in ruins, and the way ahead is nothing but stonecrop and muck. Our doctoral students tell us that the world of the founding critics is dead—as distant from us intellectually as Paracelsus, as far from the heart as the Tuscan villages of St. Frances. Thus, the hyperbole of the young. Of course, it is really a very old charge. Ninety years ago Julian Benda had already indicted intellectuals for gravitating to power. Although a few enlightened ones challenged the accuracy of Wander's charges, many of us beat our breasts, shouting, "Mea mega culpa!" thus echoing the very cry we had used to receive uncritically Black's work. Finally, Herman Cohen's slanted history of "the old days" struck the few remaining traditionalists a physical blow. His indictment lies heavily upon our will.[11]

But if these works and others have torn the scales from our eyes, they have had other effects as well. In exposing our Great Critics, the ideologies have carried out their own ideological mission. Now everyone is marginalized. We are all "out in the cold," as it were. A generation of hard chargers who professed to hate hierarchy has won the day but in so winning has almost lost the means to write sensibly and at length on any subject. In the new hierarchy, relativism, timidity, and antifoundationalism have tied our tongues.

The New Norms of Street and Media Rhetoric

During the 1960s the body rhetoric of the streets eclipsed the sober citizen rhetoric that our early textbook writers idolized. The polite institutional rhetoric that had been the gold standard of rhetorical discourse suffered a "legitimation crisis" from which it never fully recovered. Much of our semiofficial identification with the margin comes from the era. At some point during the late 1960s that "group production," the mediated text, became our primary research focus. The individual speaking in real time seems quaint, even a little shameful to some. When we heard of the late Professor Hunt telling of his youthful excitement during a speech given by William Jennings Bryan in the dusty heat of a South Dakota day, we felt as great a separation as we would have felt had someone told us about Alexander addressing his troops in Nether Persia.[12] Truly, the virtual and the ersatz have taken on a reality that original events have lost.

The Epistemic Frontier

In 1976 Robert L. Scott extended Vico's notion of the loom of rhetoric: rhetoric as a producer of knowledge. Into the yawning void of relativism crept the drive for personal and social power. Our present obsession with power is one of the unintended consequences of Scott's work, for he associated Truth claims with tyranny and certainty with statism. So where are we? Other academic disciplines have crossed the same frontiers. Other disciplines have rejected their patrimony. Other disciplines have suffered a sea change in consciousness. Other disciplines have realized that a denial of continuity and an exaggeration of change have been better for careerism rather than disciplinary health.

CONCLUSION

We believe that the life and work of our own foundational scholars can serve as a corrective for this situation. We believe that discerning readers will discover losses as well as gains. If these earlier writers seem methodologically or ideologically more innocent, they are generally better stylists. Their work may lack anger and a special sense of mission, but it has a dawn quality and a feeling of scholarly community that we have lost. These writers felt that they were building something; they were members of the guild, while today we work as lonely virtuosi, struggling to find our own voices.

Like the myth of our domination by a single school of criticism, much of our belief about the founders is grossly oversimplified or is crudely false. As John Tapia has pointed out, Wilbur Samuel Howell was an astute theorist of rhetorical power. He merely located it in less fashionable places. To read the chapters contained in this book about the actual lives and careers of the founders is a necessary corrective to those who believe the world began in the middle of the 1960s. Many so-called frontier crossings were attempted earlier, and many "new" concepts were discussed in a fashion that seems startlingly eloquent when honestly contrasted to the present moment. We believe with Richard A. Cherwitz and T. J. Darwin that "there is no real distinction between modernity and postmodernity" but that the supposed "tension between them may be enlightening."[13]

We urge you to read about some of the Great Critics of the century that has just passed away. These scholars built the foundation upon which our new temples rise. We must pay attention to that foundation for it is our launching pad and our point of departure. That is our fate. To cut our roots is to die.

NOTES

1. National Center for Education Statistics of the U.S. Department of Education, *Digest of Education Statistics* (Washington, DC: U.S. Department of Education, 1994).

2. Edwin Black, *Rhetorical Criticism: A Study in Method* (Madison: University of Wisconsin Press, 1978), 35.

3. Thomas Benson, "The Study of American Rhetoric," *American Rhetoric: Context and Criticism*, Thomas Benson, ed. (Carbondale: Southern Illinois University Press, 1992), 5.

4. Martin J. Medhurst, *Landmark Essays in Public Address* (Davis, CA: Hermagoras Press, 1993), xxi.

5. Hoyt Hopewell Hudson, "The Tradition of Our Subject," *Quarterly Journal of Speech* 17.3 (1931): 326.

6. Black, 30.

7. Loren D. Reid, "The Perils of Rhetorical Criticism," *Quarterly Journal of Speech* 30 (1944): 421. Everett Lee Hunt's study of Matthew Arnold was an early example of anti-Aristotelianism. See *Historical Studies of Rhetoric and Rhetorician*, Raymond Howes, ed. (Ithaca, NY: Cornell University Press, 1965), 322–344.

8. Black, 33.

9. Ibid., 30.

10. Ibid.

11. Herman Cohen, *The History of Speech Communication: The Emergence of a Discipline, 1914–1945* (Annandale, VA: Speech Communication Association, 1994).

12. Everett Lee Hunt, private communication to Andrew King.

13. Richard A. Cherwitz and T. J. Darwin, "The Utility of Argument in a Postmodern World," *Argumentation* 9 (1995): 181–202.

1

Everett Lee Hunt and the Humanistic Spirit of Rhetoric

THEODORE OTTO WINDT, JR.

> The case for rhetoric as a humane study may be stated with deceptive simplicity. Rhetoric is the study of men persuading men to make free choices.[1]

During his long career as an active academic and later in retirement, Dean Everett Lee Hunt championed the cause of humanism in education. It was his persistent thesis whether applied in his early years to rhetoric or later to literature and to his stewardship as dean of men at Swarthmore College or in retirement as he thought about the places of education, religion, and rhetoric in contemporary society.

Teacher, writer, administrator, critic, counselor, rhetorician, educational philosopher, horseman, mountain climber, singer of hymns and Irish songs—in all these activities a self-styled "amateur," Everett Lee Hunt belonged to no pattern, no academic stereotype. He fashioned his own matrix; it left an impression of an uncommon diversity upon those who knew him or read his works. Herbert Wichelns, his onetime colleague at Cornell University, described him accurately: "[T]he originality and subtlety of his insights did not lend themselves to systematic formulation . . . but his example of the true scholarly mind, inquiring, noting, combining, has put the present generation of graduate students and their teachers heavily in his debt."[2]

Everett continually insisted that he was neither a professional nor an expert, contrary to the usual ways in which academics prefer to describe themselves then and even more so now. He wrote more polemics than scholarly pieces. He loved debating ideas of culture, education, and politics. Early in his teaching

Everett Lee Hunt. Photo courtesy of the National Communication Association. Used with permission.

career he had read Bliss Perry's article "The Amateur Spirit." It had a lasting influence on him. Perry had divided his time between the academic and literary worlds and moved easily back and forth between the two, teaching at Williams, Princeton, and Harvard but also editing the *Atlantic Monthly* for ten years. Perry eschewed professionalism in academe and exalted the intellectual amateur who could roam over various fields of knowledge with no special claim to expertise other than his own inquiring and imaginative mind as a guide. The amateur "works for love, and not for money," he wrote, and cultivates an art or a study because "he is attached to it, not because it gives him a living, but because it ministers to his life."[3] Such a person, Perry believed, would not be constricted to any specific field of study but would feel equally at home in any intellectual activity. He concluded about this amateur: "The highest service of the educated man in our democratic society demands of him breadth of interest as well as depth of technical research. It requires unquenched ardor for the best things, spontaneous delight in the play of mind and character, a many-sided responsiveness that shall keep a man from hardening into a mere high geared machine. It is these qualities that perfect a liberal education and complete a man's usefulness to his generation. Taken by themselves, they fit him primarily for living, rather than for getting a living."[4] Reading these words early in his career made an indelible impression on Hunt. Henceforth, he would be that educated amateur and live his life in accordance with its ideals. Throughout his career he would persistently deny that he was a professional *anything* in preference for calling himself an amateur, who is usually defined as "one who follows a pursuit without proficiency or a professional purpose." It can hardly be said that Everett lacked proficiency in rhetoric or literature, but it might be said that he pursued his teaching of rhetoric and literature with a personal, rather than a professional, purpose. But he also meant, as he said on various private occasions, that he was an amateur in its older meaning—as a "lover" (from the Latin *amator*), a lover of debate, of language, of ideas, of all things human and interesting. In his pursuit of what interested him, he produced only a few pieces of what we might call modern scholarship. Yet, his "example of the true scholarly mind," as evidenced in his polemical essays as well as in his guidance of students, colleagues, and others who came in contact with him, marked Everett Hunt as one of the premier figures in rhetorical education from the founding of the National Association of Academic Teachers of Public Speaking to his death in 1983.

Everett Lee Hunt was born October 14, 1890, in Colfax, Iowa, to Charles Reeve Hunt, a peripatetic Presbyterian minister and sometime schoolmaster, and his wife, Anna Belle. Then as now, ministers move from call to call, and the Hunts were different only in the many times that they moved. Hunt could remember at least ten different moves, ranging as far south as Deming, New Mexico, and as far north as the small hamlets of South Dakota. The Christian home and church were centers of Everett's life. The family conducted daily Bible readings and prayers. These instilled in him religious habits of thought, especially that habit of seeing life as whole and purposeful. In one of his early essays he lamented that students often did not realize that "we live in a universe instead of a multiverse."[5] The rugged life on the harsh prairies was hard and left a lasting impression on him. Through much of his life he dressed in clothes that emphasized his western heritage.

In 1909 Everett entered Huron College, which the Presbyterians had founded in 1883 but which is now defunct. The college had not yet adopted the curriculum of more advanced, eastern schools and had not yet instituted the electives system. The classics in which Hunt majored and Christian ideals constituted the core of a liberal education. Hunt spent five years at Huron (he missed a year because of illness associated with his clubfeet) and was a whirlwind of activity: running the college bookstore, serving as junior class president, editing the college newspaper in his senior year, and debating. For several professors who stopped at his father's house, he learned about the tradition in public speaking at Hamilton College and about Dr. Henry Mandeville's belief in its power.[6] In college he became a fierce debater.[7]

Upon graduation in 1913 he was appointed instructor in Latin, oratory, and debate at Huron, a position for which, he said later, he had little technical preparation:

I majored in Greek and Latin because my father had done so in his preparation for the ministry, but I had not the least expectation that it was a specialized training for a career. My real enthusiasm was for debating, and especially debating both sides of a question. This did lead to my appointment as an instructor with a minimum of anything like technical training. I rejoiced in the freedom to argue about almost anything that interested me, especially if it had a touch of philosophy about it. I was enthusiastic about the "field" I had entered, although it did not really occur to me to call it a field.[8]

To compensate, Hunt went to Chicago in the summer of 1913 to take private lessons in oral reading and speaking from A. E. Phillips, whose book, *Effective Speaking*, was described as a "logical, practical, beautifully clear theory of speech composition."[9] After assuming his first academic position, Hunt went about changing the ways in which public speaking was taught at Huron to suit his own preferences and interest. His background in the classics provided him with a very different model of what public speaking ought to be, one thoroughly grounded in rhetoric rather than elocution. His interest in current affairs, undoubtedly motivated by his experience as a college debater, gave substance to his courses. In his 1915 "Teacher's Report" he explained his emphasis on contemporary themes and issues because "very few courses in the college curriculum do creative work upon present day themes."[10] The most important change that he initiated was to emphasize substance over form. Hunt later stated that he thought it of greater importance "to make an undergraduate want to make a speech than to tell him how to make it and that the acquiring of any new intellectual interest is of equal importance with improvement in formal argumentation."[11] These changes foreshadowed the arguments that Hunt would soon make in pressing for the primacy of substance over form and his insistence that teachers of public speaking concentrate on current issues.

THE SCIENCE VERSUS HUMANISM CONTROVERSY

In 1914 a small group of teachers of public speaking broke away from English departments and formed the National Association of Academic Teachers of Public Speaking, now called the National Communication Association. These teachers created the association to signal their separation from departments of English and from the dominance of elocution in teaching public speaking. To give themselves a distinct professional identity, they turned to major questions about what directions teaching and research in public speaking ought to take, about how their new academic departments ought to be organized, about the goals for the association and its members.

One of the most prominent issues involved research. To be accepted as a legitimate academic and scholarly association, members had to define and describe the kind of scholarly research that they intended to do. In the first issue of the new journal that they created, *The Quarterly Journal of Public Speaking* (now called *Quarterly Journal of Speech*) James Winans of Cornell University asserted that scientific research into various aspects of speaking was needed to establish public speaking as a respectable member of the academic community. He called for scientific studies that would advance knowledge in public speaking in a way comparable to the advances made in medicine and economics.[12] In the second article, "Research in Public Speaking," the Research Committee of the association maintained, "Some academic subjects have arisen as pure sciences and later been applied to the practical problems of life. Public Speaking has come by the other road, having been first a practical or semi-practical subject and then aspiring to become more like a pure science."[13] Research, the report concluded, would produce technically trained teachers for the profession. More important, the committee knew that it had to produce a body of scholarship to qualify in its eyes and in the eyes of others as a legitimate academic discipline. Little did it anticipate that Hunt would challenge the very bases of these recommendations.

Everett Lee Hunt—a twenty-five-year-old instructor at an obscure college in South Dakota with only two years' teaching experience under his belt, a young man with only a B.A. degree in classics and a few private lessons in public speaking—raised his voice in opposition. His article "The Scientific Spirit in Public Speaking" set off a vigorous controversy with the new profession when it was published in the second issue of the new journal.

Hunt wrote that public speaking is more akin to literature than physics. Thus, it should not be studied as a technical, specialized science. He did not object, he said from his lofty perch in Huron, to research that would dispel misconceptions about public speaking, but he feared that excessive specialization and scholasticism would minimize the human element in speaking and be "as fatal to

enthusiasm and inspiration in public speaking as they have been to broad and
sympathetic development in many of those [branches of learning] where they
now prevail."[14] He feared that technical research would become an end unto
itself and would eventually replace teaching and learning as the principal force
in academics. In voicing these fears, he struck a note that was to become his
theme for life: "May we never substitute imitation for originality. May we never
exalt learning above sincerity, academic recognition above service, or logic
above life."[15]

Hunt soon found himself engaged in a series of debates with leading members
of the association, among them Charles H. Woolbert, a prominent figure in the
movement to separate speech from English. In his article "The Organization of
Departments of Speech Sciences in Universities," Woolbert, who later received
his doctorate in psychology from Harvard, described the kinds of departments
that teachers of speech should create. Research and teaching in these departments should include phonology, techniques of expression, psychology of expression, application of laws of expression, the acting drama, extempore
speaking, argumentation and debate, persuasion, pedagogy of oral expression
and aesthetics of speaking.[16] The issue about the substance and direction of
departments of speech was joined when the July 1916 issue of the *Quarterly
Journal* published Hunt's attack on Woolbert's article and Woolbert's reply.

In "General Specialists" Hunt wrote that Woolbert's vision of the department
of speech sciences "gives rise to the conception that the technique of a speech
can be successfully abstracted from the subject matter and formalized; whereas
it is a truism that you cannot separate the style from the man."[17] He urged that
speaking not be placed in the laboratory. Techniques cannot be so easily separated from ideas. Instead of a scientific department Hunt advocated a department
of "general specialists":

The Public Speaking department is to serve as a clearing house of ideas. The instructor
should inspire in his students a vital interest in the affairs of the world, in politics,
sociology, economics, literature, and art. He must realize with Cicero that all the arts
which pertain to culture, have as it were, a common bond; and he should make his
students realize it. Too many students are graduating without the slightest realization of
the relationship of the various departments in which they have worked. They have no
vivid sense that we live in a universe instead of a multiverse. To the question, "Has't
any philosophy in thee?" they can only reply with a stare.[18]

Hunt called teachers of speech to return to the intellectual ideal of the nineteenth-
century college president who could occupy any chair in a college. He saw
departments of public speaking fulfilling the need for men and women of general
culture to bind together the fragments of knowledge that specialists create.

In his reply, which was commissioned by editor James O'Neill presumably
to erase Hunt's heresy, Woolbert remarked that he and Hunt shared no common
ground on these issues: "Mr. Hunt and I are of different epochs and countries.

He is a romantic golden age, I, of the common, ignoble now. He is from Greece, I am from Germany (!)—he probably by choice, I perforce. He cries out for the glory that was Greece and the grandeur that was Rome; I am surrounded by laboratories and card catalogues."[19]

Woolbert went on to describe Hunt as "a sort of lay pastor, an intellectual and spiritual knight errant, an educational court physician."[20] Such characteristics belong properly to college teachers where they are appreciated, but they are, Woolbert implied, inappropriate and impractical for university professors. Research and specialization are required in universities. Professors must have a distinct and clear field of knowledge and research. Thus, Woolbert maintained that speech should be studied as an academic discipline—a field whose content should be carefully detailed analysis, experimentation, identification, and description of effective speaking techniques.[21] "I stand for a search for the fact; the facts of how speaking is done; of what its various effects are under specified conditions; how these facts can be made into laws and principles," he wrote.[22] He believed that the only means for discovering these facts lay in scientifically conducted investigations and research.

The debate continued at the 1916 national convention in New York. Hunt entitled his address "Academic Public Speaking." His presentation was divided into two parts: (1) a defense of his ideas against the attack from Woolbert in "A Problem in Pragmatism" and (2) a brief exposition of what he taught in his courses at Huron College.[23] He began by stating: "Professor Woolbert . . . almost dealt a death blow to all my ambitions by declaring that I am not modern. I belong to the age of Greece and Rome, he says. It is a terrible thing not to be modern. It is almost the worst thing that could be said about a man. But I recall Bernard Shaw's remark about Ruskin. It was easy, he says, for Ruskin to declare that it is better to die than to do an unjust act, for dying is a very simple matter; but when it comes to determining what justice is, there is a difficulty."[24]

So, too, Hunt continued that it was easy to condemn a "man for not being modern, but to determine what it is to be modern, that is another matter."[25] Everett went on to repeat his arguments against specialization and to call for those who teach by example rather than precept. He concluded that "it seems to me to be greater to make an undergraduate want to make a speech than to tell him how to make it."[26]

His argument was not persuasive. Woolbert's rejoinder playfully predicted that in the future Hunt would achieve fame through research and experimentation.[27]

The debates between Woolbert and Hunt began to focus the disparate ideas that floated about at professional meetings regarding what it meant to be a professional in speech. Each in his own way defined public speaking within the context of American colleges and universities. After the break with English departments, Woolbert's concern (which was shared by most others in the association) was that speech be accepted as a separate and responsible academic profession. He knew that research provided the foundation for any academic discipline in a university, and he promoted research. He recognized that prestige was accorded scientific studies and encouraged scholars in speech to conduct scientific research. He saw specialization proliferating among other academic departments and urged that teachers of speech specialize. "I can only say that in an age of organization and specialization I am for specializing and organizing," he wrote.[28] It was a problem in pragmatism for Woolbert, who at age thirty-nine had taught at the University of Illinois and had experienced advanced graduate work at Harvard. He wanted to create professional speech departments that would educate professional scholars.

Hunt was cut from a much different cloth. He was in his mid-twenties, had only a B.A. degree from an obscure church college in the raw lands of South Dakota, had never taken a graduate course, and did not know much about graduate schools. Thus, he shared little of Woolbert's sense of urgency in developing public speaking as a technical department, nor was he overly concerned about creating a separate and distinct field of knowledge based on research. Undoubtedly, he was influenced by his (limited) experience as an undergraduate teacher. But he primarily was interested in questions other than those posed by Woolbert. What interested Hunt were the effects of specialization on knowledge and what service teachers of public speaking could perform in educating liberal students who would, in turn, be interested in service and ideas. He believed that the plain purpose of a liberal education was to prepare young men and women to assume their public responsibilities. Teaching techniques without real concern for ideas or ideals undermined this goal because it ignored the unity among ideas and the differences among students. Hunt wrote: "The kind of students we as teachers of speech want in our classrooms are not plodding scientists, effeminate aesthetes, or scholastic prodigies. We want men who are to be leaders of men, who will have an active share in all public affairs."[29]

The goals proposed by Hunt constituted a far higher calling for teachers in the new profession than the curriculum of mechanics and techniques. Public speaking courses, as Hunt viewed them, would necessarily draw heavily on information and ideas from other disciplines and would require speech teachers to be broadly read in a variety of areas other than the field of speech. Consequently, students and teachers would have to leap over the boundaries that Woolbert strove to place around speech. Specialization would not serve or be served.

But professionalism and specialization, as Woolbert correctly noted, were the emerging standards of the day in both academic and cultural life.[30] Hunt could devise an undergraduate curriculum but had little idea how a graduate curriculum might be developed that would satisfy the standards for a scholarly graduate department or the emerging academic profession. To Woolbert and other leaders of the national association, that was the most pressing issue facing them. But Hunt, always the gadfly, was too wary of regimented theories and too fond of debating ideas to be concerned with such matters. Furthermore, Hunt's slender experience at that time had been spent solely in a small, provincial, undergraduate college. Even more to the point, he did not realize the politics of establishing a new discipline within a university. Hunt's ideas might serve as an inspiration to individual teachers, but they would hardly persuade a hard-pressed dean to grant money and facilities for a new department.

Hunt had his sights on an even greater problem, one that transcended academic and professional concerns. He saw not only knowledge fragmenting but modern American life as well. The old order of the nineteenth century was passing away as a consequence of World War I, but a new order had not been created to replace it. Certainty had been lost, tradition ridiculed, and authority diminished (except when enforced by brute force). The problem with which Hunt was grappling was one that a number of other intellectuals were also addressing in different ways.[31]

Scientists proposed science as a method of dealing with this new world, but Hunt found that solution wanting when it came to confronting the daily problems of living and the practical problems of governing in a democratic society. In a world of science and specialization, Hunt would divide problems between those that scientists and experts could address and those that resided in the realm of probability. These latter problems would be his principle concerns. If belief could no longer be discovered in the nature of things and if authority no longer had power to compel belief, he would find in public persuasion, in rhetoric, the method for attempting to address and resolve such problems. In this new world of uncertainty and probability, he sought to create a modern conception of rhetoric as the humanistic instrument for grappling with the great problems of government and morality as well as the daily problems of living. Hunt's humanism was not a strictly rational humanism but a rhetorical one based on sympathetic appeals to all of a person's senses, not merely to the mind. Indeed, the final essay written while he was at Huron expressed this skepticism. In "An Adventure in Philosophy," written in response to separate attempts by Woolbert and Mary Yost to find a single theoretical unity in the profession, Everett retorted: "Yost proclaims that the real fundamentals are to be found in the field of sociology, and that distinctions not arising from the social situation are antiquated in oratory. And now Professor Woolbert from his psychological laboratory, announces that 'since mental processes can be described and explained (I have yet to learn of anything 'explained' by science) only in terms of psychology,' the solution of the difficulty is to be found in psychology alone."[32]

Hunt saw no such thing as fundamental or, at the very least, that "any claim that one branch of learning is to be final or 'fundamental' should be very carefully examined."[33] The central and controlling idea of this rambling essay was what was to become a distinctive mark of Everett's thinking: the direct questioning of any idea or theory that presumed to be fundamental, all-inclusive, or final. Life was problematic. Although Hunt had celebrated the unity of life, he was equally persistent in disclaiming that any substantive discipline or theory or idea could find or express that unity. Paradoxically, even as he pointed to anomalies and particulars, he also insisted that people go beyond them to seek the principles exemplified by those particulars, if only to see the competing principle about which people would argue. Thus, trying to pin down Everett Lee Hunt in the way in which other intellectuals or theorists can be cataloged or consigned to a specific school of thought is a fruitless and maddening task. He fashioned his own matrix based on his love of debating all sides of an issue.

THE CORNELL SCHOOL OF RHETORIC

When Everett Hunt left Huron College to join the faculty at Cornell University, he embarked on a new educational adventure. Only two years before, James A. Winans had persuaded the president of the university to separate public speaking from the English Department so as to form a department of its own. In the next few years the department would consolidate its position as a separate unit and develop a graduate program. For Hunt it meant joining a notable faculty that included Lane Cooper, Alexander M. Drummond, Herbert Wichelns, and Harry Caplan, soon to be joined by Hoyt Hudson and William Utterback—both from South Dakota and Huron College—who would do graduate work there. For Hunt this was an entirely new experience. To acquire the appropriate academic credentials necessary for a university instructor, Hunt ventured to the University of Chicago for the next four summers to do graduate work in philosophy, concluding with a thesis on Plato's dialectic.[34]

The 1920 Seminar in Classical Rhetoric

Alexander Drummond became chair of the Department of Public Speaking when Winans left for Dartmouth. Drummond wanted to build up graduate work in rhetoric. Prior to this time, only general subjects had been offered in seminars, usually taught by Winans. Of all the possible subjects that could have provided the focus for building up graduate courses in the department, classical rhetoric was chosen. So, he and Everett founded a seminar in classical rhetoric. Among the members of the seminar were Hunt, Drummond, Harry Caplan, Herbert Wichelns, and Hoyt Hudson. These were the "young turks" from Cornell, who, now free from Winans' leadership and his emphasis on the psychology of public speaking, would create a different form of leadership at Cornell and later throughout the profession.[35]

The seminar lasted the entire academic year. As Hudson recalled, Hunt and Drummond "took a few of us through Aristotle's *Rhetoric* (it is quite possible that we were the only group in any American university then giving attention to what is now a perennial best-seller), Cicero's *De Oratore*, and Quintilian's *Institutions*. The three works occupied most of the academic year, though somewhere early in it we also polished off Plato's *Phaedrus* and picked up something about Isocrates and the Sophists."[36] This was the first graduate seminar in classical rhetoric taught in a department of public speaking in the twentieth century and became a landmark in graduate education in rhetoric as well as a touchstone for publication by the small band of scholars at Cornell.

In actuality, Hunt was the driving force behind the seminar. It was his brain-child. Drummond was listed as teaching it because he was the only one on the faculty (Lane Cooper was in the English Department) with a doctorate. Hunt still had not completed his master's and therefore could not officially offer a graduate course. He chose the readings and made the assignments. Judging from his later long work on Plato, Aristotle, and the sophists, which covers much of the ground that was explored in the seminar, one can imagine the significant role that he played in directing it.

Each member of the seminar was thoroughly conversant with Greek. Caplan, of course, was a classics major. Wichelns had won a Greek prize in high school. Hunt and Hudson had read Greek with a clergyman instructor at Huron College. Drummond's role, as was his preference, was to ask questions to help clarify thinking or point people in new directions. (Hudson remarked: "There was Drummond, you see, asking questions, never knowing anything but showing an almost pathetic willingness to learn. He wasn't exactly dull, but he was stubborn as all get out. Somehow we couldn't let him down; we had to educate him.")[37] More important was the fact that this small band became excited about applying classical principles to a modern study of rhetoric and public speaking. They were not content to be philologists of classical rhetoric but sought, as Donald C. Bryant noted, to find the "relation of rhetoric to the modern world and for a definition of [the] function of rhetoric" in the twentieth century.[38] With such enthusiasm, little wonder that Hudson wrote of the seminar: "Things began to happen. We found that there were articles we wanted to write. We saw chances to apply classical dogmata in our dealings with the modern material. We suddenly discovered that swatting over old books, or swinking over long papers was fun."[39] And write they did.

Between the years 1920 and 1925, Cornellians were prolific in their contributions to the *Quarterly Journal of Speech*. The following are examples:

Hunt: "Plato on Rhetoric and Rhetoricians" (June 1920); "Dialectic: A Neglected Method of Argument" (June 1921); "Adding Substance to Form in Public Speaking Courses" (June 1922); "Knowledge and Skill" (February 1923); "The Teaching of Public Speaking in Schools of Theology" (November 1924).

Hudson: "Can We Modernize the Study of Invention?" (November 1921); "The Field of Rhetoric" (April 1923); "Rhetoric and Poetry" (April 1924).

Wichelns: "Research" (June 1923); "Our Hidden Aims" (November 1923); "Analysis and Synthesis in Argumentation" (June 1925).

Caplan: "The Latin Panegyrics of the Empire" (February 1924).

Drummond: "Graduate Work in Public Speaking" (April 1923).

If one adds to these the articles by other Cornellians (usually graduate students) such as William Utterback (two articles), Wayland Parrish, Raymond Howes, Robert Hannah, and Marvin Bauer, the impact was enormous. No other single school—college or university—could match this explosion of research and writing during this formative period. Their work culminated in the landmark book *Studies in Rhetoric and Public Speaking*, published in 1925.

Studies in Rhetoric and Public Speaking

By 1925 the little group at Cornell had achieved stature in the profession. They served on major committees and constituted a significant presence on the committee on public speaking for secondary schools that the national association had created. But a Festschrift to honor James Winans, who they believed was dying of cancer, marked the full flowering of the Cornell School of Rhetoric.

Studies in Rhetoric and Public Speaking in Honor of James Albert Winans by his pupils and colleagues was published in 1925 in a limited edition of 400 copies. The eleven essays—all original works—that made up the volume ranged from a long opening essay on classical rhetoric (Hunt), to a psychological study of argumentation (Utterback), from a theory of rhetorical criticism (Wichelns), to specific examinations of Bacon, De Quincey, and Emerson (Hannah, Hudson, and Theodore Stenberg, respectively), from a translation of a medieval tractate on preaching (Caplan), to two investigations of stuttering (Smiley Blanton and Margaret Blaton), from the rhythms of oratory (Parrish), to a study of phonetics and elocution (Lee Hultzen).

Hunt's "Plato and Aristotle on Rhetoric and Rhetoricians," the lead essay, was the most impressive and sustained piece of scholarship published in the first two decades of the profession. If it is not the definitive word on classical Greek rhetoric, it remains an indispensable study that any scholar who came to the same subject afterward had to acknowledge and master if he or she disagreed with Hunt. The long essay contained Hunt's sympathetic survey of the various sophists and his delineation of Plato's attacks on rhetoric as well as Plato's conception of a "true" rhetoric, his description of Aristotle's answers to Plato, and his summary of the main points of Aristotelian rhetoric. The publication of his essay established Hunt as a formidable scholar in his own right, so much so that his lack of a doctorate (which he never achieved) did not diminish his authority on rhetorical matters within the profession from that time on.

But "Plato and Aristotle" was more than distinguished scholarship. The opening line was pure Everett Hunt: "The art of rhetoric offered to the Athenian of the fifth century B.C. a method of higher education and, beyond that, a way of life."[40] Rhetoric was truly a method of higher education, as he had repeatedly stated in his arguments with Woolbert. Among the ancient Greeks he found an intellectual base and tradition for his claims that studies in rhetoric and public speaking should produce enlightened citizens: "In the problems of the relations of Plato to Protogoras, of philosopher to sophist and rhetoricians, are involved the issues which we debate when we discuss the aims of a liberal education, the desirability of government by experts, the relations of a university to the state, the duty of a scholar in a democracy, the function of public opinion in a popular government, the difference between a conventional and a rational morality, to say nothing of more speculative questions."

These were some of the public questions that Hunt sought to have students address, and here was the justification for rhetoric's using them as the focal point in education. His study, then, of Greek rhetoric was not a dry, philological study of limited academic value but a living testament and guide for modern rhetoricians who would apply their own imaginations and intellects to contemporary problems.

Beyond that, rhetoric was a way of life. Everett saw life rhetorically, and the Greek idea of rhetoric guided him. In this sense, he could be mistaken for some of the postmodern literary and rhetorical theorists. But unlike them his key word for unlocking his vision of rhetoric was not *persuasion* or even *identification*, but *probability* and *public judgment*. Hunt eschewed certainty in life and found little in common with those who sought certainty. He was interested in public issues that resided in the realm of probability, significant issues about which people debate and that they must decide through participation in political and civic life. His emphasis on ideas within the realm of probability accounts for his disdain of specialized scholarship that searched for the facts and his persistent criticism of science (be it natural, physical, or social science) that sought certainty. Discovering facts gave him only a basis for argument. They did not tell him anything significant about how to conceive of, or relate to, the ideas that he wished to conceive of and relate to. The idea that rhetoric was based on probabilities led Hunt to develop a humane rhetoric. Such a rhetoric required one to explore ideas with imagination, to express them with intelligence, and to view opposing opinions with sympathy. This emphasis on sympathy for the opinions of others certainly separates his ideas from those of postmodern cultural and Marxist critics. Such was his view of a humane rhetoric and a humane life.

Studies in Rhetoric and Public Speaking was a landmark book. Reviewing its original publication, James O'Neill stated: "The work is of great professional interest, first, because we have not had anything like it before. It is not a textbook, but a volume of scholarly papers for teachers and scholars of the profession."[41] O'Neill quickly noted the three most distinguished essays—Hunt's "Plato and Aristotle," Wichelns' "Literary Criticism of Oratory," and Caplan's "A Late Medieval Tractate"—and observed that the others were "less brilliant achievements" when compared to these "pre-eminent examples of interesting and scholarly additions to the literature of our field."[42] He predicted that teachers would direct their future graduate students to these studies not only as examples of contemporary scholarship but as standards to aspire to. He concluded his long, ten-page review by describing the book as a "distinguished achievement," the "most significant volume offered to workers in the field of speech in a very, very long time."[43]

Form versus Content Controversy

Between the inauguration of the 1920 seminar and the publication of the book honoring Winans, Everett served as president of the Eastern Public Speaking Conference, the oldest continuing professional organization for teachers of public speaking. At Christmas 1922 the Eastern Conference was held in conjunction with the national association and highlighted the "form versus content" controversy, which was in reality a continuation of the previous Woolbert–Hunt debate, only along different lines.

The point of contention specifically concerned how much attention a teacher should pay to the substance of students' speeches. Should teachers limit their instruction solely to the form or techniques of speaking? Hunt had sparked the controversy when he wrote in "Adding Substance to Form in Public Speaking Courses" that teachers should pay more attention to *what* students say than to *how* they say it. He argued that the content of a course in public speaking should "include as source material a group of essays or addresses which treat a limited number of fundamental subjects upon which any liberally educated man should be able to speak intelligently and effectively in public."[44] He stated that ideas within the realm of probability, controversial public issues of enduring interest, should provide topics for students' speeches. He excluded informative or other forms of speeches from his courses.

Teachers from the Midwest, especially James M. O'Neill, were incensed by Hunt's ideas. Marshaling all his authority as first president of the national association and first editor of the *Quarterly Journal*, O'Neill came to the joint meeting prepared to exorcise Hunt's heresy.

In his speech to the convention O'Neill charged that "Adding Substance to Form" and William P. Sandford's article "The Problem of Speech Content" made "the most thorough-going attack upon the worth and dignity of instruction in public speaking that has appeared in our generation."[45] He predicted that if Hunt's and Sandford's ideas were ever adopted by teachers of speech, that "courses known as courses in public speaking should, and will, soon disappear from our colleges and universities."[46] O'Neill accused Hunt of undermining the dignity of teaching the mechanics of speaking, the primary duty of a teacher of speech. He said that the subjects that students chose for speeches concern teachers or critics only incidentally: "Ideas, facts, information, therefore, about tariff, diplomacy, and poverty, and the great principles of liberty, religion, and progress, are legitimately given attention in public speaking only incidentally, only insofar as giving them attention promotes the real purposes of such courses— knowledge of, and proficiency in, public speaking."[47] O'Neill defined teaching public speaking as teaching techniques of speaking. It was as simple as that. Teachers had no right to venture into the areas of politics, sociology, economics, or ethics, except for academic or professional ethics of, say, plagiarism. Teachers should not prescribe topics for students. They should not provide reading materials for students. O'Neill objected to Hunt's limiting students to speeches on controversial public problems and accused him of being an undemocratic dilettante.

At the meeting Hunt replied that knowledge is more important than skill. Public speaking, he said, is a liberal art, and the liberal college is a "standing protest against the subordination of life to routine."[48] Teaching only form or skills involved routine and resulted in drudgery. In addition, these skills seldom influence important decisions in life. We should do better, Everett said, if we were to cultivate a philosophic attitude toward problems and a system of values by which to judge what we ought to do rather than concentrating on acquiring proficiency in the mechanics of speaking: "If we are free men we do not cast our votes as a result of a particular skill; most of us ought not to choose our profession because of skill; we do not marry through skill, or accept or reject religions through skill, or become conservative or radical, or appreciate nature or select our friends or love our country or hate lying, through skill. For the direction of the choices there is needed all the knowledge that can be obtained in the four short years of its unhampered pursuit."[49] Instead of drilling students in routine techniques, Hunt would encourage them to explore controversial ideas and policies for the purpose of deciding what values that they believed most important. As particular speeches or essays were studied, the specific techniques used by the advocate could be discussed, but that was about the only context in which Hunt was interested in studying them. He asserted his persistent thesis that methods could not be separated from ideas.

The charge that he was undemocratic involved greater difficulties, especially for Hunt, who was a prairie socialist. He replied that restricting students to public issues as subjects for speeches reflected the tradition of the liberal arts, not a political tradition. The liberal arts college, he noted, is exclusive, not inclusive. Some ideas are more important than others. Courses in public speaking should strive to be liberal by limiting the topics for student speeches to public issues and the purpose to persuasive speaking.

Wichelns summarized the debate and its effects on members attending the conference:

Involved was the speech teacher's interpretation of the range of his responsibility. O'Neill would take the student as he was and develop his ability to communicate his present thought by giving him better technical command of the resources of expression. Hunt wished to stimulate thinking, give wider perspective and deeper insight; in consequence he put less stress on technical improvement. O'Neill was concerned to find a clearly delimited departmental field. Hunt, who had come to the east from the open prairie, naturally said: "Don't fence me in." It was a great battle, in which the attacker's [O'Neill's] hard debating style was well contrasted with his opponent's [Hunt's] thoughtful reflective approach. It left the members of the Eastern [Conference] unmoved in the end.[50]

But more was at stake than the range of teachers' responsibilities.

Hunt contended that the examination of public issues and the persuasive arguments used to justify them formed the essence of a liberal education and that teaching only skills diverted teachers from their primary responsibility: the education of the liberal person. The controversy no longer involved the academic topic of specialization but now overflowed to the aims of a liberal education. Hunt was asking explicitly whether public speaking can claim to be a liberal art when its teachers eschewed public ideas. O'Neill said yes. Hunt said no and provided an alternative perspective to the curriculum of skills and mechanics advocated by O'Neill.

But it went beyond even these topics. It was a battle between East and Midwest, between two different conceptions of the purpose and content of public speaking. On the one side were O'Neill, Woolbert, and others. On the other side were Hunt, Hudson, Wichelns, and the other Cornellians as well as W. P. Sandford. Hoyt Hudson would eventually emerge as chief spokesman for the Cornell group with his essays "Rhetoric and Poetry" and "The Field of Rhetoric," but the essence of the liberal definition of rhetoric and public speaking originated with Everett Hunt.

Five issues distinguished the two groups from one another. First, the easterners insisted that speech—oral as opposed to written language—was the defining feature of the new profession.

Second, the easterners sought to develop a curriculum that would draw together all subjects that relied primarily on spoken language, from public speaking, to drama, to speech correction, and oral interpretation.

Third, they sought to make the study of speech a specialized study that would produce specialized research and professionals for the new discipline.

Fourth, they insisted that the proper subject matter for teaching and research was the techniques of how oral language is used and how it can be improved; ideas about public issues interested them only incidentally.

Fifth, the easterners sought to establish a professional academic discipline that would train undergraduates to become proficient in speaking and that would prepare graduate students to become experts in research on oral language.

The Cornellians, led by Hunt and Hudson, came in direct conflict on each of these. First, the Cornellians insisted that rhetoric was the defining feature of the new profession. Hudson said it well: "Rhetoric does not include all the work done by our present departments of public speaking: it does not include the oral interpretation of literature, nor dramatics, nor studies designed to improve the pronunciation and diction of ordinary conversation."[51]

Second, the Cornellians wanted a curriculum that would be broadly liberal and draw together studies of all subjects that depend on persuasion. Drummond listed these subjects in a catalog of topics taught at Cornell, a curriculum that Hunt was instrumental in developing. Among the 129 subjects he listed were "Rhetoric and Logic," "Rhetoric and Dialectic," 'Rhetoric and Probability," "History of the Feud between Philosophy and Rhetoric," and so on.

Third, they believed that the study of rhetoric ought to be liberal and humane, not scientific or specialized. Hunt was especially adamant on this point from his first published essay at Huron to his last public statement a year before his death. He believed that making the study of rhetoric specialized or scientific would make it into a modern scholasticism cut off from the lifeblood of politics and ethics. Instead, he insisted that public speaking could be liberal and humane only if teachers and scholars concentrated their attention on ideas in the realm of probability and examined the various persuasive arguments that prominent figures had used to address similar public issues.

Fourth, Cornellians, led by Hunt, sought to ally the study of rhetoric with the liberal arts, with ethics and politics, with history and literature rather than concentrating on the mechanics of public speaking. They would broaden the studies to include editorial writers, pamphleteers, advertisers, preachers, propagandists, and all sorts of others who depended on persuasion. Writing later, Loren Reid noted that the Cornell tradition was "more concerned with rhetorical theory than with the criticism of speakers. . . . Its standards are classical, applied venturesomely and imaginatively; it is deeply rooted in literature."[52]

Finally, Hunt and the Cornellians sought to establish the intellectual bases for research and the teaching of rhetoric in colleges and universities. Hunt, in particular, believed that if this intellectual base were established and connected with the ancient Greek and Roman conceptions of rhetoric as the center of liberal arts and as the most appropriate preparation for public life (be it in public affairs or education), then professional recognition would follow.

On this final issue Hunt greatly miscalculated. The result of Hunt's conception of rhetoric would have been that all other departments within colleges and universities would have been subservient to rhetoric and that rhetoric would have emerged as a "general clearing house for ideas," as Hunt once phrased it. At this time in the development of the fledgling new discipline, no dean would ever have accepted such an expansive mission for a new department, and certainly no faculty committee would have approved establishing such a department that would have made all other departments second-class citizens. The tide of organizing higher education and creating academic departments was moving in the opposite direction, the direction that Woolbert and O'Neill outlined. In his later years, Hunt admitted that he had misunderstood the drive for professional recognition and that his ideas about rhetoric would not have achieved that recognition.

But that is not to say that Hunt's vision of rhetoric was without value. He added substance to form in public speaking in a fashion that *individual* teachers and scholars, if they were so moved, could use to justify forays into politics, ethics, history, literature, and other fields of knowledge. To aid such teachers, Everett edited a new textbook for such use.

Persistent Questions in Public Discussion was ostensibly edited by Drummond and Hunt, though Drummond did little more than lend his name to it so as to get a publisher. It was a different kind of textbook from Winans' *Public*

Speaking or the other texts current at the time. John Dolman Jr. noted that prior
to its publication no such anthology had been produced for courses in public
speaking: "But here is a book of the same kind [as those used in English de-
partments] edited by teachers of public speaking and prepared especially for
their own classes—not a book of model speeches for study as such, but a book
of stimulating source material, selected with reference to its actual helpfulness
in arousing discussion. Those who know the work of Mr. Drummond and Mr.
Hunt in other connections need not to be told that the book is well done."[53]

Certainly, it was a different textbook. In the preface Hunt wrote: "Selections
have been sought which, whatever their date, will provoke further thought concerning fundamental issues on which an educated citizen should have enlightened opinions, and which he should be able to discuss intelligently."[54] He chose
two or three essays or speeches to illustrate these persistent public questions.
Topics in the volume included American Character and Ideals, Democracy, Liberty of Thought and Discussion, Economic Society, Education, Religion, Racial
Problems (which included an address by W. E. B. Du Bois), War and Peace,
International Relations, Public Duty and Public Discussion. "In a Word to
Teachers," Hunt wrote that he had "sought stimulating and provocative readings
which adequately state conflicting views on a series of selected public questions"
and that these selections were intended "to arouse interest in further investigation
and discussion of ideas which are central in our political and social thinking."[55]
Persistent Questions represented the marriage of form and content that Hunt
believed should be the center of public speaking courses, with a heavy emphasis
on content over form. The book was widely used by the next generation of
Cornellians as they issued forth to teach at various colleges and thus to publicize
the Cornell School of Rhetoric's unique approach to the ways that speech and
rhetoric should be studied.

By 1925, when *Studies in Rhetoric and Public Speaking* was published, the
small band at Cornell had created an impressive record. The seminar in classical
rhetoric had set graduate education in rhetoric on a different course. The irony
of it was that this was the only graduate course that Hunt would teach during
his active academic career. Not until retirement and his appointments as a visiting professor would he again teach graduate students.

There was little doubt, though, that these original Cornellians were the dominant group in the new profession now celebrating its eleventh anniversary. As
Edward P. J. Corbett concluded, Everett Hunt and Hoyt Hudson were the cat-
alysts for the Cornell movement in the renaissance of interest in classical rhetoric.[56] The articles and books that flowed from this intellectual headwater had
created streams of scholarly interest to other points in the country far beyond
the Finger Lakes of New York.

But at the very time of their triumph, they were also breaking up. Winans
had already departed for Dartmouth. Drummond turned his attention to his first
love, drama. Caplan left public speaking to join the Classics Department. Hud-

son had graduated and gone off to Swarthmore and then to the University of Pittsburgh. Cooper remained in the English Department but would soon become a one-man Department of Comparative Literature. In 1925 Hunt left to replace Hudson at Swarthmore. Only Wichelns remained when he returned from the University of Pittsburgh in 1925.

SWARTHMORE COLLEGE

Everett Hunt had high hopes when he arrived at Swarthmore College. The Department of Public Speaking that he inherited from Paul Pearson was the largest department on campus. Hunt intended to do graduate work with Charles Sears Baldwin, author of *Ancient Rhetoric and Poetic*, at the University of Pennsylvania and later Columbia University. In 1927 Hunt was elected editor of the *Quarterly Journal of Speech*.

But just as quickly his high hopes were dashed. In 1929 Baldwin informed Hunt that Sister Marie Therese had just published her translation of St. Augustine's fourth book of *De Doctrina Christiana*, the subject for Everett's dissertation, and "that the subject was therefore no longer acceptable."[57] Hunt gave up on completing his doctorate. Then Frank Aydelotte, the new president of Swarthmore College, abolished the public speaking department along with courses in composition, contending, as Everett later said, that any student admitted to Swarthmore already knew how to speak and write. In 1932–1933 Hunt was given a leave of absence to find a new field of study, which turned out to be Milton and seventeenth-century English Literature and later the "Wisdom Literature" of the Bible. He was promoted to professor of English and appointed dean of men, positions he would hold until his retirement.

Literary Criticism as Rhetorical Criticism

Now teaching in the English Department, Hunt sought to adapt to the professional responsibilities of a professor of literature. That meant attending academic conferences and writing and publishing essays on literary topics. But even as these topics were ostensibly literary, each had a strongly rhetorical perspective and in one way or another reflected Hunt's continuing intellectual concerns.

At a symposium in 1934 on "Literature and Society" at the College Conference on English in the Central Atlantic States, Hunt appeared with the communist Granville Hicks. Only the year before, Hicks had published *The Great Tradition: An Interpretation of American Literature since the Civil War* while he was very much under the spell of Marxism, so much so that he had joined the editorial staff of *New Masses*. In his address, "Literature and Revolution," Hicks defended the pathetic proletariat novels, arguing that they were in their infancy and needed time to mature. But his principal argument—the one that had brought him prominence in the first place—was that writers must develop a class consciousness to produce significant social literature and that critics should do the same, that is, adjust their standards to meet Marxist interpretations of society.[58]

In "The Social Interpretation of Literature," Hunt wryly admitted that Hicks' doctrine had virtues. It "orders all our conflicts, divides our writers neatly into schools, explains all their failures, and fills us with a long unfelt glow."[59] But he retorted that to insist on "praising the strength and worth of the proletariat, to demand an optimistic faith in the revolution, is to compel authors to write by formula and to substitute rhetoric for art."[60] Writers would no longer be free to write as they wished but would be confined to hymns of praise to Marxism. In addition, critics would judge literature not on its own merits but by the standard of particular political or economic criteria. Such an economic or political basis for literary criticism was no worse, Hunt slyly noted, than a particular theological or psychological basis, but such criticism would necessarily ignore great works of literature to distort them to fit a reductive method of criticism.

Hunt did agree with Hicks on the need for studying literature to produce an imaginative realization of the worldview of writers, rather than have criticism concentrate on the minute techniques of writing:

Anyone who has gone through the controversy over Matthew Arnold's "criticism of life" knows how inadequate that formula has been found. In the face of all that, I am willing to subscribe to it, for purposes of teaching at least. I hope teachers will always recognize the large element of enjoyment in literature, beyond all the explaining or interpreting, and will to some extent leave students alone to enjoy. But so far as the intellectual processes of teaching are concerned, a discussion of the world-attitude of the author seems to me to be the most truly liberal way of teaching.[61]

Hunt proposed to study the variety of "world-attitudes" created by authors rather than subordinating art to a particular and reductive "world-attitude." The conflicts among such attitudes created the literary equivalent of the conflicts of ideas and policies that he had included in *Persistent Questions*.

His mention of Matthew Arnold was not incidental. In the 1930s Hunt published two essays on Arnold: "Matthew Arnold: The Critic as Rhetorician" (1934) and "Matthew Arnold and His Critics" (1936). In the first he sought to present Arnold's conceptions of criticism and in the second to note Arnold's critics and to defend him against them.

Although Matthew Arnold condemned the rhetoric practiced in his time, he did so, Hunt believed, because it "lacked the tolerance and detachment and wisdom that come from a wide acquaintance with the best that has been said and thought."[62] Hunt pointed out that Arnold distinguished between "rhetoric," which he saw as flattery, and "persuasion," which he thought of as a method of expressing criticism. Arnold attacked the former while praising the latter. Thus, what he attacked was a certain constricted notion of rhetoric. What he practiced was the Aristotelian conception of rhetoric.

Arnold believed that the critic should examine literary ideas as a guide to conduct, as a criticism of life. (In nineteenth-century parlance, literary ideas were social, political, educational ideas that public figures discussed and debated.) To do so required that the critic persuade his reader that particular ideas are more desirable than others. Thus, Arnold enlarged the conception of literary criticism to encompass more than technical or aesthetic evaluations of creative works. In fact, his conception often had little to do with literature at all: "It is criticism of all branches of knowledge—theology, philosophy, history, art, science, to use Arnold's list—if the tone and temper and method, and oftentimes the scale of values, are taken from literature. That is, literary criticism takes its meaning from its method and tone, not its subject matter."[63] The methods and aims of Arnold's literary criticism coincided with Hunt's view of the function and methods of rhetoric. Such an approach to criticism, Hunt observed, contrasted sharply in method and purpose from contemporary scholastic criticism written principally for other scholars for professional purposes. Arnold, as critic and thinker, defied simple classification, but Hunt concluded that "the intuitions of a disciplined spirit and the persuasion of an accomplished rhetorician will always have their place in criticism."[64]

In "Matthew Arnold and His Critics" Hunt ventured to summarize many of the criticisms that arose over Arnold's conception of criticism. The main controversies concerned these assertions: "As a literary critic, Arnold too often abandoned literature; he trespassed flagrantly in the realms of theology, philosophy, and social science; his criticism was authoritarian and rationalistic; he commended poetry to his readers, not for its own sake, but as a guide to life, and thus he is inevitably a hopeless moralist."[65] Hunt began his essay with a survey of each of these accusations, but in so doing, he was surveying the same accusations that had been hurled at him. Woolbert and O'Neill had accused him of leaving speech to trespass into other fields. In defending Arnold, he was defending himself. The issues, whether they arise in literature or rhetoric, concern one fundamental question in criticism: "[I]s the literary critic a technical analyst of literature, asking only, what does the author propose to do and how does he do it, or does the critic make use of his own values derived from all the living that he can encompass, and insist upon discussing any values that seem relevant?"[66] However, Hunt argued that the questions that Arnold asked admitted of no authority higher than the continuous discussion of critical minds. He noted that they could not be solved by scientists or experts or even people like Arnold and himself. They remain unsettled for they are the persistent problems confronting practical public figures in every civilization about how to educate, how to govern, how to live. These were the questions that intrigued Hunt, and in Matthew Arnold he had found a model.

Return to Rhetoric

In 1949 Hunt discussed the Harvard report *General Education in a Free Society* at the Eastern Public Speaking Conference and later had his remarks published in the *Quarterly Journal of Speech*. The Harvard report proposed to establish a body of courses bound together by the general knowledge and common objectives that, it believed, students should possess. It was an answer to the intense specialization that had grown up in higher education: "Special education instructs in what things can be done and how to do them; general education, in what needs to be done, and to what ends."[67] In his address "Rhetoric and General Education," Hunt argued that general education finds its ultimate goal in the creation of the liberal person, "the good man skilled in speaking." He adapted the recommendations of the report to place rhetoric at the center of the plan for general education by making it the core that would hold together the different subjects that would constitute this kind of education. Hunt's proposal meant that courses in rhetoric would not be given separately but in connection with the courses in general education. They would lose their identity as a distinct discipline but would serve a higher purpose of integrating separate fields of knowledge by concentrating on themes that "present the greatest, most universal, most essential human preoccupations first."[68]

Hal Harding, editor of the *Journal*, circulated Hunt's article for responses from academics both from the speech profession and from without. Once again, Hunt ignited controversy. Howard Mumford Jones asked plaintively: "What does Mr. Hunt mean by rhetoric?" Others embraced his humanistic approach and saw in it the proper role for rhetoric. But W. Norwood Brigance wrote that if teaching speech did not remain separate from general education, "after twenty years no genuine rhetoric would be taught in these courses, and after forty years no semblance of rhetoric would be taught."[69] Hunt replied briefly to these criticisms and endorsements. He reiterated that he still believed that rhetoric could be and should be a central study integrating various specialties into a coherent set of general questions about significant issues in education and politics. There was little more that he could say. He had heard it all before, and his position remained as steadfast as ever.

Five years later at a program honoring Wayland M. Parrish of the University of Illinois upon his retirement, Hunt delivered his most succinct and eloquent statement about his conception of a humane and intellectual rhetoric: "The case for rhetoric as a humane study may be stated with deceptive simplicity. Rhetoric is the study of men persuading men to make free choices." But choices should not only be free but also be enlightened: "An enlightened choice is a choice based upon a wide knowledge of all the alternatives, but knowledge about the alternatives is not enough. There must be imagination to envisage all the possibilities, and sympathy to make some of the options appeal to the emotions and powers of the will. Such dignity as man may have is achieved by the exercise of free choice through the qualities of learning, imagination, and sympathy; and we should add to these qualities as a fitting accompaniment, what may be called civility."[70] In this brief paragraph Hunt summarized his conceptions of rhetoric.

The key words for Hunt were *probability, knowledge, imagination, sympathy,* and *civility.* Hunt was concerned with the public and practical issues upon which all people are called to deliberate and decide, issues that reside in the wide spaces of probability rather than in the closed corridors of scientific or specialized knowledge. To decide these questions would require all the knowledge that one could gather. But knowledge, even of the best that had been said and thought, was not enough. Hunt tempered his admiration for intellect with a recognition of the limits of intellect. He was humanist enough that the claims of the rational intellect to be a complete guide to conduct in life was only one step away from dogmatism or intellectual arrogance. Thus, to knowledge, he added imagination and sympathy as two preeminent qualities needed to temper, expand, and humanize intellect. He used imagination as Arnold had used intuition, as a means for discovering the truths that intellect, dependent as it is on logic, cannot imagine. But the "truth" of which Everett spoke was an individual truth, very much like that inner light of his Quaker heritage, and even it had to be tempered by a sympathy for the inner lights and individual truths of others. Sympathy, as Hunt conceived of it, was not sentimental but respectful, a knowledge and feeling for the beliefs and emotions of others. To balance one's own convictions with a genuine sympathy for the convictions of others was to understand truly what Hunt meant by addressing ideas in the realm of probability. If such issues could not be decided decisively, then a humane rhetoric would be one that, at the very least, addressed issues with civility. Once again he turned to classical rhetoric for the foundations for these beliefs:

Isocrates . . . defined the liberally educated man as one who, in an uncertain situation, could make the best guess as to what he ought to do next. Making these guesses upon the basis of whatever learning, imagination, and sympathy he could command, and strengthening all these qualifications by attempting to make himself and his conclusions acceptable to others, he might well acquire dignity and civility and become a persuasive man, a rhetorician, in the best ancient sense of that now debased word. He would become acquainted in a general way with those persistent questions about which generations of men continually debate. He would know the characteristics of different types of audiences, what kind of ends, aims, values would appeal to them, and without necessarily attempting to be all things to all men, would both consciously and unconsciously attempt to commend himself as a personally trustworthy agent of the policy he was supporting.[71]

In these brief words, Hunt summarized forty years of thinking about rhetoric, its place in a democratic society and in education, and the qualities needed to cultivate and use it humanely. It was his personal credo stated with simple elegance. Much of it came down to concern for *ethos,* which Aristotle wrote was probably the most potent force in persuasion.

RETIREMENT

Everett Hunt retired from Swarthmore College in May 1959. That same year Raymond Howes edited a volume of celebrated essays that represented the Cornell tradition, including, among others, Hudson's "The Field of Rhetoric" and "Rhetoric and Poetry," an excerpt from Wichelns' "The Literary Criticism of Oratory," and his own "Plato and Aristotle on Rhetoric and Rhetoricians." *Historical Studies in Rhetoric and Rhetoricians* was dedicated "To Everett Lee Hunt[:] a pioneer in the Cornell movement to revive classical rhetoric and the author of distinguished rhetorical studies."[72] The volume, handsomely edited by Howes, went through two printings.

At the same time Everett was at work on a book of his own. For several of his last years at Swarthmore, he had team-taught with Dr. Solomon Asch and Dr. Leon Saul a seminar in emotional maturity. It centered on the problems of emotional life that occur frequently in the process of growing to maturity and addressed the special problems that students encountered in that transition from adolescence to the beginning of adulthood that we call the college years. As Hunt had listened to students during that time, he had gathered materials for a book about college students and especially about the changes among them that had occurred over his long tenure as dean at Swarthmore. *The Revolt of the College Intellectual* was published in 1963. In his book *Puritan Boston and Quaker Philadelphia*, E. Digby Baltzell noted: "The book was not widely read, yet it is a perceptive predictor of the anomie and student unrest that marked elite campuses all over America in the 1960s."[73]

During the first decade or so in retirement, Hunt accepted a number of visiting positions at universities as widespread as the University of Hawaii and Cornell. In addition, he occasionally wrote a brief article or gave a paper at a professional convention. Few of these merit our attention, with the exception of his address at the 1960 meeting of the National Communication Association in New York. His subject was "Lincoln's Rhetorical Triumph at Cooper Union," and he delivered his speech at the union. With his customary orderliness he deftly set the historic stage for Lincoln's speech and noted its most characteristic, persuasive ideas and appeals. But his sustaining focus was what the speech revealed about the man and about the qualities of practical leadership that he demonstrated. Hunt concluded:

This Cooper Union Address was persuasive in that it was the mature expression of the characteristic beliefs and reflections of a man of sound judgment, informed by historical research, and concerned with a choice between civic goods. It argued for a middle ground between extremists. It appealed to the intelligence and moral convictions of his listeners. It made an American tradition out of the startling contrast between his Western frontier appearance and speech on the one hand, and his good manners, with the wisdom and common senses of his conclusion, on the other. Where can we find a better example of the Aristotelian faculty of discovering all the available means of persuasion in a given case? The Cooper Union Address was a rhetorical triumph in that it was perhaps an unprecedented combination of political skill with a nobility of purpose and lofty qualities of ethical persuasion, which are a permanent need of democratic society.[74]

The speech was printed in *Representative American Speeches, 1969–1970.*

Much of Everett's time during retirement was spent meeting with young scholars in rhetoric who sought him out. He corresponded with them and encouraged them in their writings and careers.[75]

Everett Lee Hunt died on April 30, 1984. He was ninety-three years old.

CONCLUSION

What, then, can we say about Everett Hunt's place in the history of our profession? He created no new theory of rhetoric. He developed no new method for criticism. He founded no system of scholarship that eager young scholars could apply. He was too individualistic for that. At his retirement, the citation accompanying the John Nason Award that he received aptly captured his special gifts:

Opponent of the too frostily rational, his affectionate skepticism has shown a right knowledge of the occasion and the man, an Aristotelian knack for the proper hunch at the proper time. As dean, so also as teacher—no man of hard facts and regimented theories, but rather an issuer of invitations to the art of enjoying and of wondering, a person too well acquainted with human affairs to let them be over-simplified, too aware of their ultimate individuality to see them overgeneralized. He knows our human as well as our scholarly frailties, and has doctored both of them with a similar prescription—one that combines perceptive listening, imaginative suggestion, and friendly, educated laughter. We who have learned that in college one studies not courses, but men remember Milton, yes, but Everett Hunt perhaps more.[76]

Surely this brief statement captures the influence that he exerted with people.

But he was more than that. During his ninety-three years he produced one landmark work of scholarship, "Plato and Aristotle on Rhetoric and Rhetoricians." It was landmark in several senses. As O'Neill pointed out in his original review, it gave the profession its first sustained piece of scholarship. Beyond that, "Plato and Aristotle" grounded the study of rhetoric firmly on classical principles. That gave a base, a starting point for the study of rhetoric, its history, and influence.

Hunt also defined the humanistic tradition in rhetoric and sought to apply it to the modern world. He was seldom interested in historical or philological studies of rhetoric, be they ancient or modern. He sought instead to find a humane function for rhetoric in our times. He wanted to use the perspective of classical rhetoric to roam over those general ideas whenever he was moved to do so, rather than settle down on an academic homestead to till a single piece of scholarly land. In sum, he wanted the profession to be creative and to take upon itself its public responsibilities beyond scholarship. To achieve that goal, he wanted to marry substance and form. The "rhetorical turn" of the past decade or so may not be attributable to Everett Hunt's polemic essays, but he certainly would smile with approval at the variety of ways in which rhetoric is now used in various disciplines to criticize life and to recognize some common method of analyzing current issues. Charles Woolbert, his early antagonist, was prophetic when he described Hunt as "a sort of lay pastor, an intellectual and spiritual knight errant, an educational court physician." As Everett himself sometimes remarked, the description turned out to be an accurate prophecy of his career.

NOTES

1. Everett Lee Hunt, "Rhetoric as a Humane Study," *Quarterly Journal of Speech* (hereafter cited as *QJS*) 41 (April 1955), p. 114. The national journal has had a variety of names since the formation of the association. I use *QJS* throughout to refer to it for the sake of consistency.

This chapter is an adaptation of my book about Dean Hunt, *Rhetoric as a Human Adventure: A Short Biography of Everett Lee Hunt* (Annandale, VA: Speech Communication Association of America, 1990). Since Everett and I were close friends during the last several decades of his life, as I have recounted in my biography of him, I hope the reader will understand when I refer to him by his first name on occasions throughout this chapter.

2. Herbert A. Wichelns, *A History of the Speech Association of the Eastern States* (Mineola, NY: Speech Association of the Eastern States, April 1959), p. 7.

3. Bliss Perry, "The Amateur Spirit," *The Amateur Spirit* (Boston: Houghton Mifflin, 1904), p. 4.

4. Ibid., pp. 32–33.

5. Hunt, "General Specialists," *QJS* 2 (July 1916); p. 262.

6. Taped interview with Everett Hunt, August 10, 1967, in Swarthmore, Pennsylvania.

7. For Hunt's activities as a student and debater, see Windt, *Rhetoric as a Human Adventure*, pp. 24–27.

8. Hunt, "General Specialist: Fifty Years Later," a speech delivered at the Conference on Rhetoric and the Modern World, Bowling Green State University, July 1964.

9. Karl Wallace, quoted in Raymond G. Smith, "Modern Pioneer in Public Speaking," *QJS* 35 (February 1949), p. 50.

10. Hunt, "Teacher's Report," for the school year 1914–1915. For an overview of the changes enacted by Hunt after he became an instructor, see Donald W. Rasmussen, "A History of Speech Education at Huron College, 1883–1943," M.A. thesis, University of South Dakota, 1949; Windt, *Rhetoric as a Human Adventure*, pp. 27–32.

11. Hunt, "Academic Public Speaking," *QJS* 3 (January 1917), pp. 34, 35.

12. James A. Winans, "The Need for Research," *QJS* 1 (April 1915), pp. 20–21.

13. Research Committee, "Research in Public Speaking," *QJS* 1 (April 1915), p. 25.

14. Hunt, "The Scientific Spirit in Public Speaking," *QJS* 1 (July 1915), p. 191.

15. Ibid., p. 193.

16. Charles H. Woolbert, "The Organization of Departments of Speech Sciences in Universities," *QJS* 2 (January 1916), pp. 265–266.

17. Hunt, "General Specialists," *QJS* 2 (July 1916), p. 258.

18. Ibid., p. 262.

19. Charles H. Woolbert, "A Problem in Pragmatism," *QJS* 2 (July 1916), p. 265.

20. Ibid., pp. 265–266.

21. Ibid., pp. 268–271.

22. Ibid., p. 268.

23. On the curriculum that Hunt developed at Huron College, see Windt, *Rhetoric as a Human Adventure*, pp. 29–30.

24. Hunt, "Academic Public Speaking," *QJS* 3 (January 1917), p. 27.

25. Ibid.

26. Ibid.

27. C. H. W. to L. E. H. [*sic*]; a rejoinder, p. 3, 6. On Christmas Day 1917 Woolbert wrote a long letter to Hunt urging him to leave Huron and seek an advanced degree, preferably in the Department of Philosophy and Psychology at Harvard, where Woolbert was working on his doctorate. Woolbert generously offered to help him in this pursuit. Hunt applied and was accepted. However, it did not materialize. A sudden financial crisis in the family did not allow him to live on a graduate student's stipend. Fortunately, he was offered a position at Cornell University that he accepted instead. See Woolbert's letter published in *Rhetoric Society Quarterly* 14 (1986), pp. 251–259. I have provided opening and closing commentary.

28. Woolbert, "A Problem in Pragmatism," p. 274.

29. Hunt, "The Scientific Spirit in Public Speaking," pp. 191–192.

30. Burton J. Bledstein, *The Culture of Professionalism: The Middle Class and the Development of Higher Education in America* (New York: W. W. Norton, 1976).

31. See, for example, Walter Lippmann, *A Preface to Morals* (New York: Macmillan, 1929). Quoting Aristophanes, Lippmann observed: "Whirl is King having driven out Zeus."

32. Hunt, "An Adventure in Philosophy," *QJS* 3 (October 1917), p. 298. Words in parentheses are Hunt's.

33. Ibid., p. 299.

34. See Hunt, "Dialectic: A Neglected Mode of Argument," *QJS* 7 (June 1921), pp. 221–232.

35. For a description of Hunt's revolt against Winans, see Windt, *Rhetoric as a Human Adventure*, pp. 49–58.

36. Hoyt H. Hudson, "Alexander M. Drummond," *Studies in Speech and Drama in Honor of Alexander M. Drummond* (Ithaca, NY: Cornell University Press), p. 4.

37. Ibid., p. 3.

38. Donald C. Bryant, "The Founders of the Cornell Tradition of Rhetorical Study," a paper presented at the Speech Association of America convention, 1957, p. 5.

39. Hudson, "Alexander M. Drummond," p. 4.

40. Hunt, "Plato and Aristotle on Rhetoric and Rhetoricians," *Studies in Rhetoric and Public Speaking in Honor of James Albert Winans* (New York: Century, 1925), p. 3.

41. James M. O'Neill, "New Books" review of *Studies in Rhetoric and Public Speaking in Honor of James Albert Winans, QJS* 11 (November 1926), p. 368.

42. Ibid., p. 369.

43. Ibid., p. 377.

44. Hunt, "Adding Substance to Form in Public Speaking Courses," *QJS* 8 (June 1922), p. 257.

45. James M. O'Neill, "Speech Content and Course Content in Public Speaking," *QJS* 9 (February 1923), p. 27.

46. Ibid.

47. Ibid., p. 30.

48. Hunt, "Knowledge and Skill," *QJS* 9 (February 1923), p. 69.

49. Ibid.

50. Wichelns, *A History of the Speech Association of the Eastern States*, p. 7.

51. Hoyt H. Hudson, "The Field of Rhetoric," *QJS* 9 (April 1923).

52. Review by Loren Reid of *The Rhetorical Idiom: Essays in Rhetoric, Oratory, Language and Drama Presented to Herbert August Wichelns*, edited by Donald C. Bryant (Ithaca, NY: Cornell University Press, 1958), in *QJS* 44 (October 1958), pp. 316–317.

53. John Dolman Jr., review of *Persistent Questions in Public Discussion* in *QJS* 9 (November 1924), p. 396.

54. "Preface," *Persistent Questions in Public Discussion*, edited by Alexander M. Drummond and Everett Lee Hunt (Century, 1924), p. v.

55. Ibid., p. 486.

56. Edward P. J. Corbett, "The Cornell School of Rhetoric," in *Essays on the Rhetoric of the Western World*, edited by Edward P. J. Corbett, James J. Golden, and Goodwin F. Berquist (Dubuque, IA: Kendall/Hunt, 1990), p. 295.

57. Letter from Hunt to Windt, April 5, 1968.

58. Granville Hicks, "Literature and Revolution," *English Journal* 24 (March 1935), pp. 219–239.

59. Hunt, "The Social Interpretation of Literature," *English Journal* 24 (March 1935), p. 214.

60. Ibid., p. 217.

61. Ibid.

62. Hunt, "Matthew Arnold: The Critic as Rhetorician," in *Historical Studies of Rhetoric and Rhetoricians*, edited by Raymond F. Howes (Ithaca, NY: Cornell University Press, 1962), p. 342.

63. Ibid.

64. Ibid., p. 344.

65. Hunt, "Matthew Arnold and His Critics," *Sewanee Review* 44 (October–December 1936), p. 449.

66. Ibid., p. 450.

67. Quoted by Hunt, "Rhetoric and General Education," *QJS* 35 (October 1949), p. 276.

68. Ibid., p. 278.

69. "W. Norwood Brigance, A Symposium on Rhetoric and General Education," *QJS* 35 (December 1949), pp. 421–425.

70. Hunt, "Rhetoric as a Humane Study," p. 114.

71. Ibid., pp. 114–115.

72. Dedication in Howes, *Historical Studies in Rhetoric and Rhetoricians*, n.p.

73. E. Digby Baltzell, *Puritan Boston and Quaker Philadelphia* (Boston: Beacon Press, 1979), p. 513.

74. Hunt, "Lincoln's Rhetorical Triumph at Cooper Union," in Lester Thonssen, ed, *Representative American Speeches 1969–1970* (New York: H. W. Wilson, 1970), pp. 195–196.

75. For only one example, see my first chapter in *Rhetoric as a Human Adventure*.

76. Xeroxed copy of statement issued from the Office of the President, Swarthmore College, n.d., two pages.

BIBLIOGRAPHY

Arnold, Carroll C. "Rhetoric in America since 1900." In *Re-Establishing the Speech Profession: The First Fifty Years*, edited by R. T. Oliver and M. G. Bauer. N. p.: Speech Association of the Eastern States, September 1959, pp. 3–7.

Corbett, Edward P. J. "The Cornell School of Rhetoric." *Rhetoric Review* (September 1985).

Drummond, Alexander M., and Everett L. Hunt, eds. *Persistent Questions in Public Discussion*. New York: Century, 1924.

Horton, Garner, ed. *Pioneer College: A History of Pierre University and Huron College 1883–1958*. Special edition of the *Huron College Bulletin* (July 1, 1958).

Howes, Raymond F. *Notes on the Cornell School of Rhetoric*. Riverside, CA: Privately printed, 1976.

Howes, Raymond F., ed. *Historical Studies of Rhetoric and Rhetoricians*. Ithaca, NY: Cornell University Press, 1961.

Hunt, Everett Lee. "Academic Public Speaking." *QJS* 3 (January 1917), pp. 27–36.

Hunt, Everett Lee. "Adding Substance to Form in Public Speaking." *QJS* 8 (June 1922), pp. 256–265.

Hunt, Everett Lee. "An Adventure in Philosophy." *QJS* 3 (October 1917), pp. 297–303.

Hunt, Everett Lee. "Content and Form." *QJS* 9 (November 1923), pp. 324–329.

Hunt, Everett Lee. "Creative Teaching in Wartime." *QJS* 4 (October 1918), pp. 386–397.

Hunt, Everett Lee. "The Dean and the Psychiatrist." *Mental Health* 37 (April 1953), pp. 177–196.

Hunt, Everett Lee. "Dialectic: A Neglected Mode of Argument." *QJS* 7 (June 1921), pp. 221–232.

Hunt, Everett Lee. "Frank Aydelotte." *Swarthmore College Bulletin, Alumni Issue* (February 1957), pp. 5, 28–31.

Hunt, Everett Lee. "From Rhetoric Deliver Us." *QJS* 14 (April 1928), pp. 261–268.

Hunt, Everett Lee. "General Specialists." *QJS* 2 (July 1916), pp. 252–263.

Hunt, Everett Lee. "General Specialists: Fifty Years Later." *Rhetoric Society Quarterly* (Spring 1987), pp. 167–176.

Hunt, Everett Lee. "Hoyt Hopewell Hudson." *QJS* 31 (October 1945), pp. 272–274.

Hunt, Everett Lee. "Humanism and Dogma." *Sewanee Review* 43 (1935), pp. 501–503.

Hunt, Everett Lee. "Knowledge and Skill." *QJS* 9 (February 1923), pp. 67–76.

Hunt, Everett Lee. "Lincoln's Rhetorical Triumph at Cooper Union." In *Representative American Speeches: 1969–1970*, edited by Lester Thonnsen. New York: H. W. Wilson, 1970, pp. 189–196.

Hunt, Everett Lee. "Matthew Arnold and His Critics." *Sewanee Review* 44 (October–December 1936), pp. 449–467.

Hunt, Everett Lee. "Matthew Arnold: The Critic as Rhetorician." *QJS* 20 (November 1934), pp. 483–507.

Hunt, Everett Lee. "Music in a Liberal Arts College." In *Society for Music in a Liberal*

Arts College, seventh annual meeting, Princeton University, proceedings, 1956, pp. 22–26.

Hunt, Everett Lee. "Nason at Swarthmore." *Swarthmore College Bulletin Alumni Issue* (February 1953), pp. 1–2.

Hunt, Everett Lee. "Persuasion: Ancient and Modern." *Pacific Speech* (December 1966), pp. 5–8.

Hunt, Everett Lee. "Reading for Honors and Common Sense." *School and Society* 42 (November 30, 1935), pp. 726–732.

Hunt, Everett Lee. "Rhetoric and General Education." *QJS* 35 (October 1949), pp. 275–279.

Hunt, Everett Lee. "Rhetoric and Politics." *Pennsylvania Speech Annual* 21 (September 1964), pp. 10–16.

Hunt, Everett Lee. "Rhetoric as a Humane Study." *QJS* 41 (April 1955), pp. 114–117.

Hunt, Everett Lee. "The Rhetoric of Violence." In *California State [University-Hayward] Conference in Rhetorical Criticism*, ed. by James Johnson, 1969, pp. 1–5.

Hunt, Everett Lee. "The Rhetorical Mood of World War II." *QJS* 29 (February 1943), pp. 1–5.

Hunt, Everett Lee. "The Scientific Spirit in Public Speaking." *QJS* 1 (July 1915), pp. 185–193.

Hunt, Everett Lee. "The Social Interpretation of Literature." *English Journal* 24 (March 1935), pp. 214–219.

Hunt, Everett Lee. "Thinking about Feeling." *Swarthmore College Bulletin Alumni Issue* (May 1958), pp. 2–4, 29.

Hunt, Everett Lee. *The Revolt of the College Intellectual*. Chicago: Aldine, 1963.

"Rhetoric and General Education: A Symposium Continued." *QJS* 36 (February 1950), pp. 1–19.

Studies in Rhetoric and Public Speaking in Honor of James Albert Winans. New York: Century, 1925.

Wichelns, Herbert A. *A History of the Speech Association of the Eastern States*. Mineola, NY: Speech Association of the Eastern States, 1959.

Windt, Theodore Otto, Jr. "Everett Lee Hunt on Rhetoric." *Speech Teacher* (September 1972), pp. 177–192.

2

Henry Lee Ewbank, Sr.: Teacher of Teachers of Speech

HENRY L. EWBANK, JR.

PROEM

How does a man born on a farm in southern Indiana in 1893 and raised as the eldest of seven on a farm in northeastern Ohio become the mentor of twenty-five who became heads of academic departments of speech and thirty-six additional doctorates in the field whose teaching interests have spanned the field from rhetoric, to interpretation, to theater, to radio and speech pathology, and whose research methods have been critical, historical, empirical, and rhetorical?

There is no brief answer to this question, but the combination of opportunities and choices that trace his life reveals the ways in which Henry Lee Ewbank the elder influenced and contributed to the development of rhetorical studies in twentieth-century America. In the metaphor of this volume, it is the function of a "root" to provide undergirding and nourishment to a growing, living organism so that it can flourish and flower. This was what Heinie Ewbank did so well for so many as the nineteenth-century study of elocution transformed into the multiple areas of specialization that surround the central concerns of rhetoric.

For a year or so after he graduated from high school, Ewbank taught grade school students at Mansfield [Ohio] Academy. During that time—or as he attended Ohio Wesleyan University—he worked during the summer on a tent crew for the Chautauqua Lecture Series. Neither documentation nor memory attests to the names of the speakers whom he may have heard from just inside the flap or outside the tent, but it is not impossible that he was able to hear Harry B. Gough, William Jennings Bryan, or other luminaries of the platform.

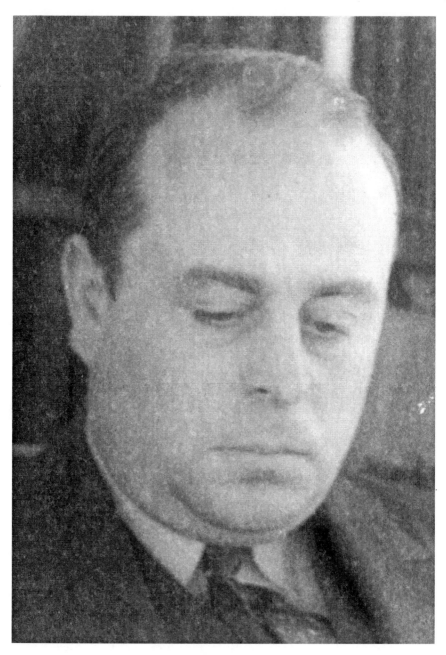

Henry Lee Ewbank, Sr. Photo courtesy of Hank Ewbank, Jr. Used with permission.

Something in his experience brought him to the School of Oratory at Ohio Wesleyan and the tutelage of Robert Irving Fulton.

WESLEYAN DAYS

Robert Fulton, together with Thomas Trueblood, bridged the gap between the itinerant or visiting teacher of elocution and the establishment of bona fide academic instruction in oral expression as a means of communication of ideas, rather than simply a means of entertainment. In 1893, after ten years of offering brief, eight-day courses in elocution at Ohio Wesleyan, Fulton gave up the school that he and Trueblood operated in Kansas City and announced the Ohio Wesleyan School of Oratory, which was incorporated in 1894. Soon the school was engaged in debate and oratory leagues with other Ohio colleges and institutions in adjacent states. By 1913, when Ewbank arrived, a range of courses was offered, including advanced study leading to master of arts degree conferred by the university.[1]

The Ohio Wesleyan yearbook, *Le Bijou*, for 1918, which includes individual pictures and activity records of the class of 1917, reports that "Heinie" Ewbank of Ashland, Ohio, was awarded a "B.A." in oratory. His speech-related activities included "Jesters, Toastmasters . . . Histrionic Club, Freshman Debate, Varsity Debate (2,3,4), Coach Freshman Debate (4). . . . [and] Oratory Instructor, Delaware High School (4)." His debate activity qualified him for membership in Delta Sigma Rho, of which honor society he was president his senior year. Apart from these extensions of his academic concentration, he was freshman class treasurer, a member of Chi Phi social fraternity, editor of *Le Bijou*, which qualified him for membership in the journalism society of Pi Delta Epsilon, and the class football player for three years.[2] Professor Emeritus Robert Crosby of Ohio Wesleyan, who brought together this information from university records, noted that Jesters and Toastmasters were "honoraries for senior men in the teen years."[3] During his junior year, when he was one of six associate members of the Histrionic Club, Heinie became aware of the interests that he shared with Rachel Angelina "Billie" Belt, one of the senior members of the club. Rachel was two years younger but had proceeded to college without interruption, so she graduated in 1916 and returned to her home town of Kenton, Ohio, to teach English and direct plays at the high school. They kept in close contact as he completed his studies and got established in his own teaching position.

Because the records for the class of 1917 are not extant, verification of the specific courses in which Ewbank enrolled is impossible.[4] However, the bulletin of the School of Oratory and the 1915 catalog of Ohio Wesleyan are clear in their agreement on the courses necessary for completion of the baccalaureate degree in oratory. Principles of Elocution is the first of the series. Here one became acquainted with "man's triune nature (i.e., The Vital Nature, The Mental Nature, and The Emotive Nature"[5]) with the vocal mechanism, with action, and with gesture, through reading, reciting, and memorizing literary selections. This course of study was "designed to give the student the basic principles of the philosophy of expression for guidance through the following courses and in all forms of public speaking."[6]

While it is not certain which of those "following courses" Ewbank took, his enrollment in Argumentation and Debate and in Advanced Debate seems obvious from his three-year involvement with this intercollegiate activity. A picture in the 1915 *Le Bijou* shows him as one of four members of an affirmative team that met at the University of Rochester, and the next yearbook pictures him again on an affirmative team that debated Colgate.[7] A family joke, given his long tenure as a debate coach and his later eminence as coauthor of a leading debate text, was that he was never a member of a winning team in intercollegiate debate. It must be noted, however, that enrollment in Advanced Debate was open only to "the twenty-two students who have won in preliminary debate contests."[8] In addition, he may have enrolled in either or both of the elective courses Literary Analysis and Interpretation and Junior Shakespeare.

Because both Oratory and Rhetorical Criticism were listed among the specified courses "bearing more directly upon original public speaking," it is certain that these two were a part of Ewbank's program. Both of these courses listed Professor Fulton as the teacher; however, Fulton's death in 1916 leaves doubt about who taught the course when Ewbank was enrolled. Given that *Le Bijou* reported that he was an instructor in oratory at Delaware High School as well as a coach of freshman debate during his senior year, it seems certain that Ewbank took the Normal Course. The description of this course noted that students gave "didactic instruction in the principles of Elocution" and illustrated vocal and action phases of expression "subject to the criticism and guidance of the Dean of the School of Oratory." They would then have the opportunity to teach other classes under the direction of the professor in charge. Finally, there were variable hours of credit offered in Junior Private Lessons and Senior Private Lessons and/or the Oratorical Seminar or the Interpretative Seminar that would count toward the necessary total of twenty-six hours for the public speaking major.[9] Very little additional information is available to tell what studies Ewbank pursued aside from those in oratory except for a handwritten schedule for an undated semester in which he was enrolled in English 5 at 7:45 A.M. Tuesday, Thursday, and Friday, and he had chapel daily at 8:40. At 9:10 on Monday and Wednesday there was History, with Economics at the same time on the other days. At 10:10 on Tuesday, Thursday, and Friday there was Oratory. Biology Lab was crossed out at 11:10. At 1:30, Monday, Wednesday, and Friday, he had German, and at 3:00, Tuesday through Friday, there was Debate.[10] The days were full. His work pattern of long days and evening study was set for the remainder of his professional life.

Two yellowing papers remain that are manuscripts of presentations made to the English Seminar taken during the spring semester 1917. The first, partly typed with the last four pages handwritten in pen, then pencil, bears the title, "Bernard Shaw as a Satirist." In good debate style, Ewbank notes the variety of interpretations applied to Shaw's plays, provides his own definition of "satire," and offers numerous examples wherein Shaw had made humorous and exaggerated attacks on the social order to support his position. The second, presented on May 15, 1917, explores "The Idealism of H. G. Wells." This piece is entirely handwritten, with some editing in pencil. As was true of the earlier paper, there is very little use of direct citation except for general references to Wells' specific books. He alludes to "a biographer" whose words were quoted verbatim. A wide range of quotations and paraphrases illustrates Wells' changing focus from past to future, but with a growing concentration on the importance of religion. Ewbank concluded, "His pictures of the future have changed and will continue to change as greater light and greater wisdom are granted him but always they are activated by a common ideal—that of a contented and beautiful world in which the humblest of God's creatures may be well clothed and well fed—a world in which there shall be neither wars nor rumors of wars but everywhere happiness, everywhere peace."[11] This was Ewbank's appraisal, just five weeks after the United States had declared war on Germany and three days before the Conscription Law was passed by Congress.

It is apparent that Ewbank earned high regard from Professor and Dean Fulton, as well as from the other three members of the faculty of the School of Oratory and his teachers from the other departments at Ohio Wesleyan. His excellent academic record led to his election to membership in Phi Beta Kappa, and he was one of six or seven students listed in the 1917 commencement program as those graduating with high honors.[12]

Through some quirk of fate there remains a looseleaf notebook containing the series of nineteen papers, ranging from seven to twelve tightly packed, handwritten pages, that Ewbank wrote for his course in Rhetorical Criticism, together with a few notes taken during class lectures. The general assignment appears initially to have been to write a "History of Oratory" in a number of "chapters" dealing with eras, geographical divisions, and/or significant individual orators from Athenian to contemporary times.[13]

The initial paper in this collection provides a clear statement of Ewbank's view of rhetorical criticism at this stage in his life—as he concluded his undergraduate studies at age twenty-three. His "Introduction to the History of Oratory" emphasizes the importance of oratory, which was the word then in vogue for "rhetoric" or "public speaking." The orator, he wrote, "has ever been the mouthpiece of the people in their struggle for self government. In his hands lies a power so great that its magnitude cannot be calculated,—the power of the spoken word to influence the minds and action of men." He avers that "so vital a force in shaping history is worthy of . . . study" and that any addition to the long list of books devoted to that study needs no apology. The scope of "oratory" is broad but is limited to thought "prepared with the idea of its being spoken on a particular occasion before such an audience as would gather at such a time. Thus the circumstances and the purpose for which an oration is intended unite to give it a style and an appeal that is different from all other classes of literature." Although orations may be written and preserved for study by those "who were denied the privilege of hearing them delivered . . . [t]he printed page records only the words uttered. It does not record those subjective elements that thrilled the crowds on the day of their delivery—and that entitled them to a place in the history of American eloquence." The purpose of a speech "arose from some crisis in the cause in which the speaker was vitally interested." "Oratory is always the outgrowth of the age which produces it." "[T]he orator must have some message which he feels compelled to deliver. . . . True oratory is born in some great crisis when there is a real problem to be presented. It consists not in the musical utterance of euphonious words alone. Only as they are used in the deliverance of a real and vital message do they reach the heights of real oratory." Finally, Ewbank concluded, "oratory must have a lofty theme . . . one that concerns the betterment of a state or a nation or a race." As he set forth each of these criteria, references were made to speakers and situations exemplifying the point being made.[14]

Having stated criteria for evaluating the oration, Ewbank turned to the characteristics of the successful orator. First listed as desirable were "certain natural physical endowments," including large stature and a clear, strong voice. Immediately, he cited exceptions, noting, among others, Demosthenes and Lincoln, who overcame physical limitations to achieve success. No one, however, could succeed without a comprehensive knowledge of his subjects in order to be able to answer questions and, more important, to speak "with that force and conviction that comes only when one knows whereof he speaks." "A wide and well chosen vocabulary and a wealth of illustrative material" make it possible to express "the exact shade of thot [sic]" and to "sound well when spoken." A "mastery over those mechanical devices that pertain to his art" is needed. The voice must be able to express emotion and shades of meaning. The "tricks of stage gesture and of stage department" must be mastered in order to appear at ease. The variables of force, pitch, quality, rate, and emphasis "play their part to make a finished production." All great orators "have been ardent students of the science of oratory," making the mechanics "seem no longer mechanical." "But above all these the orator must have an honesty and sincerity of purpose that causes his message to ring true." Other factors can be offset by sincerity, but nothing—neither a mellifluous voice nor a ponderous vocabulary—can cause an audience to heed the grandstander who doesn't believe in his or her own message.[15]

Although the concluding sentences of this first paper of Ewbank's study of the history of oratory illustrate the more formal writing style of the times, they express a philosophy that was made manifest in much of his own work and the one that served as his legacy to those whom he taught and to others whom he influenced throughout the remainder of his life. He wrote, "Our purpose has been to mark out more or less distinctly the limits of the fields of oratory and to set up a standard by which public speakers may be judged. We have done this that the reader might have some standards and criteria for judgment as we take up the study of the lives and the orations of those men who have swayed audiences to their bidding—who have torn down and rebuilded empires—who have shaped the onward march of events thru that most wonderful of all forces—the power of the spoken word."[16]

In this and each of the remaining papers written for the oratory course, it is perhaps important to note that the approved style did not include footnotes or citations. This is not to say that there were no direct or specific references to individual orators or speeches. That was not at all the case. Such references were frequent. Brief fragments of sentences were included as illustrations of judgments made. However, two important differences come to the fore. First, the references to speakers and to phrases suggest that they were chosen because they were familiar to the writer-rhetor (Ewbank) and to the reader-audience (the professor). They were included in order to illustrate a point, rather than to convey an impression that the writer had searched widely, thus demonstrating his research prowess, in order to discover an example not already known to the professor. In sum, they were included because of their appropriateness, their rhetorical impact. Perhaps the shared knowledge of the time was better defined than it is today. Still, a familiar referent conveys a clearer message than a footnote. Second, placing students in the position of forming and framing ideas and expressing them in their own words, rather than in a passage quoted from some "authority," causes the responsibility for the ideas to rest on the students themselves, without permitting them to shift the burden to someone else or suggesting that the students ought not to express views that cannot be corroborated in print. Footnoting as evidence of "research" has gained academic acceptance and has come often to supersede the importance of developing the faculty of informed, independent judgment by students who feel that they must cite an "authority" for each of their critical statements.

Of the remaining papers in this series, seven focused on American speakers. Orators of the "American Colonial Period" were grouped, as were those of the "British Colonial Period." Senators John Calhoun, Henry Clay, and Daniel Webster formed one group. Senators Edward Everett, Rufus Choate, and Charles Sumner were treated as "Occasional" speakers, rather than lawmakers. Attorney Wendell Phillips, Reverend Henry Ward Beecher, and Reverend Phillips Brooks represented the antislavery reform speakers. Prime Minister William Gladstone, President William McKinley, and his defeated opponent William Jennings Bryan were treated together, despite their differences in nationality and official positions. Abraham Lincoln merited a paper alone, which elicited the professorial comment "fine writing." Finally, David Lloyd-George and Woodrow Wilson were the focus of separate papers. Together with Bryan, they constituted essays in rhetorical appraisal of then-current speakers. This final paper presented different challenges to the student critic. It was not as if Ewbank and his classmates had firsthand opportunity to see and hear Wilson or Lloyd-George. They necessarily relied on newspaper and periodical accounts and an occasional speech manuscript. These resources, without the possibility for long-range evaluation of the significance of issues, the attitudes and responses of audiences, and the effect of messages, presented a different sort of challenge from the judgments of orators long silent. Ewbank's experience in writing these critical papers was reflected in his later teaching and publications and in the rhetorical studies executed by the succeeding generation of rhetorical scholars.

THE STATUS OF THE PROFESSION

Those who have looked back at the beginnings of the field of speech are aware that the initial gathering of seventeen men know now as the "founders" took place in December 1915, as Ewbank was in his sophomore year at Ohio Wesleyan. Thomas Trueblood, while not a founder, joined the National Association of Academic Teachers of Public Speaking soon after its formation. Had it not been for Fulton's death, it seems reasonable to expect that he would have shared in the association's work, because the curriculum in his school conformed to the shifting emphasis from elocution to the broader scope of rhetoric and public speaking. This does not mean that either man would have abandoned all of the grounding in elocutionary training that each had taught for so many years. The view that speech—and particularly public speech—demands an understanding of, and control over, the physiological aspects of voice production, as well as a thorough command of the ideas and an ethical perspective of the potential impact and, therefore, the responsibilities of the speaker, is one that is not lightly set aside. Nor should it be abandoned in favor of a quick survey of the appeals that one might make to secure quick and uncritical acceptance of spur-of-the-moment proposals.

Ohio Wesleyan already offered a master's degree in oratory, granted to those who took a fifth year of study consisting of additional individual instruction; preparation for, and execution of, public recitals; and submission of an acceptable thesis. Apparently, this was intended principally for students who had completed a baccalaureate degree in another field and then decided to enhance their caliber of public performance. The course work cited is essentially that of the senior year for those who had declared a major in oratory. Elsewhere, several state universities in the Midwest and some colleges and universities in the Northeast were not only establishing academic departments of speech, separate from the more traditional English departments, but also offering graduate degrees and building research programs that would secure their position among other liberal arts or arts and sciences departments.

Intercollegiate competition in debate and oratory was well established and strong. Literary societies provided noncurricular opportunities for presentation of oral reports, for parliamentary practice, and for intracollegiate competition. Numbers of the topics chosen for presentation to audiences in these years dealt with matters of public policy concern as the United States came closer to involvement in the war that was tearing up Europe. On April 6, 1917, some two months before Ewbank's graduation, the United States declared war on Germany. On May 18, 1917, the Conscription Law was adopted.

The Albion Years

A card in his "chapbook," where he jotted down stories and jokes for possible later use, as was the way of speakers of the time, shows that Ewbank registered for the draft on June 5 in Delaware, Ohio. Prior to that time he had accepted a position as instructor at Albion College in Albion, Michigan, which he held until 1921, when he was promoted to professor. Having fulfilled his contract to teach during the 1917–1918 academic year, Ewbank's sense of obligation led him to ask for a leave of absence so that he could enlist and serve in the U.S. Navy. Entering as a seaman, because of his college degree he was made a midshipman and had some training aboard a coaling vessel on the Great Lakes. He was then commissioned ensign and shipped overseas on the USS *Leviathan* as she brought troops home after the armistice. After his release from active duty he returned to Albion in time to resume his teaching position for the fall 1919 semester. With classes well under way, on October 15 he married Rachel Belt. Her experience as a teacher and her shared interest in oral communication made their forty-one years together a time when they entertained others through interpretative readings and conversed understandingly about professional as well as personal thoughts.

Heinie Ewbank coached Albion debaters and orators, in addition to teaching courses offered to Albion students. As a member of Delta Sigma Rho, he also served as adviser to the Albion chapter. During the summer of 1923 he was a lecturer at Michigan State Normal School in Ypsilanti. Other summers were spent studying in Ann Arbor. In 1924 he completed the requirements for the M.A. degree at the University of Michigan, having studied with the coauthor of the speech books popular at the time, Thomas C. Trueblood. At that time Ray K. Immel moved from the University of Michigan to become dean of the School of Speech at the University of Southern California and, having served for five years as treasurer, was elected president of the National Association of Teachers of Speech (NATS). It seems probable that Immel, having known Ewbank as a graduate student and a faculty member of a respected Michigan college, might have proposed his name as a prospective nominee for association treasurer. In any event, 1925 was Ewbank's first year as NATS treasurer, a position that he held for three years until the title and responsibilities were redefined as executive secretary. From that point, 1928, through 1930 he continued to serve as executive secretary. In 1931, as he described it, he "took the treasury of the Association from my watch pocket and transferred it to Gail Densmore" of the University of Michigan, who continued in the job until 1939.

In addition to undertaking organizational work at the national level, April 2, 1925, found Ewbank among 29 speech teachers in Michigan who constituted

the Charter membership of the Michigan Association of Teachers of Speech. He
became the first president of the association of college and high school teachers.
Reelected to a second year term, he served from 1925 to 1927. At the Silver
Anniversary meeting of the renamed Michigan Speech Association, Ewbank and
other founders were presented with life membership in the association.[17]

The fact that Ewbank had completed a master's degree in 1924 did not mean
an end to his summer course work at the University of Michigan. The fact that
there was a well-established department about sixty miles from Albion meant
that he had access to further study that he chose not to ignore. Five papers
remain from his summer study in 1926. Three were papers for Rhetoric 117s,
dealing with linguistic and grammatical "problems" designated by number. The
problem 2 paper is titled "A Question of Loyalties." It explored differences
between British English and American English, noting that soon after the Revolution the British had scorned "Americanisms" as they had previously sought
to avoid "Scoticisms." Americans reciprocated by identifying "Briticisms,"
words that the British used "improperly." As time passed, Ewbank noted, and
ocean travel became more routine, usage had become less clearly distinguishable. In addition to several other sources, he cited Mencken's lists in *The American Language* of fifteen pairs of terms, such as "drug store" versus "chemist's
shop," "saloon" versus "public house," or "shoes" versus "boots," as instances
where neither choice is inherently superior to the other. His conclusion is that
each nation will doubtless enrich the shared, but not really common, language
and that Mencken's thought that the American language will prevail over the
British is "a bit of the flagwaving that [Mencken] condemns so heartily in Bab-
bits and Rotarians." The "Problem 3" paper explored "English and American
Dialects." He traced the emergence of East Midland dialect into the standard of
English literature, noting that while it was the language of Oxford and Cambridge and became the language of the court, the Welsh, Scottish, and Irish
dialects had not been lost. In America the standard dialect came first, through
preachers and teachers, and the regional variations developed as immigrants
came to different parts of the nation. Ewbank relied repeatedly on ideas cited
to "Professor Krapp," without further identification, and illustrated his position
that dialectal differences really do exist with quotations from casual conversation, with examples from Ring Lardner's writing, and with references to the
traces of "Russian, Mexican . . . and Shanty Irish" present in the conversations
of the railroad section gang on which Ewbank had worked. "Grammar at the
Crossroads" was the title of Ewbank's paper for "Problem 4." As he had done
in the two previous papers, Ewbank's introduction set a scene that illustrated
his thesis. In this case, he saw the tension between teachers of grammatical
purity and the lack of concern of students who cared not for structure and rules.
From that point he dealt almost completely with the ways in which grammatical
rules yield to the creation and understanding of idioms. Among many such
phrases that he included, perhaps the most odd was that of "the Japanese student
who wired a friend to tell him of his mother's death: 'The hand that rocked the

cradle has kicked the bucket.' " In conclusion, Ewbank said that most will avoid the posture of didactic grammarian or the attitude of the advocate for "English as she is spoke," taking his cue from the couplet:

> Be not the first by which the new is tried,
> Nor yet the last to cast the old aside.[18]

That same summer, 1926, Ewbank wrote at least two papers for a course in Advanced Public Speaking and preserved two sets of lecture notes. The paper for July 2 was a "Brief of Lincoln's Speech in Jonesboro Debate." Ewbank phrased the question for debate as follows: "Resolved that Senator Douglas, representing the Democratic Party, should be returned to office in the coming election." He noted that while there was "no one clear cut issue in this series of debates," three questions pervaded the debate: "(1) the relative merits and practices of the two parties and of the candidates themselves, (2) the question of states rights, and (3) the question of the extension of slavery in federal territories." The brief of the speech was divided into three major headings: "I. Admitted Matter," "II. Refutation," and "III. Presentation of Argument." The first category said, simply, that Lincoln agreed that states have the right to do what they please about slavery, and that he had said so many times, and that "Judge Douglas insists on placing me in the wrong light." Lincoln's refutation was set forth under five headings ranging from the "half slave, half free" idea, to Douglas' holding Lincoln responsible for the expressed ideas of his followers. Each refutation was met with reference to previous rebuttal, and/or with countercharge that Douglas' followers—both individuals and party conventions—have taken positions at variance with those expressed by Douglas. Lincoln's presentation of arguments noted that Douglas had not objected to Lincoln's answers to questions posed but rather had ignored the answers. Beyond that, Lincoln restated four questions that he had put to Douglas and challenged Douglas' responses. Finally, Lincoln addressed a new question to Douglas, asking how he would vote on any proposed legislation granting federal protection for private property in U.S. territories. This paper provided evidence that Ewbank's experience as a debater and as a debate coach enabled him to elicit the argumentative structure from a rhetorical artifact, one critical function necessarily performed in the process of rhetorical criticism.[19]

The second paper for the course was an outline extracted from Wendell Phillips' lyceum lecture "The Lost Arts." This was a speech "said to have been repeated . . . more than two thousand times"[20]; thus the print version was an arbitrary selection from the array of texts that might have been presented to any given audience. Only the "Conclusion" stands as one major division of the outline. The ten preceding divisions are substantive, with the first three apparently constituting the introduction. Phillips' thesis was that much of what passes as "current knowledge" was known to ancient cultures, that there is a risk in the "self conceit" of ignorance of the many facets of what we call "civilization" that were part and parcel of the lives of the ancient Chinese, Turks, and Egyptians. Glass, metals, dyes, canals, and even games had been in use for more than 2,000 years. The outline showed several examples under each major category, bolstering the central thesis. This selection illustrated the way the informer-entertainer-lecturer on the lyceum circuit chose a central theme and title and regaled numerous audiences who gathered for social as well as educational reasons.[21]

Apart from these two papers there are two handwritten manuscripts. One is labeled "Adv. P. Spkng. Lecture I Principles of Attention." This, according to marginal notes in several places, followed James Winans' discussion of the psychological concept of attention as it relates to the speaking situation. The introduction cited a "threefold relation of attention to speech: (1) primary aim of speaker to hold attention of audience, (2) attention or 'thinking at instant of delivery,' (3) attention in preparation of speeches." The "Body of Lecture" set forth three forms of attention: involuntary or primary, secondary, and derived primary, which is the kind sought by speakers who themselves are consumed with their message and who want their audiences to sustain their active listening without repeated effort. Derived primary attention is developed largely through interest, as James had said. Interest, in turn, grows with knowledge and through association with already known information and ideas. After an internal summary of that major point, Ewbank proceeded to the consideration of the need for concreteness and specific words over abstractions and general terms. He summed this thought with the sentence, "Think out your subject in terms with which you are so familiar that no translation is necessary." The final concept dealt with was "imagination," which he explained in terms of creating different kinds of sensory images, not simply indulging in fanciful flights. An abundance of facts is necessary to the creation of images, and the person with much material must have imagination in order to make effective use of that material with an audience. The lecture outline seems to have been cut short or abandoned, because it lacks any gesture at a final summary or conclusion.[22]

A more detailed, though not completed, manuscript is entitled, "The After Dinner Speech." It is introduced by a bit of verse attributed to Wallace Irwin on the theme that after dinner speaking is frequent and too often worthless, comprised of ill-told old saws. The manuscript concludes, "And may the wight who comes this way with nothing or too much to say, in heaven's name, keep still." Ewbank noted that, except for pulpit oratory, the after dinner speech was the most prevalent form of public speaking in America. He cited a variety of situations that create expectations for dining followed by one or more speakers. Contrary to the circumstances that bring the people together, "the popular conception of an after dinner speech seems to be that it must above all things else produce laughter." But most speakers are not humorists so they tend to "resort to the jest book and drag in venerable and bewhiskered jokes by their hoary whiskers." At that point, having demonstrated his own ability to focus attention by creating sensory images, the manuscript ends, midpage, with three blank pages included in the paper clip, indicating yet another interrupted foray into the appraisal of the status of contemporary rhetorical practices.[23]

At this stage in his career, Ewbank was thoroughly grounded in the physiological aspects of speaking through the perspective of elocution: the intellectual demands on the speaker through his practice and study of argumentation and debate, the cultural traditions of rhetoric through his study of the classical writers, and the linguistic dimensions of communication as he had explored grammar and literature.

As of September 1, 1926, Heinie Ewbank became a vice president of Delta Sigma Rho (DSR). Seven of the eight vice presidents were responsible for chapters in the seven executive districts of the organization. Ewbank's was the fourth district, which included chapters at Albion, Chicago, DePauw, Illinois, Knox, Michigan, Northwestern, and Wooster. One of the important concerns that led to the founding of DSR was recognition that the efforts of students who participated in forensics were truly central to the educational and scholarly purposes of colleges and universities but that these students had been accorded far less recognition than others who spent their time in athletic pursuits. The nine men who had met in Chicago on Friday, April 13, 1906, to found the society had been intent upon a remedy. Thomas Trueblood presided. "Almost from the start," a recorder of the history of the society wrote, "the principle was recognized that the member himself, by faithful and excellent work in forensics, really earns the honor which the society merely recognizes in making him a member."[24] By extension, in electing the national officers of the society, Ewbank had demonstrated his continuing "faithful and excellent work in forensics," which the society again recognized. He held the office of vice president through 1931 and again from 1939 to 1947.

"ON WISCONSIN!"

During the summer of 1927 the Ewbank family moved from Albion to Madison, where Heinie had accepted the position of assistant professor of speech and director of forensics at the University of Wisconsin. This move provided the opportunity for him to pursue additional graduate study toward the Ph.D. degree. He took with him his responsibilities as treasurer of NATS, which entailed serving as business manager of the *Quarterly Journal of Speech*, vice president of DSR, and secretary of the Interstate Oratorical Association, a position that he had held since 1923. The timing of his arrival in Madison was such that he just missed the opportunity to work with yet another of the early leaders who was one of the founders and the first president of the National Association of Academic Teachers of Public Speaking, James M. O'Neill, who moved that year after his long tenure in Madison. Still, Wisconsin was the scene of active study of all aspects of speech, including rhetoric. The university had been represented not only at the inception of the organization that had become NATS but also at the formation of DSR. There were the beginnings of work in developing the use of radio as a means of gaining a broader distribution of educational opportunities to the citizens throughout the state. Things were in ferment.

Throughout the twelve years during which the *Quarterly Journal of Speech* had been published, one ongoing concern had been that the newly independent field of speech should develop a body of research that would establish it as a discipline comparable in stature to other academic departments. One strong line of argument was that there was no methodology for investigating the process, the mechanisms, or the situations of speaking that was not already employed by one or another of existing academic departments. This, some argued, made speech only a "derivative" area of study. One way to meet the criticism was to pursue a strong minor in a department that relied on a research method that was useful in rhetorical studies and to make effective use of that method in examining oral rhetorical phenomena. Perhaps his familiarity with the texts by Winans and Arthur E. Phillips led Ewbank into the study of social psychology as a minor. His undergraduate and master's study had familiarized him with the physiology of voice production and the physical dimensions of presenting messages persuasively. He was also well schooled in matters of organization of ideas and in the stylistic aspects of effective rhetoric. Psychology, particularly social psychology, had been more recently established as an academic discipline. Speech textbooks had adopted and adapted some of the psychological principles, as noted in Winans' discussion of "attention." The ways in which multiple observations were made and observations recorded and results interpreted were to be studied in an attempt to explore new paths to understanding the ways in which oratory works—or doesn't. O'Neill had been engaged in publishing varying views of directions that research should take and methods that should be used in testing ideas about speaking that would yield publishable results. The curriculum that he had fostered at Wisconsin had led to the granting of the first doctor of philosophy degree in speech in 1922.

At some point in Ewbank's studies he took a psychology seminar in which he wrote a paper on "Aphasia and the Localization of Cerebral Lesions," which, together with a "Partial Bibliography of the Literature on Aphasia with Special Reference to Cerebral Localization," is in possession of the author. The subject matter of the paper is not so unusual for a rhetorician of that generation, in particular for one schooled in the elocutionary tradition where physiology was the basis on which oral communication was built. Further, the studies of the processes of speech were few and were scattered among many disciplines. The forty-page paper was "a selective rather than exhaustive" historical survey of writings about aphasia from its first identification in 1798 to a 1926 work by Sir Henry Head. The thirteen-page bibliography is partially typed with many additions made in pen. It includes numerous citations in French and German and cites books as well as articles in medical, physiological, and psychological journals and proceedings of professional meetings.

It should be borne in mind that during the first third of the twentieth century the concept of "speech" was more global, perhaps less detailed, but more encompassing than is now the case. Though we may smile patronizingly at the elocutionist's concern for the physiology and the "Mental Nature" of the speaker, there is much to be gained through an understanding of how the vocal mechanism works and the ways in which fatigue or illness can affect one's ability to express oneself. Doctoral candidates studied larynxes as well as dramatic theory, oral interpretation of literature as well as phonetics, and radio as well as rhetoric. As they took teaching positions, they did not "teach their thesis" to senior or graduate students; rather, they introduced undergraduates to the experience of speaking to different audiences in various situations.

Ewbank's dissertation represented a social science exploration of one dimension of rhetorical theory that was, perhaps, the easiest to approach through quantifiable method: style. It was titled, "Objective Studies in Speech Style with Special Reference to One Hundred English Sermons." He noted that other observers had seen a significant reduction in sentence length in writers of English language, both American and British, over the previous two centuries. Some of this was due to the number of predications, which make for complex, rather than simple, sentences. Use of shorter words, greater brevity, and variety in sentence length is thought to make ideas more accessible to a broader audience. But little study had been directed toward testing these "commonsense" ideas. The first chapter became the manuscript for an article that appeared in *The Quarterly Journal of Speech* in November 1931, under the title, "Four Approaches to the Study of Speech Style."[25] Here, Ewbank described a "Subjective Method," in which the speech is studied "quite apart from the audience for which it is intended." This, quite obviously, does not qualify as a "rhetorical study." It explores only grammar and composition, resulting often in praise or condemnation depending on the preferences and prejudices of the scholar. Second is the "Case Method," which demands that the scholar be present at the speaking occasion to describe the event and report the effect of the speech on its audience. This method makes the critic an observer of others, rather than the source of evaluation. The third, "Laboratory Method," avoids a genuine rhetorical situation in favor of measuring the effect of a specially constructed message by means of objective testing of a controlled audience. Here, Ewbank observed, the advantages of replacing the critic's subjective judgment with statistically analyzed objective data from a number of observers might outweigh the disadvantages of artificiality and difficulty of control over the complex nature of a rhetorical event. Finally, he described "The Method of Statistical Analysis" of effective composition. This involved gathering data "as to sentence length, predication, subordination, word length, the percentage of structure and content words, the relative frequency of the various parts of speech, the proportion of loose and periodic sentences, the number of repetitions of key words and ideas," and such other items as are subject to observation and counting with some degree of accuracy. One cannot explore the qualities of abstractness or concreteness with this method. Assessing the significance of data can be difficult.

"It is easy," he wrote, "to get lost in a wilderness of data, deviations, and differences; it is easy to look at the trees so minutely that we fail to see the forest." On the other hand, Ewbank continued in another analogic statement, "The microscope does not give us a picture of the whole man in action, but its use has enabled the trained observer to classify and conquer armies of dangerous germs whose existence was before unknown. The use of the microscope marked a new epoch in the study of medicine: it may be that the use of similar methods in the field of rhetorical analysis will yield commensurate results."[26]

Explaining his rationale for choosing sermons, Ewbank noted that ministers rely consistently on oral style, they speak in more uniform situations than others, and their themes and purposes are consistent within occasions and with other ministers, so this category of speech form offers essential similarities in prose speech style. Two other Wisconsin dissertations had compared written prose style with oral prose style and had explored Wendell Phillips' oral style at different stages of his career. Ewbank's choice was to analyze complete manuscripts of sermons by ministers who were acknowledged leaders, to sample different periods of time from the sixteenth to the twentieth centuries, to diversify denominations, and to minimize multiple sermons by the same minister. Eighty-nine ministers were represented in his survey. He explored sentence length, variations in length, predication and percentages of simple sentences, and word length. The background for his study came from the theoretical prescriptions of rhetoricians from Greece and Rome, from eighteenth- and nineteenth-century England and America, and from contemporary American writers. The few statistical studies of sentence length were cited. Adding a new dimension to such studies, Ewbank investigated the questions: "What do these data mean in terms of audience response? Is there any correlation between sentence length, for example, and the judgment of the listener to the merit of the style?"[27] This added line of investigation maintained the link between the numerical concerns of the social psychologist and the situational focus of the rhetorician. Using 500-word excerpts from introductions to sermons, he tested audience response by asking groups of students and others to rate "qualities of good speech style." Audiences listened to oral readings of eight selections and rated each on a 100–50 point scale. Neither sentence nor word length was noted as a criterion. Expectations were set according to the theories offered in textbooks; that is, when a text proposes that shorter words should be preferred to longer words, it could be expected that listeners would, if theory is borne out, respond more favorably to monosyllables than to more complex words. Still, theory suggests that variety is desirable, which then modifies the earlier expectation. Though statistical sophistication in 1931 was not what it is today (correlation coefficients were used), multiple audiences of different composition hearing different orders of presentation and five repetitions of the experiment were used to control for possible variables. Because he dealt with a limited number of variables, Ewbank felt able to make only a "beginning" of the determination of "the essential elements affecting the listener's judgment of speech style."[28]

Overall, Ewbank concluded that many simply reject any and all objective analyses of speech style as "word counting," inadequate to deal with the more aesthetic characteristics of mood, rhythm, unity, or realism. He conceded in another of his analogies that this microscopic method—used alone—would not tell all of the story. Still, he wrote, "a laboratory study of drops of blood and muscle cells will not yield a picture of the runners in a hundred-yard dash: but such a study may give a more adequate explanation of why one runner wins and another goes limping than any amount of looking at the race from a place in the grandstand. So, we like to think, it may be with the study of style. Investigations of sentence length and variation, in word choice and arrangement, in simplicity or complexity of sentence structure, may be to the study of speech composition what researches on the eye-wink and the kneejerk, on blood pressure and respiratory changes, have become in investigations of human behavior."[29]

Having chosen to employ statistical methods in his dissertation, Ewbank was equipped to pursue both the more traditional, historical, biographical studies with which he had worked as an undergraduate and the newer, more objectively defined numerical analyses. He could observe from the grandstand, or he could use the microscope, whichever might provide the sort of answer he sought. He was also better qualified to interpret the research of others and to guide the studies of graduate students who chose to work at the University of Wisconsin.

In 1931, just prior to the completion of his doctoral work, Ewbank was elected president of Delta Sigma Rho. He followed Stanley B. Houck, an interstate commerce attorney who had held the office since 1917.[30] Ewbank's first presidential message invited suggestions for "defining and redefining our place and function in the educational scheme of things" because "[n]ew occasions teach new duties."[31]

While teaching, coaching debate and oratory, continuing his professional activities, and chairing the University Radio Committee from its initiation in 1928, his was the eighth doctorate awarded by the department. This represents a significant concentration of effort on his part, a characteristic that was manifested throughout his life. He invariably opened his office door about eight o'clock in the morning and kept it open to all comers except when he was in class. Lunchtime was usually spent with colleagues or committees, followed by afternoons in the office or the library until five or after. Almost invariably, a part of the evening was spent in his study at home, with thirty minutes to an hour for relaxation with double solitaire or Scrabble with Rachel before retiring. The final waking moments were devoted to reading mystery novels, which he regularly passed on to colleagues who shared his penchant for whodunits. Weekends were more social and flexible, a time for bridge or the theater or dinner with friends. But the press of student concerns was never far away.

Dean Ray Immel invited Ewbank to serve as visiting professor at the University of Southern California for the 1933 summer session, to teach some graduate courses and provide guidance in the structuring of the curriculum in radio. That provided the occasion for the family to have a vacation trip in the drive from Wisconsin, to see some of the sights of the great West and the Pacific Ocean. This was also a time when Ewbank was preparing for his year term as president of the National Association of Teachers of Speech, which began in December 1933 and concluded at the convention in New Orleans in December 1934.

At the New Orleans meeting the Committee on Research in Oratory was appointed by President Ewbank. W. Norwood Brigance served as chair. Members included H. A. Wichelns, W. H. Yeager, A. Craig Baird, G. W. Gray, Louis Eich, C. C. Cunningham, G. P. Tanquary, F. M. Rarig, and Ewbank. Its report stated: "The Committee is commissioned with the definite purpose of preparing and publishing a volume of studies on the *literary criticism of American orators*, something to become in a broad way to the field of speech what the *Cambridge History of American Literature* is to the field of English."[32] That challenge to the committee led Brigance to say that the volumes of *A History and Criticism of American Public Address* were "made possible by Henry L. Ewbank, then president of the National Association of Teachers of Speech," and that Ewbank "was not to escape so easily, however, for after his presidential term had ended he was drafted by the editorial board for active service."[33] Some eight years elapsed before the 1943 publication of the two-volume work, which was attributed by Brigance to the fact that historians and authorities in various fields, such as law, religion, and statecraft, were consulted for guidance regarding individuals and periods that would be significant and that coordination of forty-one authors, working on thirty-four essays as each author simultaneously carried out regularly assigned duties, took time and patience. Each essay was read by five members of the editorial board as the essay was developed. That board, which ultimately was comprised of Dallas Dickey, Lester Thonssen, and Lionel Crocker, together with Baird, Cunningham, Rarig, Tanquary, Wichelns, Yeager, and Ewbank, included some who had agreed to serve as authors or coauthors but who found the press of editorial work great enough that they "were forced to give up the writing in order to meet their editorial obligations. Their influence," Brigance concluded, "is important, although their names do not appear at the beginning of chapters."[34] Ewbank is one who chose not to coauthor a study. He had been named to share writing of the study of Robert LaFollette Sr. with Carroll Lahman, who had done the work on his subject under Ewbank's direction. It is significant to note that, in addition to his appointment of, and membership on, the research committee and his work on the editorial board, of those forty-one authors, six completed their doctoral dissertations under the direction of Henry Ewbank. Of course, the Brigance series chapters were not the only contributions of those scholars to rhetorical studies. For example, Marie Hochmuth is one of the six. She did not finish her own doctorate until two years after these volumes were published, and she later edited the third volume in the series.

One interesting note arises from a handwritten list of doctoral advisees that Ewbank created on a yellow legal pad sometime late in his life. He listed Marvin Bauer, who contributed the study of Henry W. Grady to the first volume of *A History and Criticism of American Public Address*, as his first candidate, completing his degree in 1936. At this time, especially in the field of speech, where graduate degrees were just becoming available, the usual practice for those who elected to pursue graduate study was to continue teaching wherever they were employed and to take summer session courses at an institution that offered the desired degree. The records of the Wisconsin department and of the Graduate School show that Bauer, a member of the Brooklyn College faculty, was an advisee of Andrew T. Weaver. Given that Weaver's major interest was in voice science, it seems possible (1) that Bauer had started his study under Weaver's aegis before Ewbank was available to serve as chair and (2) that Ewbank, as a member of Bauer's dissertation advisory committee, worked closely enough with the candidate that later recall made it seem as if he had had major responsibility.

In any event, Robert T. Oliver did complete his doctorate under Ewbank's direction in 1936. Oliver went on to become one of the more prolific publishers in a wide range of subject matter during his long career at Pennsylvania State University. His first book, *Four Who Spoke Out*, published in 1946, was a popular revision of his dissertation, surveying the oratorical careers of Edmund Burke, Charles James Fox, Richard Brinsley Sheridan, and William Pitt the Younger.[35]

In 1937 two men completed their dissertations with Ewbank as major professor. Rexford Mitchell, who became president of LaCrosse State Teachers' College, was one of the authors included in the Brigance volumes. His dissertation and chapter dealt with William L. Yancey, a speaker for the Southern Rights movement and officer in the Confederacy. Nemias B. Beck, who became professor and director of forensics at Purdue University, studied the speaking of another Southern orator, Alexander Stephens. Beck later relied heavily on his dissertation resources for a chapter in J. Jeffery Auer's 1963 *Antislavery & Disunion 1858–1861*,[36] which followed the three volumes of the *History and Criticism*. In its Preface, Auer noted that Ewbank, together with Craig Baird, had been "essentially co-editors" in the planning stages of that volume.[37]

Including these men, during the twenty-three years before his death in 1960, Ewbank served as dissertation director for a total of sixty-one doctorates. Given that his was the eighth Ph.D. awarded at the University of Wisconsin and that a total of 201 had been awarded through 1960, this meant that Ewbank directed one of every three degrees completed in the department. Except for 1944, 1954, and 1957, when none of his students finished, and six years when only one candidate completed, at least two and as many as seven candidates completed their dissertations and final oral examinations with Ewbank each year. Some were war years, when the earlier pattern of summer study in between full-time faculty status during the academic year created delays.

After the first few years Ewbank's involvement with the development of public radio broadened his span of interest and competence beyond strictly traditional rhetorical studies. Students began to take advantage of his work with experimental and statistical methods, leading to empirical studies of persuasive messages that then went on to test the rhetorical dimensions of audience response. There were historical studies, such as John Penn's study of the development of WHA, the Wisconsin state radio station that had been sustained and developed by the Radio Council chaired by Ewbank. In addition to his work with doctoral students, there are names and numbers of master's degree candidates, to say nothing of undergraduate students who were in his classes and who worked with him in debate and oratory, whose records are in the files of the years that he spent in the classroom. These students, too, share the growing comprehension of the ways in which rhetoric pervades our everyday lives. John V. Irwin, who returned to Madison as a faculty member after World War II, said to this author one day, "I used to wonder how such a small faculty turned out as many students and as much work as they do. Now, I've found out. It's just that everyone does the work of five people!" This was certainly true of Ewbank.

But it wasn't just that he was in the office with his door open. Especially during the days of the Great Depression, when he had just completed his own doctorate, and in all of the years before and shortly after World War II, throughout the summer and occasionally during the academic year, a group of graduate students and their wives was at the Ewbank house on Sunday evening for supper and conversation. Not only Ewbank's advisees but others in his seminars were present. On occasion there was "shop talk," but more often it was just a sharing of views and viewpoints on topics of the day. Often the screened porch offered an evening breeze to make informal conversation comfortable. Of course, all of this meant that Rachel Ewbank, daughter Barbara, and son Hank were necessarily involved in the preparation, participation, and cleanup for the evenings. Heinie Ewbank's personal family was a nucleus for his extended professional family of students who were welcomed and encouraged cordially and warmly as they pursued their goals and remained colleagues and friends throughout their careers.

During these same days Ewbank extended his professional reach through two more avenues. On the one hand, he was a practicing public speaker, responding to frequent requests from high schools throughout the state of Wisconsin and northern Illinois to speak at their commencement ceremonies. One of this themes for such occasions was "Time Marches On," the title of a radio series of the day sponsored by *Time* magazine. A fragmentary manuscript records that he observed that "much of the marching is around in circles, change is not always progress. But even between two generations there has been so much change in customs, fads, and fashion that it seems unusually hard for parent and children to speak the same language." He then cited several changes that had occurred during his lifetime—being able to see women's shoes because skirts got shorter, the development of radio, the war that didn't end all wars, banks closing, and the dust bowl created by midwest drought—and emphasized the growing importance and availability of a high school education.[38]

The other activity that took Ewbank to numbers of Wisconsin towns was an appointment that he held for a time in the Department of Rural Sociology. In the Depression days, when it was said that "people had very little to spend but the evening," they would gather to talk about problems that confronted their communities and their common difficulties in farming and local business. Ewbank was sought by the Cooperative Extension people for help in organizing community meetings in such a way that they might have a better chance of arriving at constructive solutions, rather than simply sharing grievances. His response was to serve as a moderator for meetings that focused on a specific problem or agenda, steering the contributions so that they worked their way through a reasoned problem-solving pattern. One of his recollections told of a meeting called to consider whether or not the salary of the county nurse should be raised, in the face of a dwindling county budget. After twenty minutes or so of statements pro and con, Ewbank asked what the nurse's salary was at the time. No one in the room knew. So one person was deputized to secure the information in order for the group to arrive at a rational recommendation.

At one stage in his teaching, Ewbank reportedly became a sort of target for the then-current group of doctoral candidates. As they conversed among themselves, perhaps in the fabled Rathskeller of the Memorial Union, the perception grew that no one in the group had been able to tell Ewbank about a book or an article in the Wisconsin State Historical Library, which served as the university library, with which he did not already seem familiar. That, then, became a sort of challenge: find *some* arcane source that will finally get him to admit that he had not seen or read it. The half dozen or so students then set about to meet the challenge. They worked at it a while, when it slowly dawned on one or another that as they said, "I found . . . in this article," or "This author said . . . , have you seen it?" the response from Ewbank was sometimes a yes, but it was never a no. What usually happened was that he acknowledged the finding and then referred the student to another, related source. Then, apparently, Ewbank would track down the initial reference, digest the contents, and in the next conversation he would be able to comment at length. The ultimate conclusion was that perhaps Ewbank had *not* read everything in the entire library before his students got to it but that he was able to follow their tracks so closely that he could help in evaluating the ideas and information that they were gathering. In the process, he led them to broader inquiry and consideration of more resources than they might otherwise have encountered. This is a valuable, if difficult and demanding, pedagogical practice that certainly contributed to the scholarly works produced by those who had studied with him.

In two subject areas within the broad field of Speech, or Speech Communication Ewbank was among the "pioneers." First was his interest in the rhetorical uses of radio both for communicating information and for persuasive messages. As noted earlier, this interest was piqued shortly after his arrival at Wisconsin through his appointment as chair of the University Radio Committee. This group soon grew to become the State Radio Council, charged with operating the educational broadcasting station, WHA, which later became a statewide FM radio and television network. The council dealt directly with the legislature for funding. The need to justify appropriations stimulated the need for supporting evidence that radio could and did contribute to the educational opportunities in the state. The School of the Air programs aimed at public schools to provide instruction in music, art, and writing became the focus of master's theses and dissertations—some descriptive, some critical, some empirical. All explored the effectiveness of messages created and delivered without use of the visible code. The whole problem of assessing "effect" on radio audiences lacked both theoretical grounding and tested means of measurement. Ewbank and some of his students bent their efforts to developing audience measurements. This portion of his interests and his work led Conrad A. Elvehjem, president of the University of Wisconsin, to write at the time of Ewbank's death, "Among the little group of far-sighted men gathered around primitive radio equipment in a painting on the wall of Radio Hall . . . is Henry Lee Ewbank, pioneer in educational radio. A kindly man with sly wit, an ability to make friends easily, and a rare knowledge of his subject, he was a national leader in the work to make the electronic communication media a force in social and cultural betterment, an idealist who lived to see many of his goals achieved not only in this state but, to some degree, throughout the nation."[39]

The other academic area in which his teaching, through a popular textbook, was extended nationally was in discussion and debate. Ewbank had an unbroken connection with debate since his undergraduate days through coaching, teaching courses in argumentation and persuasion, and the national offices he held in Delta Sigma Rho. A manuscript recently sent to the author by J. Jeffery Auer[40] recounts that soon after he had completed his doctorate, Ewbank had signed a contract to produce a textbook on argumentation and debate. In the summer of 1936, when Auer returned to Wisconsin to pursue his own doctorate, A. T. Weaver, who was to be Auer's adviser, had consulted with Ewbank about the potential for merging Auer's proposal for a book about discussion with the projected debate text. From that point, as Auer describes it, the effect was "to invigorate Heinie by teaming him with an ambitious and eager young coauthor." This was the beginning of the collaboration that resulted in the 1941 publication of *Discussion and Debate: Tools of a Democracy.*[41] The collaboration extended through the completion of Auer's degree, which was delayed until 1947 by his full-time teaching and some war years in the U.S. Navy, as well as the publication that same year of *Handbook for Discussion Leaders,*[42] a rewrite for civilian use of a navy bulletin created by Auer. The collaboration continued through second editions of each in 1951 and 1954, respectively. The friendship and mutual admiration between the men, twenty years apart in age, were unending.

Tools of a Democracy, the subtitle of the text, distills the perspective that was significant to both authors. The Greek philosophers knew rhetoric to be the handmaiden of politics, and dialectic to be the counterpart of rhetoric. Treating the analysis of existing situations and identification of existing problems, the gathering of pertinent information, its evaluation as useful or irrelevant evidence, and the exploration of a number of alternative solutions under the rubric of "discussion," Ewbank and Auer presented debate, then, as the means of publicly testing the acceptance of any given "solution" through the processes of a representative democracy. The authors shared a deep and genuine devotion to the form of government under which both lived, as well as the conviction that free speech and instruction in the ways of effective speaking carry great responsibilities to the society in which they lived. Each had chosen to serve the nation in time of war. Each saw the significance of an alert and enlightened citizenry making choices among policies advocated by diverse interests. There is need for experienced, critical auditors as well as for experienced, articulate rhetors in a democracy. The continuum "of inquiry and judgment, or investigation and decision"—of discussion and debate—provides such experience.[43]

The initial sentence of the *Handbook for Discussion Leaders* provides an excellent example of the sense of style as well as the sense of humor that pervaded Ewbank's speaking and writing. "Americans are a talkative people, generally speaking" is the sentence.[44] The schooling that he had received, at least from his elocutionary days at Ohio Wesleyan, had made him highly conscious of the multiple meanings of words that make puns possible and make misunderstandings probable. This sentence, which he created with a twinkle in his eye, had a highly intentional double meaning. First, it affirmed that "most Americans are talkative." Second, it said that talkative people, including most Americans, are usually ("generally") speaking. This style, which Auer described as "direct, sharp, sometimes abrupt, and in short sentences that contributed to a staccato effect," contrasted directly with Auer's style, self-described as "meandering, indirect, non-aggressive, with long sentences that suggested hidden Germanic antecedents." Through a "partnership of equals," despite differences in age or academic status, they arrived at the expectation and acceptance of frank questions and criticisms of drafts initially prepared by each author, which led to a blending of styles. A first draft, once prepared, passed through however many iterations were necessary—once it took seven exchanges—to lead to a final "joint production."[45]

That same "partnership of equals" attitude characterized Ewbank's advisory interactions with doctoral candidates, contributing to the strength of their dissertations as well as to their later contributions to rhetorical scholarship. William S. Howell, who later chaired the department at the University of Minnesota, recalled that Ewbank directed his study of the effects of high school debate on critical thinking ability. Howell wrote that Ewbank "did a splendid, tactful yet exacting job of supervision." When Howell experienced problems in interpreting the test results, he reported that Ewbank "calmed me down and provided essential helpful advice. Our personal relationship," he noted, "was warm and friendly. When the ordeal was over I know that nobody in the world could get as high quality work out of me as H. L. E."[46] In similar vein, Paul Boase commented on Ewbank's work with candidates as they studied their way toward the process of dissertation writing. "In his seminars on persuasion, radio and society, group discussion and the history of American public address [Ewbank] never talked very much, but his incisive criticism and comments on our reports were always right on target. His critiques, oral and written, always contained a skillful balance of the historical and rhetorical aspects of public address. . . . He was a master of promoting fertile productive classroom discussions." Boase did note that the graduate students of the 1930s through the 1950s were a "more mature group . . . than we had the pleasure of working with in the late 60s and 70s." That, in addition to the requirement that one study the broad spectrum of speech education and/or reeducation (i.e., rehabilitation), theater and/or interpretation, sciences basic to speech, and public address and radio/television, is certainly critical to bear in mind as one looks back on graduate study during the time when Ewbank was such an important force.

Boase went further in his assessment of the manner in which Ewbank helped his students learn better to organize and present the information that they gathered in their studies of rhetoric. "I learned a tremendous amount about the processes of skillful editing from those little quavery brackets that he used to cut out my redundancies and his always insightful comments not only on style but content as well," Boase wrote in his description of Ewbank's "editorial genius."[47]

As still further evidence of Ewbank's editorial guidance, Boase provided some of the comments that Ewbank had written as he reviewed drafts of Boase's dissertation. The drafts themselves had not been preserved, so the "little quavery brackets" cannot be reviewed, but the "partnership of equals" attitude is clear, as is the concern for both content and style. Ewbank submitted his questions, comments, and suggestions for the consideration of the dissertation writer, whose name, after all, would be listed as author of the study. Boase's dissertation assessed the speaking of Methodist circuit-riding ministers in Ohio. Ewbank made occasional suggestions that lengthy chapters be recast into two shorter units, more proportional with others. In one note, Ewbank questioned, "[W]ill the average reader know what 'Invention' and 'disposition' mean to the rhetorician? A descriptive phrase in parentheses: Invention might help the uninformed without offending the scholar." Earlier, Ewbank had suggested that the material in one of the chapters was "interesting—but I think most of it could be saved for use in an article. Maybe I'm wrong—I have been." He then wrote, "I have made some more of those irritating editings—cutting such expressions as 'he moaned,' 'he wailed,' and turning a few sentences into a simple past tense."

That note concluded, "Through blood and sweat—perhaps not with tears—you are making this material interesting." As Ewbank returned each draft chapter and comments, he enclosed a brief note about what he was doing. Among other things, he was putting final touches on *Broadcasting: Radio and Television*,[48] classes were starting, and dissertation chapters were being read for others who were writing during the summer of 1951 and into the 1951–1952 academic year. Each letter was signed, "As ever, HL."[49]

Among the other claims on Ewbank's time and thought as Boase, James Lennon, Ted McLaughlin, Mason Hicks, Marcus Boulware, and Thorrel Fest were completing their dissertations was one rare example of published rhetorical criticism by Ewbank. This appeared in the symposium of critical comment on General Douglas MacArthur's address to the Joint Session of Congress on April 19, 1951, edited by Frederick Haberman. Among comments from congressmen and senators, journalists, and academic critics, Ewbank chose to base his assessment on a standard closely reflective of that which he used in his own dissertation. Rudolf Flesch had published *The Art of Plain Talk* in 1946,[50] which considered sentence length and syllables per hundred words and percentages of "personal words" and "personal sentences" to measure "ease of reading" and "human interest." Using that formula, Ewbank found that MacArthur's speech was much more difficult to read than Lincoln's Gettysburg Address and that his "human interest" score was only "mildly interesting." He concluded that, though it was, "in many ways, . . . a great speech, . . . it will not find an enduring place in our literature as a model of speech composition."[51] This study, employing social science methods to assess the effect of a message delivered orally to a radio, television, and face-to-face audience, through a manuscript analysis measuring "plain talk," was unique in its use of an "objective" standard. At the same time, it made use of the only kind of measuring techniques accepted by operators of the electronic media.

Edgar E. Willis was one of the early candidates to share Ewbank's interest and concern for the ways in which radio might function as a means by which attitudes could be influenced. Willis, now an professor emeritus at the University of Michigan, recalled several ways in which Ewbank had facilitated and guided his graduate study. First, Ewbank secured a fellowship award that enabled continued residence and full-time study, so that what had been projected as a four-year summer school project was completed in two years. "During that period," Willis wrote, "[Ewbank] was an invaluable source of advice and encouragement. No one could have served a student better as a guide and mentor." He noted, too, that Rachel Ewbank helped as the Willises combined pursuit of the degree with the onset of parenthood. Second, Willis recalled that much of Ewbank's importance as a mentor was generated "by guiding his students as they developed their studies and he encouraged them to make their findings known through publication . . . his influence on criticism was manifest in his critical appraisals . . . of papers by the large number of people with whom he worked as they developed their own styles and critical standards." As an example, Willis noted that Ewbank had commented on a seminar paper, "This would make a good journal article." After a number of years, Willis came upon the paper and submitted it "almost as I had written it for [the] seminar—to the *Central States Speech Journal*, and it was accepted and published." In addition, at a later time, Willis saw in another article a reference to his article. "With an unerring eye [Ewbank] had recognized something that others would also find worth reading." Beyond that incident, Willis recalled that Ewbank "put pressure on me to abstract an article from my Ph.D. dissertation and get it published. As I recall he was the one who actually submitted the article I wrote—with his help and counsel—to the then fledgling *Speech Monographs*—and it was duly published."[52] Evidence that such "pressure" or at least encouragement was applied to, or felt by, others can be found in the fact that the names of forty-five Ewbank doctoral advisees (three of every four) are found among the authors listed in the Matlon–Ortiz *Index to Journals in Communication Studies through 1990*.[53] Of the remaining sixteen, one additional name appears among the authors in the *History and Criticism* volumes, and yet another in *Antislavery & Disunion*. Several spent their careers coaching forensic activities, which may have diverted time and energy. Two became university presidents. One became governor of the state of Wisconsin, with statements published in other venues. On the other hand, such names as Robert Oliver, J. Jeffery Auer, Robert Gunderson, and Marie Hochmuth are familiar enough as authors of books and articles to raise the average of published rhetorical studies to even more significant proportions.

John Penn, now retired from the University of North Dakota, struck a rather different note as he recalled "a great teacher and a wonderful human being." He wrote that "a delightful facet of his teaching was the use of an anecdote to make a point." Following that example, Penn recalled a conversation in which Dean James McBurney of Northwestern had asked who had been Penn's major professor. When told that it was Heinie Ewbank, McBurney replied, "Say no more. That is the greatest recommendation you could possibly have. You are most fortunate to have been a student of this great teacher." Continuing, Penn listed four judgments that establish for him the contribution and the impact that Ewbank made on the field of rhetorical studies:

1. The high esteem in which he was held by other greats—Brigance, Wallace, Monroe, Rarig, Howell of Cornell, McBurney, Hance, Mabie, etc. 2. The achievements and status of his students whose articles appeared in the Journals and who appeared on the programs at national conventions—in the day when there were limited opportunities due to few sections. 3. The great impact by his students who achieved leadership in the profession and in the strongest departments across the country—the Auers, Hochmuths, Olivers, Gundersons, etc. 4. The love and admiration demonstrated by some 30–40 of his students who gathered in Chicago, flying in from across the country during the Christmas holidays for a surprise recognition dinner honoring him.[54]

The specific occasion for that surprise recognition dinner, which assuredly took place in conjunction with a Speech Association of America convention, has not been identified, but one such recognition occasion was the Golden Jubilee Congress of Delta Sigma Rho, which was held at the Hotel Sherman, April 12–14, 1956. In addition to the Student Congress, which had been held in alternate years since 1939, except for the World War II years, there was a special banquet at which nineteen distinguished members of the honor society were cited as "examples of the best traditions of Delta Sigma Rho." The nineteen honorees included four university presidents, two U.S. senators (Wayne Morse and Hubert Humphrey), Justice William O. Douglas, the librarian of the U.S. Supreme Court (Helen C. Newman), two prominent ministers, Erwin Canham of the *Christian Science Monitor*, Hans von Kaltenborn, the radio news commentator, David Lilienthal, who had headed the Tennessee Valley Authority (TVA) and the Atomic Energy Commission, Chief Justice Arthur Vanderbilt of the New Jersey Supreme Court, Inland Steel president Clarence Randall, and four prominent men in the field of speech: James A. Winans, A. Craig Baird, Andrew T. Weaver, and Henry L. Ewbank. Ewbank's citation included the comments, "By precept and example he has increased our knowledge of and faith in the basic tools of our democracy. . . . Delta Sigma Rho bears the impress of the guidance and wisdom of the man who was its national president from 1931 to 1939."[55] Elsewhere it is noted that he was also a vice president from 1926 to 1931 and from 1939 to 1947. Thorrel B. Fest, who had become president in 1953, had just completed his Ph.D. as a Ewbank student. Six former Ewbank students—one as an undergraduate and five doctoral candidates—were members of the seventeen-member Jubilee Committee. Ewbank had written the six-page "Bits and Pieces of Delta Sigma Rho History," which was a part of the souvenir booklet for the occasion.

Among those "Bits and Pieces" was mention of a significant development that had taken place within the honor society during Ewbank's presidential years. He explained that in "the 1922 revision of the Constitution the phrase 'not a Negro' was inserted" in the article defining membership qualifications. He commented that he did not know just when or why this was done and added, "I was present, however, when steps were taken for its removal." That was an understatement. He described the 1931 council meeting, the first in five years, when student delegates criticized the rule requiring approval of four-fifths of the chapters to amend Article II on membership. The presiding officer sought to stop a delegate from speaking about racial segregation, saying that the topic had been thoroughly debated at previous meetings and that little good would result from repeating the arguments. Ewbank then "rose to remark that the student delegates were not present when the issues were discussed, and anyway why shouldn't a debating society decide what it wanted to debate?"[56] At that meeting Stanley Houck was reelected president and then resigned in favor of Ewbank. It took much of Ewbank's term of office for him to communicate the merits of striking those restrictive words from the constitution, but after several years the words "not a Negro" were stricken by an affirmative vote of four-fifths of the chapters. Evidence of the "impress of the guiding wisdom" of Ewbank's presidency was one of those nineteen members who were honored at the Golden Jubilee—Dr. Benjamin Elijah Mays, an African American debater and graduate of Bates College with a doctorate from the University of Chicago, recipient of honorary degrees from Bates, Boston University, Yale, and elsewhere, and president of Morehouse College. In this, as in other endeavors, Ewbank demonstrated his own rhetorical skills in the service of education and democracy.

One especially important factor characterizes the significance of Heinie Ewbank's place among those who gave strength to the growing enterprise of rhetorical studies through the middle third of the twentieth century: the broad range and scope of the students and their studies that he helped to generate and bring to fruition. The examples that follow cite dissertation studies that, with whatever modification was appropriate, found their way into the published literature of the field.

In biorhetorical studies, such as those that constituted most of the three volumes of *History and Criticism*, one can cite from among others such examples as Walter Emery's chapter on Samuel Gompers, Louis Mallory's study of Patrick Henry, and A. E. Whitehead's examination of the speaking of William E. Borah.

Closely related but representing a different perspective on rhetorical events were historical-rhetorical background studies of an era or a period of time, such as George V. Bohman's work on "The Colonial Period" in volume 1 of the series.

Again, the dissertation research that employed a variation on the major and interlocking perspectives of history, biography, politics, and rhetoric, Robert G. Gunderson's study of the 1840 presidential campaign, became his book *The Log Cabin Campaign*.[57]

Another historical emphasis was developed with less direct relevance to traditional rhetoric in John Penn's historical study of the development of WHA, the University of Wisconsin educational radio station that became the flagship of the statewide FM broadcasting network providing School of the Air programming for public schools, information for farmers and businessmen throughout the state, and other public service functions. To a great degree, this study represented the history of an important dimension of Ewbank's rhetorical impact on the state as he sought and received legislative authorizations and funding for the State Radio Council program.

Explorations of Wichelns's view that "effect" is the distinguishing characteristic of rhetoric constitute an identifiable segment of the rhetorical studies undertaken by Ewbank advisees. In 1939 P. E. Lull reported his study of the effect of the presence or absence of humor in persuasive speeches. His method was that of a controlled laboratory experiment measuring audience acceptance of the speaker's position on current controversial topics.[58]

The effects of training in argumentation on high school and college students were explored and reported by William S. Howell and Winston Brembeck in 1942 and 1947, as they tested the critical thinking abilities of debaters and students before and after their classes and activities. The rhetorical canons of invention and disposition were in sharpest focus as the student subjects' performance both as rhetors and as audience was tested.[59] Similarly, Robert Capel assessed the effect of high school debate participation on the information and attitudes acquired by the students.

Ewbank's interest in the use of radio as a rhetorical medium presented unique challenges to the enterprise of assessing effects on audiences. Without the element of face-to-face relationship between rhetor and audience, the rhetorical situation was substantially changed. There was no potential for use of the visual elements of delivery. There were severe limitations on the potential for inter-stimulation within the audience and no way to determine the importance, if any, of interactions among listeners. Reliability of any analysis of the potential audience was highly questionable. Estimates of who would listen under what circumstances and with what prior knowledge were only guesswork. In sum, important elements of the traditional aspects of preparation were not available or not dependable. Methods of organization and presentation needed to be tested to discover how information and how persuasive messages might best be adapted to the new medium. Edgar Willis was among the early experimenters. He tested three forms of radio presentation in influencing attitudes.[60] Five years later, in 1945, John Dietrich reported the findings of his study of the effect of two modes of delivery on the attitudes of radio listeners.[61] Within the next ten years, John Highlander explored the informational effects of speaker variables in radio talks, using a mechanical audience analyzer, and Erling Jorgenson tested the relative effectiveness of three methods of television newscasting.

Second only to the number of studies of individual rhetoricians executed by Ewbank's students was the number of studies of persuasion in political campaigns for election to office and in debates focusing on specific issues. Some of these studies reached back in time as did Robert Gunderson's 1949 study of the 1840 *Log Cabin Campaign*[62] or Donald Olson's 1959 exploration of the persuasion in debate on the Kansas-Nebraska Bill in 1853–1854. Looking at more recent campaigns, Cyril Hager evaluated the persuasive strategies in the 1916 presidential campaign in 1942, while Rex Robinson reported his examination of the 1940 presidential campaign in 1947. Issue campaign studies included J. Calvin Callaghan's work on the Lend-Lease debate, concluded in 1949, and Ordean Ness's 1953 assessment of the administration's oral persuasive efforts to secure adoption of its 1951 Universal Military Training Proposal. In the non-governmental efforts to persuade American citizens, Orland Lefforge analyzed the efforts of the American Medical Association to defeat national health insurance. His findings were concluded in 1953. In 1955 Stanley Wheater presented his study of persuasion in the citizen-organized "Save the Union" meetings of 1859–1861.

Closely related to these rhetorical studies were four dissertations dealing with persuasion in legislative bodies. Paul Brandes looked at the use of evidence by selected U.S. senators (1953). In 1958 Lee Dreyfus, later governor of Wisconsin, reported his study of persuasive techniques in modern congressional debate. At the level of state legislatures, Fred Alexander looked at debate in the 1953 Michigan legislature (1955), and Charles Monnier reported in 1958 his assessment of the persuasion in the 1953 Wisconsin legislature.

Despite Ewbank's encouragement to publish papers or articles derived from graduate research, it is obvious that not all of the dissertations executed under his guidance found their way into print. Some of the authors succumbed to the pressures of teaching in institutions that put more value on the classroom than on publications. At various times, administrative positions occupied time and energy. At one time, near the academic year 1960–1961, this author noted that twenty-five of Ewbank's erstwhile doctoral candidates were serving as chair or head of the Department of Speech at their respective institutions. Others found that the time commitment to working with forensic activities left little room for writing. A few moved into careers away from academe and may have done their writing in different venues. Of course, numbers of his students published widely on topics not directly related to their dissertations. The sixty-one people who executed their major early rhetorical study with Heinie Ewbank have, in the intervening years, not only done more rhetorical studies of their own but also encouraged and influenced others to do the same.

One measure of encouragement of rhetorical studies can be inferred indirectly from contributions to the national professional association. It is scarcely possible to explore all of the program and committee assignments that have been held by his doctorates, but because that activity often leads to elective office, it seems appropriate to note that five presidents and two executive vice presidents of the (now) National Communication Association had earned their terminal degrees with Ewbank's guidance. Marie Hochmuth and Robert Gunderson edited the *Quarterly Journal of Speech*, and Jeffery Auer edited *Speech Monographs*. Those same three people have received the association's Distinguished Service Award.

From a different, more localized perspective, Frederick Haberman, who chaired the department at Wisconsin during Heinie Ewbank's final years, called attention to one of the important rhetorical strategies that Ewbank used in his teaching and speaking and writing. In the memorial notice printed in *The CHAPA Letter* of March 1961, Haberman wrote that Ewbank "was without rival in his mastery of the analogy. With analogy, he could charm and conciliate the hostile, he could make brilliantly clear a point formerly vague, or he could unmask the true triviality of an idea to which had been ascribed world-shaking significance; or, best of all, he could puncture the balloons of bombast and conceit."[63] This appreciation of the ways in which analogy and its close cousin metaphor function makes clear the fact that Ewbank used the analogy effectively both to clarify and to frame hypotheses for rhetorical studies.[64] Witness the opening sentences of *Discussion and Debate*: "Discussion and debate are not simply courses in a college curriculum. They are the essential tools of a democratic society. To train students in the intelligent and effective use of these tools is the aim of this book."[65] Earlier reference has been made to Ewbank's use of analogy in his collegiate papers and his dissertation. Yet another indication of his appreciation for the associative process of analogy and metaphor is found in his citation of a statement by Aristotle in a paper entitled "A Working Definition of Rhetoric," which may have been a proposed first chapter for a manuscript of a basic text sought by Harper Brothers. The citation read that "clearness, pleasure and distinction are given in the highest degree by metaphor, and the art of metaphor cannot be taught."[66] The significant determinant in thinking and speaking analogically is the identification of the important principle that links the factors or the thoughts being compared. Ewbank's talent for perceiving inherent, rather than superficial, factors made his rhetorical use of the analogy one of *thought* rather than *style*. This was both the heuristic ground for rhetorical studies by his students and the organizational ground for his own system of classification.

One general historical fact should be noted as we think now of the ways in which rhetorical and other studies were pursued prior to Ewbank's death in 1960. Investigations were executed either in libraries accessed by card catalogues and reference book sources or by experimental means that were compiled by hand and computed manually. There were no electronic information retrieval systems and no computers with programs to produce statistical analyses. Manuscripts were typed on manual typewriters—either portable or office models—using carbon paper when more than single copy was to be made. When each committee member was to read a draft, five copies might be the norm, necessitating typing each draft at least twice. Any typographical errors were corrected by erasing each copy, taking care not to smudge the carbons. When a draft was submitted and when elections or additions were to be made, at least the entire page was retyped, if not the entire chapter or unit. Because the University of Wisconsin Graduate School and Library required the use of footnotes rather than endnotes, changes in pagination usually demanded changes in footnotes, even if there were no additions or deletions in the notes themselves. Corrected or altered drafts were necessarily presented as "clean copy," so that the professorial reader would not be distracted by obvious deletions or marginal notes. All of these mechanical considerations, of course, were as important to the production of manuscripts for books and articles as they were to the completion of master's theses and doctoral dissertations. Heinie Ewbank's manuscript writing was further affected by the fact that he was a self-taught typist who used only the thumb and first two fingers on each hand to strike the keys. This meant much more hand movement and a much slower rate of speed than when using the touch method. Because, with manual typewriters, the "shift" key meant that there was an actual shift upward of the paper carriage, it meant that he frequently did not synchronize the "shift" and the letter keys, causing the capital letter to hit the page about half of a line above the rest of the text. This created a sort of "hiccup" pattern that made his typing readily identifiable, but not acceptable to typesetters.

Similar note should be taken of the production of rhetorical studies that appeared at professional conventions and in the scholarly journals. As John Penn noted, programs for the meetings of the National Association of Teachers of Speech, which met during the days between Christmas and New Year's Day, were a rather far cry from those of the 1990s. Not only was there no "preconvention" schedule, and not only were the programs limited to the normal workday hours of eight to five, but also the number of programs at any given hour was closer to ten than to the forty listed, for instance, at 8:00 A.M. on the opening day of the 1996 Speech Communication Association (SCA) Convention in San Diego. Because program papers often relate directly to publications, limitations on convention appearances led to smaller numbers of manuscripts submitted to the journals of the profession. Also the number and size of speech journals were smaller in the days when Ewbank was writing and advising doctoral candidates. The *Quarterly Journal of Speech* was, of course, well established. *Speech Monographs* appeared in 1934. The Southern and Western regional journals began in 1935 and 1937, respectively, with central following in 1949. *Communication Quarterly (Today's Speech)* was started in the East in 1953, one year after the *Speech Teacher* was added to the national scene. Apart from these journals, two of Ewbank's doctoral candidates published articles in the *Journal of Communication*, which started in 1951, and one article appeared in the *Journalism Quarterly* which had been in existence since 1924. *Philosophy and Rhetoric* (1968) and *Human Communication Research* (1974) came along later, as have a number of other journals. This is not to say that there were no other avenues for publication of rhetorical studies. Journals of history at the state, regional, and national organizational levels, as well as those focusing on specific eras, carried articles by several of those who had explored speakers or issues appropriate to the readership. Political science journals, too, accepted certain studies of candidates and campaigns. In this way the fields were sometimes drawn a bit closer.

True, much of the focus here is on Ewbank's work as major professor for sixty-one doctoral candidates, a number of whom made outstanding contributions to the quantity and the quality of rhetorical studies. It should not be overlooked that he served as adviser to candidates for the master's degree, some of whom continued to work with him and others of whom pursued further study with other mentors at other institutions. These numbers have not been compiled, but it can be affirmed that, for example, as two doctoral candidates completed their degrees in 1947, Ewbank also chaired the committee for eight master's theses. In 1949, when another two dissertations were completed, Ewbank chaired eight M.A. theses and six M.S. theses.

Evidence of his influence on students who were not his doctoral advisees is found in letters sent shortly after his death. Keith St. Onge, who wrote a basic speech text after a number of years of teaching, wrote "[Ewbank] left a legacy of kindness and tact which I like to think is reflected somewhat in my treatment now of students as forlorn as I was then. In spite of a foot of paper work on his desk, he always had time to help the student find himself and did it with young people of unstable temperament and little sense of direction. In courses he taught . . . the student was expected to find his own way under benign guidance and most of us did. Now after the passage of years, I see what [he] was doing, and doing so well, to our great profit."[67] In similar vein, Charles T. Brown wrote that "he was a sharply unique and penetrating personality and so he is indestructible so long as you and I and many others live. . . . for me some people die and others don't . . . he's around just as he was before I heard his mortal life had closed."[68]

A more recent reflection on Ewbank's influence was provided by Winston L. Brembeck, more than fifty years after he had written his dissertation under Heinie Ewbank's guidance and stayed on in the Wisconsin department to direct forensics and, ultimately, to teach some of the courses that Ewbank had taught. Brembeck said that for him and for others who studied with Ewbank,

he opened my mind into the many parts of public address I had only narrowly known as an undergraduate elsewhere. No one in his seminar which examined critically the subject matter in the *History and Criticism of American Public Address* volumes could come away without a keen sense of the elements of speech communication. In this and other Ewbank courses there were emphases on language usage, style, organization, finding the available means of persuasion, the classical proofs of ethos, pathos, and logos, and more. When I turned in a paper or a portion of a thesis which I was certain had great economy of style, my returned paper had some words or phrases penciled out, words I did not need at all in making a point clear or supported.

Brembeck concluded, "It came to seem that Herbert Spencer was looking over my shoulder every time I reached for a pen. 'Heinie' . . . didn't trust verbosity in either print or speech. That speaker was especially suspect 'whose expenditure of speech exceeded his income of ideas.' " Brembeck's response to those who asked why Ewbank had not published more is that, first, *Discussion and Debate* had "defined these fields for many years," emphasizing the significance of ideas more than the quantity of publishing, and, second, "Ewbank opted for instructing the more rather than the fewer, thus permitting less time to be in the library carousel [*sic*] to write. During this professional life he directed dozens of masters and doctoral candidates who, in turn, most certainly have taught many hundreds in the nature of the various theories and practices of human communication." In sum, Brembeck expressed his gratitude for working and socializing with "this great teacher" who "seemed to see life steadily and see it whole, which . . . allowed him to see much of the humor of life. I shall never forget the joy he received when he heard an aptly stated joke or story."[69]

A characteristic of Ewbank's speaking as well as his writing was his forceful use of proofs. Despite, or perhaps because of, the fact that he never was a participant on a winning debate team, Ewbank sought out and used opinion and fact from a wide variety of sources calculated to support his positions in the minds of his audiences. One of his frequent references was to the British political economist Walter Bagehot, whose book, *Physics and Politics*, published in 1869, included these thoughts: "One of the greatest pains to human nature is the pain of a new idea. . . . Naturally, therefore, common men hate a new idea, and are disposed more or less to ill-treat the original man who brings it" and "Tolerance . . . is learned in discussion, and, as history shows, is only so learned."[70] These thoughts, obviously relevant to the text and the subjects of discussion and debate, are found again in Ewbank's Phi Beta Kappa address at Albion College, in his published speech manuscripts, "What's Right with Debate" and "Teaching Speech for Human Relations," and in the *Broadcasting: Radio and Television* chapter dealing with public discussion. The same is true of references to Walter Lippmann whom Ewbank referred to as "America's counterpart to Bagehot." Lippmann's point was that "freedom of speech is established to achieve its essential purpose only when different opinions are expounded in the same hall to the same audience." Thus, "while the right to talk may be the beginning of freedom, the necessity of *listening* is what makes the right important."[71] The ubiquity of these ideas is patently due to their fundamental significance to the entire realm of rhetoric and the frequency with which many people ignore or forget their importance.[72]

PERORATION

Marcus Tullius Cicero said that "the aim of forensic oratory is to teach, to delight, to move."[73] Centuries later, Henry Brooks Adams added the observation that "a teacher affects eternity."[74] Henry Lee Ewbank was a forensic orator (and writer) of great accomplishment. His impact on, and his contribution to, the rhetorical studies of the twentieth-century America endure. He taught. He delighted. He moved.

NOTES

1. Bulletin of the School of Oratory of Ohio Wesleyan University, catalog number 1915–1916 (Vol. 14, No. 5, September 1, 1915), Delaware, OH, 5, 14–29; photocopy in possession of the author.

2. *Le Bijou* of 1918, 170; photocopy of page in possession of the author.

3. Letter from Robert Crosby, September 18, 1997, in possession of the author.

4. Ibid.

5. Robert I. Fulton and Thomas C. Trueblood, *Practical Elements of Elocution* 3d ed. (Boston: Ginn, 1896), 8.

6. "Seventy-First Catalogue of Ohio Wesleyan University," Delaware, OH, 1915, 121.

7. Crosby letter cites page 82 of the 1915 *Le Bijou* and page 182 of the 1916 edition, in possession of the author.

8. Ohio Wesleyan Catalog, 1915, 123.

9. Ibid., 124–126; School of Oratory Bulletin, 14–25.

10. Small "Chap Book" in possession of the author.

11. Manuscripts of "Bernard Shaw as a Satirist" and "The Idealism of H. G. Wells," presented to English Seminar February 15, 1917, and May 15, 1917, respectively, in possession of the author.

12. Crosby letter.

13. Notebook in possession of the author.

14. H. L. Ewbank, "Introduction to 'A History of Oratory,' " handwritten manuscript, 4–7, in possession of the author.

15. Ibid., 8–11.

16. Ibid., 11.

17. Silver Anniversary Program, Michigan Speech Association, April 28, 1950, in possession of the author.

18. Papers for Rhetoric 117s, dated July 8, 1926; July 15, 1926; and July 22, 1926, in possession of the author.

19. "Brief of Lincoln's Speech in Jonesboro Debate," July 2, 1926; paper in possession of the author.

20. Willard Hayes Yeager, "Wendell Phillips," in William N. Brigance, ed., *A History and Criticism of American Public Address*, Vol. 1 (New York: McGraw-Hill, 1943), p. 349.

21. "Outline of 'The Lost Arts,' " July 12, 1926, paper in possession of the author.

22. "Principles of Attention," Lecture I outline for Advanced Public Speaking, manuscript in possession of the author.

23. "The After Dinner Speech," manuscript in possession of the author.

24. "History of Delta Sigma Rho," *The Gavel* 15.2 (January 1933), 6.

25. Henry L. Ewbank, "Four Approaches to the Study of Speech Style," *Quarterly Journal of Speech* 17 (1931), 458–465.

26. "Objective Studies in Speech Style with Special Reference to One Hundred English Sermons." Draft manuscript of Ph.D. dissertation, 1931, in possession of the author, 9–10. Degree was conferred in 1932.

27. Ibid., 23–24.

28. Ibid., 229–272.

29. Ibid., 296.

30. *The Gavel* 11 (March 1929), 9.

31. *The Gavel* 14 (November 1931), 3.

32. *Quarterly Journal of Speech*, 21 (1935), 154.

33. Brigance, *A History and Criticism*, vii.

34. Ibid., xi.

35. Robert T. Oliver, *Four Who Spoke Out: Burke, Fox, Sheridan, Pitt* (Syracuse, NY: Syracuse University Press, 1946).

36. J. Jeffery Auer, ed., *Antislavery and Disunion, 1858–1861: Studies in the Rhetoric of Compromise and Conflict* (New York: Harper and Row, 1963).

37. Ibid., ix.

38. "Time Marches On," typescript of notes in possession of the author.

39. Quoted by Andrew T. Weaver in "Henry Lee Ewbank, 1893–1960," *Quarterly Journal of Speech* 46 (December 1960), 459.

40. J. Jeffery Auer, "I'd Like to Say a Few Words about Writing," unpublished manuscript provided to, and in possession of, the author.

41. Henry Lee Ewbank and J. Jeffery Auer, *Discussion and Debate: Tools of a Democracy* (New York: Appleton-Century-Crofts, 1941).

42. J. Jeffery Auer and Henry Lee Ewbank, *Handbook for Discussion Leaders* (New York: Harper and Brothers, 1947).

43. Ewbank and Auer, *Discussion and Debate*, 20.

44. Auer and Ewbank, *Handbook*, 1.

45. Auer, "I'd Like to Say a Few Words," 20.

46. Letter from William S. Howell, December 3, 1997, in possession of the author.

47. Letter from Paul H. Boase, December 29, 1997, in possession of the author.

48. Henry L. Ewbank and Sherman P. Lawton, *Broadcasting: Radio and Television* (New York: Harper and Brothers, 1952).

49. Penciled letters and notes, undated, sent with the letter from Boase to the author, passim.

50. Rudolf Flesch, *The Art of Plain Talk* (New York: Harper and Brothers, 1946).

51. Frederick W. Haberman, "General MacArthur's Speech: A Symposium of Critical Comment," *Quarterly Journal of Speech* 37 (1951), 330–331.

52. Letter from Edgar E. Willis, December 2, 1997, in possession of the author.

53. Ronald J. Matlon and Sylvia P. Ortiz, eds., *Index to Journals in Communication Studies through 1990* (Annandale, VA: Speech Communication Association, 1992).

54. Letter from John S. Penn, December 5, 1997, in possession of the author.

55. "Delta Sigma Rho 1906–1956 Golden Anniversary," 23, 24.

56. Ibid., 11.

57. Robert Gray Gunderson, *The Log Cabin Campaign* (Lexington: University of Kentucky Press, 1957).

58. P. E. Lull, "The Effectiveness of Humor in Persuasive Speeches," *Speech Monographs* 7 (1940), 26–40.

59. William Smiley Howell, "The Effects of High School Debating on Critical Thinking," *Speech Monographs* 10 (1943), 96–103; Winston L. Brembeck, "The Effects of a Course in Argumentation on Critical Thinking Ability," *Speech Monographs* 16 (1949), 177–189.

60. Edgar E. Willis, "The Relative Effectiveness of Three Forms of Radio Presentation in Influencing Attitudes," *Speech Monographs* 7 (1940), 41–47.

61. John E. Dietrich, "The Relative Effectiveness of Two Modes of Radio Delivery in Influencing Attitudes," *Speech Monographs* 13 (1946), 58–65.

62. Robert Gray Gunderson, *The Log Cabin Campaign* (Lexington: University of Kentucky Press, 1957); also Robert Gray Gunderson, "Presidential Canvass, Log-Cabin Style," *Today's Speech* 5 (1957), 19–20.

63. Frederick Haberman, "In Memoriam," in *The CHAPA Letter*, Committee on the History of American Public Address, Department of Speech, Queens College, Flushing, NY, March 1961, 1.

64. For a discussion of the rhetorical functions of analogy, see James R. Wilcox and H. L. Ewbank [Jr.], "Analogy for Rhetors," *Philosophy and Rhetoric* 12 (Winter 1979), 1–20.

65. Ewbank and Auer, *Discussion and Debate*, 3. Also in the 2d ed. (1951), 3.

66. Henry Ewbank, "Chapter One. A Working Definition of Rhetoric," 15, typescript in possession of the author.

67. Letter from Keith R. St. Onge, September 7, 1960, in possession of the author.

68. Letter from Charles T. Brown, December 2, 1960, in possession of the author.

69. Winston L. Brembeck. "Some Personal Reflections on the Life of Professor Henry Lee Ewbank, Sr.," March 16, 1998, in possession of the author.

70. Walter Bagehot, *Physics and Politics: or, Thoughts on the Application of the Principles of 'Natural Selection' and 'Inheritance' to Political Society* (New York: Alfred A. Knopf, 1948), 169, 168.

71. Walter Lippmann, "The Indispensable Opposition," *Atlantic Monthly*, August 1939, 186–190.

72. See H. L. Ewbank, "Free Speech in Times of Crisis," Phi Beta Kappa Address at Albion College, May 16, 1951, typescript in possession of the author; "What's Right with Debate," *Quarterly Journal of Speech* 37 (1951), 197–202; "Teaching Speech for Human Relations," *Speech Teacher* 1 (1952), 9–13; Ewbank and Lawton, *Broadcasting*, 206.

73. M. Tullius Cicero, *De Optimo Genere Oratorium*, 16.

74. Henry Brooks Adams, *The Education of Henry Adams* (Boston: Massachusetts Historical Society, 1907), 20.

BIBLIOGRAPHY

Primary Sources

Manuscripts and Scrapbooks

"Chap Book" of Henry L. Ewbank.
"Chapter One. A Working Definition of Rhetoric."
"Objective Studies in Speech Style with Special Reference to One Hundred English Sermons." Draft manuscript of Ph.D. dissertation, 1931.
"Time Marches On" (typescript notes).

Articles, Monographs, and Lectures

"Free Speech in Times of Crisis." Phi Beta Kappa Address at Albion College, May 16, 1951.
Papers presented to spring semester 1917 English Seminar.
Papers submitted in History of Oratory class, fall semester 1916.
Papers submitted in Rhetoric 117s, University of Michigan, summer 1926.
Papers submitted in Advanced Public Speaking, University of Michigan, summer 1926.
"Teaching Speech for Human Relations." *The Speech Teacher* 1 (1952), 9–13.
"What's Right with Debate." *Quarterly Journal of Speech* 37 (1951), 197–202.

Organization Documents

Bulletin of the School of Oratory of the Ohio Wesleyan University, catalog number 1915–1916, vol. 14, September 1, 1915, 14–29.
"Delta Sigma Rho 1906–1956 Golden Anniversary."
The Gavel of Delta Sigma Rho, March 11, 1929.

The Gavel of Delta Sigma Rho, November 14, 1931.
The Gavel of Delta Sigma Rho, January 15, 1933.
Le Bijou of 1918.
"Seventy-First Catalogue of Ohio Wesleyan University," Delaware, OH, 1915.
Silver Anniversary Program, Michigan Speech Association, April 28, 1950.

Books and Articles

Auer, J. Jeffery, and Henry Lee Ewbank. *Handbook for Discussion Leaders*. New York: Harper and Brothers, 1947.
Ewbank, Henry L., and Sherman P. Lawton. *Broadcasting: Radio and Television*. New York: Harper and Brothers, 1952.
Ewbank, Henry Lee, and J. Jeffery Auer. *Discussion and Debate: Tools of a Democracy*. New York: Appleton-Century-Crofts, 1941.
Ewbank, Henry L. "Four Approaches to the Study of Speech Style." *Quarterly Journal of Speech* 17 (1931), 458–465.

Secondary Sources

Letters

From Paul H. Boase, December 29, 1997 (included penciled letters and notes, n.d.).
From Charles T. Brown, December 2, 1960.
From Robert B. Crosby, September 18, 1997.
From William S. Howell, December 3, 1997.
From John S. Penn, December 5, 1997.
From Keith R. St. Onge, September 7, 1960.
From Edgar E. Willis, December 2, 1997.

Unpublished Works

Auer, J. Jeffery. "'I'd Like to Say a Few Words about Writing." N.d.
Brembeck, Winston L. "Some Personal Reflections on the Life of Professor Henry Lee Ewbank, Sr." March 16, 1998.

Books

Adams, Henry. *The Education of Henry Adams*. Boston: Massachusetts Historical Society, 1907.
Auer, J. Jeffery, ed. *Antislavery and Disunion 1858–1961: Studies in the Rhetoric of Compromise and Conflict*. New York: Harper and Row, 1963.
Bagehot, Walter. *Physics and Politics: or Thoughts on the Application of the Principles of 'Natural Selection' and 'Inheritance' to Political Society*. New York: Alfred A. Knopf, 1948.
Brigance, William N., ed. *A History and Criticism of American Public Address*. Vol. 1. New York: McGraw-Hill, 1943.
Flesch, Rudolf. *The Art of Plain Talk*. New York: Harper and Brothers, 1946.
Fulton, Robert I., and Thomas C. Trueblood. *Practical Elements of Elocution*. 3d ed. Boston: Ginn, 1896.

Gunderson, Robert Gray. *The Log Cabin Campaign*. Lexington: University of Kentucky Press, 1957.

Matlon, Ronald J., and Sylvia P. Ortiz, eds. *Index to Journals in Communication Studies through 1990*. Annandale, VA: Speech Communication Association, 1992.

Oliver, Robert T. *Four Who Spoke Out: Burke, Fox, Sheridan, Pitt*. Syracuse, NY: Syracuse University Press, 1946.

Articles

Brembeck, Winston L. "The Effects of a Course in Argumentation on Critical Thinking Ability." *Speech Monographs* 16 (1949), 177–189.

Dietrich, John E. "The Relative Effectiveness of Two Modes of Radio Delivery in Influencing Attitudes." *Speech Monographs* 13 (1946), 58–65.

Gunderson, Robert Gray. "Presidential Canvass, Log-Cabin Style." *Today's Speech* 5 (1957), 19–20.

Haberman, Frederick W. "General MacArthur's Speech: A Symposium of Critical Comment." *Quarterly Journal of Speech* 37 (October 1951), 321–331.

Haberman, Frederick W. "In Memoriam." *The CHAPA Letter*, Committee on the History of American Public Address, Department of Speech, Queens College, Flushing, NY, March 1961, 1.

Howell, William Smiley. "The Effects of High School Debating on Critical Thinking." *Speech Monographs* 10 (1943), 96–103.

Lippmann, Walter. "The Indispensable Opposition." *Atlantic Monthly*, August 1939, 186–190.

Lull, P. E. "The Effectiveness of Humor in Persuasive Speeches." *Speech Monographs* 7 (1940), 26–40.

Report of Committee on Research in Oratory. *Quarterly Journal of Speech* 21 (1935), 154.

Weaver, Andrew T. "Henry Lee Ewbank, 1893–1960." *Quarterly Journal of Speech* 46 (December 1960), 459.

Wilcox, James R., and H. L. Ewbank [Jr.]. "Analogy for Rhetors." *Philosophy and Rhetoric* 12 (Winter 1979), 1–20.

Willis, Edgar E. "The Relative Effectiveness of Three Forms of Radio Presentation in Influencing Attitudes." *Speech Monographs* 7 (1940), 41–47.

Hoyt Hopewell Hudson. Photo courtesy of the Princeton University Library, Manuscript Division, Department of Rare Books and Special Collections. Used with permission.

3

Hoyt Hopewell Hudson's Nuclear Rhetoric

JIM A. KUYPERS

Note for a Fly-Leaf

So that a cool wind in June's dawn blowing
Across a hill-top makes furrows, momently
Tossing the glass-green lengths of grasses and
Bright heads of daisies: so that twigs of spicewood
Bitten bring moisture in the mouth and sharpness
On the tongue,

            what matter then our words?
Let words and craft of words be held in secret,
Words beaten light and thin with ringing hammers,
Metal that floats like smoke, ingots made sheer
To gossamer that barely glints with any lustre.

If only the slant axe cleave the yellow fibres
Of hemlock, compressing the pith in the clean-cut
Edges of chips, then if only my instant
Become yours too, and if it could be his
Who goes by on the street—

            I say what matters is

This glancing instant with its frost of light,
These crystal blue and silver shells of air
That isolate the instant, redolence too
And texture that rests the eyes.

These are what matter.
And only then our words without noise or effort
As the mind works in secret, as clear water
Seeps in a mountain, laying beneath the rock
Multiform seams of metal and all in secret.[1]

And only then our words. . . . That a man whose very craft was words would write such as a sentence bespeaks his profoundly complex nature. Hoyt Hopewell Hudson was one such man. He was teacher, rhetorical theorist, critic, translator, editor, academic administrator, poet, chain smoker, tennis player, father, husband, humanitarian—all these and more. The purpose of this chapter, however, precludes reference to all aspects of his life; indeed, it is impossible to show all aspects of a man in but a chapter. It is possible, however, to highlight the fundamental contributions that Hudson made to our discipline, and that is the foremost purpose of this chapter.

Hoyt Hudson's profound, but slighted, contributions advanced extensively our understanding of rhetorical theory, rhetorical criticism, and the very essence of our budding discipline. Everett Lee Hunt hit home when, writing of Hudson's fecund contributions, he stated: "No other contemporary writer has related rhetoric to so many subjects, has illustrated its possibilities with such variety, and has placed it so well in the tradition of liberal education."[2] Hunt was dead-on, for Hudson was the first to begin the project of discussing modern rhetorical theory for the discipline and also the first to advance seriously a disciplinary definition of rhetoric. High praise from Hunt would be ambrosia for anyone, yet the relationship between Hunt and Hudson was reciprocal, for Hudson was greatly influenced by Hunt and echoed his call for the primacy of humanistic methods in the sprouting speech profession. This, of course, came at a time when the profession was developing along two interanimated, yet potentially antagonistic, lines of thought: humane and scientific.

The more humane view during this early period has traditionally and narrowly been called the Cornell school of rhetoric. Whether of Cornell or not, those exemplifying this view have been labeled Cornellians and are credited with developing a historical-critical approach to the study of speech. This approach, although not limited exclusively to classical rhetorical theory, did rely a great deal upon the rhetorical texts of ancient Greece and Rome. Many practitioners would later be called "neo-Aristotelians."[3] In direct contrast to this approach, scientifically oriented researchers focused upon the orality of speech.[4] Departments whose scholars stressed the scientific approach desired to make the study of speech specialized and in keeping with the scientific standards of the day. These scholars often focused research and teaching on discovering and understanding the techniques of oral language usage. They saw speech as a rather distinct field of study in which any course in any department dealing with human communication would belong to speech.

Theodore O. Windt, echoing Everett Lee Hunt, believed Hoyt Hudson to be the spokesman for the Cornell school of rhetoric.[5] Whether Hudson knew of this role or not, his seminal essays planted plentiful ideational seeds; these ideas would later be expanded by others and grouped together under the heading of the Cornell school of rhetoric. Speech was a humane study for Hudson, not scientific. His work made the argument for the centrality and importance of rhetoric at the heart of a liberal arts education. Rhetoric was not to devolve into a specialized type of training. For Hudson, ideas were inseparable from techniques; content, inseparable from form. As Hudson's essays demonstrate, rhetoric, not techniques for studying oral language, was at the heart of the new profession. Although routinely ignored today, Hudson's work is crucial for understanding the development of rhetorical studies, for it removed rhetoric from the realm of composition studies and literary criticism, forcefully argued for understanding rhetoric as an art, and made the case for rhetoric as an independent disciplinary study. This chapter thus proceeds in four sections: first, a brief biography of Hudson is presented; second, Hudson's contributions to rhetorical theory are discussed; third, Hudson's contributions to rhetorical criticism are examined; and finally, an outline of Hudson's contributions both to our disciplinary pride and to a liberal arts education is given.

BRIEF BIOGRAPHY

Hoyt Hopewell Hudson was born 6 July 1893, in Norfolk, Nebraska. His father, Reverend Fletcher Edward Hudson, was an itinerant minister, and thus Hudson's early life was marked by wide roaming through the West and Midwest. Eventually, the Hudson family settled in Huron, South Dakota, and Hudson graduated from Huron College with his A.B. in 1911. At Huron he majored in classics; he also met Everett Lee Hunt, establishing a relationship that would eventually bring Hudson to Cornell. He received his A.M. in 1913 from the University of Denver. After graduation, he taught at various high schools from 1913 through 1920 as a teacher of English and public speaking; this period was punctuated with study at the University of Chicago from 1916 to 1917.[6] No doubt Hudson impressed Hunt during his stay at Huron, for in 1920, at Hunt's invitation, Hudson began studying at Cornell for his doctorate. While at Cornell he was also an instructor of public speaking and graduated with the Ph.D. in September 1923. Although Hudson's rhetorical training had begun long before he matriculated to Cornell, the influence of the Cornell program is not to be treated lightly. While there he worked with Everett Lee Hunt, Alexander Drummond, and Lane Cooper; he was a fellow graduate student with Harry Caplan.[7]

From 1923 to 1925 Hudson taught at Swarthmore as an assistant professor of English and public speaking, and from 1925 to 1927 he taught at the University of Pittsburgh as a professor of English. In 1928 Princeton University hired him as associate professor of English. He was promoted to professor of public speaking in 1931; shortly thereafter, in 1933, he became the editor of the

Quarterly Journal of Speech. Also in 1933 he was named chairman of the English Department and professor of rhetoric and oratory. This was an amazing feat for someone who considered himself a teacher of speech, especially given the blatant bigotry exhibited toward the profession in the Ivy League. The following excerpt from the announcement in the *Princeton Alumni Weekly* of his appointment as English Department chairman attests to this:

PUBLIC speaking teachers are divided into two armed camps. The classicists find their beginnings (and also their endings, if detractors are believed) in Cicero and Demosthenes; the scientists babble of Jung and Freud, draw diagrams of the larynx, and (again believing the opposite school) have no knowledge of grammar or literature. But esteem between the two camps is cordial compared with the attitude of many pedagogues toward the whole field of public speaking, the country cousin of English literature. This is set down to emphasize the abilities of Hoyt H. Hudson, professor of public speaking, and new English Department chairman. Under any circumstances the chairman must have unusual qualities, but to gain appointment under the handicap of being known as a public speaking teacher requires character and scholarship of superlative excellence.[8]

Hudson was presented with an honorary doctor of letters from Huron College in 1938. He stayed at Princeton as chairman of the English Department and professor of rhetoric and oratory until 1942, when he left Princeton for Stanford University.[9] Although his academic contributions are found both in speech and in English, the remainder of this chapter concerns itself almost exclusively with his work in speech. We now turn to Hudson's most profound and genesic contributions, his early writings on the nature of rhetoric.

RHETORICAL THEORY

Much of Hudson's work in rhetoric is a delightful blend of theory and criticism. Accordingly, readers will find in almost any given work the existence of a sentence here, a paragraph there that enlighten them to the nature of rhetoric. Hudson propounded no system of rhetoric. He did, however, leave us with a wealth of observations and admonitions concerning the nature of rhetoric, many of which were seminal for the discipline. This section presents Hudson's theoretical contributions in three parts. The first explains his definition of rhetoric. The second describes his use of disassociation through comparison to describe rhetorical theory. The third consists of his comments on the rhetorical notion of effect. The last section could have been placed under the heading of "Rhetorical Criticism," but I treat it in the theory section to highlight Hudson's sophisticated understanding of effect. Considering that Hudson is thought by many to represent the Cornell school of rhetoric and that the development of neo-Aristotelianism is attributed to this school, I feel that Hudson's use of effect bears added scrutiny.

Definitions of Rhetoric

Hoyt Hudson was the first scholar in the discipline to both seriously and publicly advance a disciplinary definition of rhetoric. Throughout his writings he stressed that both oral and written discourse could be of a rhetorical nature and that both ought to be included in our disciplinary definition. He also advanced a modern conception of the classical canon of invention. Beyond this he differentiated between rhetoric and composition, and put forth a rather detailed explanation of rhetoric as historically situated.

Oral and Written Discourse

Herbert Wichelns is routinely given credit for broadening the discipline's rhetorical horizons to include written as well as oral discourse in his famous 1925 essay, "The Literary Criticism of Oratory."[10] Hudson is deserving of this credit, however, since in his 1921 essay "Can We Modernize the Theory of Invention?" he implied the use of topics for "speech or argument."[11] "The Field of Rhetoric," published in 1923, contains more explicit definitions. In this essay Hudson fully defined the term "rhetoric," which included the study of written as well as oral discourse. Because rhetoric is the "faculty of finding, in any subject, all the available means of persuasion," the rhetorician is "a sort of diagnostician and leaves it to others to be the practitioners; the rhetorician is the strategist of persuasion, and other men execute his plans and do the fighting. In practice, however, and in any study of the subject, this distinction can hardly be maintained, since the person who determines the available means of persuasion . . . must also be, in most cases, the one to apply those means in persuasive speech and writing."[12] Like others, Hudson recognized that the ancients communicated almost exclusively by the spoken word. Yet he also recognized that after the

invention of the printing-press we find persuasion carried on more and more by writing . . . until in our own day if we run over the principal manifestations of the persuasive art we find as many of them in type as in the spoken word. Yet in spite of our habit of thinking of writing and speaking as separate processes, the practice of persuasion is essentially one, in that the same principles apply everywhere in the field. A writer on public speaking at the present time would hesitate to call his work "Rhetoric," because the word is now usually applied to written discourse. But less than a hundred years ago the case was exactly reversed.[13]

This idea is again encountered in "De Quincey on Rhetoric and Public Speaking." Writing of the multiplication of mediums of expression for the rhetorician, Hudson asked, Will "all this have its effect upon the speaker and writer?"[14] Hudson cited a telling passage of De Quincey's thought on style and then provided an eye-opening interpretation: "Incidentally, the point of this passage supports the position of those of us who hold that the norm of good writing is good

speaking. And it is to be observed that never does one realize the artificiality
of punctuation so much as when one attempts by reading aloud to translate
writing into speaking."[15] Given the examples listed earlier, Hudson is certainly
one of the first in our field to recognize and advocate that our conception of
rhetoric include oral and written discourse.

Modernized Topics

Hudson believed strongly in the place of logic in rhetorical studies, and he
placed the study of invention firmly within the realm of rhetorical studies. His
first *Quarterly Journal* article, "Can We Modernize the Theory of Invention?,"
forcefully argued that logic's proper place is within rhetorical studies.[16] With
this article, Hudson was one of the first to consider this subject in the new field
and the first to explore it in depth. Specifically, Hudson presented the classical
theory of invention with applications to the knowledge of the 1920s. Following
the ancients, Hudson defined rhetorical topics as "places where arguments and
ideas may be found and whence they may be derived." He also asked us to
consider them as "suggesting what questions to ask."[17] Even though he drew
heavily upon the ancients for his conception of topics, he eschewed strict adherence to ancient texts. More fruitful discoveries would be had through a reexamination of classical invention with an eye toward opening, rather than
closing, discussion on the question of the proper breadth and depth for including
the classical theory of invention into our pedagogical practices and actual speech
making.

Hudson's concern with the importance of rhetorical invention was maintained
throughout his career. In "The Field of Rhetoric," he took rhetorical scholarship
well beyond the study of embellishment. He explained how rhetoric had once
been reduced to embellishment and then disclosed how to keep that from happening again: "[I]t is plain that in any period when subject-matter was conven-
tionalized, the consideration of invention would be neglected. Disposition would
require only the slightest attention, whereas stylistic embellishment, memorizing,
and delivery would constitute the orator's task. In any and all times the tendency
is present—the tendency to depend upon tradition or convention for material
and devote oneself wholly to style in writing and delivery in speaking."[18] In
"De Quincey on Rhetoric and Public Speaking," he again made the distinction
between invention and style yet showed marked sophistication. He used De
Quincey's work to demonstrate that "invention and style are two phases—an
inner and an outer phase—of the same process."[19] Viewed in this manner, rhetorical invention is a mental discipline that blends logic and style. According to
Hudson, the "first [logical invention] is a mode of thinking about one's subject,
turning the subject over in one's mind, and viewing it in as many relations as
possible. The second [stylistic invention] is the incarnation in speech of the
thoughts (or of a selection from the thoughts) engendered by the preceding
mental activity."[20]

Rhetoric and Composition

Also important for the early field was Hudson's differentiation between rhetoric and composition, a differentiation that broke ranks with the conception of rhetoric held by teachers of English. Hudson knew well that the thought of the time was to equate rhetoric with composition: "We are all familiar with the word 'rhetoric' in the titles of textbooks on writing, of which many . . . have been named 'Composition and Rhetoric'; though I am tempted to believe that if you asked the authors of these books to tell you which pages were composition and which were rhetoric, they would be at a loss."[21] Hudson wrote that careful writers have kept a distinction, maintaining that composition produces discourse and that rhetoric analyzes it—thus, the applied and the pure science. Yet Hudson's view goes well beyond this simplistic differentiation. Speaking and writing were part of the same process when viewed through the perspective of persuasion. The principles that apply to persuasive writing apply to persuasive speaking when one traces the roots back to the process of rhetorical invention: "The formal arts which underlie both composition and public speaking are grammar and rhetoric. Grammar assumes to teach the logic of words in relation, and rhetoric adds operational (tactical and strategic) dimensions to that logic, teaching ways of adapting discourse for the production of certain effects and the achievement of certain purposes."[22]

Rhetoric as Historically Situated

For Hudson, rhetoric was most easily conceived when located in an immediate historical situation, usually involving a specific audience. This conception flowed easily from two wells of thought: the emphasis that the speech discipline placed upon pedagogy and the ancient rhetorical texts used by speech scholars. Like many in his time, Hudson did feel that the audience was "likely to be a certain limited group." With this in mind, then, the rhetorician would ask specific questions: " 'What will this mean to them?' 'Will they be ready for this step?' and "How can this be illustrated so as to show its connection with their interests?' Moreover, the rhetorician wants actually to do something with the audience—and usually something quite specific."[23] Although Hudson did not limit the scope of rhetoric to a single audience, he often fell back upon this conception when providing examples. A good indication of this practice is found in "Rhetoric and Poetry." Hudson used Lincoln's Gettysburg Address as an example of the distinction between an oration viewed poetically and rhetorically. In so doing, he shared his belief in the historically situated nature of rhetoric: "But at the time it was a piece of persuasive discourse with a very specific end in view." This assertion was in contradistinction to the then-common reading of Lincoln's address as a "poetical discourse by a man who had brooded much in solitude."[24]

"De Quincey on Rhetoric and Public Speaking" has suffered from disciplinary neglect. Even so, its importance to the early discipline cannot be overlooked. With this study, Hudson produced the first major manuscript in the discipline to systematically analyze the work of a rhetorical theorist who lived outside Greco-Roman times. Moreover, Hudson relied upon his own close textual reading of De Quincey's work, which was a clear deviation of the standard of the day, which was to rely heavily upon secondary sources for interpretation. The De Quincey essay also demonstrated that Hudson did not engage in the practice of so many writers today—imposition of contemporary views upon the writings of our predecessors. Hudson situated his study of De Quincey historically. This was not a simple diachronic positioning within the flow of time; rather, Hudson presented a deeply synchronic understanding of De Quincey. Scholars who intend to engage in historical-critical studies received a clear message from this essay: the culture, society, and technology of the period under investigation must be taken into consideration.

Disassociation through Comparison

One often hears of early speech scholars attempting to legitimate our field by borrowing ideas and examples from other disciplines. Hudson is a good example of one who used such comparative reasoning; he is a poor example, however, of one attempting to borrow legitimacy or ideas from other fields. It was quite natural to contrast speech with English during the early years of the discipline, because the majority of those who taught speech had backgrounds in English. What is more natural than beginning with what is known and moving to what is unknown? Hudson did not limit himself exclusively to literary examples, however. In "Can We Modernize the Theory of Invention?" he brought notions of psychology and art into his discussion; he cited drama and poetry as well. He explained, "I have touched upon these other fields in order to suggest that in rhetorical invention as taught and practiced in ancient times there was the recognition of a method that is fundamental to all inventive thinking."[25] For Hudson, rhetoric was the center; he touched upon other disciplines to show rhetoric's centrality to all human thought.

Hudson's use of disassociation through comparison is most clearly presented in his essay "Rhetoric and Poetry." The contrast with poetry worked well because poetry was something with which most of his readers would be familiar. His example was less the desire to model rhetorical studies upon literary studies as it was to make his case to his readers. With this article, therefore, he disassociated rhetoric from poetry and thus rhetorical studies from literary studies. Hudson was seminal here. Although we may not know for certain that he originated the idea, we do know that his treatment of rhetoric in this manner was among the first that the discipline encountered. The essay was presented at the 1923 National Association of Teachers of Speech convention and published prior to Wichelns's 1925 essay, "The Literary Criticism of Oratory" and also prior to James M. O'Neill's "The Relation of Speech to Philology and Linguistics," Everett Lee Hunt's important 1935 article "Rhetoric and Literary Criticism," and Ross Scanlan's 1936 essay "Rhetoric and the Drama."[26]

Even a cursory reading of "Rhetoric and Poetry" reveals that Hudson gave to rhetoric the same honor afforded poetry. He began his comparison by citing a litany of greats—Wordsworth, Tennyson, Shelley—to present us with the distilled essence of the poet: "The poet . . . keeps his eye not on the audience or the occasion, but on his subject; his subject fills his mind and engrosses his imagination, so that he is compelled, by excess of admiration or other emotion, to tell of it; compelled, though no one hear or read his utterance."[27] For the sake of discussion, Hudson drew a line in the sand to better differentiate between where rhetoric begins and poetry ends: "For the moment, then, we shall say that poetry is for the sake of expression; the impression on others is incidental. Rhetoric is for the sake of impression; the expression is secondary—an indispensable means."[28] This distinction is subject to exceptions, and here Hudson showed a tremendous and discerning grasp of the differences between rhetoric and poetry. He provided examples of how a poet might stray into the field of rhetoric; for example, a poet envisioning a speaker attempting to persuade listeners must use rhetoric. Mark Antony in Shakespeare's *Julius Caesar* and the speeches of the Fallen Angels in the first and second books of *Paradise Lost* are two such examples. He calls this imitative rhetoric, which may be studied for its own sake. A poet may at times consider the audience (a drama, e.g.), but there exist differences in the conception of the audience: "The poet thinks of a more general and more vaguely defined audience than the orator. The poet may even think of all mankind of the present and future as his audience."[29] Hudson even provided a loose scale to show the relationship between the most purely poetical—personal lyric and rhapsodic poem; then idyll, pastoral poetry; then narrative poetry, romance, the epic—and the more purely rhetorical—tragedy and comedy; finally, didactic poetry, satire, odes, and epigrams. Hudson also demonstrated how an orator may cross over into the field of poetry: "Though the orator's end is persuasion, it is not hard to believe that there are moments in his discourse when this end is forgotten in his delight or wonder before some image which fills his inner eye. In such moments he has his eye on the subject, not the audience."[30]

Notion of Effects

I am inclined to believe it unfortunate that so many students of rhetoric uncritically accept the folklore of neo-Aristotelianism given birth by Edwin Black, who stated that neo-Aristotelian criticism comprehends "rhetorical discourse as tactically designed to achieve certain results with a specific audience on a specific occasion."[31] For Black and later critics of neo-Aristotelianism, the primary indictments were that neo-Aristotelians limited criticism to "the evaluation of rhetorical discourse in terms of its effects on its immediate audience" and that they thought of the discourse as "discrete and its relevant effects [as] immediate."[32] In addition, they were said to follow too closely the rhetorical grammar set out in Aristotle's *Rhetoric*. Hudson had moved, however, well beyond

Black's conception of effects in his essay penned with Wilbur Samuel Howell, on Daniel Webster. This essay, contained in *History and Criticism of American Public Address*, advances a notion of effects that flows from the intention of the communicator as well as the impact that the discourse might have upon *multiple audiences*. Moreover, their conception of effects was not limited to immediate results from an effort at persuasion. Intention to persuade is, however, central to a rhetor's potential effect.[33] Prior to the Webster essay, Hudson contrasted the poet and the rhetorician to make a distinction between their intended effects: "[T]he poet tends to look for an audience suitable to his subject and the resultant discourse, rather than to seek, as does the rhetorician, a subject and discourse suitable to the audience."[34] Of course, it has already been noted that Hudson's distinction between poetry and rhetoric is not rigid. The rhetorician may well give flight to fancy and enter into the domain of the poet; in such an instance, the effect often is to please the reader or listener. The student of rhetoric is interested, "for the most part," in imparting "broader effects" than simply leaving an aesthetic impression or giving vent to personal expression. The student of rhetoric, for example, might well be interested in the wielder of public opinion: "What are the secrets of his power?"[35] Of course, this question takes us well beyond a notion of immediate effects, and Hudson provided several examples of broader effects in the Webster essay. He cited the 1884 defeat of Blain, whose campaign manager launched the disastrous "Rum, Romanism, and Rebellion" campaign against the Democrats. Here, of course, effects move well beyond a single speech before a single audience. He also cited the wielding of public opinion by Theodore Roosevelt and Woodrow Wilson. Indeed, Hudson is well beyond his contemporaries with the type of questions he asked: How, for instance, is rhetoric used as a "technique of power"? Or broader still, what of propaganda, as in the case of the Russian Revolution?[36]

In Daniel Webster the notion of effect is cast wide indeed. Although immediate effect is considered, effect is broadened to account for how Webster, throughout many orations, considered the various constraints that he faced. Howell and Hudson discuss Webster's effectiveness as political orator in toto, not in terms of his moving a particular jury or the Senate on a particular case or vote. These authors viewed effect along the lines of situational perspicuity. They trod two paths here: one, they described the "resistance" that Webster "encountered because he was a member of the Whig party, and [two] the resistance that came from the public reputation fixed upon him by his opponents." They then discussed the relation of his speeches to that resistance, with an eye toward measuring his effectiveness as a political orator. In doing so, Howell and Hudson were actually on the cusp of examining the impact of Webster's "discourse on rhetorical conventions, its capacity of disposing an audience to expect certain ways of arguing and certain kinds of justifications in later discourses that they encounter, even on different subjects."[37]

CRITICISM

Hudson advanced no formal method of rhetorical criticism. Instead, his ideas were disseminated widely in his works; we glimpse a glitter of gold here, a glimmer of silver there. As Everett Lee Hunt said, with "inexhaustible fertility he was always casting out ideas for others to play and work with."[38] However, when one pulls together these scattered ideas, one finds that they can be grouped together to better appreciate their merit. In this section I first provide these general guides that Hudson provided his readers, and then I present examples of how Hudson actually performed criticism.

With Hints to Guide Us By

On Expanding Communication Artifacts

Hudson continually advocated expanding the field of study from single speeches to include other communication artifacts. He was well aware that different mediums of expression had different effects that needed to be considered in our theory and criticism. In "De Quincey on Rhetoric and Public Speaking," Hudson advocated broadening the paths of study to include radio, pamphleteering, newspapers, radio broadcasting, and others—what he called commercial rhetoric. The importance of this was stressed in the "Field of Rhetoric": "with modern wielders of publicity to observe, and with the increasing use of a method for sending human speech broadcast, so that a speaker may address thousands where he once addressed scores, the significance of persuasive discourse is continually being enhanced."[39] Along these same lines, Hudson provided clues for still other venues of critical endeavor: "Editorial writing . . . the immense business of advertising and the still more immense business of propaganda—these are occupations which modern rhetoricians may follow."[40] With this line of thinking, Hudson was charting a course for the discipline that moved beyond what other disciplines had theretofore realized. In addition to the medium of transmission, the "De Quincey" essay sowed other ideational seeds for those engaging in rhetorical criticism. For example, one could consider the effects upon style of varying methods of publication, as well as "the influence of national or racial characteristics, as present in audiences, upon rhetorical style."[41] Hudson also took into account the impact of everyday realities upon those whom we study; he believed that "such factors as freedom or censorship of speech and the press, the rise of cheap printing, the convenience of assembly or communication are too often overlooked."[42] Hudson was not content to allow his ideas to lie upon fallow ground, so he presented a few germinated seeds: "Will the English of headlines and the devices of billboard advertising invade poetry and uncommercial rhetoric? What of the appalling multiplication of pictures in recent publicity, and of pictorial communication?"[43] Through De Quincey, Hudson was able to offer other suggestions for criticism as well: "[De Quincey's] discussion of Herodotus may be said to set a model for the most fruitful type of rhetorical criticism. He considers the character of the historian, his audience, and his method of publication."[44] Although Hudson graciously attributed these ideas to De Quincey, it is clear that Hudson's understanding allowed them to be so forcefully articulated.

On Using Topics and Canons for Criticism

In "Can We Modernize the Theory of Invention?" Hudson presented a solid overview of rhetorical invention as viewed by the ancients, but did so with his eye on the rhetorical knowledge of the 1920s. According to Hudson, rhetorical topics are "places where arguments and ideas may be found and whence they may be derived. . . . We shall understand topics most readily if we think of them as suggesting what questions to ask. They are considered as places whence arguments and means of persuasion may be derived."[45] Although Herbert A. Wichelns is usually given credit for advancing the idea of using the classical canons and topics for rhetorical criticism, this distinction should go to Hudson. As early as 1921 Hudson wrote of using topics for rhetorical criticism: "Perhaps we should be more certain that the mind, in the invention of rhetorical discourse, works most efficiently along certain routines or paths, if we found it working at other tasks of invention in that manner. In art criticism we read of composition and sometimes of invention. . . . [W]e are inclined to see not only an analogy but a fundamental identify [sic] between pictorial and rhetorical composition."[46] He also wrote, "A research student might profitably trace this topic [equality of opportunity] through American oratory, finding it heavily drawn upon in Blain's famous Eulogy of Garfield as well as in the campaign speeches of 1920—and in many earlier years. He then might turn to his Aristotle and find in this topic only a concrete application of one of Aristotle's topics of the greater and lesser good."[47] In discussing the modern uses of invention, Hudson suggested that topics be used in pedagogy but also implied that they be used in criticism: "Perhaps in argumentation the various forms of reasoning and argument can be presented not merely as canons of criticism, to test the works of others, but as topics, to aid the invention of the student's own arguments."[48]

Hudson did not advocate a strict adherence to the letter of the ancients' law but rather a restudying of classical invention, this with an eye toward opening, rather than closing, discussion on the question as "to how far we can embody the classical theory of invention in our teaching or argument and speech making."[49] In the "Field of Rhetoric" Hudson provided unambiguous suggestions for using both topics and the canons in rhetorical criticism:

[T]he student of rhetoric investigates eloquence, not for its graces and ornaments, and not with regard to its effect upon him as he reads it; our admiration may be excited by a splendid figure in Burke or Canning; we may gain considerable pleasure from perceiving the skill with which words have been joined euphoniously and rhythmically—

but such admiration and pleasure are incidental and are shared by the student of literature or the general reader. The student of rhetoric looks upon each oration as an effort in persuasion; he must learn what he can of the audience to which it was addressed; he takes note of the appeals that are made, with reference to the motives that are touched, the emotions that are aroused. He must know the character and reputation of the speaker at the time when the speech was made; for a speech otherwise persuasive may fail of effect because the speaker lacks a persuasive *ethos.* . . . [W]e must also take into account matters of style and ornament and delivery; but these, too, are to be estimated with reference to their persuasive effect."[50]

On the Power of Imagination

Although he never made an explicit call to include imagination in criticism, his work fully demonstrated the necessity and power of imagination; indeed, his work is a cogent argument for inclusion of imagination in all that we do. Hudson's thoughts on the importance of imagination are highlighted in his posthumously published book, *Educating Liberally*. Although Hudson was writing of liberal arts education, the spirit of what he wrote speaks to his conception of criticism and bears mentioning here. In the chapter "Arm of Imagination," Hudson stated that one ought not associate imagination with the untrue. Instead, one must possess the truth by first imagining it—or realizing it. Imagination "is a power or activity of the mind whereby concepts, ideas, recollections, impulses, sensations, and other phenomena of consciousness (and we need not exclude phenomena of the unconscious and subconscious mind) are fused into what appears to be a fresh, perhaps temporary or tentative, perhaps enduring, entity; one which has enough clearness of outline to deserve being called an image or mental picture, though not necessarily visual in character."[51] This characterization of imagination allows for the consideration of emotions. Hudson supported the position that a critic must realize and accept his feelings on a matter but refrain from allowing his emotions to guide his criticism. There are objective standards, but they exist in the mind of the critic, so they are problematic: "So long as we inhabit a body of flesh and blood, bones and nerves, brain cells and marrow, we are bound to have feelings, emotional attitudes toward the objects of consciousness."[52] Hudson, with characteristic prescience, wrote: "Is it possible that a man may feel deeply, may take a strong, positive attitude toward the object of his thought, and yet maintain the fine impartiality of discursive thought, the detachment, the disinterestedness which science and criticism call for? The answer is 'Yes.' "[53] He continued that "to recognize our emotional drives, to be aware of their force in directing and even in methodizing our thought, to make allowance for them but on no account to deny that they exist or to be deceived as to their force and direction—this is to minimize, if not to cancel out, the famous dangers of emotional thinking. This is another truism, but it must be kept in the foreground."[54] Hudson seems here to anticipate our contemporary theoretical discussions concerning the objectivity of the critic.

Imagination is not a separate way of knowing, not a separate entity. It is vital to a complete knowledge, a knowledge that includes a "sense of fact" and also the "operation of reason." Furthermore, imagination allows for ethical reasoning in our criticism: '[K]nowledge which is informed by imagination must by its very nature lead to social sympathy and active regard for others."[55] Hudson cited Shelley to clarify how sympathy and regard ought not be mistaken for, or justify, advocacy: "The great instrument of moral good is the imagination. Sympathetic understanding is the secret to morals. We appreciate the existence of other objects and persons, and this is similar to Shelley stating, 'going out of our own nature, and an identification of ourselves with the beautiful which exists in thought, action, or person, not our own.' "[56] Hudson does not use the term "appreciate" to mean "unquestioning admiration"; rather, he means that "we can realize, and respect, the identity of something, without respecting the thing itself."[57] With that sentence Hudson speaks to many today, especially those who tread the tortuous path of advocacy based rhetorical criticism. We may remain objective and appreciative, regardless of our personal wish to confirm or confute.

Hudson's writings demonstrate his fecund imagination and his ability to step beyond the customary thoughts on criticism during his day. His imaginative reading of De Quincey has already been mentioned. Other examples of his use of imagination are contained in "Jewel's Oration against Rhetoric." At a time when rhetoric was openly denounced by some in the pages of the *Quarterly Journal* and at national meetings, Hudson identified through a novel reading of Jewel how rhetoric was being used by speech scholars to denounce rhetoric.[58] The common interpretation of Jewel's oration was that he was arguing against rhetoric. Hudson invited his readers to engage in a close textual analysis entrenched theoretically in irony and burlesque. In a mere nine paragraphs, Hudson advanced a new interpretation of Jewel's "Oration against Rhetoric," and provided a subtle perspective from which to evaluate any future offerings from those who would lambaste rhetorical studies.

Examples of Criticism

Writings in English

In the *Epigram in the English Renaissance* Hudson brought to the study of the epigram a distinctly rhetorical understanding as he traced the birth and development of the English epigram.[59] Although he offered a general definition of epigrams, he also offered a "slight amendment" that is based "upon the rhetorical teachings of the sixteenth century, and the resultant practice."[60] Moreover, when speaking of the development of the epigram, Hudson linked the differences between early and later styles to "changes in the rhetorical taste and practice from age to age."[61] The opening essay of this book is a good example of Hudson's ability to delight readers with his effortless blending of theory and criticism; never does he kowtow to theory as do so many of our critics today. Rather, theory informs practice; one does not find the rather awkward division of theory section followed by commentary section.

In his introductory chapter to his translation of *The Praise of Folly*, Hudson advanced a reading of Erasmus that is firmly rooted in rhetorical theory. He asked how Erasmus could relate classical art, classical poetry, and mythology to Christian doctrine and life. Erasmus never wrote about these issues except to make fun of the classics, yet all who read him know instinctively where he stood:

> He was revealing, not stating, that poetry may be read and enjoyed without being treated either as an insidious intoxicant or as the vehicle of sacrosanct wisdom, and that the better a person knows poetry the more fun he can have with it. The reader is aware, long before laying down the book, that Erasmus cares deeply for classical poetry, and that he believes a Christian will be better off for knowing Greek—though he also believes that among unlettered folk will be found some of the best and most admirable Christians. How did this subtle and complex construction come into being?[62]

Hudson's chapter-long answer to this question began with rhetorical theory. He advanced a notion of "eulogy or panegyric, a species of the genus oration," and spoke also of how a "rhetorical game" developed "in which one might compose a eulogy on one of the gods . . . pronounce a panygeric upon baldness, or write a praise of darkness."[63] Hudson mentioned that Erasmus referred to *Praise of Folly* as a declamation, which is, of course, "another rhetorical term, with the special suggestion that the speech was thought of as an academic one, or as a 'showpiece.' "[64] Hudson believed that *Praise of Folly* could be analyzed most fruitfully if thought of as a speech before "a gathering in a college hall, before which a senior sophister, or even a distinguished visiting scholar, might well appear with a learned declamation."[65] Hudson also suggested that the tradition of eulogy, as handed down from Aristotle, undergirded Erasmus's book: "And while a feigned speech is as much a piece of fiction as any other feigned action, a book like this, which is nothing but a speech, can hardly be completely poetic. That it is a public address, constructed on obvious rhetorical lines, harms it as a poetic or fictional creation."[66]

"Daniel Webster"

This massive essay, penned with Wilbur Samuel Howell, is divided into five sections: a brief biographical portrait, the influences of literature and law upon Webster's orations, the analysis of six epideictic speeches, the debate between Webster and Hayne, and Webster as a Whig political icon. Howell and Hudson separated oratorical technique from content to ascertain Webster's educational underpinnings. Their theoretical frame for investigation was never fully outlined; however, justification was provided, and this justification allows us insight into the thoeretical foundations of their criticism:

However much we may be biased against the orator and however much we may have been led by literary critics and aesthetes to believe that the main lights of national thought are reflected by creative artists and philosophers, it is well to temper our prejudice with the reflection that the American genius flowered in a very real sense before the advent of the literary movements of the nineteenth century and that this genius expressed itself in the Declaration of Independence, the Constitution, the *Federalist* papers, the fierce partisanship of political debates, the huge political meetings, the vitriolic editorials . . . the Fourth of July orations.[67]

The Webster essay will be a revelation of sorts to many who have uncritically accepted the folklore of neo-Aristotelianism passed on to us from the mid-1960s. Although a brief biography is provided, and the authors looked into how Webster studied the art of speaking, their general observations led to a closer look at selected orations, namely, six of Webster's epideictic attempts and selections of the Hayne–Webster debate. In the section Literature and Law, the authors looked closely at the content of Webster's speeches to ascertain the educational influences operating across his orations. In the section Epic Vein, Howell and Hudson looked at how Webster could impart to his audience those intangibles of imagination, "common government" and "national heritage." According to the authors, Webster "dramatized the nation's tradition and charged with power the less concrete symbols of our political life."[68] Only a modicum of time was spent describing the physical circumstances of the speeches.

In the section the Great Debate the authors looked at the "relation between [Webster's] habits of procedure and the true opposition" that he faced."[69] This section stressed the importance of speaker intention, especially when critical judgments on effectiveness are made: "What [Senator] Benton said is also of importance, if we wish to understand the purposes of the speakers. And only when we have a clear definition of these purposes are we able to appreciate the tactics of each man and the considerations that led each to select his topics of discussion."[70] Although the Great Debates occurred in the U.S. Senate, Howell and Hudson made the point that the immediate audience was much larger; it was the American people at large. We see in this article, then, an expansion of the notion of the immediate audience attributed to neo-Aristotelian criticism.

Howell and Hudson also discussed effectiveness, not in terms of moving a particular audience on a particular vote but rather in terms of Webster's general effectiveness as a political orator; in this context, too, they explored the notion of Webster as a political symbol. Thus, a broad notion of the constraints upon Webster's oratorical creations was included in their idea of effectiveness. Perhaps most notable is an early comparative analysis between one of Webster's speeches published in a newspaper and that same speech as Webster later published it. The authors examine the various modifications and how these were inserted by Webster to take into account his larger audience—his political supporters and detractors. Moreover, these authors were able to move beyond the strict reporting of the inventional resources that Webster used on any given

audience; instead, the authors looked at the resistance that Webster faced as a
member of Whig Party and his imputed reputation as constructed by his rivals.
With this in mind, the authors stated: "[W]e shall discuss the relation of his
speeches to this resistance, our primary object being to measure his effectiveness
as a political orator."[71] Thus, effectiveness, for these authors, embraced more
than moving a particular audience during a particular speech.

DISCIPLINARY PRIDE

Essays

At first glance "Can We Modernize the Theory of Invention?" seems to follow
the blueprints of numerous works in the early issues of the *Quarterly Journal*
since it borrowed examples and ideas from other disciplines. As previously
stated, however, Hudson did this with his eye toward elevating our appreciation
of rhetoric by disassociating it from other studies: "I have touched upon these
other fields in order to suggest that in rhetorical invention as taught and practiced
in ancient times there was the recognition of a method that is fundamental to
all inventive thinking."[72] Note well this sentence. Hudson placed rhetoric at the
heart of the liberal arts. The centrality of rhetoric permeates his writings and is
an exceptionally important contribution to the development of our field. Everett
Lee Hunt said of the early members of the speech profession:

All the instructors believed in what they were doing but felt the urge to know more of
the history and tradition of the subject. They were conscious of being pioneers but
preferred to be pioneers with a tradition. They were attracted to the great names in the
history of rhetoric. In spite of these names, however, rhetoric seemed somehow at best
a poor relation, if not actually disreputable—the harlot of the arts. Still they suspected
that if the kinship of rhetoric to logic, ethics, politics, poetry, and psychology could be
established, and if a real function were defined for it, there would come a sense of
belonging to the academic royal family.[73]

I am inclined to believe that Hunt's statement slightly exaggerates the case;
nonetheless, it is representative of many attitudes then and now. At a time when
many were uncertain, at a time when many were daunted by the task ahead, at
a time when many were faced with charges of teaching the "country cousin" of
English literature, Hudson unabashedly proclaimed our discipline's proud pedigree. There was no hesitation; there was no apology.

In the "Field of Rhetoric" Hudson opened a new door for the discipline. In
contradistinction to the theoretical roots of many early speech scholars, much
of Hudson's understanding of rhetoric was informed by postclassical authors.
He traced our roots to the ancients, but not blindly. Although he cited Aristotle,
Isocrates, Cicero, and Quintillian, he cited St. Augustine, Melancthon, and Erasmus as well. Furthermore, he cited Hugh Blair, Lorenzo Sears, and Henry Pee-

chem. The list grows: Coxe, Wilson, and Bacon; Ben Jonson, Thomas Hobbes, Isaac Barrow, Adam Smith, and John Quincy Adams; Bishop Whately and Alexander Bain. Not only was this the first serious attempt by a well-respected speech scholar to define rhetoric, but Hudson did so in part by differentiating between rhetoric and composition. This was the first of many wedges that he would drive between speech and English.

Hudson believed that rhetoric ought to be separate from English; however, if English departments were to absorb the field of rhetoric, they must do so knowing full well the differences between the study of rhetoric and the study of philology, literature, poetry, and so on. English deals with fine arts; rhetoric, the useful. On this point Hudson wrote:

As for showing this distinction in our curricula, might it not be possible to put all study of exposition and argumentation into a course or group of courses together with other work in rhetoric and public speaking; while the teaching of narration and description, or of such literary forms as the short story, the familiar essay, and the play, might be kept in closer relation to the courses in literature and in distinction from the forms of writings and speaking as a useful art. There is surely a closer kinship between writing a piece of argumentation and the delivery of an argumentative speech than between the writing of the same piece of argumentation and the reading of Tennyson's poems.[74]

This proposal to group courses in speech and English based upon thematic content was nothing short of revelatory. Hudson later asked, Has not the speech of great orators—the Bunyans, Jeremy Taylors, Pitts, Foxes, and Burkes—"exerted as great an influence upon the language as the poets and essayists? Yet the speakers are too often overlooked when investigations are made upon these points."[75]

Hudson never lost sight of the importance of studying rhetoric as a means to better understand our changing world. He urged us to learn from the past and to keep our eye on the present: "In addition to all we inherit from the past, with modern research in psychology to draw upon, with modern wielders of publicity to observe, and with the increasing use of [radio broadcast] the significance of persuasive discourse is continually being enhanced. Surely it would be a mistake to overlook this significance, and in proportioning our emphasis I do not see how we can give any but a central position to rhetorical study."[76]

He explored the pedagogical ramifications of rhetoric while justifying its close association with so many other disciplines. He fully realized that rhetoric drew content from other fields and that this violated the divisions among various college departments. Hudson, though, pointed out what was often overlooked by those in other disciplines: they, too, borrow from others. For example, a student of architecture must draw knowledge from the field of engineering, painting, sculpting, surveying, and landscaping. This student learns much from many fields but is, in the end, just an architect. Of course, rhetorical training is analogous to this. The rhetorician must learn from the psychologist, social psychologist, and publicist, as well as more traditional subjects: finance, war and peace, defense of the country, imports and exports, and legislation. Be that as it may, "the rhetorician does not necessarily become an expert in those fields. He learns, in any given situation, what questions to ask—and to answer."[77]

Hudson firmly believed that the study of rhetoric was equally important as the study of literature, and his belief is most forcefully apparent in his essay "Rhetoric and Poetry." Citing James Russell Lowell, who made a "distinction 'twixt singing and preaching,' " Hudson intrepidly added, "I wish to urge that the distinction is an important one in literary criticism; I would urge especially that we who claim to know something about preaching have as great an interest in making clear the distinction, and can contribute as much to this end, as the student of 'pure literature,' whose attitude toward preaching too often lacks both sympathy and understanding."[78] Hudson concluded "Rhetoric and Poetry" with the following adjuration: students of literature and literary criticism should study rhetoric. Hudson clearly advanced rhetoric's importance in relation to other fields when he stated: "[P]oetry in some of its most usual forms is more or less strongly tinged with a rhetorical element. . . . [C]riticism will walk with surer feet if it can learn to isolate and analyze this rhetorical element. Hence it follows that a part of the equipment of a literary critic, and, we may add, of an interpreter of literature, must be knowledge of the devices for getting and holding attention, the technique of adaptation to audience and occasion; which are the stock and trade of teachers of public speaking."[79] In this he predated Wichelns' condemnation of those using literary methods of study for rhetorical criticism and assigned to rhetorical studies the same significance as literary studies.

By 1925, when some speech scholars seemed to respect other disciplines more than their own, Hudson was in the vanguard advancing rhetoric as a respectable area of study. With the publication of "De Quincey on Rhetoric and Public Speaking" he daringly begat a new form of scholarship for the field. He relied on his own mind for his ideas, not other disciplines; he relied on his own insights for confirmation, not secondary sources. His essay on De Quincey set a precedent in two major ways by systematically engaging the work of a rhetorical theorist who lived outside of Greco-Roman times and by relying on his own close textual reading of De Quincey's work. In addition, this essay showed remarkable insight into the history of rhetorical education in the West. Moreover, Hudson demonstrated his ability to proudly claim our own good theorists: "Rhetorical invention is a mode of thinking; and if the school rhetorics of the nineteenth century had followed De Quincey, Whately, and Newman, instead of Blair and Bain, we should not now find rhetoric so far from the minds of educators when they are looking about for 'some way to make students think.' "[80]

Perhaps one of Hudson's best cheerleading essays is "The Tradition of Our Subject," published in 1931. In this essay he unabashedly restated his 1923 message: our discipline emerged from a long and proud tradition, and we ought to be aware of this history. This essay greatly contributed to the intellectual underpinnings of our discipline and is indicative of Hudson's well-developed conception (both historical and theoretical) of rhetoric. Eschewing the greats—Aristotle, Cicero, and Quintillion—Hudson began with theorists and practitioners of the eighteenth century, demonstrating how common it was to find at universities professors who taught rhetoric and public speaking. He traced problems that we today think are new back to roots centuries old. For example, he linked the controversy surrounding the use of the term "speech" to a poem published by Sir John Davies in 1599. Hudson argued that we must know our tradition before we do anything else:

We have in keeping a discipline and a body of knowledge and an approach to education which have commanded the interest and the devoted labors of men in . . . sixty-five generations. Surely we are in a rather graceless position if we act as people without a history, as though wisdom had been born with us, and hence would die with us. Surely there is place for that natural piety which bids us survey with some affection the pit from which we were digged and the rock from which we were hewn. I do think a knowledge of our tradition, beginning with a realization of our need for such knowledge, will make for a salutary and becoming humility on our part. Paradoxically enough, I think it will also make for a wholly justifiable pride. But another positive motive to studying our tradition is that study gives us perspective upon our own labors and our own place, if any, in the sun.[81]

Unfortunately, Hudson's admonition was largely ignored—it is too often ignored even today. Hudson thrust our tradition upon us; we failed his call. His idea was for us to "become acquainted with ourselves" through understanding how rhetorical training and theory developed through the centuries. He envisioned self-reflexive scholars who would understand what they would be like if born earlier. More to the point, Hudson felt we could see how we "shall look to teachers of the future, when time has brought perspective."[82] Much like today, when it is too common to find departments in which social scientists and rhetoricians contend with each other, Hudson's time felt the first pangs of contention. He was concerned and felt that knowing our common past, regardless of contemporary application, would help strengthen us: "[I]t seems to me that the strongest motive to a study of our tradition is our need for unity. A common tradition may be a stronger tie than a common language; it is a tie which we have almost overlooked."[83]

Rhetoric and the Liberal Arts

In *Educating Liberally* Hudson set out his conception of a true liberal arts education. Liberal education, he posited, has something to do with freedom—one frees the mind. One comes to understanding, not just recognition or acquaintance. Rhetoric was an indispensable and central component of such an education. Hudson's book was posthumously published, and he had finished only the section dealing with his framework for a liberal education; the envisioned second section, never completed, would have dealt with the practical applications. Donald C. Bryant wrote of this book: "No finer contribution to the interpretation and definition of liberal education has appeared in recent years. Few have surpassed it from Plato or Quintillion to the Harvard Report."[84]

Hudson saw "Three Foes" to a liberal education and "Three Arms of Attack" to ensure such an education. The foes are ignorance, muddleheadedness, and crassness. One may also call them "lack of information, lack of operative logic, and lack of imagination."[85] These are not separate entities but rather three phases of the same activity. The first two phases establish and recognize the relations between facts and also among our inferences; thus, we have the acquisition of factual knowledge and operative logic. The teaching of facts is important, but the relationship between them must be stressed—in short, harmonizing the knowledge difference between knowing a definition and assimilating it. Hudson's third phase involves imaginative insight or sympathetic contemplation. At this third level we find "the creation in the mind, or revelation to the mind, of a unified entity with a character of its own."[86] Imagination "fights against isolation and abstraction; for it is a synthetic power and catches up all matters of knowledge with and into itself."[87] Educators are often guilty of ignoring the second and third aspects, simply because of the difficulties in setting an examination for them; too, there is the inordinate amount of time necessary just for making certain that one's facts are correct.

Hudson's notion of "operative logic" bears scrutiny. Here we are getting at "a clear vision of the relevance of facts" and the "active following out and testing of lines and links of relevance."[88] Hudson stressed that everyone deals with probabilities—the working tool of practical people. This involves everyday affairs that often are worked out only through common sense and a little imagination, for instance, a faculty meeting. He used this example as a segue to bring up then-recent arguments that every field has its own logic. If so, which is most important to liberal education? Which is most important for academic unity? Hudson argued for the importance of a general, cross-disciplinary application of Aristotelian logic. This would allow for an elevation of criticism and communication between various disciplines. At present, the liberal arts teach "types" of logic: mathematical, economic, historical method, physics, chemistry, and so on. Hudson admonished us to do better, to seek out principles of unity, parallels between one field and another, or, with what sounds eerily similar to contemporary interdisciplinary studies, to "encourage cross-fertilization from one field to another."[89] Hudson drew upon the few comparative studies of his day (comparative literature, comparative anatomy, comparative philology) and suggested that fruitful cross-fertilization was to be had between fields of knowledge.

In advancing his notion of a common inventional resource, or unifying logic, Hudson thoughtfully advanced rhetoric. He was very aware that academics were "somewhat blind to the extent to which they now accept writing and speaking as the *Organon*, or universal logic, of all studies."[90] He asked, How often must students give oral or written reports of papers? Are not colleagues judged by how well they teach and write? This universal logic is a type of methodology of communication and expression: "The formal arts which underlie both composition and public speaking are grammar and rhetoric. Grammar assumes to teach the logic of words in relation, and rhetoric adds operational (tactical and strategic) dimensions to that logic, teaching ways of adapting discourse for the production of certain effects and the achievement of certain purposes."[91] Here we come to the distinction between the fine and useful art of discourse: fine (as in the art of the novelist or poet) and useful (as in the art of the logical expositor, disputant, or persuader). If composition and rhetoric are to be used as organons of learning, then "teachers must have a clear concept of expository, argumentative, and persuasive discourse and must be willing to train students in it. Accuracy, clarity, order, logical soundness, and force—these are the primary canons; for they are canons of thinking itself."[92]

Altogether, Hudson's writings clearly demonstrated discernment and deep love for the field of rhetoric. Moreover, he unabashedly proclaimed the centrality of rhetoric to all academic studies. This was no idle speculation on his part, but rather the fruit of painstaking examination of the literature available to him from the past 2,500 years. His feeling of pride for the discipline clearly showed: "I have tried to show that in the field of persuasive discourse, which traditionally and still to a great extent practically is to be identified with oratory and public address, we have a rather definite body of theory and practice, with an honorable history and an excellent academic pedigree."[93]

PRÉCIS

Hudson is truly an ignored giant. His eloquent, yet forceful, style of writing; his penetrating insight; his prescient admonitions; and his unflagging assertion that we have a proud and noble tradition to guide us deserve much fuller treatment than received from our discipline. Hudson accomplished so much for us; indeed, it seems as if he was perpetually at efflorescence. Two of his earliest essays, "The Field of Rhetoric" and "Rhetoric and Poetry," deserve landmark status. Two others, "De Quincey on Rhetoric and Public Speaking" and "The Tradition of Our Subject," might deserve this status as well.

One is astounded when one compares the attention that Hudson heretofore received and his actual contributions to our discipline and our understanding of rhetoric. His contributions, judged by the standards of the time when they were offered, were invaluable, often prescient, often seminal. Hudson was among the first to cogently and consistently expand the study of speech to include oral and written discourse. Although he traced the roots of rhetoric to the ancients, he was ever aware of the 2,500-year continuity of rhetorical studies. Thus was he able to present a classical theory of invention integrated with the rhetorical understanding common to the 1920s. He was the first to provide the discipline with a well-developed and serious definition of rhetoric, and may have been the first to differentiate between composition and rhetoric. Hudson was also the first to discuss rhetorical criticism differentiated from literary criticism; moreover, he was the first to suggest using topics and the classical canons as theoretical touchstones for rhetorical criticism. Although he spent his career in departments of English, Hudson firmly defended the separation of rhetorical studies from English; additionally, he envisioned a thematic grouping of courses in English and speech based upon the fine and useful arts inherent within discourse. At a time when many borrowed from other disciplines, Hudson consistently engaged readers with trenchant, argumentative contrasts between rhetoric and art, poetry, drama, and so on that distinguished well the field of speech from other disciplines. I am inclined to believe that he was the first to treat the subject of rhetoric consistently in this manner. He further advanced the importance of our discipline by arguing forcefully that students of literature and literary criticism ought to study rhetoric; for Hudson, rhetorical studies were as significant and honorable as literary studies.

Hudson shared with us the importance of imagination in expanding knowledge of the field. While others were relying on secondary sources and other disciplines for interpretations and theoretical groundings, Hudson relied on his own imagination and intellect for his close textual readings. When others were arguing whether to limit rhetoric to oral discourse, Hudson was prescient in his call for broadening the paths of study to include pamphleteering, newspapers, radio broadcasting, and other forms of communication. He also suggested that one might profitably take into account methods of publication, as well as the effects of national and racial characteristics upon rhetorical style. Hudson may well have foreseen the impact of photojournalism when he suggested analyzing "pictorial communication." While others were looking almost exclusively to the ancients for their understanding of rhetorical theory, Hudson was the first to show a serious and sustained interest in postclassical rhetorical theorists. His grasp of the tradition of our subject abounds throughout his work; its immensity staggers the mind. He was the first well-known and respected scholar to unabashedly state that our discipline emerged from a long and proud tradition. He thrust this tradition upon us, contributing greatly to our intellectual understanding of our field. We are, I firmly believe, deeply obliged to this man.

I leave you with a poem that he penned:

Winter Evening

I had a mile to tramp, due eastward, when
I turned and, walking backward, saw the snow
Rolled out, a cold deserted beach below
The ebbing waves of day: I stopped again.
"Twilight will come," I said, "and night, but still
It's day: and I shall wait to watch it go."
I watched until the iced wind let me know

That standing is no remedy for chill,
Then turned to travel on across the field
Into a purple alcove of the night.
"Still it is day," I said, and would not yield
To dusk and dark and stars by dark revealed
So long as far behind me there was light
Enough to keep a crimson cloud-rim bright.[94]

Hoyt Hopewell Hudson died 13 June 1944. He was fifty years of age.

NOTES

1. Hoyt Hopewell Hudson, *Celebration: A Book of Poems* (San Francisco: Grabhorn Press, 1945),. 3.

2. Everett Lee Hunt, "Hoyt Hopewell Hudson," *Quarterly Journal of Speech* 31.3 (1945): 273. Unfortunately, since the rush to posthumously publish several of his works in progress, Hudson has been neglected by our discipline; many previous histories of the field did not so much as mention him, for example, Karl R. Wallace, ed., *History of Speech Education in America* (New York City: Appleton-Century-Crofts, 1954). Donald Bryant's *The Rhetorical Idiom* (Ithaca, NY: Cornell University Press, 1958) makes reference to him only in passing. Three notable exceptions are Raymond F. Howes, *Historical Studies of Rhetoric and Rhetoricians* (Ithaca, NY: Cornell University Press, 1961), in which no less than three of Hudson's essays are reprinted; Theodore Otto Windt Jr., "Hoyt H. Hudson: Spokesman for the Cornell School of Rhetoric," *Quarterly Journal of Speech* 68.2 (1982): 186–200; and Herman Cohen in *The History of Speech Communication: The Emergence of a Discipline, 1914–1945* (Annandale, VA: Speech Communication Association, 1994). Cohen primarily addressed Hudson's *Quarterly Journal* essays.

3. Representative examples of this work are contained in the three volumes of *History and Criticism of American Public Address*. Disciplinary folklore imposes a rather narrow and rigid view of rhetorical criticism upon the neo-Aristotelians. For example, criticism is said to have been tidily divided between intrinsic and extrinsic aspects of the speaking situation. Intrinsic aspects of the critical effort were limited to the examination of the five classical canons; extrinsic aspects were limited to the setting and the discovery of the immediate audience and the immediate effects that the speech had upon that audience. Ideas expressed by speakers were to be described but not critically engaged. William Norwood Brigance, ed., *History and Criticism of American Public Address*, vols. 1, 2 (New York: McGraw-Hill, 1943); Marie Kathryn Hochmuth, ed., *History and Criticism of American Public Address*, vol. 3 (New York: McGraw-Hill, 1955).

4. Indeed, J. M. O'Neill stated: "[W]hat is speech? To us speech is the oral use of language, and also some other muscle movements, in human behavior for the purpose of direct and immediate communication. Speech is the field of human communication without the aid of papers and pencils, typewriters, printing presses, chisels, brushes, or musical instruments. Speech is not essentially and primarily concerned with words as printed or written symbols; and so, of course; the printed manuscript of a so-called speech is not really the speech itself, only the plan of the speech." James M. O'Neill, "The

Relation of Speech to Philology and Linguistics," *Quarterly Journal of Speech* 14.1 (1928): 2–3.

5. In his excellent essay, Windt stated that Hudson "cast about" a wide range of ideas in essay form and that these ideas "provided the foundation for what we now call the Cornell tradition in Rhetoric and Public Address." Windt examined Hudson's contributions with an eye toward his being spokesman for the Cornell school of rhetoric, a school characterized by "an adaptation of classical rhetoric to modern conditions" but also a school that "sought to delineate ways in which those ideas could be brought to practical, intellectual fruition in pedagogy and scholarship." Windt spoke of Hudson's biography, the major tenets of the midwestern school of speech, and major tenets, as inferred from Hudson, of the Cornell school of rhetoric. Windt, 187.

6. High school posts included Coeur d'Alene, Idaho; Duluth, Minnesota; and Cleveland, Ohio.

7. Hudson took courses in both speech and English at Cornell. In 1920–1921: Philosophy 5: History of Philosophy, with James E. Chreighton; Public Speaking 20: Seminary, with Alexander Drummond and Everett Lee Hunt (given throughout the year); English 44: Shakespeare, with Joseph Q. Adams; English 41: The English Drama to 1642, with Joseph Q. Adams. In 1921–1922: Public Speaking 20: Seminary, with Alexander Drummond; for the study of special subjects in the history, literature, psychology and pedagogy of public speech; English 72: Principles of Literary Criticism, with Lane Cooper (a study of the chief theories of poetry and chief kinds of literature, with illustrations drawn from writers both ancient and modern). In 1922–1923: Philosophy 16: Reading of Philosophical German, with William A. Hammond; English 53: Old English, with Benton S. Monroe.

8. "A New Department Chairman: English—Hoyt Hopewell Hudson," *Princeton Alumni Weekly*, 12 January 1934. The high esteem given to Hudson by his colleagues, even in the face of his "handicap," is evinced by the last line in this article: Hudson "was called to Princeton from Pitt in 1927 by Robert K. Root [previous English chairman] who considers that act his greatest service to Princeton."

9. Hudson was also the managing editor for the *Step Ladder* and a trustee and member of the committee on publication of the Princeton University Press. Also in 1938, Hudson was an editor for the *Popular Educator*, a weekly serial composed of fifty-three issues. Each issue contained articles dealing with almost every cultural and practical field: Accounting, Anthropology, Penmanship, Philosophy, English. Hudson taught the occasional summer course at Cornell, University of California at Los Angeles, Stanford, Colorado and Northwestern Universities, and Harvard. In addition to many intellectual pursuits, he also participated in the everyday life of his local community. For example, he was a trustee of the Princeton Country Day School and was the first president of the Princeton Committee on Russian War Relief. He was also a member of Phi Beta Kappa, the Modern Language Association, and the National Association of Teachers of Speech, the Book Fellows Club of Chicago, and the Princeton Club of Philadelphia.

10. Herbert A. Wichelns, "The Literary Criticism of Oratory," *Studies in Rhetoric and Public Speaking in Honor of James Albert Winans by Pupils and Colleagues*, A. M. Drummond, ed. (New York: Century, 1925).

11. Hoyt Hopewell Hudson, "Can We Modernize the Theory of Invention?" *Quarterly Journal of Speech Education* 7.4 (1921): 326.

12. Hoyt Hopewell Hudson, "The Field of Rhetoric," *Quarterly Journal of Speech Education* 9.2 (1923): 169–170.

13. Ibid.

14. Hoyt Hopewell Hudson, "De Quincey on Rhetoric and Public Speaking," *Studies in Rhetoric and Public Speaking in Honor of James Albert Winans by Pupils and Colleagues*, 148.

15. Ibid., 148–149.

16. Hudson, "Can We Modernize," 325–334.

17. Ibid., 326.

18. Hudson, "Field of Rhetoric," 177–178.

19. Hudson, "De Quincey on Rhetoric," 139.

20. Ibid., 141–142.

21. Hudson, "Field of Rhetoric," 168.

22. Hoyt Hopewell Hudson, *Educating Liberally* (Stanford, CA: Stanford University Press, 1945), 46.

23. Hoyt Hopewell Hudson, "Rhetoric and Poetry," *Quarterly Journal of Speech Education* 10.2 (1924): 145.

24. Ibid. H. L. Mencken would later make this same distinction, but with remarkably different conclusions:

The Gettysburg speech was at once the shortest and the most famous oration in American history. Put beside it, all the whoopings of the Websters, Sumners and Everetts seem gaudy and silly. It is eloquence brought to a pellucid and almost gem-like perfection, the highest emotion reduced to a few poetical phrases. Lincoln himself never even remotely approached it. It is genuinely stupendous. But let us not forget that it is poetry, not logic; beauty, not sense. Think of the argument in it. Put it into the cold words of everyday. The doctrine is simply this: that the Union soldiers who died at Gettysburg sacrificed their lives to the cause of self determination that government of the people, by the people, for the people, should not perish from the earth. It is difficult to imagine anything more untrue. The Union soldiers in the battle actually fought against self-determination; it was the Confederates who fought for the right of their people to govern themselves." (H. L. Mencken, *A Mencken Chrestomathy* [New York: Vintage Books, 1949], 222–223)

25. Hudson, "Can We Modernize," 331–332.

26. O'Neill, 1–7; Everett Lee Hunt, "Rhetoric and Literary Criticism," *Quarterly Journal of Speech* 21 (1935): 564–568; Ross Scanlan, "Rhetoric and the Drama," *Quarterly Journal of Speech* 22 (1936): 635–642.

27. Hudson, "Rhetoric and Poetry," 145.

28. Ibid., 146.

29. Ibid., 148.

30. Ibid., 153.

31. Edwin Black, *Rhetorical Criticism: A Study in Method* (Madison: University of Wisconsin Press, 1978), 33.

32. Ibid., 30–33. The full text on page 30 reads: "The primary and identifying ideas of neo-Aristotelianism that we can find recurring in the critical essays of this school are the classification of rhetorical discourses into forensic, deliberative, and epideictic; the classification of 'proofs' or 'means of persuasion' into logical, pathetic, and ethical; the assessment of discourse in the categories of invention, arrangement, delivery, and style; and the evaluation of rhetorical discourse in terms of its effects on its immediate audience."

33. Wilbur Samuel Howell and Hoyt Hopewell Hudson, "Daniel Webster," *History*

and Criticism of American Public Address, vol. 2, William Norwood Brigance, ed. (New York: McGraw-Hill, 1943), 711.

34. Hudson, "Rhetoric and Poetry," 149.

35. Hudson, "Field of Rhetoric," 175.

36. Ibid.

37. Black, 35. Which, of course, is exactly what Black stated that neo-Aristotelians ignore in their criticism.

38. Hunt, "Hoyt Hopewell Hudson," 271.

39. Hudson, "Field of Rhetoric," 180.

40. Ibid., 171.

41. Hudson, "De Quincey on Rhetoric," 149.

42. Ibid.

43. Ibid., 147–148.

44. Ibid., 149.

45. Hudson, "Can We Modernize," 326–327.

46. Ibid., 329–330.

47. Ibid., 333.

48. Ibid.

49. Ibid.

50. Hudson, "Field of Rhetoric," 174. This, along with Hudson's 1921 essay, clearly demonstrates that he advanced canons and topics prior to Wichelns. It is generally assumed that Hudson studied with or under Wichelns at Cornell during the years 1920–1923. However, according to Dartmouth College records, Wichelns came to Dartmouth with James A. Winans in 1920 and left only in June 1921. Raymond F. Howes stated that he first met Wichelns in 1921 and that he "was then completing his Ph.D. under Lane Cooper and was an instructor in the Department of Public Speaking [at Cornell]." See Raymond F. Howes, *Notes on the Cornell School of Rhetoric* (Riverside, CA: Privately printed, 1976), 13.

51. Hudson, *Educating Liberally*, 59.

52. Ibid., 62.

53. Ibid.

54. Ibid., 63.

55. Ibid., 72.

56. Ibid.

57. Ibid., 12.

58. A spirited exchange between Paul Shorey, a professor of classics, and Everett Lee Hunt is recounted in Herman Cohen, *The History of Speech Communication: The Emergence of a Discipline, 1914–1945* (Annandale, VA: Speech Communication Association, 1994), 223–229. Also see Hudson, "Jewel's Oration against Rhetoric," *Quarterly Journal of Speech* 14.3 (1928): 374–397. See, too, the article which that precedes "Jewel's Oration," which offered a negative, but thoughtful, critique of rhetoric: V. E. Simrell, "Mere Rhetoric," *Quarterly Journal of Speech* 14.3 (1928): 359–374. Hudson clearly allies himself with Everett Lee Hunt in the arguments with Shorey, Woolbert, and O'Neill concerning both orality and the nature of the new discipline.

59. This is shown well in the following two paragraphs. Hudson, in *The Epigram in the English Renaissance* (Princeton, NJ: Princeton University Press, 1947), 16–17, cited

F. E. Schelling in *The English Lyric* to begin his discussion of the rhetorical nature of the epigram:

"In conclusion of these matters, be it remarked that in anthologies of English poetry the epigram has sometimes trespassed on the domain of the lyric. The epigram is often musical and commonly short, and here the resemblance between it and the lyric ends. For the epigram is intellectual, rhetorical, and conscious, addressed to stir in the hearer an approval of art; the lyric is emotional, poetic, and unconscious, in so far as a piece of artistry often involving a loving elaboration may exist for its own end and only secondarily for the pleasure which is its legitimate function to occasion in the hearer or reader."

There was much confusion—indeed, virtual identification—of rhetoric and poetry in the period of the Renaissance, as there has also been later. "My greatest approbation," wrote Erasmus, "is reserved for a rhetorical poem and poetical oratory . . . the rhetorical art should transpire through the poem." This idea is strong in literary theory and practice for many years both before and after Erasmus wrote. Considering rhetoric as discourse which is designed primarily for the sake of an effect (either as display or as persuasion) upon a certain audience, and poetry, in its pure state, as "the spontaneous overflow of powerful feeling," we see that the rhetorical impulse colored most of the literature of the period we wish to consider. Even lyrics, as Professor Schelling would agree, did not escape this coloring; and at best he can be sure of distinguishing only the predominantly poetical from the obviously rhetorical. But he is right when he puts epigrams in the realm of rhetoric. "Eloquence is written to be heard, poetry to be overheard," is Mill's famous apothegm. Epigrams are always written to be heard. Their authors address them to an audience. They have the touch of epideictic rhetoric, the touch of display; and they frequently have as well the persuasive purpose. This last is stated epigrammatically by Robert Hayman in his *Quodlibets* (1628):

> TO THE READER
> Sermons and epigrams have a like end,
> To improve, to reprove, and to amend.
> Some passe without this use, 'cause they are witty;
> And so doe many Sermons, more's the pitty.

60. Hudson, *Epigram*, 4.

61. Ibid., 8.

62. Desiderius Erasmus, *The Praise of Folly*, trans. from the Latin, with an essay and commentary by Hoyt Hopewell Hudson (Princeton, NJ: Princeton University Press, 1941), xiv.

63. Ibid., xv.

64. Ibid.

65. Ibid.

66. Ibid., xxvi.

67. Howell and Hudson, 673–674. The first section was equally penned by both men. Although both men worked on the entire essay, Hudson worked as principal author on the influences of literature and law upon Webster's orations and the analysis of six epideictic speeches; Howell was principal author on the debate between Webster and Hayne and on Webster as a Whig political icon.

68. Ibid., 691. This early analysis suggests some rough parallels to our contemporary notions of ideographical analysis. See ibid., 677.

69. Ibid., 692. I would be remiss if I did not mention that this particular section, The Great Debate, worked principally upon by Howell, smacks of anti-Southern bias so common among intellectuals of northern schools. Several examples should suffice: said of the arguments used by Senators Hayne and Benton: "These tactics are familiar to the

student of modern propaganda" (p. 698). Said of Hayne's speeches: "the most sinister force yet encountered by the American republic" (p. 699). The South's feeling toward the tariff of 1828 is slighted, and its explanations of how the Northeast used western support to pass the tariff was discounted. Bias is more readily apparent in their essay when Howell and Hudson stated Hayne's "sympathy for the poor workers of the North being hardly a sentiment that would occur to a defender of slavery unless he had an ulterior purpose in dwelling upon it" (p. 700). Moreover, they left out the responses given by Hayne after Webster's "Third Reply to Hayne," thereby allowing Webster the last word on the matter. I am inclined to believe these instances of bias due more to Howell than Hudson considering Howell was principal author.

70. Ibid., 696.

71. Ibid., 711.

72. Hudson, "Can We Modernize," 331–332.

73. Everett L. Hunt, "Introduction: Herbert A. Wichelns and the Cornell Tradition of Rhetoric as a Humane Study," *The Rhetorical Idiom: Essays in Rhetoric, Oratory, Language, and Drama*, Donald C. Bryant, ed. (Ithaca, NY: Cornell University Press, 1958), 1–2.

74. Hudson, "Field of Rhetoric," 177–178.

75. Ibid., 179.

76. ibid., 180.

77. Ibid., 176–177.

78. Hudson, "Rhetoric and Poetry," 143.

79. Ibid., 154.

80. Hudson, "De Quincey on Rhetoric," 140–141.

81. Hudson, "Tradition of Our Subject," 326–327.

82. Ibid., 328.

83. Ibid. On the following page Hudson stated: "We want to feel ourselves in touch with our kind, belonging to something of continuing dignity among mankind, something which will outlast our own brief career. However far we may have come, whatever new ground we may have advanced upon, we shall go farther more surely, we shall hold that ground permanently, if we take care not to cut our lines of communication with the past."

84. Donald C. Bryant, Book Review, *Educating Liberally*, by Hoyt Hopewell Hudson, *Quarterly Journal of Speech* 32.1 (1946): 116.

85. Hudson, *Educating Liberally*, 8.

86. Ibid., 14.

87. Ibid., 66–67.

88. Ibid., 32.

89. Ibid., 39. I would again be remiss if I did not mention Hudson's ambitious program for reorganizing the university to accomplish his goals for a true liberal arts education. For Hudson, history and philosophy, broadly construed, are that from which all other fields flow. He would place the social sciences under the humanities, where studies are generally directed at humans and nature. Central areas of study, then, are humanities and sciences, "considered historically and philosophically." Of course, central to all is communication. The importance of placing the sciences under the humanities seems to foreshadow the very problems that we have today: "As we usually put it, Science by itself and as such does not furnish the criteria for its evaluation or the directives for its application" (ibid., 82–85). Hudson clearly understood the need to add a humanizing element to scientific inquiry and training. He considered God as well. Theology is often

the blind spot in any liberal arts education; its strength as a social force is too often ignored. So many professors will confess

the death of Christianity, or of the church, or the disappearance of religion . . . overlooking mean-while the immense strength of such bodies of believers and the Catholic Church, overlooking the millions of people in our own country who hold fervently to an evangelical faith of some sort, and overlooking the millions more who find religion to be a reality and a human necessity even though they are not identified with either the Catholics of the Protestant evangelical denominations. So far as this is true, it is a charge of illiberality against these teachers, since like illiberal people in general they are ignoring facts, or, if they recognize the facts, are refusing to carry out the processes of thinking which the facts call for. (p. 83)

90. Ibid., 45.
91. Ibid., 46.
92. Ibid., 50.
93. Hudson, "Field of Rhetoric," 179.
94. Hudson, *Celebration*, 50.

BIBLIOGRAPHY

Black, Edwin. *Rhetorical Criticism: A Study in Method*. Madison: University of Wisconsin Press, 1978.

Bryant, Donald C. *The Rhetorical Idiom: Essays in Rhetoric, Oratory, Language, and Drama*. Ithaca, NY: Cornell Univeristy Press, 1958.

Bryant, Donald C. Rev. of *Educating Liberally*. Stanford, CA: Stanford University Press; London: H. Milford, Oxford University Press, 1945. In *Quarterly Journal of Speech* 32.1 (1946): 116–117.

Cohen, Herman. *The History of Speech Communication: The Emergence of a Discipline, 1914–1945*. Annandale, VA: Speech Communication Association, 1994.

Erasmus, Desiderius. *The Praise of Folly*. Translated from the Latin, with an essay and commentary by Hoyt Hopewell Hudson. Princeton, NJ: Princeton University Press, 1941.

Hebel, John William, and Hoyt H. Hudson, eds. *Poetry of the English Renaissance, 1509–1660*. New York: F. S. Crofts, 1929.

Herrick, Marvin Theodore, and Hoyt H. Hudson. *That Upper Forty*. New York: Samuel French, 1928.

Hoskins, John. *Directions for Speech and Style*. Introduction and notes by Hoyt H. Hudson, ed. Princeton, NJ: Princeton University Press, 1935.

Howell, Wilbur Samuel, and Hoyt Hopewell Hudson. "Daniel Webster." *History and Criticism of American Public Address*, vol. 2. William Norwood Brigance, ed. New York: McGraw-Hill, 1943.

Howes, Raymond F. *Notes on the Cornell School of Rhetoric*. Riverside, CA: Privately printed, 1976.

———, ed. *Historical Studies of Rhetoric and Rhetoricians*. Ithaca, NY: Cornell University Press, 1961.

Hudson, Hoyt H. "Alexander M. Drummond." *Studies in Speech and Drama in Honor of Alexander M. Drummond*. Ithaca, NY: Cornell University Press, 1944.

———. "Bibliographical Note." *Epigrams, the Forest Underwoods*, by Ben Johnson. New York: Columbia University Press, 1936.

————. "Bright Ware." *Midland* 18 (1931): 93.

————. "Can We Modernize the Theory of Invention?" *Quarterly Journal of Speech Education* 7.4 (1921): 325–334.

————. *Celebration, a Book of Poems.* San Francisco: Grabhorn Press, 1945.

————. "*Compendium Rhetorices* by Erasmus: A Translation." *Studies in Speech and Drama in Honor of Alexander M. Drummond.* Ithaca, NY: Cornell University Press, 1944.

————. "De Quincy on Rhetoric and Public Speaking." *Studies in Rhetoric and Public Speaking in Honor of James Albert Winans by Pupils and Colleagues.* A. M. Drummond, ed. New York: Century, 1925, 133–152.

————. *Educating Liberally.* Stanford, CA: Stanford University Press; London: H. Milford, Oxford University Press, 1945.

————. "Edward May's Borrowings from Timothe Kendall and Others." *The Huntington Library Bulletin* 11 (1937): 23–58.

————. *Elizabethan and Jacobean Epigrams.* Diss., Cornell University, 1923.

————. *The Epigram in the English Renaissance.* Princeton, NJ: Princeton University Press, 1947.

————. "The Ethics of Public Speaking." *Literary Scroll* 2 (1929): 2–6.

————. "Everybody Reads This." Editorial. *Quarterly Journal of Speech* 20.1 (1934): 116–117.

————. "The Field of Rhetoric." *Quarterly Journal of Speech Education* 9.2 (1923): 167–180.

————. "The Forum." *Quarterly Journal of Speech Education* 12.3 (1926): 207–208.

————. "The Forum." *Quarterly Journal of Speech* 15.2 (1929): 256.

————. "A Glance Back." Editorial. *Quarterly Journal of Speech* 21.1 (1935): 96–97.

————. "The Growth of the English Novel." *The English Novel: An Exhibition of Manuscripts and First Editions, Chaucer to Conrad.* San Marino, CA: Henry E. Huntington Library and Art Gallery, 1934, 3–5.

————. "Jewel's Oration against Rhetoric: A Translation." *Quarterly Journal of Speech* 14.3 (1928): 374–397.

————. "Publication for Researchers." Editorial. *Quarterly Journal of Speech* 20.1 (1934): 117–118.

————. "Rhetoric and Poetry." *Quarterly Journal of Speech Education* 10.2 (1924): 143–154.

————. "John Hepwith's Spenserian Satire upon Buckingham: With Some Jacobean Analogues." *The Huntington Library Bulletin* 6 (1934): 36–71.

————. "John LeLand's List of Early English Humanists." *The Huntington Library Bulletin* 11 (1939).

————. "The Knees of Demosthenes." *American Speech* 2.8 (1927): 337–340.

————. "Notes on the Raleigh Canon." *Modern Language Notes* 46 (1931): 386–389.

————. "The Oblique Approach." *Princetonian* (Tuesday, January 17, 1939).

————. "Permanance and Change." *Stray Shot* (May 1942).

————. "Sid." *Midland* 15 (1929): 41.

————. "Sonnets by Barnabe Googe." *Publications of the Modern Language Association* 48 (1933): 293–294.

————. "The Tradition of Our Subject." *Quarterly Journal of Speech* 17.3 (1931): 320–329.

————. "Two Poems." *Midland* 14 (1928): 294–295.

Hudson, Hoyt Hopewell, and W. Lee Ustick. "Wit, 'Mixt Wit' and the Bee in Amber."
    The Huntington Library Bulletin 8 (1935): 103–130.
Hudson, Hoyt Hopewell, and James A. Winans. *A First Course in Public Speaking.* New
    York: Century, 1931.
Hunt, Everett Lee. "Hoyt Hopewell Hudson." *Quarterly Journal of Speech* 31.3 (1945):
    271–274.
Kant, Immanuel. *Religion within the Limits of Reason Alone.* Translation by Theodore
    M. Greene and Hoyt H. Hudson. Chicago and London: Open Court, 1934.
Moffett, Thomas. *Nobilis; Or, a View of the Life and Death of a Sidney; and Lessus
    Lugubris.* Introduction, translation, and notes by Virgil B. Heltzel and Hoyt H.
    Hudson. San Marino, CA: Huntington Library, 1940.
"A New Department Chairman: English—Hoyt Hopewell Hudson." *Princeton Alumni
    Weekly* 12, January 1934.
O'Neill, J. M. "The Relation of Speech to Philology and Linguistics." *Quarterly Journal
    of Speech* 14.1 (1928): 1–7.
Reeves, J. Walter, and Hoyt H. Hudson. *Principles of Argument and Debate.* Boston:
    D.C. Heath, 1941.
Wallace, Karl R., ed. *History of Speech Education in America.* New York: Appleton-
    Century-Crofts, 1954.
Wichelns, Herbert A. "The Literary Criticism of Oratory." *Studies in Rhetoric and Public
    Speaking in Honor of James Albert Winans by Pupils and Colleagues.* A. M.
    Drummond, ed. New York: Century, 1925.
Windt, Theodore Otto, Jr. "Hoyt H. Hudson: Spokesman for the Cornell School of Rhet-
    oric." *Quarterly Journal of Speech* 68.2 (1982): 186–200.

4

Wilbur Samuel Howell: The Trilogy of Rhetoric, Logic, and Science

JOHN E. TAPIA

"Rhetoric educator" is the occupation listed for Wilbur Samuel Howell (1904–1992) in the June 29, 1992, edition of *Who's Who*.[1] Professor Howell continues to be a rhetoric educator. His scholarship provides a useful paradigm apropos of explaining how rhetoric and logic responded to the cultural and social changes in sixteenth-, seventeenth-, and eighteenth-century England. Howell argues that by the end of the seventeenth century a separation between logic and rhetoric had begun, resulting from reforms in British education, class structure, and religion. With the rise and acceptance of modern-day science in the following century, the split between rhetoric and logic became permanent. Professor Howell's prototype for interpreting the transformations that took place in British logic and rhetoric broke new ground in the field of rhetoric history. There were no forerunners, and as a result he had to invent the genre as well as account for the history of change.

At about the same time that Professor Howell's 742-page *Eighteenth-Century British Logic and Rhetoric* was published in the early 1970s, I was a new graduate student at the University of Massachusetts. I was assigned to review the book for a rhetoric course in which I was enrolled. Four or five days prior to when the review report was due, I went to the library to get this book. I was taken aback by the length of the book and was even more horrified to learn that to understand this book, I would need to be familiar with at least two of Howell's other books—*The Rhetoric of Alcuin and Charlemagne* and *Logic and Rhetoric in England: 1500–1700*. Diligently, I outlined the trends in British logic and rhetoric as suggested by Howell. Shortly after this Herculean effort (or so I thought at the time) was completed, I had the opportunity to talk with

Wilbur Samuel Howell. Photo courtesy of the Seeley G. Mudd Manuscript Library, Princeton, NJ. Used with permission.

Professor Howell at some Speech (it was speech then, not communication) convention. Proud of my accomplishment, I conveyed to Professor Howell that I had outlined three of his major works, to which he responded that "these works are a trilogy and have to be understood as such." In writing this chapter about Wilbur Samuel Howell's contributions to the history of rhetoric, I relied, in part, on these "trilogy" notes outlined almost thirty years ago.

The major works of Professor Howell include his translation of *The Rhetoric of Alcuin and Charlemagne*, printed in 1941, the *Problems and Styles of Communication*, appearing in 1945, *Fenelon's Dialogues on Eloquence*, published in 1951, *Logic and Rhetoric in England: 1500–1700* in 1956, and, in 1971, *Eighteenth Century British Logic and Rhetoric*, which was awarded the James A. Winans Book Prize and the Golden Anniversary Book Prize by the Speech Communication Association in 1972. Howell's *Poetics, Rhetoric and Logic: Studies in the Basic Disciplines of Criticism* was published in 1975 and granted the Golden Anniversary Book Prize in 1976. His last major scholarly effort was the editing of *Jefferson's Parliamentary Writing*, which appeared in print in 1988. Howell also published in such journals as the *Quarterly Journal of Speech*, of which he was editor in chief from 1954 to 1956, *Speech Monographs, William and Mary Quarterly,* and *Philosophy and Rhetoric* and an article on rhetoric in the *Encyclopedia Britannica*.

Professor Howell was born on April 22, 1904, in Wayne, New York, as the son of Wood Augustus and Edna (Hanmer) Howell. Howell received his bachelor's degree from Cornell University in 1924 and that same year accepted a position as an instructor of public speaking at Iowa State College. In 1925 he left Iowa State to accept a position as an instructor of public speaking at Washington University. In 1928, the same year that he married Charlotte Comb, Howell received his A.M. from Cornell University, doing postgraduate work at the University of Paris at the Sorbonne. Between 1929 and 1930, he was an instructor of public speaking at Cornell. While working on his doctorate at Cornell, granted in 1931, Howell accepted the position of instructor of public speaking at Harvard University. Leaving Harvard in 1933, he joined Dartmouth College as an assistant professor.

The following year, Professor Howell accepted a position with Princeton University as an assistant professor, continuing his association with the university until his retirement. He was promoted in 1940 to the rank of associate professor and, in 1955, named to the rank of professor of rhetoric and oratory. His wife, Charlotte, passed away in 1956, and in 1962 he married Cecilia Jonkman van Eerden. In 1972 Howell retired from Princeton, being granted emeritus status.

THE CORNELL SCHOOL OF RHETORIC

Professor Howell's *Poetics, Rhetoric, and Logic: Studies in the Basic Disciplines of Criticism*, published in 1975 by Cornell University, is dedicated to "Harry Caplan and to the memory of Lane Cooper and Herbert A. Wichelns in honor of their brilliant contributions as scholars and teachers to what their grateful students proudly regard as The Cornell school of Rhetoric."[2] The direction and ideology of the Cornell school of rhetoric were influenced by Cornell professor of English James A. Winans. Throughout the early teens and into the 1920s, Winans sought to establish public speaking as an independent discipline apart from departments of English.[3]

As departments of English evolved in American public education during the aftermath of the Civil War, they generally assumed "control over the teaching of writing, and such teaching of speaking as was included in the curriculum."[4] The link that tied writing with rhetoric, which frequently included literary studies at the college and university levels, "was the fact that the study of English literature appeared in the curriculum as the protégé of the venerable study of rhetoric" following a trend begun in the Middle Ages and reaffirmed by Ramus in the sixteenth century.[5]

Not until the twentieth century did the separation of public speaking from departments of English begin to occur in academic curricula. Under the guidance of Winans, Cornell was one of the first universities to treat public speaking as a field of graduate study apart from a department of English. (Winans later held the Chair of Rhetoric at Dartmouth College and established a second Ivy League outpost for public speaking.) Cornell began its graduate instruction in speech in 1916, awarding its first M.A. in 1922 and first Ph.D. in 1926. Throughout this period Howell was either attending or in contact with the university. One of the major offshoots resulting from the efforts to separate public speaking from English was that scholars of rhetoric and public address sought to reclaim the traditional tie between rhetoric and logic that had been set aside by departments of English.[6] The Cornell school of rhetoric was, to say the least, an advocate of the reclamation of rhetoric and logic as a unified field of study. This chapter explains Howell's critical and historical approach in tracing the intellectual relationship between rhetoric and logic and how modern science, based in empirical methodology, ultimately separated rhetoric and logic into two distinct disciplines.

THE ENGLISH TRADITION

The beginning of the English tradition in both rhetoric and logic originates for Howell with an eighth-century Englishman by the name of Alcuin. Alcuin was born in England in about 735 and attended the prestigious Cathedral School of York. The school was heavily influenced by the scholar Venerable Bede, whose early eighth-century work *Liber de schematibus et tropes*, Howell claims, "ranks as the earliest fragment of Ciceronian rhetorical theory [in regard to stylistic devices] to come from the pen of an Englishman."[7]

In 782 Alcuin traveled to France at the personal invitation of Charlemagne, and "there [he] became the most illustrious of the learned men assembled to rebuild in the new Carolinian empire the half-obliterated educational system of the earlier imperial epoch."[8] While in France, Alcuin wrote his rhetoric and a separate work on dialectic, both of which are written in the form of a dialogue between Charlemagne and himself. In subsequent publications of Alcuin, the two works are frequently published as companion pieces and by the tenth century were treated as one unified text. Until Howell's translation of Alcuin into English from Latin, the last published translation was that by Karl von Halm in 1863.

Most of Alcuin's rhetoric is devoted to the first Ciceronian canon of rhetoric, invention, as it relates to logic in terms of Cicero's doctrine of positions. The doctrine of positions is based on two assumptions. First, the controversies that confront judicial, deliberative, or epideictic oratory can be classified into one of two analytical categories: the first of general characteristics and the second of particular circumstances—each with its own specific subdivisions. Second, an orator having sound knowledge of these categories can synthesize arguments for a given dispute by relating his particular subject to its proper class and by examining the subject in relationship to the known characteristics of that class. Through this method of analysis and synthesis, the speaker not only generates arguments but also is provided an arrangement pattern.[9]

Despite using different terminology other than that provided by Cicero when discussing his doctrine of positions, Alcuin adopts Cicero's system when discussing invention. Due to his reliance on Cicero's doctrine of positions, Howell concludes that Alcuin was responsible for carrying ahead the tradition of invention that lies at "the heart of the Latin scheme of rhetorical analysis."[10] When discussing the remaining canons of rhetoric—arrangement, style, memory, and delivery—Alcuin primarily relies on Julius Victor's abridgments of Cicero's *De Orator* and *Orator*.[11]

Alcuin's treatment of rhetoric and logic, for Howell, represents the first work written by an Englishman pertaining to these disciplines, one that extends the traditional or Ciceronian view of invention into English rhetorical theory—a method that is both practical and intellectual. "The first function . . . assumes rhetoric to be a method of procedure, and seeks to place at the disposal of a student the tools of oratorical power. The second function, a kind of by-product, recognizes that intellectual method can only be studied in relation to the intellectual content with which it deals, and that rhetoric tends inevitably to provide instruction in the subjects toward which its methods are habitually adjusted."[12] Howell's translation of *The Rhetoric of Alcuin and Charlemagne*, published by the Princeton University Press in 1941, is the first of the chronological trilogy describing how he views the development of logic and rhetoric in England. Howell's next major book, the second in the trilogy, was *Logic and Rhetoric in England, 1500–1700*, also published by the Princeton University Press, fifteen years later.

RENAISSANCE RHETORIC AND LOGIC

After Alcuin, both the English and European rhetoric traditions became increasingly oriented toward style, with rhetoric becoming increasingly associated with writing and, more specifically, poetry.[13] This trend became so prevalent that by the fourteenth century, the Ciceronian system of rhetoric, by and large, meant applying stylistic tropes and figures to poetry.[14] The association of rhetoric with grammar and poetry, as it continued into the sixteenth century, laid the groundwork for Ramus' separation of logic and rhetoric and, as a consequence, relating rhetoric to style and delivery.

The period between 1500 and 1700, Howell notes, "is the one point in the history of Western Europe where the communication theory of ancient Greece and Rome and that of modern Europe and America are ranged side by side, the older one still alive but losing ground, the younger one still immature but growing."[15] Throughout the sixteenth century, rhetoric, as one of the "two great arts of communication," generally maintained its tie with the other great art of communication—logic.[16] By the end of the seventeenth century, however, social and intellectual transformations that had taken place in England resulted in a somber move toward the separation of rhetoric and logic.

The changes that gradually took place within Renaissance England that resulted in a new way of viewing rhetoric and logic are outlined by Howell: (1) there was a movement away from the deductive method of scholasticism in the new field of science toward the acceptance of empirical methodology that favored induction; (2) as the aristocracy of the late medieval period was shoved aside by the emerging merchant middle class, conciliatory stylistic rhetoric lost its usefulness; and (3) with the Reformation the Catholic reliance on religious commonplaces gradually gave way to skepticism.[17]

Howell's *Logic and Rhetoric in England, 1500–1700* begins by claiming that Renaissance rhetoric and logic began with the writings of Cambridge's Thomas Wilson—the sixteenth-century counterpart to Alcuin.[18] Wilson was the first to write the first English version of scholastic logic, the *Rule of Reason*, published in 1551—the "greatest Ciceronain rhetoric in English"—and *The Arte of Rhetorique*, published in 1553.[19] Howell maintains that scholastic logic dominated English treatises on logic throughout most of the Renaissance, as evidenced by its continuous history in England "between the age of the first English logician, Alcuin, and the mid-sixteenth century."[20] Throughout most of the Renaissance, scholastic logic functioned much the same way that it had in the ancient world. At its heart was disputation, which pragmatically constituted the basis of "scholarly and scientific discourse and . . . the theory of communication in the world of learning."[21] Rhetoric, on the other hand, although still leaning toward stylistic embellishment, was also generally viewed in the same way as it had been in the ancient world. Rhetoric was treated as a theory of communication that served as a bridge "between the learned and the lay world."[22]

Responding to the emerging communication needs of a "modern" sixteenth- and seventeenth-century England, traditional perspectives concerning rhetoric, logic, and the interconnection between the two began to change. Until the 1570s, English logic generally was based on the logical treatises and interpretations of Aristotle.[23] Rhetoric was viewed in terms of its ties with ancient Greek and

Roman rhetoric vis-à-vis Ciceronian theory in three distinct patterns, according to Howell.[24]

1. The Ciceronian school considered most, if not all, five canons of rhetoric as assigned by the *ad Herennium*, Cicero, and Quintilian. The traditional pattern, Howell maintains, became associated with English rhetoric first through Alcuin, then, in the thirteenth and fourteenth centuries by the numerous works on grammar and poetry that relied on Ciceronian terminology, finally resulting in Thomas Wilson's *Rhetorique*.[25]

2. The stylistic school recognized all of the five parts of traditional rhetoric but was committed to style. Tracing this pattern back to Venerable Bede's eighth-century work, this trend frequently involved the cumbersome classification of the figures and tropes of rhetoric as prescribed by grammars for poetry. In part because of the long association of rhetoric with style after Alcuin and, in part, because of the reforms proposed by Ramus, the stylistic school was and remained the most popular trend in England until 1700.[26]

3. The formulary school acknowledged all of the Ciceronian parts but believed that the most effective way to study and teach rhetoric was through prescriptive guides. Formulary rhetorics were frequently written in the form of schoolbooks for the teaching of public speaking in secondary schools.[27]

Ramus and the Split between Rhetoric and Logic

In the last quarter of the sixteenth century, based on the teachings of Peter Ramus, a revolt occurred "against scholastic logic and traditional rhetoric."[28] French logician and educator Pierr de la Ramee, or, in Latin, Petrus Ramus, carrying on the work begun by Ramon Luu in the thirteenth century, separately treated rhetoric, logic, and grammar in both his *Dialectique* and *Dialecticae Libri Duo*, published in Paris in 1555 and 1556, respectively.[29] The basic schemes of division proposed by Ramus relegated etymology and syntax to grammar, invention, and arrangement to logic and reduced rhetoric to style and delivery. Under his scheme the canon of memory was omitted.

The teachings of Ramus spread throughout Northern Europe after his death in 1572, roughly paralleling the expansion of his popularity in England.[30] The first publicist of Ramastic logic was a Scot by the name of Roland MacIlmaine. He published both a Latin and an English version of *Dialecticae Libri Duo* in 1574. The first Englishman, according to Howell, to interpret Ramus to his compatriots was Gabriel Harvey, who delivered a series of lectures on Ramus at Cambridge in 1757.[31] Interest in Ramus was also indicated by the many translations of *Rhetorica* written by Ramus' protégé Omer Talon (also known as Audomarus Talaeus) that appeared in England.[32]

Ramus's views about logic and rhetoric did encounter resistance by (1) those who had been influenced by the educational reforms proposed by the Continental logician Melanchthon in which rhetoric was reduced to invention, judgment, arrangement, and style, (2) the adherents to an unscathed scholastic logic, and

(3) those who valued the completeness of the five-part Ciceronian tradition.
Between those who either accepted or rejected the teachings of Ramus was,
however, a middle ground for both logic and rhetoric: The systematic school
for logic and the variations of neo-Ciceronian rhetoric—the Ciceronian school,
the stylistic school, and the formulary school.

The systematic school of logic embraced Ramus's pedagogical scheme of
having logic encompass invention and giving disposition to logic. Systematics,
however, also held on to the communicative function of logic by acknowledging
the importance of style, delivery, and, on occasion, memory to the presentation
of argument.[33] The neo-Ciceronian rhetoricians acknowledged the first four canons—invention, disposition, style, and delivery—and almost universally excluded memory. Their discussions of invention and disposition, however, fell
under the consideration of logic as Ramus had it.[34]

Francis Bacon: Toward a New Rhetoric and A New Logic

Another reaction to Ramus is found in the writings of Francis Bacon. His
early sixteenth-century writings, particularly *The Advancement of Learning*, published in 1605, oppose not only Ramus but many of the neo-Ciceronian trends
as well. Bacon does not reject the method of the formulary approach but believes
that it needs to be enriched by utilizing better instructional models. He equates
stylistic rhetoric with the disease of excessiveness that, he assumes, undermines
cultural ideology. Under his plan, Ciceronian rhetoric is reduced to four procedures: the Art of Inquiry or Invention, Art of Examination or Judgment, Art
of Custody or Memory, and the Art of Elocution or Tradition under which style
and delivery are unified.[35]

Viewing invention from a Ciceronian perspective, Bacon argues that only
what is already known can be discovered through the first canon of rhetoric. In
turn, he conceptually separates logic from rhetorical invention and assigns to
logic the process by which new knowledge is discovered. Logic, in Bacon's
view, involves "subjecting physical and human facts to observation and experiment, and of accepting as new truth only what could be shown to conform to.
the realities behind it."[36] Whereas Ramus divides rhetoric and logic based on
subject matter, Bacon relegates logic and rhetoric to two different spheres of
communication, the former operating in the world of learning and the other in
the world of practical affairs.[37] Bacon's treatment of rhetorical invention allows
the speaker to assimilate existing knowledge about the subject. But, as he suggests, the classical construction of invention cannot provide new facts about the
subject. New facts evolve from the logical scrutiny of the subject. This perspective concerning rhetoric and logic was another step toward their separation.

Descartes and the Port Royalist: A New Epoch

Rene Descartes's *Discours de la Methode* first appeared in France in 1637
and, by the late 1600s, had become a popular English textbook, commonly

referred to as a Discourse on Method. *Discours* called for a logic that would (1) accept experiment rather than disputation as the method for the quest for truth, (2) function as theory of inquiry rather than theory of communication, and (3) be practical rather than speculative.[38] This work became influential in England at about the same time as another book, also of Continental origin, entitled *La Logique, ou L'Art de Penser*, began to gain popularity.

The *La Logique, ou L'Art de Penser* was published anonymously in Paris in 1662 and enjoyed great success in France and on the Continent into the late 1870s. Before being translated into English in 1685, the work appeared in England in three separate Latin editions. In England the work was commonly referred to as *The Port Royal Logic*, and its adherents were referred to as Port Royalists. Considering some of the reforms proposed by Bacon and Descartes concerning the function of logic, apart from traditional rhetoric, the Port Royalists, according to Howell, developed a "system of communication suited to the transfer of information from one scientist to another, and from scientist to public," which resulted in a significant "step toward the creation of a new rhetoric."[39]

EIGHTEENTH-CENTURY BRITISH LOGIC AND RHETORIC

Howell's *Eighteenth-Century British Logic and Rhetoric* is the last of his trilogy that outlines the changes that took place in English logic and rhetoric, *The Rhetoric of Alcuin and Charlemagne* being the first in the trilogy and *Logic and Rhetoric in England: 1500–1700*, the second. *Eighteenth-Century British Logic and Rhetoric* is presented in a chronological pattern so that the reader, according to Howell, may view the trends in logic and rhetoric "in relation to their antecedents in the seventeenth and their consequences in the nineteenth centuries."[40]

For Howell, the eighteenth century is the point in history at which the split between rhetoric and logic, encouraged, in part, by Ramus, and forecast, in part, by Bacon and Descartes, becomes permanent and irreversible largely due to the influence of John Locke. During this century, as England responded intellectually and practically "to the new science," logic "dissolved its alliance with the communication arts and aligned itself instead with the theory of scientific investigation."[41]

Although scholastic logic had been under scrutiny during the sixteenth and seventeenth centuries, scholasticism persisted well into the eighteenth century. The scholastic method of inquiry, which consisted of "subjecting traditional truths to syllogistic examination, and of accepting as new truth only what could be proven to be consistent with the old," dating back to Aristotle and Cicero.[42] Moreover, scholastic logic continued to be viewed as a theory of communication the world of learning.[43]

Onto the eighteenth-century scene, however, arrived John Locke, who, according to Howell, changed the intellectual and practical course of both traditional logic and traditional rhetoric. Inspired by the writings of Bacon and Descartes, and from his association with the Royal Society of London, Locke produced, in the 1690s two remarkable treatises, the *Essay Concerning Human Understanding*, published in 1690, and an intended supplement to it entitled *Of the Conduct of the Understanding*, published in 1706. Together these works caused a great stir in Europe and exerted a powerful influence upon the intellectual life of the eighteenth century. So far as its dominant thrust may be said to be embodied in the works of one man, the movement . . . is hardly anything more than the expression of Locke's influence.[44]

Through the influence of Locke, logic became separate from learned communication and became solely a method of inquiry.

The Old and New Logic

The differences between Locke's conception of the "new" logic as contrasted with the principles of "old" logic are summarized by Howell as follows:

1. Method of communication versus method of inquiry. The old logic was conceptualized in such a manner as to operate both as a method of inquiry and as a model of presentation. The new logic was only a method of scientific inquiry.
2. The syllogism versus example. The old logic regarded the syllogism as the preeminent instrument of inquiry and proof. The instrument of inquiry for the new logic was empiricism.
3. Deduction versus induction. The method of investigation for the old logic was that of subjecting axioms and verbal propositions to deductive analysis, whereas, the new logic relied on the inductive method.
4. Disputation versus experimentation. The old logic believed that disputation was the means of philosophical inquiry. The new logic viewed controlled experimentation and observation in relationship to physical data as the main method of philosophical inquiry.
5. *Topoi* versus invention. The old logic utilized the topics of invention as the machinery for subjecting questions to systematic investigation. The new logic emphasized a factual approach that was tied to a particular situation as a means of investigation.
6. Consistency versus observation. The old logic conceived of truth in terms of consistency in relationship to self-evident truths. The new logic considered a statement as true only when it conformed with the facts under observation.[45]

The Old and New Rhetoric

As logic moved from being a method of scholastic inquiry toward a method of scientific inquiry, it also became disassociated from operating as a theory of learned communication. As a result, rhetoric tried to fill the vacuum created by logic's abandonment of communication. Rhetoric came to be viewed as an art that governed "all forms of verbal expression, whether popular or learned, persuasive or dialectic, utilitarian or aesthetic" and no longer functioned as a method of inquiry—scholastic or otherwise.[46] "Its special purpose begins to communicate truths through a process that, on the one hand, blended scientific conclusions with popular opinions and manners, and, on the other hand, transmitted that blend to the general population."[47] Howell identifies six issues differentiating the "old" rhetoric from the "new" rhetoric.

1. Popular oral discourse versus all types of exposition. The old rhetoric limited itself to popular oral discourse, whereas the new rhetoric, as logic became less and less associated with learned exposition and debate, began to encompass all types of exposition, both oral and written.

2. Artistic proof versus inartistic proof. The old rhetoric carried on the tradition of viewing the artistic proofs—*logos, pathos*, and *ethos*—as the means of persuasion. The new rhetoric considered both artistic and inartistic proof as means of persuasion and equated inartistic proof with the empirical method.

3. Deductive versus inductive method. The old rhetoric viewed the deductive method, via the enthymeme, as the basis of rhetorical argument. The new rhetoric was concerned with creating argument inductively through the examination of the facts surrounding or emerging out of a case.

4. General versus situational probability. The old rhetoric believed in arguing from probable premises to a probable conclusion. The new rhetoric viewed truth in relationship to a specific situation and rhetorical argument as emerging from the specifics of the situation.

5. Complex structure versus simple structure. The old rhetoric generally followed the six-part Ciceronian structure in structuring or ordering the message. The new rhetoric advocated a simple and natural structure, in part, dictated by the situation.

6. Ornate style versus simple style. The old rhetoric considered effective style to be ornate and intricate and was heavily committed to the use of figures and tropes. The new rhetoric, on the other hand, relied on the use of the plain style.[48]

The Elocutionary Movement

So powerful was the influence of Locke, argues Howell, that by the end of the eighteenth century the new logic and the new rhetoric stood side by side with their traditional counterparts, including an offshoot that emphasized delivery and was known as the elocutionary movement.[49] Why the focus on delivery became important to eighteenth-century England is attributed to several factors. (1) Delivery was the only canon of Ciceronian rhetoric that had not been under attack or revised during the seventeenth century. Thus, delivery, as the least controversial of the five canons, could easily be the focus of those who wanted to keep classical rhetoric or some aspect thereof alive. (2) Due to the emphasis on the readings from the *Book of Common Prayer* by the Church of England, delivery seemed especially pertinent to the early training of English pulpit orators. (3) There was an awareness on the part of British educators and politicians by this time that the numerous English dialects spoken throughout the empire were becoming a hindrance to its cultural, political, and economic welfare.[50]

The theory of elocution as the movement emerged in eighteenth-century England had two theoretical extremes—one being the mechanical school and the other the natural school—and, in practice, many variations in between.[51] (1) The mechanical school assumed that individuals, in general, share universal passions. These passions could, in turn, be aroused through prescriptive and universal rules derived from the study of the universality of passions. As a result, rules, models, and script notations were viewed by the adherents of the mechanical school to be the best way in which to learn delivery techniques.[52] (2) The natural school theorized that people vary as to how and under what circumstances passions are elicited. As a result of this perspective, they argued that prescriptive and universal rules were not fruitful to the reader. What the reader should do, according to the proponents of the natural approach, is use intuition and insight in adapting the text to the audience. They believed that script notation and prescriptive models hinder the creative process.[53]

In actual practice, however, the extremes expressed by the natural and mechanical schools were frequently blurred. Both schools agreed that elocution embodied the use of both voice and body, strongly recommended that the reader understand the literature or discourse he is presenting, and believed that the ultimate goal of the reader is to achieve a natural manner in delivery.[54]

POETICS, LOGIC, AND RHETORIC IN A MODERN-DAY WORLD

In 1975, four years after the publication of *Eighteenth-Century British Logic and Rhetoric*, Cornell University Press published Howell's *Poetics, Rhetoric, and Logic: Studies of the Basic Disciplines of Criticism*. Dedicated to "The Cornell School of Rhetoric," the eight essays making up the book chapters were first written by Howell as self-contained articles that had appeared elsewhere in publication or had been presented at scholarly conventions.[55]

Up to this point, nothing has been said of Howell's view of the poetic in relationship to its sister arts of logic and rhetoric. This is not to imply that Howell has neglected to mention the art of poetry within the works that constitute his "trilogy."[56] But when he does, it is either by way of explaining that poetics does not have the same connection as rhetoric and logic to the ancient world or in passing while discussing where he believes poetic is erroneously treated as rhetoric or rhetoric mistakenly considered as poetic.[57]

The "Proper" Relationship among Poetic, Rhetoric, and Logic

Poetics, Rhetoric, and Logic: Studies of the Basic Disciplines of Criticism, in fact, directly addresses the "proper" treatment of rhetoric and logic in relationship to poetry. The book is designed to combat two trends in current poetic theory: (1) "the exclusion of rhetoric and logic from literary theory" and (2) "the practice of allowing rhetorical and logical writings to have a place of honor in the firmament of genuine literature only if they can be shown to differ from their fellows by possessing a quality quite beyond anything to be expected of them as true representatives of their genres. They must in other words have an element of magic in them, and it must be understood that the magical element is not rhetorical or dialectical in its genesis."[58]

Literary theory, for Howell, should be construed as broad enough to include nonfiction and, as such, to include rhetoric and logic under appropriate conditions. The conditions of appropriateness are found in Howell's distinction between rhetorical and poetical functions: literature that is poetic accomplishes its purpose through poetic mimesis or fiction; whereas rhetoric relies on statement and proof for its effectiveness.[59]

Howell acknowledges two exceptions under which poetic can operate within the framework of rhetoric and rhetoric within the parameters of poetry. The first occurs when a mimetic discourse, such as a fable, is used within the context of a rhetorical or nonmimetic presentation.[60] The second happens when a speech is used within the context of literary mimesis, such as occurs in a drama or poem as a speaker addresses an audience within its context.[61] Howell argues that this distinction between rhetoric and poetry has been misinterpreted by the Chicago school of literature, as well as by some well-known literary critics. As a result, a rhetorical, rather than a literary, theory of poetry has evolved.[62]

This perspective, Howell claims, has led twentieth-century scholarship to conclude that either Renaissance poetics is essentially rhetorical, or Renaissance rhetoric is essentially stylistic, or Renaissance logic has no importance to the literary theory of the period.[63] "Their thesis has been that rhetoric assumed control over poetics . . . , and their argument in support of this thesis ha[s] made it apparent that poetics becomes rhetoric whenever it asserts its capacity for didacticism or persuasiveness, or whenever it shows concern for its audience, or whenever it makes open use of the teachings of rhetoric in regard to the thought content or the style of poetry."[64] These characteristics, as Howell argues, may be common to both rhetoric and poetic depending on their respective functions, and "if rhetoric," he maintains, "is to regain its true place in Renaissance criticism, it must be recognized, not only in its stylistic aspects, but in its full range."[65]

Modern Rhetoric

Although acknowledging that rhetoric, as a theory of communication between people, has to be modified in response to cultural and social changes, the transformation of rhetoric that has taken place since its disassociation from logic has not, for Howell, resulted in anything of positive consequence. In *Logic and Rhetoric in England, 1500–1700*, he observes, for example, that "rhetoric, popularly taken today, [is] a term for the sort of style you happen personally to dislike."[66] In his June 1963 lecture at the Henry Huntington Library, Howell notes that "modern man, in his tendency to divide learning into mutually exclusive academic departments and to prevent trespassing from one department to another, has forgotten the creative relationship once recognized between rhetoric and logic. He has tended to construct an image of logic as the antithesis of rhetoric and of rhetoric as the repository of sophisms, irrational appeals, outmoded pompostities of style, and empty, insincere declamations."[67]

Like a parent reacting to a rift between two loved family members, Howell always holds out hope for a reconciliation between logic and rhetoric. One of his reasons for writing *Eighteenth-Century British Logic and Rhetoric* is that "explaining the changes that occurred in logic and rhetoric . . . will give these two disciplines an important new set of relations in modern scholarship and criticism."[68]

CONTRIBUTIONS AND RESPONSES

The most important contribution made by Howell to twentieth-century rhetorical studies is the development of a critical model of how and why rhetoric, with respect to logic, was comprehended and transformed in England. Beginning with Alcuin, "the first" Englishman to write a rhetoric and a logic, then tracking the patterns of change in England between 1500 and 1700, and, finally, concluding with the eighteenth century, he traces how rhetoric and logic became philosophically and practically separated largely due, as he believes, to the rise of science.

By identifying and tracing these patterns, however, Howell opens himself up to the criticism to which many historians are subjected. Historical patterns are limiting, for they include some things and exclude others, and they are based on presumptions about the status quo, causal relationships, and change. The actual impact that Alcuin had on English rhetorical theory, for example, is called into question by both James J. Murphy and Charles Sears Baldwin. Acknowledging that, although Alcuin may have been the first Englishman to author a rhetoric and logic, his work was written on another continent "for a Frankish King and for students," Murphy observes, "that were Continental Europeans. . . . In terms of the later history of the arts of discourse . . . Alcuin's is still-born."[69] Baldwin notes that just because Alcuin adapted Cicero's *De Inventione* into his text does not prove the "use of the whole ancient program."[70] In addition, Howell's perspective ignores the Southern European rhetorical tradition by concentrating on Ramus and Bacon and ignoring theorists such as Giambattista Vico and Juan Vives.

As he traces how logic and rhetoric change during the seventeenth and eighteenth centuries, Howell assumes that the only philosophical and practical tie between rhetoric and logic was scholastic logic. This limited perspective, as Vincent Bevilacqua points out, does not take into consideration how the application of science to the "study of man re-oriented mid-eighteenth century rhetorical theory in terms of human nature, thereby connecting rhetoric to such related studies as ethics, aesthetics, and criticism."[71]

Howell's view of rhetoric in relationship to poetry is also criticized as being too limited. Kenneth Burke argues that modern electronic media allow the imprinting of news and other events that, when shown, symbolically appeal, at the same time, to both the imagination and the real. Under Howell's own definitions of rhetoric and poetry, then, these symbols may operate simultaneously within the realm of both.[72] They are not mutually exclusive, as Howell seems to imply. Howell himself acknowledges the limit of his perspective in a modern, technologically oriented world when he notes:

Other changes have taken place in the theory of rhetoric during the past four centuries. Some of them have come with the development of mass media of communication, some with the application of the concept of propaganda to the fields of commerce, public relations, and statecraft. Some have come as rhetoric has stated its problems in terms of the principles of modern psychology, some as means have been developed to explore the state of public opinion and to measure the effect of communications upon the audience. These changes are of course vitally important in the growth of modern rhetoric. I have not treated them here because the impulses which produced them have originated within the past half-century and thus cannot be said to have deep roots in the ancient world as well as our own.[73]

Although modern rhetoric does suffer from many "discordant and limited interpretations," to suggest, as Howell does, that the reexamination of rhetoric's past connection with logic will somehow provide a perspective about what rhetoric "needs to acquire if it is to gain a central place in the learning of our time" is not a workable assumption.[74] The fallacy in this line of argument is that somehow rhetoric and logic should operate in a time vacuum, apart from modern-day forms of communication. If rhetoric is tied to cultural and historical parameters, as Howell constantly reminds us in the approaches to his works, then to reestablish a traditional rhetorical theory would mean that the clock would have to be turned back some 300 or 400 years.[75] Rhetoric and logic, apart from other advances in the modern world, cannot stand alone as Howell may wish.

Beyond providing patterns for understanding the development of rhetorical theory as it emerged between Alcuin and the eighteenth century, Howell also reminds us time and time again that rhetoric goes beyond technique and has an intellectual and substantive heritage. (Ironically, perhaps, is the folk tradition at Princeton University that reminds us that many of Howell's undergraduate students sought careers in the largest and most powerful advertising agencies in New York City.) Howell's lifetime association with rhetoric embodies technique, theory, and intellect: "Rhetoric has been my chief scholarly interest since my undergraduate days at Cornell. Why? Because of its central importance. In its full sense, rhetoric is the study and the use of the persuasive factors inhering in the subject matter, the organization, the style, and the oral or written presentation of nonfictional verbal discourse."[76]

NOTES

1. *Who's Who in America*, 46th ed. (Chicago: Marquis, 1990).

2. Wilbur Samuel Howell, *Poetics, Rhetoric, and Logic: Studies in the Basic Disciplines of Criticism* (Ithaca: Cornell University Press, 1975). Hereafter refered to as *Poetics, Rhetoric, and Logic*.

3. Giles Wilkeson Gray, "Some Teachers and the Transition to Twentieth-Century Speech Education," *A History of Speech Education in America*, ed. Karl R. Wallace (New York: Appleton-Century-Crofts, 1954).

4. Donald K. Smith, "Origin and Development of Departments of Speech," *Speech Education in America*, 450.

5. Ibid.

6. Ibid., 467.

7. Wilbur Samuel Howell, *Logic and Rhetoric in England, 1500–1700* (Princeton, NJ: Princeton University Press, 1956), 33. Hereafter refered to as *Logic and Rhetoric*. The assertion of Bede's *liber de schematibus et Tropes* being "the earliest fragment of Ciceronian rhetoric" has been called into question. James J. Murphy, for example, argues that Bede's schemes and tropes come directly from Donatus, *Barbarismus*. See Murphy's *Rhetoric in the Middle Ages: A History of Rhetorical Theory from St. Augustine to the Renaissance* (Berkeley: University of California Press, 1974), 77.

8. Wilbur Samuel Howell, trans., *The Rhetoric of Alcuin and Charlemagne*, by "Albini Magistri," better known as Alcuin (Princeton, NJ: Princeton University Press, 1941), 3.

9. Howell, *Alcuin*, 34–61.

10. Ibid., 38.

11. Ibid., 24–33; also see Wilbur Samuel Howell's "English Background of Rhetoric," *Speech Education in America*, 7–8.

12. Howell, *Alcuin*, 62.

13. Howell, *Rhetoric and Logic*, 116–145.

14. Examples include Geoffrey of Vinsauf, *Poetica Nova* (1208–1213), *The Court of Sapience* (1481), and Stephen Hawes, *Pastime of Pleasure* (1506).

15. Howell, *Poetics, Rhetoric, and Logic*, 142. Also see Warren Guthrie, "Rhetorical Theory in Colonial America," *Speech Education*, 48–57. Guthrie discusses the influence of Ramus in colonial America and the forms through which classical rhetoric persisted.

16. Howell, *Logic and Rhetoric*, 4. Vincent Bevilacqua notes that Howell "wrongly" presumes that "in the eighteenth century as in the seventeenth century the most important philosophical connection of rhetoric was that of logic." New Books in Review, *Quarterly Journal of Speech* 58 (1962), 346.

17. Howell, *Logic and Rhetoric*, 10–11.

18. Howell says, for example, "At the middle of the sixteenth century, Ciceronian rhetoric . . . received a full-length treatment in that medium by Thomas Wilson, shortly after he wrote the first English version of scholastic logic. Thus, Wilson, like Alcuin . . . play[s] a dual role." Ibid., 7.

19. Howell argues that Wilson's *Rule of Reason* "is not a translation of Aristotle's

Organon" but "an attempt to render into English the main concepts and terms of the *Organon*, as those concepts and terms had come to be understood in the Renaissance." 13.

20. Ibid., 6. Also see James J. Murphy's discussion of how rhetoric was primarily limited to style during the period under discussion: *Rhetoric in the Middle Ages: A History of Rhetorical Theory form St. Augustine to the Renaissance* (Berkeley: University of California Press, 1974), 135.

21. Howell, *Logic and Rhetoric*, 3.

22. Ibid., 4.

23. Ibid., 6.

24. See Howell's discussion of the evolution of these traditional patterns of rhetoric in ibid., 64–144. Also see Wilbur Samuel Howell, "English Background of Rhetoric," 5–28.

25. Examples of the Ciceronian school provided by Howell include Geoffrey of Vinsauf, *Poetica Nova* (1208–1213), Stephen Hawes, *Pastime of Pleasure* (1509), Lorenzo Traversagni, *Nova Rhetoric* (1479, first work on rhetoric published in England); *Court of Sapience* (1481), Leonard Cox, *The Arte of Crafte of Rhetoryke* (1529), Thomas Vicars, *Guide to the Art of Rhetoric* (1621), Thomas Farnaby, *Index Rhetorica* (1625), and William Pemble, *Oratorical Manual* (1633).

26. Examples of the stylistic school include John of Salisbury, *Metalogicon* (twelfth century), *Poetica Nova*; John of Garland, *Exampla Honestae Vita* (thirteenth century), *Court of Sapience*; Richard Sherry, *Treatment of Schemes and Tropes* (1550); Henry Peacham, *The Garden of Eloquence* (1577); John Hoskins, *Directions for Speech and Style* (1599).

27. Examples of the formulary school include Thomas Wilson, *Rhetorique* (1553), Richard Rainolde, *Foundacion of Rhetorike* (1563); Angle Day, *The English Secretorie* (1586); and Anthony Munday, *The Defence of Contraries* (1539).

28. Howell, *Logic and Rhetoric*, 7.

29. Two earlier works on logic by Ramus, *Dialecticae Institutiones* and *Aristotelicae Animadversiones*, according to Audomarus Talaeus, had already laid out his plan for reforming the arts.

30. Howell, *Logic and Rhetoric*, 282.

31. Ibid., 247.

32. Talaeus' first work on rhetoric, *Institutiones Oratoriae*, was published in Paris in 1544.

33. *Logic and Rhetoric*, 343. Examples of the systematic school in England are Thomas Granger, *Syntagma Logicum* (1620), Thomas Spencer, *Art of Logick* (1622), and Thomas Blundeville, *Art of Logike* (1599–1619).

34. The "chief English rhetoricians of the Neo-Ciceronain school," according to Howell, are Thomas Vicars, *A Manuduction to Theologie* (1620, trans. of earlier Keckermann work), *Manuduction to the Rhetorical Art* (1628); Thomas Farnaby, *Index Rhetoricus* (1625), William Pemble, *Enchiridion Oartorium* (1633); Obadiah Walker, *Some Instructions Concerning the Art of Oratory* (1659), 325.

35. See Howell, *Logic and Rhetoric*, 366–374, and "English Backgrounds," 33–39.

36. Howell, *18th Century British Logic and Rhetoric* (Princeton, NJ: Princeton University Press, 1971).

37. Howell, "English Backgrounds," 38.

38. Howell, *Logic and Rhetoric*, 349.

39. Ibid. 9.

40. Howell, *18th Century British Logic and Rhetoric,* 5.

41. Ibid.

42. Ibid.

43. Ibid.

44. Ibid., 7. Also see Wilbur Samuel Howell, "The Declaration of Independence and Eighteenth-Century Logic," *William and Mary Quarterly* 18 (October 1961): 463–484. Howell argues that Thomas Jefferson was greatly influenced by John Locke in constructing the arguments contained in the Declaration.

45. Howell, *18th Century British Logic and Rhetoric,* 259–260. Some examples of the "old" logic included Henry Aldrich, *Artis Logicae Compendium* (1691): John Wallis, *Institutio Logicae* (1687); Bishop Sanderson, *Logicae Artis Compendium* (1615); Richard Cranathorp, *Logicae Libri Quinque* (1622); John Sergeant, *Method to Science* (1696); examples of the "new" logic following Locke are Thomas Reid, *An Inquiry into the Human Mind* (1764); Lord Kames, *Elements of Criticism* (1762); George Campbell, *The Philosophy of Rhetoric* (1776); Dugard Steward, *Outlines of Moral Philosophy* (1793); and *Elements of the Philosophy of the Human Mind* (1792); examples mixing the old with the new include Jean Le Clerc, *Logica* (1692); John Henley, *A New Treatise of the Art of Thinking,* trans. of Jean-Pierre de Crousaz (1724); Issac Watts, *Logick* (1725); William Duncan, *The Elements of Logick* (1728); Christian Wolff *Philosophia Rationalis* (1728).

46. Howell, *18th Century British Logic and Rhetoric,* 6.

47. Ibid.

48. Ibid., 441–447. Some examples of the "old" rhetoric include Thomas Wilson, *Arte of Rhetorique* (1551); Thomas Farnaby, *Index Rhetoricus* (1625); Thomas Vicars, *Manuductio and Artem Rhetorican* (1621); Obadiah Walker, *Some Instructions Concerning the Art of Rhetoric* (1659); John Ward, *A System of Oratory;* examples of the "new" rhetoric are Adam Smith, *Lectures on Rhetoric and Belles and Lettres* (1785); George Campbell, *The Philosophy of Rhetoric* (1750); those embodying both the new and old include David Hume, "Of Eloquence" (1742); John Larson, *Lectures Concerning Oratory* (1753); Joseph Priestley, *A Course of Lectures on Oratory and Criticism* (1777).

49. Howell, *18th Century British Logic and Rhetoric,* 152.

50. Ibid., 152–156.

51. For example, see Eugene and Margaret Bahn, *A History of Oral Interpretation* (Minneapolis: Burgess, 1970), 113–135; Alethea S. Mattingly, *The Mechanical School of Oral Reading in England, 1761–1821* (Ph.D. diss., Northwestern University, 1954); Daniel Vandraegen, *The Natural School of Oral Reading in England, 1748–1828* (Ph.D. diss., Northwestern University, 1949).

52. Some examples that are typically classified under the "mechanical" school include James Burgh, *The Art of Speaking* (1714); William Enfield, *The Speaker* (1745); Joshua Steele, *Prosodia Rationalis* (1775); John Walker, *Elements of Elocution* (1781), *Exercises for Improvement in Elocution* (1777); Gilbert Austin, *Chironomia* (1806).

53. Some examples that are typically classified under the "natural" school include John Mason, *An Essay on Elocution, or, Pronunciation* (1748); John Rice, *An Introduction to the Art of Reading* (1755); Thomas Sheridan, *A Course of Lectures on Elocution* (1762); *Lectures on the Art of Reading* (1775); William Cockin, *The Art of Delivering Written Language* (1775).

54. Howell, *18th Century British Logic and Rhetoric* 182–256; Bahn, *A History,* 121.

55. Each self-contained article is listed in the bibliography under the citation for *Poetics, Rhetoric, and Logic: Studies in the Basic Disciplines of Criticism*.

56. For example, Howell discusses George Puttenham's *The Arte of English Poesie* (1589) in *Logic and Rhetoric in England, 1500–1700* because "it handles the doctrine of style as a work on rhetoric would," 327.

57. See, for example, Wilbur Samuel Howell, "Oratory and Poetry in Fenelon's Literary Theory," *Quarterly Journal of Speech* 37 (1951), 1–10.

58. Howell, *Poetic, Rhetoric, and Logic*, 18–19.

59. Ibid., 31–32, 56–59.

60. Ibid., 60–61.

61. Ibid., 61–62.

62. He specifically singles out the Chicago school of Aristotelians such as Bernard Weinberg (*A History of Literary Criticism in the Italian Renaissance*, 1961), Ronald S. Crane, Richard P. McKeon, and Elder Olson. In addition, he also identifies Brian Vickers, *Classical Rhetoric in English Poetry* (1970), and Kenneth Burke as blurring the distinction between rhetoric and poetic.

63. Howell, *Poetics, Rhetoric, and Logic*, 23.

64. Ibid., 105.

65. Ibid., 121.

66. Howell, *Logic and Rhetoric*, 3.

67. Wilbur Samuel Howell, "The Plough and the Flail: The Ordeal of Eighteenth-Century Logic," *Huntington Library Quarterly* (November 1964), 63.

68. Howell, *18th Century British Logic and Rhetoric*, 9.

69. James J. Murphy, *Rhetoric in the Middle Ages: A History of Rhetorical Theory from St. Augustine to the Renaissance* (Berkeley: University of California Press, 1974), 81.

70. Charles Sears Baldwin, *Medieval Rhetoric and Poetic: to 1400* (Gloucester, MA: Peter Smith, 1959), 142.

71. Vincent M. Bevilacqua, "New Books in Review," *Quarterly Journal of Speech* 58 (1962), 346. Bevilacqua makes his case that "taking human nature as their starting point, mid-eighteenth century rhetoricians reinterpreted traditional theory in light of the developing 'philosophy of the mind' or 'pneumatics' as psychology was then termed," in "Philosophical Influences in the Development of English Rhetorical Theory: 1748 to 1783," *Proceedings of the Leeds Philosophical and Literary Society* 12 (1968), 203.

72. Kenneth Burke, "The Party Line," *Quarterly Journal of Speech* 62 (1976), 62. The argument advanced by Burke is necessary to his symbolic interaction theory, 64.

73. Howell, *Poetics, Rhetoric, and Logic*, 161.

74. Howell, *18th Century British Logic and Rhetoric*, 9.

75. Walter Ong's theory of orality and communication, for example, is not constrained by a particular historical period.

76. *Who's Who in America*.

SELECT BIBLIOGRAPHY

Howell, Wilbur Samuel. "Aristotle and Horace on Rhetoric and Poetics." *Quarterly Journal of Speech*, 54 (1968), 325–339.

———. "The Arts of Literary Criticism in Renaissance Britain: A Comprehensive View."

Based on a lecture, "Poetics, Rhetoric, and Logic in Renaissance Criticism," written for the Classical Influences on European Culture, A.D. 1500–1700 conference, Cambridge University, April 1974.

———. "The Declaration of Independence and Eighteenth-Century Logic." *William and Mary Quarterly*, 18 (October 1961), 463–484.

———. "De Quincey on Science, Rhetoric, and Poetry." *Speech Monographs* 8 (1946), 1–13.

———. *Eighteenth-Century British Logic and Rhetoric*. Princeton, NJ: Princeton University Press, 1971.

———. "English Background of Rhetoric." *History of Speech Education in America*, ed. Karl R. Wallace. New York: Appleton-Crofts, 1954.

———. "Kenneth Burke's 'Lexicon Rhetoricae': A Critical Examination." First appeared as "Rhetoric and Poetics: A Plea for the Recognition of the Two Literatures." *The Classical Tradition*, ed. Luitpold Wallach. Ithaca, NY: Cornell University Press, 1966.

———. "Literature as an Enterprise in Communication." *Quarterly Journal of Speech* 13 (1947), 417–426.

———. *Logic and Rhetoric in England, 1500–1700*. Princeton, NJ: Princeton University Press, 1956.

———. *Poetics, Rhetoric, and Logic: Studies in the Basic Disciplines of Criticism*. Ithaca, NY: Cornell University Press, 1975. This work is a compilation of articles and lectures by Howell and includes the following as ordered in the book.

———. "Ramus and English Rhetoric: 1574–1681." *Quarterly Journal of Speech* 37 (1951): 299–310.

———. "Renaissance Rhetoric and Modern Rhetoric: A Study in Change." *The Rhetorical Idiom*, ed. Donald C. Bryant. Ithaca, NY: Cornell University Press, 1958.

Howell, Wilbur Samuel, ed. *Jefferson's Parliamentary Writings: "Parliamentary Pocket-Book" and A Manual of Parliamentary Practice*. Princeton, NJ: Princeton University Press, 1988.

Howell, Wilbur Samuel, trans. *The Rhetoric of Alcuin and Charlemagne*. Princeton, NJ: Princeton University Press, 1941.

5

Marie Hochmuth Nichols: Voice of Rationality in the Humane Tradition of Rhetoric and Criticism

JOHN H. PATTON

> So far as speech communication shares in that endeavor of improvement [of humanity], it works through man's language habits and uses—language habits and uses which seem to have at least four dimensions, namely, logical, ethical, aesthetic, and rhetorical. Is excellence in our understanding and use of these dimensions the Ithaka which we seek? Are our eyes constantly on this destination, or are we all too ready to listen to Calypso urging us to forget Ithaka?[1]

There are peak experiences that make significant, even transforming differences in our lives. Knowing Marie Nichols as colleague, friend, mentor, and more during the last four years of her life was such an experience for me. I, along with several others, was near the beginning of my academic career at the University of Illinois at Champaign-Urbana, where Marie Hochmuth Nichols had been a Distinguished Professor of Rhetoric for nearly forty years.[2] Marie embraced and challenged us both intellectually and personally, leveling the playing field for us all. Hence, I make no pretense of writing about her in a detached way. What follows is an attempt to provide a comprehensive view of her remarkable career and work from as honest a perspective as I can give. The real difficulty in her case is not knowing what to write about but knowing what must be omitted, because there is so much. There is surely not enough space in a single chapter to say all that could or should be said about her scholarship, teaching, and leadership. I acknowledge any shortcomings in what I write but hope that this serves as a useful beginning.

Marie Hochmuth Nichols stands as a preeminent voice in the history of rhe-

Marie Hochmuth Nichols. Photo courtesy of John H. Patton. Used with permission.

torical theory and criticism. This chapter focuses on her distinctive role as an advocate of rationality in rhetorical thought and action. Nichols emphasized the permanent and enduring qualities of rhetoric, qualities that she consistently expressed in her role as a teacher, in her scholarship, public essays, and speeches, and in her academic leadership of the speech communication profession. She worried greatly about the fragmentation and apparent disintegration of the rhetorical tradition from its roots in classics and history. Simultaneously, her intellectual scope and expertise were among the broadest and deepest in the field, or any field, for that matter. She consistently encouraged fresh, innovative insights from diverse theoretical and critical perspectives. Within that diversity she clearly located a central core that unified the study and practice of rhetorical thought and action. One can almost hear her say, "I am interested in facts, from whatever source and by whatever method they may be obtained." More than any other teacher and scholar whom I have encountered in person or through published scholarship, Nichols took Kenneth Burke's recommendation fully to heart that in the theory and criticism of rhetoric one should always "use all that there is to use."[3] Her dedication to this principle included teaching and research reflecting a broad and deep range of rhetoric. At one point it featured neoclassical models of *ethos*, *logos*, and *pathos* in the study of public address, while at another it illuminated the core concepts of Kenneth Burke's rhetoric and grammar of motives. Imagine what scholarship in our field would be like without Nichols' meticulous introduction and development of Burke's five key terms of dramatism, "Act, Scene, Agent, Agency and Purpose."[4] This brought to the field a precise idea of Burke's "[g]rammatical resources as principles, and of the various philosophies as casuistries which apply these principles to temporal situations."[5] For example, by bringing Burke to the forefront, Nichols opened the possibility for nuances and levels of symbolic action that supplemented, without contradicting, the older, classical concepts of rhetoric. Burke's instance of the Road to Victory photographic murals at the Museum of Modern Art is instructive: "There was an aerial photograph of two launches, proceeding side by side on a tranquil sea. Their wakes crossed and recrossed each other in almost an infinity of lines. Yet despite the intricateness of this tracery, the picture gave an impression of great simplicity, because one could quickly perceive the generating principle of its design. Such, ideally, is the case with our pentad of terms, used as generating principle. It should provide us with a kind of simplicity that can be developed into considerable complexity, and yet can be discovered beneath its elaborations"[6] Simplicity within complexity is an apt description of the many layers of rhetorical knowledge examined and exposed in Nichols' long career.

From this starting point I provide an overview of Nichols's education and career accomplishments, many of which were landmark events, especially for a female scholar and teacher in the 1940s and 1950s. Then I turn to a discussion of her role as a teacher, including the typical courses and course preparations that reflected her standards of excellence; next I examine her role as theorist-critic and disciplinary leader in the humane tradition. In doing so I explore several key essays and public addresses that Nichols delivered, some unpublished, that illuminate her fundamental and enduring contributions to the understanding and practice of rhetoric.

EDUCATIONAL BACKGROUND AND CAREER ACCOMPLISHMENTS

Marie Kathryn Hochmuth was born July 13, 1908, in Dunbar, Pennsylvania, to Alexander and Mary Flydell Hochmuth. She attended Catholic school in her early and secondary years. She enrolled in the University of Pittsburgh and received both financial aid and a scholarship, while also working for her room and board in the home of Kenneth Gould, a scholastic magazine editor. The tradition of independence and hard work came early to her. While at the University of Pittsburgh she was a member of the debating team coached by Theresa K. Murphy, wife of Richard Murphy, who served as Nichols' colleague for many years at the University of Illinois.[7]

She received her B.A. degree in English and history in 1931 and her M.A. in English in 1936, both from the University of Pittsburgh. She completed her Ph.D. in rhetoric at the University of Wisconsin in 1945, writing her dissertation on "William Ellery Channing, D.D.: A Study in Public Address" under the direction of Professor Wayland M. Parrish. Although the dissertation as a whole has never been published, one of her earliest scholarly essays was drawn from it, "William Ellery Channing: New England Conversationalist,"[8] in the *Quarterly Journal of Speech*. Interestingly, at the time of her hospitalization and death in 1978, she was rereading and revising the dissertation with a view to an extended analysis based on a return to that work. Her death occurred at age seventy on Saturday, October 7, 1978, in Champaign-Urbana, Illinois, after an illness of approximately four weeks. Her husband, Professor Alan G. Nichols, had previously died in 1973. At the time of her death she was professor of Speech Communication emerita at the University of Illinois-Urbana, where she had taught for thirty-seven years.

Nichols' career pioneered landmark developments in many areas. She began her teaching responsibilities by returning briefly to the University of Pittsburgh. Then she accepted a full-time position at Mount Mercy College, Pennsylvania, from 1935 to 1939, as an instructor in the English Department. From there she joined the faculty of the University of Illinois-Urbana as an instructor in Speech in 1939. She was tenured in 1952 and held the rank of full professor for the last seventeen years of her career there. Over that time she served as distinguished visiting lecturer at several institutions, including San Fernando Valley State College in 1961 and Herbert Lehman College in 1973 and as the Green Honors Lecturer at Texas Christian University in 1975, the University of Southern California, where she met her husband, Alan and she gave the Distinguished Lectures in Speech at Louisiana State University, which were subsequently published in book form as *Rhetoric and Criticism* in 1963. One of her most insightful and comprehensive addresses, in many respects a capstone of her thinking over the years, was delivered as the commencement address at Drury College, Saint Louis, in 1977, which also awarded her an honorary doctorate on that occasion. This unpublished address deserves special comment, along with other key public discourses that she made during her leadership of the Speech Communication Association of America (now the National Communication Association).

I recall her laboring daily and on weekends in her office on the first floor of Lincoln Hall and at one of her favorite reading places, the stately Lincoln Dining Room in the center of Lincoln Square mall in Urbana. There one might easily find Nichols sipping coffee and reading the *New York Times*, an absolute ritual, each Sunday. But in this last spring of her life Marie was earnestly wrestling with what to say to the graduating class at Drury College. Notes, papers, drafts of sections written in her distinctive handwriting, always in pencil, covered the table. She typically had coffee on one side; her cigarettes and lighter and ashtray, on the other. The cigarette always glowed relentlessly as she worked.

She found her commencement voice with words like these:

One does not learn to solve problems by repeatedly asking himself the question of the late 60's and early 70's: who am I? without attempting a serious answer. What am I might be a more productive question? (*sic*). What is my vision? Which the more vocal of those students [radical students in the 1960s] did not have. What can I do? Or learn to do well? And here is a ground for studying what men and women in all times have done, for what they have done gives us some understanding of what we might do? (*sic*). Other people and we are one. We understand them better through ourselves and understand ourselves better through them. This may give us some ground for recognizing "ethics" as a human specificity, too. What do we cringe at? What do we sanction? What are the consequences to ourselves and others?[9]

The posing of these questions was vintage Nichols. None of them were rhetorical questions for her. She honestly wanted students and scholars to take seriously the issues and value questions that underlie the stark inquiry about what we "cringe at" (one can almost hear the resonance and rising inflection of her voice) and what we "sanction." In that sense, like a Socratic sage she was relentless. That was the only way to bring the intellect and the heart to deal with the ultimate concern of rational judgment: consequences.

Later in the Drury address Nichols severely critiques the 1960s and 1970s by returning to a hallmark theme: relevance, which she had strongly attacked in an attempt to rebut what she regarded as irrational extremes in her famous Speech Association of America Presidential Address, "The Tyranny of Relevance." At Drury Nichols proclaimed, "We are now admitting that we were wrong in the 60's and 70's by seeming to sanction the cry for relevance to the point of neglecting language and mathematical study—that feeling was all and that discipline should not be allowed to stifle it; that science was making us unhumane."[10] Notice that she uses the inclusive "we" when referring to the wrongheadedness of the earlier decades, a significant indication that she never operated from an exclusive or dogmatic position. Indeed, one of the principal things that one sees in Nichols' work is the importance of making strong, defensible arguments, which themselves may be contested. She actually participated in the rational worldview that the best ideas and decisions emerge through the clash of evidence and reasoning, literally enabling the rational capacity of humans to carry out the essential function of making reflective, informed decisions. Interestingly, Nichols continued this line of argument by noting,

Science is a human activity. It would not be easy for me to believe that Jacob Bronowski [one of her favorite authors], or the bone hunter Loren Eisley, or Jonas Salk, or even B. F. Skinner were less humanistic than I, and that Easy Rider was a better role model. So far as maintaining a coherent culture is concerned, one of the most destructive cliches of the 60's was the clichi [sic] "Do your own thing" and don't pay too much attention to responsibility. What is one's own thing? Smashing windows on the campus? Destroying the card catalogue in the library? Drugs on the injunction of Timothy Leary? Growth of gangs? Growth of pornographic film-making, with children from 4 to 12, under the name of creativity or artistic freedom or the right to free expression?[11]

She saw all this as an inadequate argument, for it was offered all too frequently "to the neglect of Plato, Euclid, Locke, Freud, who, by the way, a recent Yale graduate said he has passed through college without."[12] One can see the gleam in her eye and sense the passion in her voice as she makes these points. It is the passion and tone of tradition, yes. But even more it is a passion for coherence, for a sense of stability, for, in words that were to become a future theme for a Speech Communication convention, a quest for the center that holds.

In addition to career-long membership in the Speech Association of America, she was a member and fellow of the Center for the Study of Democratic Institutions and the Humanist Society of America, whose journal was a regular staple of her interdisciplinary reading. Nichols subscribed to, and poured over, every issue of *Critical Inquiry* and *Diacritics*, to digest and frequently to dispute the newest trends in literary and rhetorical theory. She was the first woman to achieve the highest leadership and scholarly levels in the profession. In 1955 she served as editor of volume 3 of the landmark series in rhetorical criticism *A History and Criticism of American Public Address*. From 1963 through 1965 she became the editor of the field's most prestigious journal, *Quarterly Journal of Speech*. She was elected and served as president of the Speech Association of America in 1969, during which time she prepared and delivered one of her most memorable addresses, "The Tyranny of Relevance." In October 1973 the community of Champaign-Urbana selected Nichols as one of twenty-seven University of Illinois scholars to be honored as distinguished, one of only two women chosen at the time. In December 1977 the then-Speech Communication Association (SCA) gave Nichols its highest recognition, the SCA Distinguished Service Award. In making this award, Joseph DeVito remarked of Nichols, "Her scholarship has shaped the discipline. She, perhaps more than any other person, has contributed to the development of the contemporary definition of rhetorical criticism. She has shown us not only how to think about and write about criticism but how to function as a critic, a role that less able rhetorical critics have shown themselves reluctant to assume."[13] The association has since established the Marie H. Nichols Award for Scholarship in Rhetoric and Public Address, given annually at its national convention.

Jane Blankenship of the University of Massachusetts, Amherst, who completed her Ph.D. under Nichols' direction, has elegantly and perceptively written that Nichols can best be described as a teacher by looking at her four fundamental beliefs: "her fundamental belief in enduring values; her fundamental belief in rational public discussion and debate; her fundamental belief that through the clear and elegant use of language we can elevate rather than diminish our lives; and, her fundamental belief in the inextricable relationship between rhetorical study and the humane tradition."[14] These beliefs apply not only to her teaching but also to the totality of her thought and work. There is a virtually straight line from the work that Nichols began in her study of Channing to the consistent themes that she emphasized throughout her career. I am indebted to Lisa Oksman, who completed a senior honors' thesis on Nichols under my direction, for the insight that there are intriguing parallels between Channing and Nichols. Both Channing and Nichols stressed the moral obligation that individuals have to develop and expand their minds. As Oksman expressed it, "Channing spent many a sermon discussing his faith in the progress of the human race and the moral obligation to progress through such an expansion and development of the mind. He also interpreted this search for progress as the route to the individual's happiness. Nichols once described the very function of the humane tradition of rhetoric as to prepare one to assume his or her place in society by providing the individual with the ability to express and discuss his or her beliefs and values in appropriate ways."[15]

In the same fashion both Channing and Nichols shared an outspoken alignment with pressing issues of their times. As Oksman says, "Nichols pointed out in her thesis that Channing associated himself with the social movements of his time: She cited his openly expressed stand against slavery. . . . Dr. Nichols herself expressed hot opinions on topics that had the potential to be less than well received. At a commencement address she gave at Drury College in 1978, only a few months before her death, she spoke of the 1960's motto 'do your own thing' as destructive. She further expressed her dismay at the growing participation of her own gender (whom she referred to as the presumably 'gentler' sex) in 'bad' things, such as crime and acts of violence."[16]

RATIONALITY IN TEACHING

From 1954 through 1977 Nichols served on numerous master's and doctoral committees at the University of Illinois. She directed thirty doctoral dissertations ranging from Wayne Brockriede's study of "Bentham's Philosophy of Rhetoric" in 1954, to J. Gregory Payne's "Evidential Analysis of the Kent State Affair: A Case Study" in 1977.

Her classroom preparation was meticulous, including lectures typed on the manual typewriter, which sat on her office desk, then edited and revised in pencil. She regularly taught courses in Classical Rhetoric, Ancient and Modern Rhetoric, American Public Address, Modern Rhetorical Theory, and Rhetorical Criticism. She also offered special seminars on Kenneth Burke, I. A. Richards, and Marshall McLuhan.

Her course schedule for a spring semester of American Public Address began with an introduction followed by detailed examinations of speakers and their discourses in successive periods. She started with the colonial period, focusing on John Cotton, the Mathers, Edwards, and Whitefield; moved to the Enlightenment and revolutionary period, treating discourses of Otis, Samuel Adams, and Patrick Henry. Next came discussion of public addresses from 1778 to 1860, including Hamilton, Madison, Jefferson, Channing, John Calhoun, and Henry Clay and culminating with Daniel Webster, William Sumner, Henry Ward Beecher, and, most importantly, Abraham Lincoln. The last part of the course dealt with discourses from 1865 to 1956 and included Booker T. Washington, William Jennings Bryan, Theodore Roosevelt, Clarence Darrow, and Eugene V. Debs and ended with major concentrations on Franklin D. Roosevelt and Adlai Stevenson. This course was accompanied with a 5½-page, single-spaced set of guidelines: "Suggestions for the Study of an Oration." It presented an outline for considering material external to the speech itself, elements of interpreting the speech itself (structure, proofs and materials of persuasion, style, the contributions of all these to the whole), and a section on means of criticism of the speech (comparison with other speeches of the same types or from the same period, evaluation of the adaptation to the audience, judgment about use of "all the available means of persuasion," and consideration of judgments of other critics.

Nichols's course on Modern Rhetorical Theory: 1890–1949, Speech 322, was one of her most significant contributions. The syllabus was six pages long, single-spaced, and contained detailed readings from a wide range of essays published in the *Quarterly Journal of Speech*. The course began with transcendentalism, elocution, and the scientific attitude and then moved to the classical tradition, where it focused on the dispute over form and content. Here Nichols assigned such classic essays as Everett Lee Hunt's "The Scientific Spirit in Public Speaking" (1915) and Herbert Wichens's "Our Hidden Aims" (1923). She included a section on significant questions pertaining to the classical tradition, which included such readings as Giles Wilkenson Gray's "How Much

Are We Dependent upon the Ancient Greeks and Romans" (1923) and Wichelns's highly influential "The Literary Criticism of Oratory" (1925), which dealt with issues raised by Hoyt Hudson four years earlier. The third section of the course focused on "The Forensic Mind: Classical Tradition and Modifications." This was followed by "The Influence of Behaviorist Psychology on Rhetorical Theory" with emphasis on Charles H. Woolbert and W. Norwood Brigance. Next came "The Influence of Gestalt Psychology" and "Rhetoric from the Point of View of Mental Hygiene" with the Classic Essays by Wayne Morse (1928) and Elwood Murray (1934). The course then considered "The Functional Approach to Rhetoric: The Influence of Business" and "Adapting Speech to Radio." It culminated with two major sections: "Toward Democracy in Rhetoric: The Influence of John Dewey," which included articles by James H. McBirney, J. Jeffrey Auer, and Douglas Ehninger; and "Propaganda Technique: The Influence of Social Psychologists" and especially "The Influence of Korzybski, Ogden and Richards, etc." This last section introduced students to essays by Irving J. Lee, Bower Aly, S. I. Hayakawa, and Ralph G. Nichols, among others.

The assignments and exams for Speech 322 were daunting and typical of Nichols's comprehensive approach. The first paper assignment, for example, was on the subject "The Meaning of Nature, Art, and Science in 18th Century England." Graduate students were to write 4000 words for one unit of credit. Undergraduates were to write 1,000 words, and their topic was refined to "The Meaning of Nature in 18th Century England." Documentation was to follow *The Chicago Manual of Style*. A list of supplementary materials for the paper was also provided, containing such weighty volumes as Ernst Cassirer's *The Philosophy of the Enlightenment*, A. O. Lovejoy's "Nature as Aesthetic Norm," and Lecky's *History of England in the 18th Century*, among other resources. Nichols' examination for this course was also typical of her challenging style. It included six questions, and there were no choices among questions as is so often the case today. Her questions were: "1. Define rhetoric. Relate it to grammar and logic. 2. Discuss the influence of science on rhetorical and elocutionary theory in eighteenth-century England. 3. Discuss the statement: 'American rhetorical theory in the eighteenth century was largely derivative.' 4. Compare George Campbell's *Philosophy of Rhetoric* with a modern textbook in public speaking, preferably, James A. Winans, *Public Speaking*, or Bryant and Wallace, *Fundamentals of Public Speaking*. 5. Briefly describe the theory of style of Swift, Biffon, and Spencer. 6. Choose one leading idea of I. A. Richards and one of Kenneth Burke relating to rhetorical theory and explain it."

Nichols designed a special seminar on McLuhan, B. F. Skinner, and selected existentialists, Speech 438A, which was extremely attractive to many graduate students. Her handout concerning the course and initial assignment are indicative of her ingenuity and inquisitiveness, which created a contagious atmosphere for knowledge among her students. In introducing the seminar, she describes it as follows:

"I regard McLuhan as one of the very few men capable of significant contribution to the problems of advanced communication theory," says Raymond Williams in the University of Toronto Quarterly. And Kenneth Boulding, economist of the University of Colorado, has argued that McLuhan's works should be required reading for all university students. What is McLuhan saying that should prompt such reactions, some friendly and some hostile? This is what the course is designed to find out. Books: Bibliography attached [this referred to a special bibliography on McLuhan prepared by Nichols's former student Richard Katula at the University of Rhode Island. In addition to biographical highlights, Katula's bibliography provided twenty-two pages of essays by and about McLuhan].

Written Assignment: After you have read the *Gutenberg Galaxy* and David Riesman's essay, "The Oral and Written Traditions," in *Explorations in Communication*, attempt in about 1,500 words to answer the following question: How does an oral culture differ from a written tradition? (Two weeks hence).[17]

Her teaching method was always to try to bring out the very best in her students, and she refused to accept superficial work or shoddy analysis. This was frequently referred to as "the Nichols treatment," described by Jane Blankenship when she attempted to short-circuit her reading for a class presentation. Nichols confronted her in front of the class and asked if she had read the entire assignment. After the initial anger and humiliation wore off, Blankenship realized what Nichols had done—made her confront her self. For Blankenship this turned into a positive learning experience because she realized not only that she could do better work but also that this particular professor would accept nothing less. Raising the stakes in effort, intellectual rigor, and committed action was a constant feature of Nichols' pedagogical regimen. Indeed, this very same quality was reflected in her final analysis of Lincoln's First Inaugural Address, one of her best-known essays. While Lincoln's speech itself did not have the hoped for effect of preserving the union at that time, the purposes for which he spoke were ultimately valuable. Thus, Nichols argued, "In speechmaking, as in life, not failure, but low aim is crime."[18]

RATIONALITY IN SCHOLARSHIP

Over her career Nichols published numerous books and scholarly articles and chapters. She was the coauthor with Wayland M. Parrish of *American Speeches* in 1954; edited *A History and Criticism of American Public Address*, vol. 3 in 1955; published *Rhetoric and Criticism* in 1963; and edited the *Abstracts of the Speech Association of America 54th Annual Meeting* in 1968. As a highlight and indication of her esteemed academic reputation she edited the *Quarterly Journal of Speech* in 1963, 1964, and 1965.

She published, in addition, twenty scholarly articles and book chapters, beginning with her article on "Phillips Brooks" in the *Quarterly Journal of Speech* in 1941 and continuing through "When You Set Out for Ithaka . . . ," her keynote address at the 1977 Central States Communication Convention, in the *Central States Speech Journal*, fall 1977.

Nichols is best known as a careful and meticulous rhetorical critic, her work on the first Lincoln inaugural being most often cited in that respect.[19] She is further acknowledged as the person who introduced the works of Kenneth Burke and Ivor Armstrong Richards to the field of speech communication in her groundbreaking essays in the *Quarterly Journal of Speech* on both theorist-critics.[20] Moreover, Nichols was immensely interested in the work of Marshall McLuhan and had well-marked copies of all of his books in her office library. In fact, Nichols may best be thought of as a theorist-critic herself, for she artfully combined the insights about language and human society from Burke, Richards, and others into her own thinking and writing. While she has been frequently held up as an exemplar of the neo-classicist or traditional method of rhetorical criticism, such a label seems far too limiting for the kinds of insights that she generated in her theorizing and critical practice. She clearly resisted the attempts to label her by any single method—no student of Burke, which she clearly was, would settle for that. It would be useful to look more carefully at some of her theoretical and critical works to see both the scope and depth of her approach. While there is not space to do so here, Nichols' early work on Channing, including part of her dissertation and an early essay, along with two essays near the end of her career, a review essay entitled "On Looking beyond One's Discipline" and her final publication, "When You Set Out for Ithaka . . . ," are especially strong candidates for further analysis.

ACADEMIC AND PROFESSIONAL LEADERSHIP

Combined with her innovative scholarship on Burke and Richards, Nichols was a firm and vibrant voice for rationality and excellence during the decade of the turbulent 1960s. In that time she achieved her highest potential as an academic leader by editing the *Quarterly Journal of Speech* in the middle of the decade and serving as president of Speech Communication Association of America in 1969, a post that offered her the willingly accepted opportunity for speaking out on the issues of the time. It is useful to examine her work as an editor, both for the types of essays published and for the attention to detail and style that marked her own writing.

As editor of the *Quarterly Journal of Speech* Nichols gave visibility to an impressive array of scholars in a variety of areas. She designed and implemented an elaborate and careful structure for manuscript review, creating an Advisory Board composed of Richard Murphy at the University of Illinois, Donald C. Bryant at the University of Iowa, and Wilbur Samuel Howell at Princeton. In addition, she consulted with an Editorial Board composed of Wayne Brockriede and Malcolm Sillars as book review editors, along with fifteen different associate editors covering specialties such as public address (Robert G. Gunderson), classical tradition (Ray Nadeau), statistical and quantitaive studies (David K. Berlo), argument and debate (Robert Friedman), preaching (Harold Brack), film (Kenneth Harwood), hearing disorders (Merle Ansberry), theater (Patricia McIlrath), interpretation (Wallace Bacon), and communication and opinion (Robert T. Oliver). This approach reflected an early version of unity within diversity, which Nichols used to garner the best scholarship from many different areas of the discipline.

In her first issue of the *Quarterly Journal of Speech*, February 1963, Nichols published Wayne Thompson's "A Conservative View of a Progressive Rhetoric" as the lead essay. The issue also included essays by Fred Casmir on "The Hitler I Heard," by Stanley Glenn on "Style and Stanislavsky," and by Ralph Pomeroy on "Whateley's Historic Doubts: Argument and Origin." Moreover, Nichols utilized the journal for a lively Forum section, which became one of the most important pathways for intellectual exchanges within the profession. R. R. Allen and J. B. Polisky contributed "The Gorgeous Debating Machine" in the first Forum section, along with Wayne Thompson's piece on "Policies for Speech Monographs 1963–65" and J. Jeffrey Auer's remarks at the Cleveland Convention Luncheon of the Speech Communicated Association of America.

Her second issue led off with J. Jeffrey Auer and Jerald Banninga's "The Genesis of John Quincy Adams' Lectures on Rhetoric and Oratory." It also featured significant essays by Loren Reid on "The Last Speech of William Pitt," by Charles M. Kelly on "Mental Ability and Personality Factors in Listening," and by Wil Linkugel on "The Woman Suffrage Argument of Anna Howard Shaw." Nichols's third issue continued the trend of publishing essays that became the foundations of rhetorical scholarship. Here the lead essay was Karl Wallace's famous "The Substance of Rhetoric: Good Reasons." This issue also covered a variety of topics from Latin American cinema attendance, to an analysis of the play *The London Merchant*. The last essay again offered a major piece of research in American colonial rhetoric, Eugene White's "Cotton Mather's *Manductio ad Ministerium*." In the final issue of 1963 Nichols published Otis Walter's essay, "On Views of Rhetoric, Whether Conservative or Progressive," along with essays about television courtroom proceedings, George Campbell, political symbolism, and semantic analysis.

In 1964 Nichols maintained the rhetorical focus of the journal while expanding its scope into new content areas. Issue number 1 included essays by Gary Cronkhite on "Logic, Emotion and the Paradigm of Persuasion" and research by Donald Dedmon on "Translating *Le Cid*" and by Gerald Miller and Murray Hewgill on "The Effect of Variations in Nonfluency on Audience Ratings of Source Credibility." Essays by Donald Bryant and Ray Nadeau, along with Sidney Kraus' lasting analysis of "Presidential Debates in 1964" provided major additions to rhetorical scholarship. Taken together, her editorial leadership of the *Quarterly Journal of Speech* undermines the notion of a rigid neo-Aristotelianism or a narrow selectivity in her appraisal of scholarship. On the contrary, Nichols's editorial acuity demonstrated a keen eye for variety and a constant attention to quality in a plurality of speech communication perspectives. The immense seriousness with which she approached her role as editor and her determination to encourage scholarship at the highest levels are clearly articulated in her comments at the end of her term as editor. She noted that "although rejecting a manuscript is never pleasant, she has had to do this—at times with great reluctance, for the line between acceptance and rejection is often thin and one needs to produce a balanced journal that will be of interest to as many readers as possible, and, at the same time, work within space limitations. She has used the best judgment she has—never too good—but still the only judgment with which she has been endowed."[21] Casting a look to the future, Nichols commented that "the editor's ambition has been to maintain the high standards left as a legacy by the long line of distinguished editors. . . . Were her term as editor longer, she would promise to try to do better, but, alas, all rewarding experiences must end, and she wishes for her successor the same happy adventure."[22]

Some of Nichols's most important and heartfelt ideas were expressed in addresses made during this period. Indeed, 1968, 1969, and 1970 marked vital periods in Nichols's career and in her leadership of the profession. These were trying times for all of academe, and the Speech Communication Association of America was no exception. In 1968 Nichols was first vice president of the association and was responsible for planning the convention program. In her convention preview remarks she noted, "In our planning, we have not neglected the traditional, nor have we avoided the controversial. These are times in which that which is tried must be reexamined for its continuing worth in giving continuity and stability, and also times when the new must be reexamined for its possible worth."[23] Interestingly, under her influence the practice of giving a presidential address was reinstituted after a lapse of three years. In her words, "Some gentle persuasion induced President Douglas Ehninger reluctantly to agree to reopen the tradition."[24] As president of the association in 1969 Nichols reflected on the 1968 convention in Chicago and published her detailed commentary, called "The Search for Excellence" in the February 1969 issue of *Spectra*. In that essay she deals with what she termed "the principle of control." Nichols frequently used a kind of oblique style of argument, and here was one of her finest. She noted that she and others had been "roundly defeated" in an attempt to introduce the principle of control into convention programming. This left her "with considerably more freedom than I had knowledge and discipline in the matter of convention programming."[25] Her response? Off to see Professors Wrage and Haberman and her colleague at Illinois, Richard Murphy about what to do with the task of reconciling freedom with control. Out of the discussions the idea of a Debut Program emerged, the term "debut" being attributed by Nichols to Richard Murphy. Her comment again shows her distinctive approach and style: "Possibly because the principle of control applied only to the young, whom we were seriously trying to encourage to participate in the convention, but who would be in no danger of losing prestige by having a paper rejected in preliminary evaluation, the idea met with great approval."[26] In addition, Nichols proudly announced that her principle of control had reemerged in agreement to publish the first volume of *Convention Abstracts*. Among other things, this helped drive up the quality of convention papers: "By requiring Abstracts prior to the Convention, we are asking for concerned scrutiny of public remarks." She adds that "my private dedicatory note for the first volume of Abstracts was mentally written for Professor Wrage, whose memory I cherish for his dedication to the search for excellence in his chosen field."[27] Finally, in "The Search for Excellence" Nichols affirmed her innovative spirit. "Rhetoric," she remarked, "is but one of our interests. As we must in that area not only reclaim but invent, so with all other areas of our discipline—drama, interpretation, therapy, behavioral studies. Lament over lost opportunity will not serve us. Our object should be to gather the splinters of language study into a central discipline that all other disciplines must respect."[28]

The center of that discipline for Nichols was the rational study of language. Gathering the splinters of language also entailed defending them against unreasonable attacks, a task that Nichols took up with dedication in her 1969 address "The Tyranny of Relevance." She began by quoting one of her favorite historians, Carl Becker, about "certain unobtrusive words with uncertain meanings that are permitted to slip off the tongue or the pen without fear and without research"[29] and become the powerful instruments of defining knowledge. Nichols singled out the word "relevance" for special examination, noting, "In its name John Gerassi at San Francisco State was hired, and in its name he was also fired. In its name Harvard's Social Studies 148 was developed and taken over by students, and in its name is also marked for elimination. In its name, both high schools and colleges have staged sit-ins, walk-outs, firebombings, and physical maiming; and on my own campus, in its name eleven files of index cards—guides to a library of more than 4,000,000 volumes—were destroyed."[30] After these stark examples Nichols argued that it was not the notion of relevance to genuine social needs and issues as Douglas Ehninger had described a year earlier to which she objected. Rather, her concern was that the term "relevance" itself had been overtaken by "more sinister aspects" until it had become "a bullying slogan, allied with power, designed to stop thought, as slogans frequently do."[31] This meant that scholars must ask "whether it fosters unreason instead of reason, whether, under it, the freedom of the teacher to teach and the student to learn are not threatened."[32]

She then identified three areas of weakness in the slogan of relevance as it is applied to education in general, to teaching and the curriculum, and to professional organizations. Although her views were then and remain today contestable and controversial, Nichols minced no words in the spirit of public debate. Responding to the newly formed Speech Association Concerned Committee of Students and Teachers about such issues as discontent with curriculum, she argued that "everywhere we hear cries that the lecture system must go, the formalized discussion must go, and every mode of instruction we have used in the past must go, this despite the fact that educators have frequently demonstrated that there is no one method of presenting materials."[33] The same Concerned Committee had issued a manifesto declaring the Speech Communication

Association Convention itself to be "irrelevant." Nichols posed a series of questions in response: "What could that mean? Does it mean 'I don't like conventions'? If so, what about them do I not like . . . The programs I did not hear? The substance of programs I did hear? . . . Could it be that in the kind of society one foresees, free and rational discussion will be out of order?" In various ways Nichols continued to raise what was for her the key question, "relevant to what?"[34]

In her concluding paragraphs Nichols posits an answer, a very large and inclusive answer to that question. In her words, "The answer to the question, Relevant to what? consists in the answer, 'Man.' There is a continuity, not of the word, but of man. Relevance is determined by what man was, is, and will be—not what he now seems to be. Whoever knows the field of speech knows that other words at other times have tried to take over. The field of speech has persisted because it has always evaluated the new idea or word in terms of man's ancient, contemporary, and everlasting needs to communicate and work with other men in changing society."[35] We must keep in mind in reading her strong words that, at the time she spoke them, campuses were in disarray, and violence and unreason on many fronts in social life had emerged. It took considerable courage to speak for a different way, for a continuity of humanity, which could thrive only if reasonable thought and action could flourish. Nichols never veered from attempting to guide her students, colleagues, and profession in that rational direction.

CONCLUSION

The most important thing to remember about Marie Nichols is that she was consistently committed to excellence in teaching, research, and academic life. Moreover, her central concern was the study of language in all of its human dimensions. She once observed, "As a humanist, I believe that I am expected to work in and through language, aiming to develop educated taste; second, to work with and on the mind, to develop educated judgment and persuasiveness; and third, operate in and on the whole person to help make a moral person and a responsible citizen or political leader—in other words a responsible citizen."[36] As a rhetorical critic she was committed to the centrality of language in history, to the substance of rhetorical argument, and to the application of enduring values to the practice of rhetoric. As a professional leader she stood for rationality and the fierce integrity of intellectual freedom. Her life and career reflected the cultivation of disciplined habits of reading, reflection, and expression and the consistent growth of both the mind and heart. I recall her fascination in the last years of her life with new findings on right-brain–left-brain developments and with the contributions of social scientists like B. F. Skinner, whose work she regarded as extremely enlightening because it helped us understand how human beings respond. Indeed, Skinner, McLuhan, Mortimer Adler, Suzanne Langer, and Michael Polanyi were all welcome participants, joining Aristotle, Cicero,

George Campbell, Donald Bryant, Jeff Auer, Karl Wallace, Richard Murphy, I. A. Richards, and Kenneth Burke under Marie's rich rhetorical tent. I also remember the last book she was reading with extreme interest: Mortimer J. Adler's autobiography, *Philosopher at Large*.[37] She gave it to me with a knowing smile from her hospital bed only days before her death, saying "Here, you might enjoy this." Soon afterward she underwent chemotherapy and almost immediately fell into a coma that preceded her passing on. In Chapter 14 of that work Adler strikingly cites a poem by Mark Van Doren dedicated to Adler and carrying the title of his life story. The poem tells the story of an "ancient garden where most men step daintily," contrasted with Adler, who "bulldozes; plows deep; moves earth; says someone must, if truth is to be found." The result of this approach has its risks, for it "horrifies those men, by hedge and dust plot, whom the top sufficed. They thought the garden theirs." That may be, writes Van Doren, but the philosopher adds essential new dimensions: "[T]he dead air is spiced with damp new things dug up. Or old, he says; like God, like buried gold."[38] Van Doren's verse could as well have been written about Nichols. She dug deeply for truth beneath every surface she encountered and taught students, colleagues, and leaders in many areas the discipline and pleasure of discovering the hidden gold of knowledge.

What did she know? Nichols knew how to live and to die with dignity. She knew how to instill in almost everyone whom she encountered a sense of integrity and an abiding respect for the rational capacity of human beings. In the fashion of most great leaders, her rationality did not exclude or run counter to strong feeling. For Nichols, *logos* and *pathos* were intricately woven together to make a lasting fabric of integrity. Her *ethos* hence remains as strong today as when she argued against the "tyranny of relevance," stood for reinvigorating the inherent connection between rhetoric and history, and expanded the horizons of rhetorical scholarship to incorporate dramatism, metaphor, orality, paradigm shifts, performance, and the emerging role of electronic media. In these and other areas of the speech communication discipline Nichols represented the highest and most demanding aspects of the spirit of inquiry, the power of contagious intellectual curiosity, and commitment to the values that bring out the best attitudes and actions in the human arena. Through her scholarship, pedagogy, and disciplinary leadership Marie Hochmuth Nichols showed us the pathway to, and the priority of, transforming our human conditions into humane practices. Her life, scholarship, teaching, and leadership leave us with strong traditions and exciting expectations in our ongoing journey on the road to "Ithaka."

NOTES

1. Marie H. Nichols, "When You Set Out for Ithaka . . . ," *Central States Speech Journal* 28 (Fall 1977), 148.

2. My close association with Professor Nichols as mentor, colleague, and friend began in 1974, while I was an assistant professor in the Department of Speech Com-

munication at the University of Illinois, Urbana-Champaign. I delivered the eulogy at her funeral, "For Marie H. Nichols," on October 10, 1978.

3. Kenneth Burke, *The Philosophy of Literary Form* (Baton Rouge: Louisiana State University Press, 1941), 3.

4. Kenneth Burke, *Rhetoric of Motives* (Berkeley: University of California Press, 1969; 1945), xvff.

5. Ibid., xvi.

6. Ibid.

7. Her colleague Professor Joseph Wenzel provided an excellent review of Nichols' life and accomplishments, "Marie Hochmuth Nichols, 1908–1978," in *Spectra* (June 1979), 3. This includes citation of the volume *Rhetoric and Communication: Studies in the University of Illinois Tradition*, published by University of Illinois Press in 1976 to honor Nichols, Richard Murphy, and Karl Wallace.

8. Marie H. Nichols, "William Ellery Channing: New England Conversationalist," *Quarterly Journal of Speech* 30 (February 1944), 429–439.

9. Marie H. Nichols, "Song of the Open Road," commencement address at Drury College, August 12, 1978, 8.

10. Ibid., 9.

11. Ibid.

12. Ibid.

13. Joseph De Vito, "Nichols Honored," *Spectra* (February 1977), 16.

14. Jane Blankenship, "The Song of the Open Road: Marie Hochmuth Nichols as Teacher," *Communication Quarterly* 34 (Fall 1986), 420.

15. Lisa R. Oksman, "Marie H. Nichols: An Analysis of Women and Public Address," unpublished senior honors thesis, Newcomb College of Tulane University, New Orleans, May 1992, 23.

16. Ibid., 22.

17. Marie H. Nichols, unpublished lecture notes, class materials, and personal papers donated to the author and to the library at University of Illinois, Champaign-Urbana.

18. Marie H. Nichols and Wayland M. Parrish, eds., *American Speeches* (New York: David McKay, 1954), 12.

19. See Nichols' essay "Lincoln's First Inaugural," reprinted in Robert L. Scott and B. Brock, eds., *Methods of Rhetorical Criticism* (New York: Harper and Row, 1972), 60–100.

20. Marie H. Nichols, "Kenneth Burke and the 'New Rhetoric,' " *Quarterly Journal of Speech* 38 (April 1952), 133–144; Marie H. Nichols, "Burkean Criticism," *Western Speech Journal* (Spring 1957), 89–95; Marie H. Nichols, "I. A. Richards and the 'New Rhetoric,' " *Quarterly Journal of Speech* 44 (February 1958), 1–16.

21. Marie H. Nichols, Editor's page, *Quarterly Journal of Speech* (1965).

22. Ibid.

23. Marie H. Nichols, "Convention-Preview Remarks," *Spectra* (October 1968), 1.

24. Ibid., 2.

25. Marie H. Nichols, "The Search for Excellence," *Spectra* (February 1969), 1.

26. Ibid., 2.

27. Ibid.

28. Ibid.

29. Marie H. Nichols, "The Tyranny of Relevance," *Spectra*, vol. 6 (February 1970), 1.

30. Ibid., 9.

31. Ibid.
32. Ibid.
33. Ibid., 10.
34. Ibid.
35. Ibid.
36. Marie H. Nichols, "Search for Identity: Who Are We?," keynote address, Illinois Speech and Theatre Association, St. Louis, MO, November 7, 1975, 3.
37. Mortimer J. Adler, *Philosopher at Large: An Intellectual Autobiography* (New York: Macmillan, 1977).
38. Ibid., 292.

BIBLIOGRAPHY

Adler, Mortimer J. *Philosopher at Large: An Intellectual Autobiography.* New York: Macmillan, 1977.

Blankenship, Jane. "The Song of the Open Road: Marie Hochmuth Nichols as Teacher." *Communication Quarterly* 34 (Fall 1986).

Burke, Kenneth. *The Philosophy of Literary Form.* Baton Rouge: Louisiana State University Press, 1941; 3d ed. Berkeley: University of California Press, 1973.

———. *Rhetoric of Motives.* Berkeley: University of California Press, 1969.

De Vito, Joseph. "Nichols Honored." *Spectra* (February 1977), 16.

[Nichols], Marie H. "Phillips Brooks." *Quarterly Journal of Speech* 27 (February 1941), 227–236.

———. "William Ellery Channing: New England Conversationalist." *Quarterly Journal of Speech* 30 (February 1944), 429–439.

———. "Kenneth Burke and the 'New Rhetoric.'" *Quarterly Journal of Speech* 38 (April 1952), 133–144.

Nichols, Marie H., and Wayland M. Parrish, eds. *American Speeches.* New York: David McKay, Longman, Green, 1954.

Nichols, Marie H. "Lincoln's First Inaugural." In *American Speeches,* ed. Wayland M. Parrish and Marie Hochmuth [Nichols]. New York: Longman, Green, 1954, 21–71.

———, ed. *A History and Criticism of American Public Address.* Vol. 3. New York: Longman, Green, 1955.

Nichols, Marie H. "Burkean Criticism." *Western Speech* 21 (Spring 1957), 89–95.

———. "I. A. Richards and the 'New Rhetoric.'" *Quarterly Journal of Speech* 44 (February 1958), 1–16.

———. *Rhetoric and Criticism.* Baton Rouge: Louisiana State University Press, 1963.

———. Editor's page. *Quarterly Journal of Speech* (1963, 1964, 1965).

———. "The Search for Excellence." *Spectra* (February 1969), 1, 2.

———. "The Tyranny of Relevance." *Spectra* 6 (February 1970), 1, 8, 10.

———. "Rhetoric and Style." In *Patterns of Literary Style,* ed. Joseph Strelka. University Park: Pennsylvania State University Press, 1971, 130–141.

———. "Rhetoric and the Humane Tradition." In *Rhetoric: A Tradition in Transition,* ed. Lloyd F. Bitzer and Edwin Black. Lansing: Michigan State University Press, 1974, 178–191.

———. "Search for Identity: Who Are We?" Keynote address, Illinois Speech and Theatre Association, St. Louis, MO, November 7, 1975.

———. "When You Set Out for Ithaka . . ." *Central States Speech Journal* 28 (Fall 1977), 145–156.

———. "Song of the Open Road." Commencement address, Drury College, St. Louis, MO, August 12, 1978.

Oksman, Lisa R. "Marie H. Nichols: An Analysis of Women and Public Address." Senior honors thesis, Department of Communication, Newcomb College of Tulane University, New Orleans, May 1992.

Patton, John H. "For Marie H. Nichols." Eulogy delivered at Champaign, IL, October 10, 1978.

Scott, Robert L., and Bernard Brock, eds. *Methods of Rhetorical Criticism*. New York: Harper and Row, 1972.

Wenzel, Joseph. "Marie Hochmuth Nichols, 1908–1978." *Spectra* (June 1979), 3.

Waldo Braden. Photo courtesy of Andrew King. Used with permission.

6

Waldo Braden: The Critic as Outsider

ANDREW KING

SYNOPSIS

Waldo Braden was a complex man. His greatest contribution to rhetorical criticism, the nature and function of myth, emerged out of his profound distrust of myth. In his view, myth was for people in headlong retreat from real problems. Braden believed in a world of limits and irreconcilable choices, of five senses, three dimensions, and foursquare accountability. In short, his view of things was tragic. Myth has a collective strategy to avoid, ignore, or transcend tragedy. Rhetors who employed it threw dust in the eyes of their auditors. In Braden's view myth provided a season of hope, but a season only. Ultimately myth failed, and its words lived on as mocking reminders of the limits of discourse.

A MOONSTRUCK NORTHSIDER

I met Waldo Braden in 1980, two years after he had stepped down from his twenty-year reign as department chair at Louisiana State University. I knew him well starting in 1985. At that time he had largely abandoned writing about Southern oratory, for he had become enamored of Abraham Lincoln and was engaged in writing three books at once, two of which appeared posthumously. Even in retirement Waldo came into the department to have morning coffee with Harold Mixon and to work in the archives of the Hill Memorial Library. When I joined the department in 1985, I was immediately invited to join Waldo's Sunday afternoon circle. Since I was the only nonretiree to do so, this resulted in not a little jealousy on the part of several rhetoricians and historians who never quite made it into the master's cadre. "You have just arrived and he treats you like a colleague. It is not fair," one senior historian expostulated bitterly. During these leisurely Sunday dinners at the Plantation Room, Waldo talked about the future of the field and also about his life and work.

He much admired Ernest Bormann's *Force of Fantasy*,[1] a work that burst upon the field in the fall of 1985. "This is a watershed work. It signals the production of a whole new culture of book writing by rhetoricians. I predict that articles will become less important," Waldo announced at one his Sunday dinners. He stroked the book as if it were a kitten and said that reading it had inspired him and made him wish he were "a young billy-buck coming up now." His smile was a slash of brilliant sunlight on a sphere of leather. Some years later, when he gave up his little house to live with his daughter and son-in-law in Columbia, Missouri, he used the same words as he gave his most prized collected volumes to Harold Mixon and me. He loved the field passionately. "I can't let go," he kept saying fiercely, the tears streaming down his face. "I want to begin all over again." If he could manage another life, he told us, he would start in the West instead of the Middle Border and the Deep South: "I'm a wanderer, incorrigible."

Despite sensibilities grounded in the forty-acre Iowa farm on which he was born, Braden was a complex, even mysterious person. There was an irony about everything that he did: Braden was the Northerner who became a leading expert on Southern oratory, the historian who wrote about a historical myth, the literary humanist who adopted the categories of social science. In this chapter I argue that those contradictions gave Waldo Braden's work a degree of complexity and a driving energy that it might have lacked had he been an orthodox Georgian or Mississippian or, as Braden liked to say, "a native product dipped in fundamentalism."

THE CRITIC AS OUTSIDER

One afternoon during a discussion of Waldo's 1983 *The Oral Tradition in the South*,[2] I observed how odd it was that he, a Yankee son of the old Middle Border, had become a noted writer on Southern oratory. I pointed out that Dallas Dickey, the man often referred to as "the founder," had had deep roots in Tennessee, north Florida, and the Carolinas. Braden sighed and told me that Dickey had been a pioneer but that he had missed the South's tragic sense. "Dickey was a local colorist and a regionalist and damned good at that sort of thing but he missed the guilt and the mendacity that an outsider sees." Braden proceeded to outline a theory of criticism that had never appeared in any of his works: the critic as outsider. He began by asserting that people inside an institution could never grasp its essence. He said that his father, a farmer turned salesman, had taught him that the hardest things to understand were your own business, your own family, and your own region.

Now take the *New Yorker Magazine*. Don't read it myself much. Don't like it. But the point is that it was started by a man from Colorado named Ross and the people he hired were mostly middlewesterners. He never hired people who were born and bred in the city to write for the magazine. That is because New Yorkers can't see New York. For them it is just a collection of crime-ridden streets, subways, big buildings, and jobs. But an outsider with a cardboard suitcase sees the dreams and the romance. The outsider sees the city as a whole and can write and speak about New York as magical, a place with a special feel and pulse. You know the sort of thing people mean when they talk about the soul of a place.

Waldo's theory was very much like that of the circle theory of organizations,[3] the idea that people inside a business are so consumed with the politics and personalities of an institution that they cannot perceive the needs of its constit- uency, the demands of its customers, or the moves of its competitors with any clarity or understanding. The outsider was the best critic, said Waldo, because that person "has a different angle of vision." That is how George Bernard Shaw wrote "such wonderful plays," said Braden; "he was Anglo-Irish, somebody who didn't quite belong in either culture, someone at the edge of it all." I asked him if his work on the state of Mississippi as "a closed society" was a product of his own outsiderliness in the secret and impenetrable heart of the South. "Of course," said Waldo, "they [Mississippians] didn't see themselves as a closed society. They were inside it and were completely focused on trying to reconcile their brutal social system with their religious guilt."

Waldo went so far as to say that insiders never know what is going on in their own worlds. They are particularly wrong about the future. He confessed that he himself became enough of an insider to be wrong about the development of the New South. His New South, he confessed, was supposed to be following a trajectory of secularism, deracination, and individualism in a direction that can only be described as North by Northwest. "I forgot about my own dictum. The New South doesn't give anybody communal identity. It's just a word for unlim- ited greed. That is why the New South remains stillborn within the Old South. The first thing a successful New South captain of industry does is to put up an Old South-style house with pillars and a Tara-like lawn. The crowning emblem of his success is drawn from the antebellum era and not from the new cosmo- politan South." As he said these words during an unbearable summer night in his un-air-conditioned study, I remember a sudden illumination of lightning. It was August 5, 1987, about midnight. His oracular words were followed by a tremendous roll of thunder, and the stars took cover.

I now know what fascinated Waldo about the South. To him it was the last place in America where actions might have real consequences and where people were unprotected from their sins. Late in life he became interested in snake- handling churches and their preachers who not only handled rattlers, cotton- mouths and copperheads but drank strychnine and handled fire. He felt that these worshipers were in rebellion against the dead consumer culture of the New

South. He had an image of a mighty swath of people, stretching from southern West Virginia all the way to East Texas, descending from the hills and festering in unhappy knots in Nashville, Birmingham, Memphis, Jackson, and Tulsa. The seed of John Knox and Cromwell, these Southern folk were revolted by the empty materialism of the cities. Like Dennis Covington, whom he befriended, Waldo believed that cultural backlash against the sterility of the secular world had caused the people to take up serpents.

THE HISTORIAN AND TIMELESS MYTH

Much to the chagrin of Marie Hochmuth Nichols, Braden never rejected the discipline of history as the gold standard of all scholarship. Braden's best friends—and he could say it without a blush—were historians or, at best, critics of public address primarily interested in setting the record straight. He admired the work of Ernest J. Wrage, who believed in the legitimacy of a rhetorical history of ideas, and of Barnett Baskerville, who unashamedly compiled a history of American public address. Toward the end of his life Braden felt that something terrible was happening to the discipline that he had so ferociously admired. In 1988 he told me with fascinated horror that History had become "unhinged," that historians were abandoning their traditional mission, and that "self-conscious historiographers" were undermining the confidence of historians. Mysteriously and precipitously, they had abandoned the breastworks of truth and were in danger of becoming "second-rate rhetoricians." Worst of all was a new kind of "self-loathing" that he sensed among his friends in history. It was very dismaying for him. He felt that historical methods had been the touchstone of all humane scholarship and, thus, that "all our standards of handling evidence are in danger of being chucked out onto the rubbish heap."

No one will deny that most of Braden's works are organized temporally or that he quotes historians at least as often as he cites other rhetorical critics. Yet here, too, one finds the Bradenesque irony. The great rhetorical historian of the South became increasingly enamored of Southern myth. Perhaps his most famous article, "Repining over an Irrevocable Past: The Ceremonial Orator in a Defeated Society: 1865–1900," is organized around four myths, psychic patterns that transcend events and transform brute facts.[4] Indeed, the article is far more about a deep human need for transcendence than about the history of a particular era.[5] Braden used to affirm that scholarship was, at bottom, about the patient rescue of a place, person, or event from the cruel indifference of time. He writes in this article about the collective need of a people, and what he is willing to say goes far beyond material conditions of the late nineteenth-century Southern region. He uses history as little more than strategically invented narrative and moves dangerously close to the "social scientist" for whom he expressed unfailing contempt. In fact, Braden saw the ceremonial orator as a opportunistic exploiter of comforting communal fictions, a shaman rescuing his people from defeat with the aid of psychic resources. He felt that the accuracy of the true historical record counted little with the Southern orator who sought to connect his audience with the permanent, the universal, the transcendent, and the time- less. In so doing, these orators ignored the true character of the place around them. The real alternatives to the witless industrial imitation of the North were never discussed; those who did not admire soil mining of large-scale agriculture were dismissed as eccentrics, and antebellum race relations were set forth as a romantic ideal. Braden saw myth as a narcotizing narrative that closed off dis- cussion. It was a quick fix: "Everything may be done—every material thing— to give a place the aspect of tolerance, benignity, friendship and humanity, but the true character of a place, like that of a human being, is a slow organic growth."[6]

Although that was his expressed sentiment, Braden the practitioner did not see it that way. "Myth is just a tool for me, King," he once told me. "Myth allows me to understand history, and it makes me a better historian of public address."[7] When I asked how that could be, he told me that it had aided him to understand the complexity of the South. He noted that the Southern fire-eaters were routinely dismissed as crude demagogues. Because of this, the dispute among historians had boiled down to an either-or issue. On the other hand, there were those who argued that these agitators had had a great deal to do with starting the War between the States. On the other, there were those who argued that the sectionalists were failed politicians whose rhetoric had little more than entertainment value. The truth, Braden ultimately concluded, was much more complex than either camp imagined, and it had to do with the ways in which the myths embedded in pathetic and ethical appeals used by the fire-eaters had resonated with their constituencies. When he examined the utterly prosaic ap- proach to the arguments of the fire-eaters and the clumsy, literal-minded boil- erplate analysis of their logic, Braden said with pride, "It was that discovery that convinced me I had something I could contribute to the study of History." But some afternoons he was in a less mellow mood. "They should read our stuff, King," he snapped one day; "they might learn something." How ironic that statement seems today when so many historians (such as Kenneth Cmiel and George Arditi) study the rhetorical practices of communities on a scale that would have delighted Braden.

Through 4½ decades, Braden remained fascinated by the culture of the South. At a deeper level he was still a son of the Middle Border. He said that he remained an Iowan "in his bones" to the last. But although he admired what he called the "straight, single sense of the the Middle West," he had the scholar's admiration for complexity, and he had come to believe that northern culture was "more thinly scratched into the soil" than Southern culture. His friend the vocal scientist Giles Wilkerson Gray had told him that Iowans spoke with only forty phonemes, while Mississippians managed sixty-two. In addition to the superior melodic line Southerners slithered between hyperbole and outright mendacity as they spoke with a conscious relish. But what most engaged him were the things they spoke about, a Southern art form that involved a dense layering of myth and symbol. He liked thinking about the way that orators managed rival myths as if they were spinning plates in the air. In 1979 he wrote about the uneasy dialogue of the South's four major myths, a dialogue that revealed much about the South's obsession with regional identity: "As a central concern, this paper is directed toward a consideration of how the orators of the South from 1865 through 1900 attempted to cope with the problems of a defeated society. Following Tindall's advice, the writer will analyze how the orators as myth makers encouraged their constituents to retreat into 'an ideal dream world of the past,' largely through the development, promotion and exploitation of four great myths, which may be referred to as (1) The Old South, (2) The Lost Cause, (3) The Solid South, and (4) The New South."[8]

Braden's treatment of the rival myths was complex. He understood that they were braided together in an uneasy alliance. Unlike his native Iowans who have the luxury of speaking more or less "straight, single sense," Southerners have always had to be code-switchers, adapting to powerful outsiders who can hurt them, nuancing their language in order to manage small incremental changes, crossing group boundaries with a special wink or a mendacious nod, fooling clumsy intruders with skillful digression, turning one's linguistic melodic line to satisfy northern expectations, and grimly dancing their local dance before the cosmopolitan culture lords of North America. The South's myths represent a series of power displacements, each new group trying to assimilate the other's past without its burdens, an objective that is utterly vain and doomed from its conception. In a place where nothing is ever wholly forgotten or forgiven, this demeaning, frustrating, and tragic legacy is not without its compensations. It has created a rhetorical artistry among native Southerners of every class and background, an artistry that is honored in the old riddle, Why is it that most of our publishing houses are in Connecticut, while most of our writers live in Mississippi?

Braden also told me that it was late, very late when the scales fell from his eyes about the final end of the South as South. Anyone who looks at his work will see that Braden often retailed the general, modernist myth of "regions." Regions are the places where the writ of the metropolis does not run, little worlds remote from the center where folk survivals abound. Later in life he had the luxury to read ever more deeply and to reflect upon what he called "the club consensus" of the academy. Braden's deep, natural sympathies were touched when he thought about the rural Midwest that he had left behind after serving in World War II. Late in life he brooded about the passing of the Iowa of his youth, a world of small farms whose sons and daughters left for agricultural college and never returned. He had also witnessed the great collective farm consolidations of the lower South and wondered if a rural South would survive the twentieth century. "It is too bad the country is passing away before it's been found. It's just been dreamed. You've got to write about it, too, but don't expect too much. It's a mystery." A spartan thread ran through his counsel, counsel that I did not follow.

Waldo sought the answers in Western European social and intellectual history. The great nation-building era of the French Revolution was a triumph of science and reason; the romantic reaction that followed discovered the folk. At best, "the folk" were a useful remnant of an older organic culture, useful in the sense that it might serve as a sort of core icon to bind the new nations together. That is, while the folk were being dispersed and assimilated into the new urban national cultures, their presence gave the enlightened leaders a kind of breathing space. The folk provided an emblematic identity and a set of historical links to an appropriately idealized past. But, of course, this celebration of the folk was a temporary expedient. Organic culture was retrograde; wherever it persisted too strongly, it served as a huge, indigestible boulder aimed against the forces of modernity. After the moral bankruptcy of Napoleon and other revolutionaries, the folk were an important ethical symbol. But they were important only as raw material, and they were uprooted by the bourgeoisie, the railroads, the Morrill Act, and nearly every effort that served to unify and consolidate the new nation-states. They were transformed into urban, middle-class citizens or agribusiness-men. Their children were seldom allowed to remain where they were, and the deepest truths of culture cannot be acquired after childhood. In the United States, the South awaited its Kemal Attaturk who would level its folkways, ridicule its mores, and bulldoze its belief systems. Governors educated in Ivy League schools and armed with the charismatic authority of the Harvard Business School would pave the steaming red earth, send Hazel Motes to Duke (an out-post of light in Mencken's benighted Bozart), and end the corrupt "familial systems" of Southern business and politics.

I have expressed the doctrine crudely? Perhaps my description needs the touch of the social scientist to redeem it. Surely, I have not expressed it any more crudely than those many who so long asserted it with the belligerent confidence so characteristic of unexamined beliefs. The point is that Braden rose to a level of complexity that exposed the modernist doctrine, and asserted that the so-called dying South is in itself just another submyth. The South (like the folk) is always dying; it is one of the oldest Southern traditions. Magnolias rot in the moonlight, but they never disappear. Today's modernists present enlightenment culture and global integration as unstoppable historical destinies, but they may prove more feeble than, and as ephemeral as, the myth of the dying South.

He often told me that compared to the Southern generals, lawyers, politicians, and preachers whom he had studied, his own life seemed a shapeless mass. He admired greatly the Southerners' dramatic flair that had given their lives an epic quality. Like a hero's life, each seemed to fly straight to its mark like a Plutar-chian tale in which everything is foreshadowed, and the stages of the heroic journey are like the flight of a javelin sailing to its mark. At the same time he knew that this fictionalizing, storyteller quality somehow flattened our sense of their humanity. In part, this was the scholar's traditional envy of the man of action, but his disciples believed that Braden's intellectual pilgrimage had its own kind of pathos and dignity.

Waldo's frustration with the ironic power of myth was expressed in his final works on Abraham Lincoln. He worried that the "adoration" of Lincoln had reduced him to a symbol of national community and "served to minimize or obscure the fact that Lincoln first won attention where he was principally concerned with persuading the common citizen."[9] He notes that Lincoln was celebrated as a literary artist by critics who deliberately ignored all but three of his major speeches. The real Lincoln disappears along with his messy, compromise-filled, embarrassingly prolix orations. The "myth-haunted Lincoln"[10] has covered up the flesh-and-blood Abraham. Perhaps we can no longer see the complex "real man who was first a struggling citizen of Springfield, then a busy country lawyer, a shrewd and ambitious politician, a rugged campaigner for the young Republican party and finally the successful wartime leader of the union."[11] Waldo believed that we wanted to view Lincoln as a child prodigy born of congenitally crazed backwoods drifters.

Braden spent decades reading Southern oratory and studying Southern orators. He found the commentary by historians, literary critics, and newpaper editors narrowly repetitious. "Like the roar of the doors of Hell swinging on rusty hinges" was Waldo's apt characterization. The question assaulted him: Had these critics actually read the body of speeches that they dismissed as florid, vituperative, and provincial? On the one hand, people who actually paid little attention to the genre could sum up the concept of Southern oratory in a few spiteful words. He who had devoted half a lifetime to reading it could barely define the concept of a Southern oratory. Suddenly, the idea leaped up as if it were in love with him. He would make the academic world deal with what Southerners had actually said.[12] This struck his friends as quite a novel idea at a time when careful analysis of texts was being abandoned and when a premium was increasingly put on rapid categorization and sophistic fluency. Waldo Braden's gift to American scholarship was to explode one of its last "style" stereotypes, the florid entertainment value of Southern oratory.

Braden noted that Lincoln invented himself, that "he changed his image when he ran for the presidency," and that he altered it with events and "monitored it carefully."[13] But Braden made it clear that he did not approve of such postmodern behavior. He did not like to think of Lincoln as a "decentered individual of the collective" or a "matrix that makes choices."[14] Lincoln's "postmodernness" disturbed Braden. He was never comfortable or happy with myth despite the fact that mythic analysis had given his career as a scholar a brilliant second wind. In his bones he distrusted it as another mass medium in an age of collective snake oil, an odd sentiment for a rhetorician whose very lifeblood was the study of the communal loci and the tribal mores. Despite his prowess as a rhetorical critic, it must be admitted that everything that Waldo admired and believed in was the product of intense individualism. Despite his doubts, he clung to his faith in the gifted individual as beads clinging to the skirts of a whirling dervish. He did not admire the collective, and the great mass ideologies and doctrines of the twentieth century revolted him. He found communism inhuman and perverse, but he had a profound suspicion of corporate capitalism as well. He once criticized my tie and searched for an appropriate image. "That tie makes you look like a depression banker trying to look sorry while he forecloses the mortgage on your farm." Again, despite the fact that he deplored many things about the South, he admired "its stark reality." He once said to me, "[W]hatever I may say in one of my moods about the South, I always come back to the fact that it is a real place." He liked to say that the South was not really an old, encrusted place but "a young country where people are eager to see you."

After forty-five years of living and working in the South, Braden was still an outsider. It was "a real place," but it was not his place. He went north to Columbia, Missouri, where his daughter and son-in-law had settled and where his lifelong friend Loren Reid remained as a keeper of the rhetorical flame. There at the edge—a place between the Midwest and the South where the alien continental plates grind and shift in ceaseless struggle—Waldo found a new home. It was neither the Midwest of his youth nor the voluptuous sleeping South of Louisiana, but a place where both worlds were locked in struggle. Waldo called me once from Columbia urging me not to tell his old colleagues that he was no longer well. "But, Waldo, they want to come and see you, especially if you cannot walk," I urged him. "No, I couldn't stand that," said he; "you see I always want them to think of me at my best."[15]

THE EVOLUTION OF BRADEN'S THOUGHT

Waldo Braden's scholarly world changed from a world of solid things into a world of frames, mind-states, community formulas, metaphors, and myths. The early Braden studied discrete texts, manifestos, broadsides, diaries, treatises, resolutions, laws, debates, and edicts. He believed that these were the decisive pieces of discourse, for they were the things that directly affected the lives of a people. Braden was fond of saying that we should direct our attention to boilerplate political communication. He had a barely disguised contempt for those rhetoricians who studied historical novels, ceremonial speeches, and pageant discourse. "One can enjoy poetry or listen to stories, but to reckon upon them like varieties of tobacco is perverse," he told me. He argued that one should look at the talk of powerful people and at the records of that talk. Like Rod Hart, Braden firmly believed that scholars should pay attention to words that have consequences for war and peace, confiscation of our money and resources, redistribution of power, and the life chances of our children and our social class. "In literature one must believe in fate to have a tragedy. It's not so in life, and that was my point; we can choose our fate. That is what I've believed," said Waldo, speaking of his early career.

Braden's fascination with Mississippi as "a closed society" changed all that. According to him, Mississippi had developed a public culture that was "modern in form" but feudal in substance. He had been impressed by R. W. Southern's

The Making of the Middle Ages and adopted Southern's thesis that much power flows beyond the government and its official works.[16] He noted that there were many private spaces and clandestine arenas in which power was exercised. Like Michael Shapiro and Deanne Neabauer, Braden came to believe in the limits of the state, that only societal agreement of limits and cultural confinements make governance possible in the first place.[17] He began to read Durkheim and Joseph Campbell. This was a difficult matter for a man who had always worried about "going soft," and he still brooded about the great sea change in the field "away from studying the discourse of great men in formal settings," to what he called the "inchoate bleating of unhappy couples" and "the small group industry who wish to enrich themselves in corporate commerce." He despised anything that might be seen as entertainment, and once he shouted at me that no human activity achieved spiritual dignity until it could be properly called work, a very unSouthern attitude by his lights.

Waldo had a great thirst to understand. From the late 1960s onward he felt that a large part of actual social change could not be explained by a narrow concentration on institutional rhetoric. He broke through his earlier beliefs about the crucial importance of the routines of historical scholarship. "They have their myths, too" became a favorite saying of his. He no longer believed that his job centered on setting the record straight about who said what to whom with what effect. "When I was a young man, I looked only at the pictures," he expostulated. "Now I look increasingly at the frames." In particular, Waldo castigated the myth of Western development inherited from the Enlightenment. He had once believed that we were on a rational and utilitarian path from the local and the tribal, to the rational and the universal. Then he had believed that the South was an atavism, a temporary obstacle to the triumph of the truly modern state. We were headed toward a global state in which regional peculiarities would soon be melted down. "I was a literal-minded Hegelian," said Braden, who had been hugely taken with Christopher Berry's famous monograph "From Hume to Hegel," which appeared in *The Journal of the History of Ideas* in October 1977.[18] Berry has always argued that diversity and empiricism did not lead to relativism, that the "local" custom never really dies out but is merely transmuted to other forms. Berry also maintains that societies can contain all sorts of apparent contradictions and subcultural islands. Waldo had always wondered about the remarkable persistence of what he believed were anachronistic ideas in the American South, and Berry's work confirmed this unevenness. Finally, Braden concluded that Southern folkways, attitudes, and beliefs were preserved by the presence of mediating concepts. Just as Hume understood the Amerinds by comparing them to the ancient Germans, Southerners fashioned paradigms of conduct like the "Marble Man," Robert E. Lee. "Progress" and "science" were other paradigmatic norms that hierarchically ordered the diverse world. Thus, "taste" recognized diversity without surrendering its social authority to it.

In his final years Braden said that his scholarship had been a quest for community. He wanted to find his identity and his people in a strange land. He believed that the community "extends" the self into the remote past and through its aspirations for its future. The community "frames" or, as Waldo would have said, "recontextualizes" all common objects and individual acts. He confessed to me that until he served in the armed forces, he had not realized what it meant to be an American. "All we ill-assorted farm boys, factory workers, and dead-end kids were given a template of conduct that we imposed on our civilian personalities. The youth who had been dipped in fundamentalism and the village atheist wore the masks of dog-faced soldiers in brutal solidarity." He told me that "everybody needs a tribe. Otherwise your words fall on the wind."

THE IDEA OF LIMITS

Braden was fascinated by the work of Richard Weaver, but he always spoke of Weaver as "an innocent man." Weaver's Platonic conception of community as "an order of goods" in which values could be placed in neat hierarchies struck Braden as absurd. Weaver's separation of dialectic and rhetoric or rhetoric as the handmaiden of a prior dialectic showed only that Weaver had never been forced to spend "a lot of time around half-wits."

Braden believed that the process of adjudicating values was the very warp and woof of rhetoric. One's bedrock axioms did not lie beneath the protective cover of rhetoric. For Braden, there was no point where the mind stopped and the heart took over. "The problem is as old as Aristotle. The old Stagirite knew that if you chose one good thing you could not choose another. He did not believe in Utopia like his mater. He knew that if you got too much of freedom you lost order. And if you really got justice, you destroyed the license of the hero or the enterprise of the rich."

Braden taught that if you got too much of one good thing, you had to forsake another good thing. The world was a world of limits. Thus, Braden's "trade-offs" were fully illustrated in his attitude toward Southern myth. Southern myth was a popular conspiracy to hide conflicts between values. It was a practical device but ultimately unstable. The myth of the Old South was a "desperate" attempt to reconcile the irreconcilable notions of liberty and slavery, of nullification and liberty, of patriotism and states' rights.

In dismissing the very notion of a distinctive Southern orator, Braden concludes that the South could not even acknowledge its own pluralism.[19] The core of the South's problem, its escape into myth, its juxtaposition of elegance and brutality, of patriotism and localism lay in its unacknowledged pluralism. Braden's famous collection, *Oratory in the Old South*, is about this failing. Every contributor faults the South for its failure to acknowledge some major policy or value conflict. Southerners attempted to assert nullification while trumpeting their loyalty to the Constitution. They eulogized both freedom and slavery in a social narrative that undermined the very fabric of the larger national ethos.

Braden's fascination and revulsion with myth came from a Middle Border childhood. He had heard how "the dry line" took revenge on his relatives, who were seduced by the maxim that "rain follows the plow" and that the climate would become benign as settlement progressed. He was both fascinated and horrified by public myth. For him myth was a first and last resort of scoundrel rhetors.

Waldo Braden was a scholar whose understanding grew until the very end. He embraced historical method early. Despairing of setting the record straight, he employed myth as a key to understanding. Finally, he used the method against itself to valdiate the importance of day-to-day rhetorical practice grounded in local practice and tangible consequences. He never finished his quest for complete understanding of his craft, but he arrived at a mature and grounded sense of rhetoric and its role in the world. His best work was his last work, the books that appeared posthumously. Like Alexander Stephens, the little Georgian whom he so much admired, Waldo Braden "went out game."

CONCLUSION

I have not written an affectionate "remembrance of things past" such as Waldo's brilliant eagles, Howard Dorgan or Cal Logue, might write. Nor have I written an encomium on the "Arch Realist," as Harold Mixon might have done. I close with an anecdote from the lips of Owen Peterson. It seems that one day Waldo returned from his dean's office and reported that the dean had shown signs of agitation.

Dean: "The provost asked me to write a succinct statement on the nature and purpose of higher education."

Waldo: "That's easy."

Dean: "Not for me. I found myself writing a bitter diatribe on how universities had lost their sense of mission and focus."

Waldo: "That's nonsense. Next time he asks you the purpose of education, say that it is to kindle old dreams in new minds. Tell him that it is about intellectual immortality."

Later, Waldo told Professor Owen Peterson that he had set him (the dean) straight on a very important matter. Waldo believed in the power of the apt word delivered at the opportune time. At certain privileged moments a single, incandescent sentence was better than volumes shouted against the wind. Whatever words are worth, Waldo Braden's words remain with me.

NOTES

1. Ernest Bormann, *The Force of Fantasy: Restoring the American Dream* (Carbondale and Edwardsville: Southern Illinois University Press, 1985). Braden praised this as the paradigmatic book of the new age. In his view, the "new" books would exploit a single methodology or theory across a varied range of texts.

2. Waldo Braden, *The Oral Tradition in the South* (Baton Rouge and London: Louisiana State University Press, 1983).

3. The circle theory of organizations was developed by Charles King, former creative director of Gray Advertising, in 1978. It has since become a familiar feature in books on organizational culture, organizational communication, and business communication. The theory states that people within an organization are more strongly influenced by internal political struggles than by the messages of their clients, customers, and other external constituencies.

4. Waldo Braden, *Oratory in the New South* (Baton Rouge and London: Louisiana State University Press, 1979).

5. In an even more famous article, "Myths in a Rhetorical Context," *Southern Speech Communication Journal* 40 (Winter 1975), 113–126, Braden served as an inspiration for rhetorical scholars. As years passed, he deepened and enriched the concept with the submyths, countermyths, and myths that operated in tandem.

6. Braden, *New South*, p. 10.

7. Like most rhetors of his age, Braden was dipped in Greco-Roman rhetorical categories. He resisted the ahistorical ethos of myth by assimilating it to temporal events and situational structures.

8. Braden, *New South*, p. 8.

9. Waldo Braden, *Abraham Lincoln: Public Speaker* (Baton Rouge and London: Louisiana State University Press, 1988), p. 2.

10. Waldo Braden, *Building the Myth: Selected Speeches Memorializing Abraham Lincoln* (Urbana and Chicago: University of Illinois Press, 1990).

11. Ibid., p. 10.

12. Braden, *Oral Tradition*, p. 21.

13. Braden, *Lincoln: Public Speaker*, p. 14.

14. For the best expression of this postmodern personality, see Douglas Madsen and Peter G. Snow, *The Charismatic Bond: Political Behavior in Time of Crisis* (Cambridge: Harvard University Press, 1991). In this book personality is dissolved into context, a concept that Braden with his individualistic, depression upbringing resisted all his life.

15. Conversation with Waldo Braden. Diary in possession of author.

16. Robert W. Southern, *The Making of the Middle Ages* (New Haven, CT, and London: Yale University Press, 1953). See pp. 80–81 for a succinct statement of the theory.

17. Michael Shapiro and Deanne Neabauer, *Contending Sovereignties* (Los Angeles: UCLA Press, 1982). Their characteristic expression of politics as "an art of confinement" was adopted by Braden.

18. Christopher J. Berry, "From Hume to Hegel," *Journal of the History of Ideas* (October 1977), p. 694.

19. Waldo Baden, *Oratory in the Old South* (Baton Rouge: Louisiana State University Press, 1970), p. 18.

SELECTED BIBLIOGRAPHY

Bormann, Ernest. *The Force of Fantasy: Restoring the American Dream*. Carbondale and Edwardsville: Southern Illinois University Press, 1985.

Braden, Waldo. *Abraham Lincoln: Public Speaker*. Baton Rouge and London: Louisiana State University Press, 1988.

————. "American Public Address as a Humane Study." *Speech Teacher* 23 (March 1974), pp. 109–114.

————. *Building the Myth: Selected Speeches Memorializing Abraham Lincoln.* Urbana and Chicago: University of Illinois Press, 1990.

————. "Eloquence as a Creative Art." *Vital Speeches* 38 (April 15, 1972), pp. 398–401.

————. "The Emergence of the Concept of Southern Oratory." *The Southern Speech Journal* 25 (Summer 1960), pp. 173–183.

————. "Myths in a Rhetorical Context." (1975), pp. 113–126. *Southern Speech Communication Journal* 40 (Winter 1975).

————. "Public Address and the Humanities." *Southern Speech Communication Journal* 41 (Winter 1976), pp. 151–157.

————. *The Oral Tradition in the South.* Baton Rouge and London: Louisiana State University Press, 1983.

————. *Oratory in the New South.* Baton Rouge and London: Louisiana State University Press, 1979.

————. *Oratory in the Old South.* Baton Rouge: Louisiana State University Press, 1970.

————. "The Quest for a New Rhetoric." *Southern Speech Communication Journal* 37 (Spring 1972), pp. 323–326.

————. "Secession Means Disunion: A Speech by Pierre Soule." *Louisiana History* 6 (Winter 1965), pp. 77–82.

————. "Southern Oratory Reconsidered: A Search for an Image." *The Southern Speech Journal* 29 (Summer 1964), pp. 303–315.

————. "Three Southern Readers and Southern Oratory." *Southern Speech Journal* 32 (Fall 1966), pp. 31–40.

Madsen, Douglas, and Peter G. Snow. *The Charismatic Bond: Political Behavior in Time of Crisis.* Cambridge: Harvard University Press, 1991.

Shapiro, Michael, and Deanne Neabauer. *Contending Sovereignties.* Los Angeles: UCLA Press, 1982.

Southern, Robert W. *The Making of the Middle Ages.* New Haven, CT: Yale University Press, 1953.

7

Carroll C. Arnold: Rhetorical Criticism at the Intersection of Theory, Practice, and Pedagogy

Carroll C. Arnold (1912–1997) taught at Cornell University, where he rose from instructor to professor and department chair before joining the faculty of Penn State University in 1963. He retired from Penn State in 1976.

Arnold was an exemplar of the high-water mark of what one of his students, Edwin Black, later called neo-Aristotelian criticism. He wrote influential critical essays on Benjamin Disraeli, Thomas Erskine, George William Curtis, the Senate Committee of Thirteen, and early debates on the constitution in Pennsylvania. As one of the great figures of midcentury rhetorical studies in speech communication, Arnold was a model of balance and disciplinary leadership. In his own work, he envisioned a nearly seamless connection among teaching, writing, editing, and preparation for citizenship. While not himself involved in community politics, he was widely sought for leadership in his department, discipline, and university. Arnold was famous among his colleagues and students as an editor who became virtually a silent coauthor, working line by line to clarify and to press forward on conceptually interesting pathways. As a teacher of group discussion, public speaking, rhetorical theory, and criticism, Arnold engaged with the same intensity. Arnold's written critiques to students reveal an extraordinarily generous sense of the obligations of pedagogy and a level of effort in teaching that would be hard to sustain in a contemporary research university.

In his criticism and in later writings on rhetorical theory and the methods of rhetorical criticism, Arnold followed the implications of a deep belief in a series of related propositions. He thought that rhetoric properly concerned matters that were public and expedient. He believed that when public debaters (or rhetorical

Carroll C. Arnold. Photo courtesy of Thomas W. Benson, The Pennsylvania State University photo service. Used with permission.

critics) invoked primarily moral or ethical justifications, they were likely to derail the possibility for public consensus and reasonable judgment. Speakers and critics needed to take into account both the generic resources of rhetorical craft and the best contemporary findings about the psychology of audiences. Public speaking, for Arnold, was the model of rhetorical performance, with persuasion as its end. Though their methods might differ, rhetorical criticism and the social scientific study of communication sought, in principle, the same sort of knowledge and belonged together as modes of intellectual inquiry. The role of the rhetorical critic was to judge the probable efficacy of a speaker's choices from among available alternatives and to contribute to gradually enlarged understandings of persuasion.

Yet Arnold, though seemingly never self-doubting or self-contradictory, was more complex than a doctrinal summary might suggest. He possessed extraordinary intellectual self-confidence, which he not only employed in his own writings but extended to others—he encouraged his own students to develop radically different methods from those that he championed. His keen intelligence, commonsense empiricism, and growing philosophical curiosity led him to see the world of rhetorical action both as deeply rooted in day-to-day action and as revealing, through practical human engagement, important truths about what it means to be human.

In this chapter, I set Arnold in the context of rhetorical criticism of his time; see his criticism as part of his larger intellectual engagement as teacher, author, and editor; and engage in close reading of several of his exemplary essays in rhetorical criticism.

RHETORIC AS PUBLIC AND EXPEDIENT

Arnold understood rhetoric as a practical human activity, an art designed to exert social force. He followed his understanding of Aristotle's *Rhetoric* in believing that rhetorical action was best employed when the speaker appealed for a decision about matters that could be decided by appeal to common standards of practical judgment, though he was convinced that public judgment is as much emotional as it is rational. He rejected notions of faculty psychology that compartmentalized the participants' minds into faculties of reason-emotion-will, and he saw logical, emotional, and personal proofs as ever-present and intermingled in discourse. In Arnold's observation, public debate tended to collapse into an impasse when one side or the other appealed to primarily moral grounds as the basis for making a judgment about a public decision. In his view, when a speaker appealed to morality as the basis for a public decision, the implication—and often the direct claim—was that the opposing side was immoral. Such an accusation was likely to render further discussion useless.

On similar grounds, Arnold advised the rhetorical critic against supposing that ethics ought to be the primary standard for critical judgment. Rhetorical criticism, in Arnold's view, was properly interested in assessing the artfulness with which a speaker employed rhetorical means to achieve a chosen effect. In his book on *Criticism of Oral Rhetoric*, Arnold wrote, "Ethical principles are principles according to which moral 'goods' and 'bads' are measured; rhetorical and speech norms are propositions that identify possibilities achievable within particular kinds of communicative interactions."[1] Arnold's was a speaker-centered criticism, both because he saw criticism as contributing to a body of knowledge that could support advice to speakers and because he understood rhetoric as a body of knowledge that was not itself capable of judging on ethical grounds the ends or means chosen by the speaker.

In his critical essays, Arnold illustrated his conviction that the rhetorical critic was properly concerned with rhetorical art, not with a speaker's ethics or politics. In his essay on Lord Thomas Erskine, Arnold observes that "we are in some danger of submerging [Erskine's] claim to greatness as a forensic *artist* beneath our enthusiasm for the political ideals into which his art breathed new life and vigor in an important but limited set of trials."[2] At the same time, Arnold, within the boundaries of what he took to be rhetorical art, was quite willing to render judgments. Though he celebrated Erskine's courtroom speeches, Arnold found that when Erskine was elevated to the House of Lords, his parliamentary speeches were of little interest. Arnold writes that "it was as if his wonted unity of thought, harmony of methods, and functionalism in style had been left among his briefs and law books. In Parliament he cluttered his speeches with *ad hominem* arguments, sprinkled them with lumbering quotations from Dr. Johnson, with commentary to match, and only now and then revealed his real powers in a telling proof of expediency or inexpediency."[3]

Despite his view that a critic should typically accept a speaker's ends as a given, Arnold's view of the responsibilities of rhetorical practice was broad, and his own critical work is full of ethical probes, as, for example, in his evident disappointment at the rhetoric of George William Curtis, in which he found a bland conservatism and the lack of a "vigorous and decisive effort to remake the future."[4]

Although he advised against short-circuiting rhetorical criticism by an appeal to predetermined ethical or political judgments, Arnold followed his own speaker-centered logic in trying to understand what personal attributes or learned skills might contribute to a speaker's success or failure. This interest in discovering the nature and sources of a speaker's craft was characteristic of an era in the discipline in which senior research professors routinely taught not only graduate seminars but also the beginning course in public speaking. The issues of how a speaker learned the skills of communicating effectively and the identification of those skills were of daily salience. For some, such a commitment to the relation between instruction and inquiry might have led to a dumbing down of the research agenda, but not for Arnold. He found in practical communication not so much a limit as a perspective that led, in his view, to profound understandings of what it means to be human. One of the reasons that Arnold's basic courses in public speaking and group discussion were so exciting and so convincing to undergraduates is that he used every student exercise as the basis for detailed critical inquiry—not simply "correction" of student errors but also reflection on what could be learned about the mysteries of communication from any and every attempt. I saw this at firsthand when, as a graduate student, I team-taught courses in public speaking and small group communication with Arnold. For example, in the group discussion course at Cornell, every student discussion was observed by the class and the instructor—Arnold or me—and recorded on tape. We would then take those tapes home in the evening and write detailed critical analyses of the discussion, running to several single-spaced pages of transcript, analysis, and advice, which were passed out to the class at its next meeting. For a graduate student learning to write rhetorical criticism, it was a memorable apprenticeship.

THE FORCE OF IDEAS AND THE PROBLEM OF EFFECTS

At the heart of rhetorical studies over many centuries has been an embarrassment about how ideas and techniques contribute to rhetorical effects. Rhetoric begins with the claim that practical people use it as a tool to choose among competing claims for public assent. Presumably, those doing the persuading and those doing the deciding are trying to separate the best from the worst claims—based on their merits according to a logic of probabilities. In this sense, content, ideas, and rhetorical rationality govern public choices under ideal circumstances. But if this is so, what is the role of rhetorical technique, of form, of emotion and self-interest in rhetorical training? Are they merely ways of corrupting persuasion, of distracting listeners (as Plato argues in the *Gorgias*), or are they, instead, the tools required to unite logic and human reality in all its complexity (as Aristotle argues in the *Rhetoric*)? Arnold clearly and explicitly declared himself an Aristotelian, in a world that he understood to be divided between Aristotelians and Platonists. Because humans are imperfect, and because the matters about which they persuade are not capable of certain proof, rhetorical practice emerges in an open society, in which, despite our flaws, "things that are true and things that are better are, by their nature, practically always easier to prove and easier to believe in."[5]

Arnold was alert to the sorts of errors that irrationality and sloppy procedure could introduce into rhetoric, but he seems ever to have returned to the power of ideas as the source of rhetorical force. This interest in ideas and Arnold's confidence in rhetoric as the study of how to produce the best possible social outcomes in situations of disagreement seem to have been a core cluster in Arnold's work. The intellectual climate in which Arnold worked—a climate that changed considerably over the course of his long career—both shaped and gave energy to his agenda even as it made theoretical harmony difficult to achieve. For example, Arnold's generation of critics worked with a vocabulary that made "effects" the motive and measure of rhetoric while at the same time it placed ideas and social goods at the center of their inquiries. This was a problem because the language of "effects," carrying the hidden assumptions of an instrumental modernism and a behavioral psychology, tended to suggest that rhetorical action sought effect through technical manipulation and that rhetorical theory sought a technology that could predict persuasive outcomes with something like scientific precision.

Arnold rejected the faculty psychology that divided the human mind into reason, emotion, and will, and he rejected firm distinctions between argument and persuasion as modes of discourse, while at the same time he employed a vocabulary of appeals to logic, emotion, and personal proof. Though deeply rooted in classical rhetorical assumptions and in his practice a rhetorical theorist and critic, Arnold was an enthusiastic supporter of social scientific studies of persuasion, and he resisted a tendency for rhetoric and communication theory to form separate factions within the discipline. Arnold shared with other critics of his generation the attempt to synthesize classical rhetoric and twentieth-century psychology through the practice of rhetorical criticism.

The strains and difficulties of reconciling rhetorical humanism with scientific modernism under the umbrella of a recovered Aristotelian rhetoric showed in the work of the best rhetorical critics of Arnold's period. For example, Marie Hochmuth Nichols's celebrated essay on Abraham Lincoln's First Inaugural Address, published in 1954, sets forth an extended description of the historical moment in which Lincoln came to speak, attempting to place the contemporary reader sufficiently into the situation to appreciate Lincoln's rhetorical achievement. Nichols's essay is rightly regarded as a classic attempt to provide a situated analysis of an important speech and to assess the issue of effects. But the essay is also a famous example of the anxieties and ambiguities of effects criticism. Nichols specifically requires of herself an evaluation of the speech that differs from that of the literary critic and the historian interested in long-range cultural values. "We must," says Nichols, evaluate the speech "as a speech, a medium distinct from other media, and with methods peculiarly its own. We must be concerned with discovering in this particular case 'the available means of persuasion' and with evaluating their worth."[6]

Nichols offers several fundamentally different versions of what she takes to be Lincoln's purpose. In one passage, she says that Lincoln "intended to take the occasion of the inauguration to declare the position of the Republican party in regard to the South, to announce his considered judgment in regard to the practical questions raised by the movement of secession, and, in all, to give what assurance he could of his personal integrity."[7] Nichols's orator is a fully purposive agent, whose intentions the critic may determine from intrinsic and extrinsic evidence. Note the operating verbs attributed as Lincoln's purposes in this passage: "to declare . . . to announce . . . to give assurance." These purposes are achievable entirely through utterance—that is, Lincoln may achieve them simply by performing the verbal acts of declaring, announcing, and giving assurance. But the analysis goes further. With respect to such purposes, Nichols puts herself in the position of assessing "effect" as an artistic issue—that is, judging the ways in which Lincoln employs the resources of rhetoric, of the situation, and of language "to declare . . . to announce . . . and to give assurance."

Elsewhere in her analysis, Nichols defines rhetorical effects not merely as the achievement of excellence but also in terms of influence over an audience, showing us how Lincoln attempts to "conciliate," to "touch off favorable responses," and even "to control the behavior of his audience." Indeed, she concludes her essay with a considerably expanded suggestion as to Lincoln's purpose, framed as an effect upon his audience, an effect that he failed to achieve. "Lincoln," writes Nichols, "had sought to save the Union by carefully reasoned argument, by regard for the feelings and rights of all the people, and by a solemn avowal of justice and integrity. That the inaugural alone could not prevent the war is surely insufficient ground to condemn it for ineptness."[8]

Nichols's analysis is by no means simple, though it strikes me, in some ways, as, necessarily, an unsatisfactory one. The reader can sense her struggle to reconcile a complex set of circumstances with an emerging theory of rhetoric, to find some consistency in competing vocabularies. Nichols's agenda of separating rhetorical criticism from literary and historical analysis seems at every turn in danger of becoming, somehow, both literary and historical. Her artistic analysis, however, is not what she would call literary since it is always framed in terms of putting rhetorical art to the purpose of immediate, situated, public use. Her historical analysis of effect differs from the view that she attributes to the historian, who redeems the speech from its immediate failure of effect by referring to its long-term effects. Nichols argues that the speech succeeded as a work of practical rhetorical *art*, while it failed in its immediate *effects*—the attempt to prevent the war.

Nichols attempts to synthesize the language of art with the language of social science to arrive at a vocabulary for rhetorical criticism. The attempted synthesis is suggested, for example, in this description of Lincoln's delivery: "With dignity and firmness coupled with mildness and humility, he sought to enforce his plea by those powers that reside in personality. That they have stimulus value one can scarcely question."[9] The vocabulary of "enforce," "powers," and especially "stimulus value" gestures toward the empiricism of social science, but empiricism is trumped by what follows in the same sentence, when we are told that "one can scarcely question." Questioning the alleged effect is, of course, precisely the point. Nichols has shown us that Lincoln's effort to be practical has led him to be artistic. But she has not shown that his art led to practical effect. Indeed, in explaining the speech's lack of a sufficient immediate effect, Nichols evokes a standard of judgment found neither in art nor in social science but in a retrospective political and moral judgment. If I read Nichols correctly, the speech ought to have worked, not only because Lincoln used rhetoric to do everything that rhetoric could do but also because Lincoln was right—he not only seemed to be but was reasonable, just, and brave. The Southern audience not only failed to be sufficiently affected but *chose* to reject Lincoln's appeal to save the Union. "The South," writes Nichols, "accepted the burden of [Lincoln's] challenge," the challenge—and here she quotes Lincoln—that "[i]n *your* hands my dissatisfied fellow countrymen, and not in *mine*, is the momentous issue of civil war."[10] Now it is certainly possible to accuse Nichols here of importing unargued moral and political standards or even regional bias into her analysis. It is possible, too, to argue that she rescues her synthesis of art and social science, a synthesis that somehow failed to work in the practical world, not by admitting Lincoln's rhetorical failure—as effects criticism would seem to require her to do—but by condemning the South for moral stubbornness or worse. But if Nichols may be accused of inconsistency, she may also be said to be demonstrating for us, admittedly unintentionally but with absolute fidelity to her good sense, that here, at the high tide of effects criticism, is a fully autonomous audience responding as it chooses.

Looking back over several decades, Nichols's essay appears to cry out for a more rigorous theorizing of its vocabulary and its premises, but we should perhaps remind ourselves that the encounter of a critical intelligence and a lively historical imagination makes the need for such theorizing evident. Theory and criticism need each other, and both appear to require the complexity that arises from taking into account the untidy contingencies of historical situations. I mean to convey my sense of the theoretical difficulties that a close reading of Nichols's essay reveals, but I mean equally to convey my admiration for her meticulous effort to think through this issue. The challenge to rhetorical theory that is posed by Nichols's essay is made possible because her essay is a work of criticism rather than a work of theory. It was much easier in 1954, just as it is today, to make a coherent theoretical statement of rhetoric as an art of practical action than it proved for the best critics when confronted with the task of analyzing situated discourses. Nichols's essay on Lincoln could be tidied up and rendered in more consistent theoretical terms, but to do this would make it less interesting both as criticism and as theory.

The problems illustrated in Marie Hochmuth Nichols's analysis of Lincoln's First Inaugural Address were faced by the best critics of her generation, including Carroll Arnold. These critics attempted to develop in critical essays and sometimes in theoretical works a vocabulary that could give a convincing account of rhetoric as a practical art aimed at immediate effects. During Arnold's early career, rhetorical criticism emerged as an intellectual practice central to uniting the discipline and driving it forward. The work of these critics attempted to hold together a synthesis of three disciplinary strands that a generation later seemed in danger of unraveling.[11] These three strands—history of public address, rhetorical criticism, and rhetorical theory—were seen by Arnold, Nichols, and their contemporaries as necessarily united, with rhetorical criticism of historically situated public address, animated by a theoretical curiosity, as the core practice. The practice can be most clearly understood if we look closely at several of Arnold's critical essays.

In his "The Senate Committee of Thirteen: December 6–31, 1860," Arnold investigates the rhetoric of the Senate committee appointed on the eve of the Civil War, just after Lincoln's election, ostensibly to discover whether it was possible to find ways in which the national legislature could usefully address the impending crisis. Arnold finds the situation in most ways not promising, since North and South had by this time taken apparently irreconcilable positions on the issue of "slavery's right to expand" and since "most legislators agreed that the final decision on this issue must come from conventions of the people," rather than from the Congress.[12] The essay begins with narrative and follows a narrative pattern throughout, weaving analysis into the unfolding story of the committee. This practice differs considerably from that followed by many contemporary critics and often imposed by gatekeepers at journals in rhetoric, who—in my view, mistakenly—argue that every critical essay should begin with a clearly stated theoretical question and a review of the relevant theoretical scholarship, to which the criticism is then subordinated as an illustration.[13] None of this apparatus appears in Arnold's essay on the Committee of Thirteen or in his other critical essays. Nevertheless, the entire essay, including its narrative, is governed by the implicit—and sometimes explicit—questions of how to understand the rhetorical practices of the committee and of the Senate debate on the committee from what might be called a theoretical perspective that is woven into the critical and historical work of the essay.

Although arguing that the Committee of Thirteen began with little hope of a compromise, Arnold nevertheless tells his story as a failed search for some way out of the impasse. Arnold's account takes notice of the personal agendas of the various committee members and of the larger historical issues at stake, but he focuses primarily on what he takes to be the rhetorical and communicative dimensions of the committee's work, which are represented in two ways—first, as a search for useful ideas or rhetorical *topoi* to reshape the debate and, second, as a search for procedures that might allow for a solution. Any hope for a solution, Arnold argues, must come from a willingness to frame ideas and arguments that would adapt to the needs of the opposition, and such ideas could emerge only if the committee adopted a procedure that avoided confrontation. Neither of these things happened, and the committee failed, as it was probably doomed to do but from whose experience, Arnold seems to say, we can learn something useful. Arnold combined his analysis of the clash of ideas and procedural rigidity in this observation:

As debaters commonly do, the antagonists in this inconclusive clash [at the opening of the committee's deliberations] assumed their ultimate positions of rhetorical defense. The Southerners took their stand upon legal rights; the Republicans dug in behind a moral justification. For the moment at least each side believed itself impregnably fortressed, and neither was disposed to reconsider any questions of probability or expediency.[14]

Even the border-state compromisers on the committee failed to adapt their ideas and appeals to the circumstances of the moment. "They argued from *topoi* that neither body of partisans accepted. For the centrists, the preservation of the Union was the highest good attainable through political action, but this was a supposition many doubted and some categorically denied."[15] Committee members on all sides seemed not to understand that "[r]hetoric could break the deadlock only by demonstrating that sectional rights and political integrity would be better served through compromise than through action in defense of rights and principles."[16] The rigidity of the committee's rhetoric was matched by the formality of its procedures.

True to the imitative spirit which touched its formation, the new committee aped the Senate in its deliberative procedures. It stifled exploratory impulses under the formality of unneeded parliamentary rules; its suggestions, resolutions, and plans were treated as "bills" to be adopted or rejected by recorded votes, but not, if we may judge from its journal and from public and private reports, to be informally examined, compared, combined, and expanded. The committee's mode of procedure and its accepted mode of discourse encouraged the processes of contention and debate rather than the processes of conciliation.[17]

Arnold's interest in the role of ideas in rhetoric stayed with him throughout his career as a practicing critic. In an early essay, "Invention in the Parliamentary Speaking of Benjamin Disraeli, 1842–1852," based on his University of Iowa dissertation, Arnold puzzled out the problem of how to account for the origins, application, and effects of a speaker's ideas. In Disraeli, he found a speaker whose speaking in the British House of Commons was consistently based in historical premises conceived as organic, thus leading him to "resist all procedural expedients which might weaken, however slightly, the evolved fabric."[18] Despite his evident admiration for some of Disraeli's intellectual achievements as a speaker and for Disraeli's conservatism, Arnold conceded that Disraeli's enthymemes would probably not have appealed to his immediate hearers and that his constructive arguments were overshadowed by the "barbed epigrams and contemptuous sarcasms that were the speaker's forte."[19] Though later biographers and historians granted "Disraeli's claims of personal integrity and consistency," his contemporaries disagreed, partly because "when Disraeli claimed credit for intelligence and acumen, he commonly did so by contrast or as a matter of right, rather than on grounds of reciprocal respect."[20] In this early work, Arnold consistently strives to maintain a rhetorical perspective, and while this permits him to introduce evidence, with admiration and evident approval, as to Disraeli's brilliance and his historical consistency, it forces him to concede the failure of Disraeli's ethical proofs. Nevertheless, Arnold is willing, as was Nichols in her analysis of Lincoln, to suggest that the audience was in some ways myopic: "Apparently his audience took the view that cleverness and brilliance were incompatible with probity."[21]

In "The Speech Style of Benjamin Disraeli," published in the *Quarterly Journal of Speech* in 1947, the same year that the study of Disraeli's invention appeared in *Speech Monographs*, Arnold again investigated the probable origins of the speaker's rhetorical skills, again admired Disraeli's conservatism, and again focused on the role of intellect in oratory. What Arnold finds most striking in Disraeli's style is what he terms "the language of intellection," characterized by "antithesis, anti-climax, humor, satire, and sarcasm," which "rested upon subjectively perceived qualities and abstractions rather than upon sense-perceptions" and which "seldom sought to touch sentiments or emotions through resorting to moralizing verbalisms or Victorian stereotypes."[22]

Arnold's essay on George William Curtis appeared in the third volume of A *History and Criticism of American Public Address*, a series that was intended to create a foundation for the discipline. In this essay Arnold anticipates by several years and perhaps provokes an interest by rhetorical criticism in issues of identification and narration.[23] Arnold agreed with Curtis' description of his own speeches on civic affairs as "lay-sermons" and found in them a self-satisfied secular piety; those favorably disposed to Curtis "did not analyze his logic," and perhaps because they did not study speech after speech, they did not notice the way that Curtis used the same arguments over and over again, suggesting "a certain superficiality in the study and treatment of his subjects."[24] Though Arnold's impatience with Curtis and his admiring audiences shines through clearly, it is also clear that Arnold is pursuing not only judgment but an understanding of what it means to read Curtis *rhetorically*—using the puzzlement of a contemporary reader who sees little to admire in Curtis as a way of provoking inquiry into the speeches as heard from the point of view of their intended audience. Hence, Arnold's assessment is disapproving, but it is also tenacious in pursuing the dynamics of speaker–audience attachment:

If Curtis succeeded with such arguments and evidence as have been described—and he did succeed in a considerable degree—it must have been because he gave dignity and attractiveness and significance to lines of thought toward which his listeners were already favorably disposed. Perhaps, had his inventive powers been greater and more original, he might have discovered fresher and stronger arguments that could move his listeners to act more and decry less; but to reach beyond the mere reinforcement of beliefs, to translate beliefs into energetic action, seems to have been either beyond his rhetorical power or outside his purpose. He was, in short, a ceremonial speaker capable of giving an acceptable dignity and moral tone to almost any theme or occasion. If he did not place a high value upon freshness in argument or upon originality in interpretation, his supporting materials still had a familiar and therefore attractive ring to those already inclined to accept his propositions. Such listeners were only the more disposed to praise his skill in exalting all received values, for they missed not at all the arguments and evidence with which another speaker might have sought to create belief in the unbelieving and turn dissatisfaction into action among the believers.[25]

The failures of Curtis, Arnold argues, were inseparable from his successes— he and his audiences were satisfied with narrow ideas and ceremonial rhetoric. With complacent audiences Curtis achieved a sort of admiration, while at the same time he left untapped the intellectual and rhetorical resources that might have made a lasting difference. In this analysis of Curtis, we see Arnold's discovering something about the nature of rhetorical analysis that is parallel to, but apart from, literature and history; we see him making a contribution to the intellectual vigor of his chosen discipline while at the same time insisting, at least implicitly, that the best theory ought to speak to present practice and that the work of professors is addressed not only to fellow professors but to students.

Arnold's essay on "Lord Thomas Erskine, Modern Advocate," published in 1958, again shows a biographical and historical focus that was characteristic of public address criticism of the era. But, as with his other essays, Arnold found himself attracted to the force of ideas that were given life by rhetorical art. Arnold found that Erskine gave his speeches a "distinctive congruity," writing,

The most striking elements in this consonance of matter and manner seem to me to be three: his ability, within a single speech, to direct effective persuasion toward the predispositions of judges and jurors even when these two classes of auditors were differently inclined; the entire harmony of language, thought, and purpose which marks all his pleas; and, above all else, his ability to discover and make inescapable the *public* significance of each case for which he accepted a brief.[26]

In Erskine, according to Arnold, rhetorical perspective-taking, rhetorical art, and a grand idea were united. In his essay on Erskine, one senses the continual maturation of these themes in Arnold's work, which here achieve an expression that is thoroughly focused on rhetorical matters, presses forward an original theoretical perception, and roots it all in close reading of speech texts, in historical context, and in biographical understanding.

Arnold found it especially interesting and significant that Erskine's courtroom speeches "suggested strongly but indirectly that judge and juror ought to *make* law, ought to refashion social patterns by *creating* precedents." This worked partly because of Erskine's skillful use of suggestion, indirection, and *insinuatio* and partly because of the predispositions of Erskine's audiences. Arnold observes that "jurors almost always, and judges very often, actively desire to influence the future, even though they know, intellectually, that they are expected to render decisions according to law and precedent alone. To put the matter another way, Erskine tempted his courtroom 'deciders' to become policy makers too, a temptation few men even desire to resist."[27] How had Arnold come to this perception of Erskine's method? We can never really know, but looking back on this essay forty years after it was published, one sees how much it is influenced by deep reflection on Aristotle's notion of the difference between forensic and deliberative genres, which Erskine so successfully violated. One wonders, too, how much Arnold's own political conservatism, in the years of the Warren Court and just following the Supreme Court's *Brown v. Board of Education* school integration decision, alerted him to what political conservatives in his own day were calling "strict constructionism" in an attempt to undermine what they thought of as an unduly activist and liberal Supreme Court. But if a "strict constructionist" sensibility partly guided Arnold to his insight into Erskine's methods, there is no trace of any deliberate political agenda in Arnold's essay; he is content to try to understand the dynamics of persuasion without imposing his own political views on Erskine or on his own readers. One can perhaps detect in this essay an underlying dynamic in which Arnold himself, brought to an insight about Erskine by his own political convictions, which lend the essay a special energy, nevertheless resists the temptation to render a decision that goes beyond the domain of the rhetorical. Readers today may object that Arnold's apparent restraint was itself a political decision, and I suppose he would have agreed to that, but I think he would still have maintained that he was working on rhetorical rather than political grounds and that outright political argument in a work of rhetorical criticism was inappropriate, not only because the rhetorical critic was not necessarily an authority on ethics or politics but also because, as a teacher—and Arnold was always a teacher, in the class-room or in a scholarly essay—it would be professionally unethical to advance a political agenda under the cover of a scholarly argument.

Late in life, long after he retired, Arnold contributed a chapter to a volume of studies in American public address that was conceived as a tribute to his colleague at Penn State, Eugene White. Arnold's "Early Constitutional Rhetoric in Pennsylvania" is an account of the seven debates in Pennsylvania in the period 1776–1790 over the formation of a state constitution. Arnold traces the competing claims and counterclaims of those who supported and those who urged amendment of the Frame of 1776, as the first of these constitutions is called. This is a masterful essay, lucidly tracing the shifting arguments and cast of characters through a period of rapid change and at the same time giving detailed narrative texture to Arnold's conviction, articulated early in his career and matured over decades, that public argument works best when, as in this case, "men finally taught themselves that a reality of democratic self-government is that the end of parliamentary procedures is to generate creative responses to the will of the popular majority, after terminable consideration of alternatives." Arnold teaches us to admire the way in which "conciliation, responsiveness to popular opinion, and regard for pragmatic necessities were by 1790 raised to high status among political values," and he singles out for special admiration James Wilson of Philadelphia and William Findley of Westmoreland County, who eventually succeeded because "each displayed from the beginning of his career personal integrity, respect for the legitimating powers of political procedures, and greater concern for ideas than for personalities."[28]

In the critical essays discussed here, as well as in a parallel series of theoretical and speculative essays, Arnold remained true to a core commitment to devote his intellectual energies to understanding what it means for humans to govern themselves through persuasion. In his view, the field of speech communication, as it came to be called, was one and not many disciplines, though Arnold's vision of the unity of the field left considerable room for diversity of views and methods. Arnold counseled that, in rhetorical studies, history, theory, and criticism were complementary enterprises; in academic life, teaching, research, and pragmatic advice about the conduct of public discourse were inseparable and mutually enriching obligations.

Arnold's work helped to advance the intellectual respectability and the organizational integrity of an emerging discipline. His published work richly and originally demonstrates what it means to think about public action from a rhetorical perspective. Many of the views that he advanced most fervently have been questioned by the generations that succeeded his, but this is the natural condition of a living intellectual practice. For scholars as well as for public advocates, Arnold teaches us, the obligation is not to settle a question for all time but to provide contributions that enhance the ongoing conversation while maintaining the values and institutions that make rhetorical and academic practice possible.

NOTES

1. Carroll C. Arnold, *Criticism of Oral Rhetoric* (Columbus, OH: Charles E. Merrill, 1974), 273.

2. Carroll C. Arnold, "Lord Thomas Erskine, Modern Advocate," *Landmark Essays on Rhetorical Criticism*, ed. Thomas W. Benson (Davis, CA: Hermagoras Press, 1993), 91.

3. Ibid., 101–102.

4. Carroll C. Arnold, "George William Curtis," *History and Criticism of American Public Address*, vol. 3, ed. Marie Hochmuth Nichols (New York: Longmans, Green, 1955), 162.

5. Aristotle, *Rhetoric*, trans. W. Rhys Roberts, *The Oxford Translations of Aristotle*, vol. 2, ed. W. D. Ross (Oxford: Clarendon Press, 1925), 1355a–1355b; quoted in Arnold, *Criticism of Oral Rhetoric*, 273. Arnold goes beyond the Plato–Aristotle pair in Carroll C. Arnold and Kenneth D. Frandsen, "Conceptions of Rhetoric and Communication," *Handbook of Rhetorical and Communication Theory*, ed. Carroll C. Arnold and John Waite Bowers (Boston: Allyn and Bacon, 1984), 3–50.

6. Marie Hochmuth Nichols, "Lincoln's First Inaugural," *Landmark Essays in Rhetorical Criticism*, ed. Thomas W. Benson (1954; rpt. Davis, CA: Hermagoras Press, 1993), 77. Nichols' essay was first published in *American Speeches*, ed. Wayland Maxfield Parrish and Marie Hochmuth Nichols (New York: David McKay, 1954), 60–100.

7. Nichols, 79.

8. Ibid., 79, 80, 86, 88.

9. Ibid., 88.

10. Ibid.

11. On the sometimes problematic relations of theory, criticism, and history in rhetorical studies, see Barnet Baskerville, "Must We All Be 'Rhetorical Critics'?" *Quarterly Journal of Speech* 63 (1977): 107–116; Thomas W. Benson, "History, Criticism, and Theory in the Study of American Rhetoric," *American Rhetoric: Context and Criticism*, ed. Thomas W. Benson (Carbondale: Southern Illinois University Press, 1989), 1–17; Thomas W. Benson, "Beacons and Boundary-Markers: Landmarks in Rhetorical Criti-

cism," *Landmark Essays on Rhetorical Criticism*, ed. Thomas W. Benson (Davis, CA: Hermagoras Press, 1993), xi–xxii; James Darsey, "Must We All Be Rhetorical Theorists? An Anti-Democratic Inquiry," *Western Journal of Communication* 58 (1988): 164–181; Roderick P. Hart, "Contemporary Scholarship in Public Address: A Research Editorial," *Western Journal of Speech Communication* 50 (1986): 283–295; Roderick P. Hart, "Doing Criticism My Way: A Reply to Darsey," *Western Journal of Communication* 58 (1994): 308–312; Roderick P. Hart, "Theory-Building and Rhetorical Criticism: An Informal Statement of Opinion," *Central States Speech Journal* 27 (1976): 70–77.

12. Carroll C. Arnold, "The Senate Committee of Thirteen, December 6–31, 1860," *Anti-Slavery and Disunion, 1858–1861*, ed. J. Jeffery Auer (New York: Harper and Row, 1963), 311.

13. I am not arguing against "theory" nor even against theory-driven criticism but against a gatekeeping practice that would require all criticism to proceed according to a single generic model.

14. Arnold, "The Senate Committee," 317.

15. Ibid., 318.

16. Ibid., 329.

17. Ibid.

18. Arnold, "Invention in the Parliamentary Speaking of Benjamin Disraeli, 1842–1852," *Speech Monographs* 14 (1947): 70.

19. Ibid., 77.

20. Ibid., 78.

21. Ibid. In another passage, Arnold even comments, "To judge what part of his ethical weakness was due to anti-Semitic prejudice would require a study beyond the scope of this paper" (78).

22. Carroll C. Arnold, "The Speech Style of Benjamin Disraeli," *Quarterly Journal of Speech* 33 (1947): 431, 435–436.

23. Kenneth Burke had by this time published his major work on rhetoric as identification, though in 1956 Burke had not been widely acknowledged among rhetorical critics working in speech departments. Burke's *Philosophy of Literary Form* had appeared in 1941; his *Grammar of Motives* in 1945; and *Rhetoric of Motives* in 1950. Marie Hochmuth [Nichols] published "Kenneth Burke and the 'New Rhetoric' " in the *Quarterly Journal of Speech* in 1952. Walter Fisher's influential *Human Communication as Narration* was published in 1987. Since the publication of Edwin Black's *Rhetorical Criticism*, the three-volume *History and Criticism of American Public Address*, whose influence had only begun to be felt in the journals, the folkloric history of the discipline has regarded the *History and Criticism* as something of a dinosaur, relegated to the dustbin of an outmoded neo-Aristotelianism. The folklore became in some ways self-fulfilling, and yet much in these volumes anticipates later developments in the discipline. On the influence of Burke in speech communication, see Herbert W. Simons and Trevor Melia, eds., *The Legacy of Kenneth Burke* (Madison: University of Wisconsin Press, 1989); on the early Burke, see Jack Selzer, *Kenneth Burke in Greenwich Village* (Madison: University of Wisconsin Press, 1996).

24. Arnold, "Curtis," 162, 167.

25. Ibid., 168.

26. Arnold, "Erskine," 92.

27. Ibid., 93.

28. Carroll C. Arnold, "Early Constitutional Rhetoric in Pennsylvania," *American*

Rhetoric: Context and Criticism, ed. Thomas W. Benson (Carbondale: Southern Illinois University Press, 1989), 192–193.

BIBLIOGRAPHY

Aristotle. *Rhetoric*. Trans. W. Rhys Roberts. *The Oxford Translations of Aristotle*, vol. 2. Ed. W. D. Ross. Oxford: Clarendon Press, 1925.

Arnold, Carroll C. "The Case Against Speech: An Examination of Critical Viewpoints." *Quarterly Journal of Speech* 40 (1954): 165–169.

Arnold, Carroll C. *Criticism of Oral Rhetoric*. Columbus, OH: Charles E. Merrill, 1974.

Arnold, Carroll C. "Debates in the Constitutional Conventions: Constitutional Eccentricity." *A History of Public Speaking in Pennsylvania*. Ed. DeWitte Holland and Robert T. Oliver. Philadelphia: Pennsylvania Speech Association, n.d.

Arnold, Carroll C. "Debates in the Constitutional Conventions: Ritual and Deliberation." *A History of Public Speaking in Pennsylvania*. Ed. DeWitte Holland and Robert T. Oliver. Philadelphia: Pennsylvania Speech Association, n.d.

Arnold, Carroll C. "Early Constitutional Rhetoric in Pennsylvania." *American Rhetoric: Context and Criticism*. Ed. Thomas W. Benson. Carbondale: Southern Illinois University Press, 1989, 131–200.

Arnold, Carroll C. "Editor's Foreword." *Early English Reading Theory*. Ed. David Bartine. Columbia: University of South Carolina Press, 1989, vi–vii.

Arnold, Carroll C. "Foreword." *The Context of Human Discourse*. Ed. Eugene E. White. Columbia: University of South Carolina Press, 1992, vii–viii.

Arnold, Carroll C. "George William Curtis." *A History and Criticism of American Public Address*, vol. 3. Ed. Marie Hochmuth. New York: Longmans, Green, 1955, 133–174.

Arnold, Carroll C. "Goodrich Revisited." *Quarterly Journal of Speech* 48 (1962): 13–14.

Arnold, Carroll C. "Herbert August Wichelns (1894–1973)." *Southern Communication Journal* 47 (1982): 124–130.

Arnold, Carroll C. "Invention in the Parliamentary Speaking of Benjamin Disraeli, 1842–1852." *Speech Monographs* 14 (1947): 66–80.

Arnold, Carroll C. "Johnstone's 'Wedge' and Theory of Rhetoric." *Philosophy and Rhetoric* 20 (1987): 118–128.

Arnold, Carroll C. "Lord Thomas Erskine: Modern Advocate." *Quarterly Journal of Speech* 44 (1958): 17–30.

Arnold, Carroll C. "The Nature of Speaking-Listening Man and His Works." *Today's Speech* 8 (September 1960): 23–25.

Arnold, Carroll C. "Oral Rhetoric, Rhetoric, and Literature." *Philosophy and Rhetoric* 1 (1968): 191–210.

Arnold, Carroll C. "Reader or Listener? Oral Composition." *Today's Speech* 13 (February 1965): 5–7.

Arnold, Carroll C. "Reflections on American Public Discourse." *Communication Studies* 28 (1977): 73–85.

Arnold, Carroll C. "Reflections on the Wingspread Conference." *The Prospect of Rhetoric*. Ed. Lloyd F. Bitzer and Edwin Black. Englewood Cliffs, NJ: Prentice-Hall, 1971, 194–199.

Arnold, Carroll C. "Rhetoric." *International Encyclopedia of Communications*. Vol. 3. Ed. Erik Barnouw. New York: Oxford University Press, 1989, 461–465.

Arnold, Carroll C. "Rhetorical and Communication Studies: Two Worlds or One?" *Western Journal of Speech Communication* 36 (1972): 75–81.

Arnold, Carroll C. "The Senate Committee of Thirteen: December 6–31, 1860." *Antislavery and Disunion, 1858–1861*. Ed. J. Jeffery Auer. New York: Harper and Row, 1963, 310–330.

Arnold, Carroll C. "The Speech Style of Benjamin Disraeli." *Quarterly Journal of Speech* 33 (1947): 427–436.

Arnold, Carroll C. "What's Reasonable?" *Today's Speech* 19 (Summer 1971): 19–23.

Arnold, Carroll C., and John Waite Bowers, eds. *Handbook of Rhetorical and Communication Theory*. Boston: Allyn and Bacon, 1984.

Arnold, Carroll C., and Kenneth D. Frandsen. "Conceptions of Rhetoric and Communication." *Handbook of Rhetoric and Communication Theory*. Ed. Carroll C. Arnold and John Waite Bowers. Boston: Allyn and Bacon, 1984, 3–50.

Baskerville, Barnett. "Must We All Be 'Rhetorical Critics'?" *Quarterly Journal of Speech* 63 (1977): 107–116.

Benson, Thomas W. "History, Criticism, and Theory in the Study of American Rhetoric." *American Rhetoric: Context and Criticism*. Ed. Thomas W. Benson. Carbondale: Southern Illinois University Press, 1989, 1–17.

Benson, Thomas W. "Beacons and Boundary-Markers: Landmarks in Rhetorical Criticism." *Landmark Essays on Rhetorical Criticism*. Ed. Thomas W. Benson. Davis, CA: Hermagoras Press, 1993, xi–xxii.

Benson, Thomas W., ed. *American Rhetoric: Context and Criticism*. Carbondale: Southern Illinois University Press, 1989.

Benson, Thomas W., ed. *Landmark Essays on Rhetorical Criticism*. Davis, CA: Hermagoras Press, 1993.

Burke, Kenneth. *A Grammar of Motives*. Berkeley: University of California Press, 1969.

Burke, Kenneth. *The Philosophy of Literary Form*. 3d ed. Berkeley: University of California Press, 1973.

Burke, Kenneth. *A Rhetoric of Motives*. Berkeley: University of California Press, 1969.

Cohen, Herman. *The History of Speech Communication: The Emergence of a Discipline, 1914–1945*. Annandale, VA: Speech Communication Association, 1994.

Darsey, James. "Must We All Be Rhetorical Theorists? An Anti-Democratic Inquiry." *Western Journal of Communication* 58 (1988): 164–181.

Douglas, Rodney B., and Carroll C. Arnold. "On Analysis of *Logos*: A Methodological Inquiry." *Quarterly Journal of Speech* 56 (1970): 22–32.

Fisher, Walter R. *Human Communication as Narration*. Columbia: University of South Carolina Press, 1987.

Hart, Roderick P. "Contemporary Scholarship in Public Address: A Research Editorial." *Western Journal of Speech Communication* 50 (1986): 283–295.

Hart, Roderick P. "Doing Criticism My Way: A Reply to Darsey." *Western Journal of Communication* 58 (1994): 308–312.

Hart, Roderick P. "Theory-Building and Rhetorical Criticism: An Informal Statement of Opinion." *Central States Speech Journal* 27 (1976): 70–77.

Hochmuth, Marie. "Kenneth Burke and the 'New Rhetoric.' " *Quarterly Journal of Speech* 38 (1952): 133–144.

Johnstone, Henry W., Jr. "Response." *Philosophy and Rhetoric* 20 (1987): 129–134.

Keltner, John, and Carroll C. Arnold. "Discussion in American Colleges and Universities." *Quarterly Journal of Speech* 42 (1956): 250–256.

Lutz, Jeanne, et al. "From the 50th to the 75th: ECA History through the Eyes of Past Presidents." *Communication Quarterly* 33 (1985): 3–16.

Nichols, Marie Hochmuth. "Lincoln's First Inaugural." *Landmark Essays in Rhetorical Criticism*. Ed. Thomas W. Benson. Davis, CA: Hermagoras Press, 1993, 51–88.

Rosenfield, Lawrence W. "The Terms of Commonwealth: A Response to Arnold." *Communication Studies* 28 (1977): 86–91.

Selzer, Jack. *Kenneth Burke in Greenwich Village*. Madison: University of Wisconsin Press, 1996.

Simons, Herbert W., and Trevor Melia, eds. *The Legacy of Kenneth Burke*. Madison: University of Wisconsin Press, 1989.

Wagner, Russell H., and Carroll C. Arnold. *Handbook of Group Discussion*. 2d ed. Boston: Houghton Mifflin, 1965.

White, Eugene E., ed. *Rhetoric in Transition: Studies in the Nature and Uses of Rhetoric*. University Park: Pennsylvania State University Press, 1980.

Wilson, John F., and Carroll C. Arnold. *Public Speaking as a Liberal Art*. 2d ed. Boston: Allyn and Bacon, 1968.

8

Robert Gray Gunderson: The Historian as Civic Rhetorician

KURT RITTER

In the final years of the twentieth century, two important books on rhetorical studies were published by university presses in the United States. Both are edited volumes of original essays growing out of scholarly conferences held in the 1990s. Both deal with the study of history and public address. Both are dedicated, in whole or in part, to Robert Gray Gunderson.[1] Graduate students entering the field of rhetorical studies in the twenty-first century may well ask: Who was Robert Gray Gunderson? What was his method of rhetorical analysis? What is his legacy in rhetorical studies? This chapter answers those questions.

James Andrews notes that Gunderson launched his academic career during "the formative years of public address scholarship."[2] He influenced the development of rhetorical studies through the substance of his scholarship and through his bold style of writing and teaching. Perhaps the most important theme of Gunderson's scholarship was his concern that American political rhetoric is debased when powerful economic interests manipulate public opinion. Four decades before Kenneth Cmiel set forth his thesis on "the fight over popular speech in nineteenth-century America,"[3] Gunderson was examining the persuasive techniques employed by political bosses seeking to harvest the votes of recently enfranchised American citizens in the presidential campaign of 1840.[4] Gunderson would have agreed with Cmiel that much of American rhetoric was little more than "bromides designed to soothe an audience into complacency or invective essaying to conjure up vague demons."[5] But Gunderson prescribed a different rhetorical medicine to cure that civic illness. Cmiel argues that the rise of the technical discourse of the expert (speaking like a "professional"), the use of the plain style, and especially the rise of colloquial political discourse "all

Robert Gray Gunderson. Photo courtesy of Jeff Gunderson. Used with permission.

corrode civic discourse." He urges his readers to "distrust the colloquial and manage the technical."[6] The thrust of Gunderson's five decades of scholarship was rather the reverse: for democracy to thrive, educators should distrust the rhetoric of the technical professional and should teach citizens how to manage their own popular or colloquial rhetoric.

The bulk of Gunderson's scholarship focused on the political rhetoric of nineteenth-century America—a century that rhetorical scholars Gregory Clark and S. Michael Halloran have characterized as featuring a rise of both individualism and professionalism in rhetorical practice. Gunderson celebrated individualism with (in Clark and Halloran's words) its "rhetoric of the charismatic or representative personality." But Gunderson was troubled when the views of professional experts displaced the voices of ordinary citizens. Like Clark and Halloran, Gunderson believed that "the rhetoric of professional expertise" not only neglects "passion and moral commitment" but also "tends to undermine their legitimacy" in public dialogue.[7] In response, Gunderson advocated rhetorical education and rhetorical scholarship as necessary elements in a democracy. In making his argument, Gunderson functioned as a scholar of both history and speech.

SPEECH PROFESSOR AND HISTORIAN

Robert Gunderson's first publication—a transcript of his speeches in a public debate[8]—appeared in 1937, when he was twenty-one years old, just as he completed his undergraduate degree at the University of Wisconsin. At the time of his death in 1996 at the age of eighty-one years, he was busy working on two book-length biographies. During the intervening six decades, he had published forty-seven articles, eight book chapters, and two university press books. He taught at a prestigious liberal arts college for two decades and then joined the Department of Speech and Theater at a "Big 10" university, where he directed almost fifty doctoral students over the course of four decades.

Throughout his professional life Gunderson managed the tension between dual careers—one as a speech professor and the other as a professional historian. That duality reached back to the University of Wisconsin at Madison, where, after being an active member of the undergraduate debating society, he received his bachelor's degree in 1937 with a major in history and a minor in speech. The next school year (1937–1938) he taught history and speech at Platteville High School in Wisconsin. Gunderson's career as a speech professor began in the summer of 1938, when J. Jeffery Auer, then the chair of the Department of Speech at Oberlin College, offered him a position as an instructor of speech.[9] He remained on the Oberlin faculty for twenty years (including leaves of absence for military service during World War II and subsequent doctoral study). During those two decades, he completed his Ph.D. in speech at the University of Wisconsin, rose in academic rank to professor of speech, and served as chair of the Department of Speech during his final six years at the college. Teaching at a leading liberal arts college at a time when speech was still emerging as an area of study, Gunderson helped secure a place for the discipline in the academy.

In 1958 he joined the faculty of Indiana University as a professor of speech and theater (later of speech communication), where he was the director of graduate studies for twenty years (1958–1977), served a three-year term (1961–1964) as the executive vice president of the Speech Association of America (now the National Communication Association), edited the book review section of the *Quarterly Journal of Speech* for two terms (1957–1963), and then edited that journal for three years (1966–1969).

Upon arriving at Indiana University, Gunderson began directing graduate students in speech; in 1962 his first two doctoral students successfully defended their dissertations. More followed, with Gunderson continuing to direct the dissertations of Ph.D. students in speech communication long after his retirement in 1985. His last two doctoral students completed their degrees in 1993, when Gunderson was seventy-eight years old. Of the forty-nine Ph.D. dissertations that he directed to successful completion, forty-eight were with graduate students in the Department of Speech Communication (or the Department of Speech and Theater, as it was called in the 1960s). A number of those graduate students earned dual degrees in speech communication and American studies, but only one of Gunderson's Ph.D. students was outside the field of communication—a graduate student with a dual Ph.D. in English and American studies.

What for many academics would have been a full career was only half of Gunderson's professional life, for he pursued a simultaneous career as a historian. When he began teaching speech at Oberlin College in 1938, he also enrolled for the M.A. degree in the Department of History at that institution. Having completed his M.A. in history in 1941, he made history the minor field in his doctoral studies in speech at the University of Wisconsin in the mid-1940s. William B. Hesseltine of the Department of History at Wisconsin became Gunderson's mentor and served on his doctoral committee.[10] Primarily a historian of the American South and the Civil War, Hesseltine was unusual among historians because of his interest in speeches as historical artifacts. A prolific author of historical articles and books, his essays also appeared in speech journals and in books on American public address.[11]

Professor Henry L. Ewbank Jr., who earned his Ph.D. in speech at Wisconsin, with Hesseltine on his dissertation committee a few years after Gunderson completed his degree, has noted that Gunderson was "as much a product of the History Department at Wisconsin as he was a doctoral recipient from the Department of Speech."[12] Donald W. Zacharias (an early doctoral student under Gunderson who later served as a university president) recalled that "during our days with Bob Gunderson, we heard stories about the University of Wisconsin and William Hesseltine, probably one of the greatest producers of historians. . . . Robert Gunderson . . . admired him and emulated his professionalism. Those of us who studied under Gunderson have a lot of Hesseltine in us."[13]

Gunderson regularly attended the meetings of historical associations, presented papers to historical groups, and published in historical periodicals. In fact, over the course of his career, half of Gunderson's articles appeared in history journals. He was particularly active in the Organization of American Historians and the Southern History Association. He became an officer in both groups, serving on the executive board of the former during the 1970s and serving as parliamentarian of the latter association well into the 1980s. Among historians, he was best known for his two books—one on the 1840 presidential campaign and the other on a 1861 political conference that constituted the last effort to avert the Civil War.[14]

American historian Martin Ridge remarked in 1997 that "neither of these works have been superseded, nor are they likely to be."[15] Indeed, in 1998— more than forty years after the publication of Gunderson's book on the 1840 presidential campaign—a highly regarded biography of Lincoln was published that relied almost exclusively on Gunderson's work to explain the political and rhetorical context of Lincoln's activities as a Whig Party campaigner in that election.[16] In 1999 Michael F. Holt, the Langbourne M. Williams Professor of American History at the University of Virginia, noted in his definitive book on the American Whig Party that Gunderson's *The Log-Cabin Campaign* "provides the fullest description of the [1840] campaign." He explained to his readers that, "unless otherwise noted, I have taken my information from him [Gunderson]."[17]

After Gunderson had been on the faculty at Indiana University for almost two decades, the Department of History invited him to hold a joint appointment in that unit as well as in the Department of Speech Communication. Gunderson made no effort to hide his dual careers, but neither did he call much attention to it. Beyond the campus of Indiana University, most of his professional colleagues in each of his disciplines were at best dimly aware of his stature in his other discipline. After Gunderson's death, Martin Ridge recalled: "When I came to Indiana thirty years ago, I was astonished to learn that Bob was in the Speech Department. . . . I had met him often at historical society meetings, where he knew everyone." Ridge went on to say that he had "assumed that he was an historian" because Gunderson's two books were "classic historical studies."[18] Similarly, academic colleagues with whom Gunderson interacted at meetings of communication associations generally did not know of Gunderson's faculty appointment in history or that he had been the interim editor of the *Journal of American History* for two years in the 1970s—a circumstance that made Gunderson the only person to have edited leading journals in both speech and history.

When rhetorical studies turned away from the historical study of public address in the 1970s and focused on competing systems of rhetorical theory and criticism, Gunderson found that American studies provided him with an academic vehicle for promoting the study of public address as vital to sustaining democracy. American studies also gave Gunderson a means for uniting his dual careers as both a rhetorical scholar and a historian. He helped to create the interdisciplinary Graduate Program in American Studies at Indiana University during the period of 1961 to 1965, when he served as chair to the university's Committee on American Studies. In particular, he was responsible for initiating its degree Ph.D. program during the 1964–1965 academic year. He fashioned a degree program consistent with his own career, for it did not offer a separate doctoral degree. Instead, a student would earn a dual degree in an established department and in American studies. Upon completing his term as editor of the *Quarterly Journal of Speech* in 1969, Gunderson became director of the American studies program—a duty he continued for ten years.

After retiring in 1985, Gunderson remained professionally active as professor emeritus—working at Indiana University during the Midwest's warm months each year and conducting research at the Huntington Library in southern California during Indiana's cold months. During the last twenty-five years of his life Gunderson suffered from an excruciatingly painful arthritic disease; yet even in retirement, he took joy in participating in the annual meetings of professional associations of historians and communication scholars. For example, in November 1985—during his first semester of "retirement"—he happily limped his way around snow-covered Denver at the annual meeting of the Speech Communication Association and then scrambled on an airplane to fly from Denver to balmy Houston to attend the Southern Historical Association.

Gunderson lived long enough to witness a renaissance in the historical study of American public address,[19] which included books written by his former students.[20] As the author of university press books published in the 1950s and 1960s, Gunderson anticipated that the field of speech would become a "book discipline" as well as a "journal discipline." Working most of his career in the era of the typewriter rather than the word-processing computer, Gunderson thought of book titles as words to be underlined, while article titles were to be set off with quotation marks. He urged his graduate students: "Don't just get quotation marks on your vita; get some underlines."[21] At the time of his death, Gunderson still maintained his passion for writing about history and speech. On the one hand, he was writing a traditional biography of the ninth president of the United States, William Henry Harrison.[22] On the other hand, he was reshaping and supplementing some of his previously published essays into a book-length study of Abraham Lincoln as a speaker.[23]

Gunderson's many publications over the course of his almost six-decade career can be grouped into four general topics: (1) American election campaign rhetoric, (2) American rhetoric of economic and social reform, (3) the rhetoric of the Civil War, and (4) American public address as both a reflection of American society and an expression of the individual speaker. His scholarship on each of those subjects reflected his dual interests in speech and history, as well as his own progressive politics. His scholarship also reflected his conviction that democracy requires citizens who are capable public speakers and discerning critics of political rhetoric.

POLITICAL CAMPAIGN RHETORIC: SHAM AND DECEIT

Gunderson devoted the greatest body of his scholarship to the historical study of American political campaign rhetoric—a topic to which he devoted his doctoral dissertation, a book chapter, seventeen journal articles, and his first book. Most, but not all, of Gunderson's analysis of American campaign rhetoric used the Whig Party's campaign in the 1840 presidential election as a case study. Gunderson recognized that the 1840 campaign was the moment in American history when political rhetoric fundamentally shifted from elevated discourse among the social elite, to a popular discourse designed to capture the enthusiasm of citizens enfranchised during the Jacksonian era.[24]

Writing with characteristically colorful detail, Gunderson described the first American presidential campaign to fully use the popular rhetoric of "image politics"—huge rallies lubricated with hard cider, campaign songs, fictionalized biographies of candidates, outrageous claims and attacks, torchlight parades, and so forth. Contrary to the general association of Abraham Lincoln with a log cabin, Whig rhetors twenty years before Lincoln ran for president made the log cabin the symbol representing the rustic virtues that they attributed to their presidential candidate William Henry Harrison—a son of an aristocratic Virginia family who earned his reputation as a frontiersman during the Indian campaigns in the trans-Appalachian West and later as a farmer and territorial governor. With that ploy the Whigs won the election, which came to be known as "the log-cabin campaign." Overwhelmed by the effective Whig campaign rhetoric, Gunderson reported, the defeated Democrats lamented that they had been "sung down, lied down, drunk down."[25]

Gunderson's procedure in writing his books was to analyze discrete portions of his topic in a series of journal articles, then to reshape the articles into a book-length study. His first essay on the 1840 campaign appeared in 1948,[26] before he had even finished his dissertation.[27] Two more essays appeared in 1949—the same year that he completed his dissertation.[28] In all, Gunderson published essays in four communication journals (then called speech journals) and in eleven history journals before publishing his comprehensive study in book form.[29] The book is an impeccably researched historical study based on over thirty manuscript collections and over forty newspapers.

In *The Log-Cabin Campaign* Gunderson acknowledges historian William B. Hesseltine for his "help and inspiration," but the influence of Hesseltine was not merely one of historical method. From Hesseltine Gunderson acquired a healthy suspicion of the motives behind campaign rhetoric. While Hesseltine viewed speeches as valuable historical documents, he argued that the scholar had to "look *through* the document at the event which produced it" and warned that "both the written document and the spoken word are used as often to deceive as to inform, to conceal rather than to reveal."[30] On first reading, Gunderson's publications on the 1840 campaign are fascinating accounts of contestants using persuasion in the hurly-burly context of nineteenth-century American politics. A closer reading, however, reveals that Gunderson sought to expose what he saw as the lies and deceit of the economic interests that supported the Whig Party in antebellum America. In order to grasp Gunderson's understated critique, one need look no further than the third chapter of his book, which he titled "Cynical Bosses and Pious Rationalizations,"[31] or his essay on Daniel Webster's speaking as a Whig in the 1840 campaign. While still in the first paragraph of that article, Gunderson noted that Webster had put "aside his satin-lined coat, white vest, diamond knee buckles, and shirt with lace-point ruffles," which he had recently worn "for his audience with young Queen Victoria," and assumed the role of the rustic in order to project the Whig's preferred campaign image. Gunderson reported that during a stump speaking tour that took him from Vermont to Virginia, "the Godlike Daniel donned a linsey-woolsey coat, a wide brimmed hat, knee-high boots, and a flowing necktie. . . . To identify himself with the new coonskin Whiggery, Webster camped with the Green Mountain boys in a pine wood before an open fire, ate meals from shingles, paid tribute to log cabins, and challenged at fisticuffs anyone who dared call him an aristocrat." Gunderson did not end his essay before noting that the Whigs rewarded Daniel Webster "with first place in the new Cabinet" as payment for his sham appeals as a common man.[32]

When writing on other election campaigns, Gunderson argued more explicitly that political rhetoric was merely a mask for hidden economic motives. In his analysis of southern Whig political rhetoric from the twenty years between 1833 and 1853, Gunderson explained that "Whig demagogues" were motivated "by economic impulses—unsophisticated hankering for office and financial advantages which accompany political success." A prime example of such deceptive rhetoric, Gunderson pointed out, was none other than Tennessee congressman Davy Crockett, who "was duped into becoming a dancing bear for the Bank of the United States." In order to pay off his financial debts to the Whig Party's kingmaker Nicholas Biddle, Crockett gave political speeches against Andrew Jackson. Gunderson described Crockett as having "aroused a great pseudoequalitarian outcry for Whiggery during his celebrated tour of the North" in 1834—just two years before he "abandoned his wife and family and set out for a hero's death in Texas." What success the Whigs achieved in presidential campaigns Gunderson attributed to their strategy of celebrating "past military victories" of their presidential nominees and to their "mindless reiteration of catchy shibboleths."[33]

Gunderson saw the deceit of nineteenth-century campaign rhetoric as a harbinger of twentieth-century American politics. On September 23, 1952, he traveled from Oberlin, Ohio, to Cleveland on assignment for the *Quarterly Journal of Speech*, which published a symposium every four years on the speaking of presidential campaigns. It had been Gunderson's intention to analyze the speech of the Republican presidential candidate, General Dwight D. Eisenhower, at a Republican Party rally at the city's Public Hall. But the normal agenda for the rally was cast aside in order for the sponsors to play on the public address system the radio version of Richard Nixon's apologia in response to charges that he had a secret slush fund. Those charges had called into question Nixon's future as Eisenhower's running mate. What Gunderson heard in Cleveland was the same thirty-minute speech that Nixon broadcast on television that same night—the famous "Checkers" speech that kept Nixon on the Republican Party ticket as its candidate for vice president. Gunderson's description of the Eisenhower rally featured the same type of compelling and colorful details that he had used to re-create the rhetoric of Whig campaign rallies held more than a century earlier.[34]

Unsympathetic to Nixon in any case and repulsed by Nixon's shameless appeals to pathos, Gunderson described the speech as "starring" not just Nixon but "his Irish wife Pat, and a cocker spaniel named Checkers." He contrasted the "tense silence" in the hall during Nixon's speech with the "inhibited smiles and whispered witticisms" in the press gallery. Eisenhower described Nixon's speech as "an example of courage" in an impromptu speech that Eisenhower used in place of the speech manuscript prepared for the rally. Unmoved, Gunderson alerted his readers that "General Eisenhower's homily on courage was a hurriedly prepared but successful diversionary maneuver" that evaded "the moral issue" of Nixon's alleged slush fund.[35]

Gunderson regarded the use of speechwriters as just one more layer of deceptive political rhetoric to be stripped away by the rhetorical scholar. In Gunderson's view, the fact that George Washington, Andrew Jackson, and Davy Crockett had all used ghostwriters was no excuse. Whether criticizing Franklin D. Roosevelt or Dwight D. Eisenhower, he rejected the notion that preparing a speech to citizens was "beneath the time, trouble, and dignity" of a candidate or officeholder. Such excuses, he suggested, revealed "indolent politicians too lazy to phrase their own thoughts."[36]

Gunderson did not portray all campaign orators as dishonest. His evaluation of Henry Clay illustrates this point. Gunderson did note that Clay's self-professed rejection of emotional appeals contrasted with his often passionate and sometimes overstated speeches in the 1840 campaign.[37] But on balance, Gunderson placed the Whig senator from Kentucky in the oratorical "tradition of responsible conservatism and moderation"[38]—which Gunderson did not exactly intend as a compliment.

In contrast to "Establishment" political speakers, Gunderson typically presented "grassroots" campaign orators as sincere advocates who were exploited by party leaders. Such speakers fascinated Gunderson. He devoted a journal article and a portion of his first book to the rhetorical exploits of one John W. Bear, "the Buckeye Blacksmith" from Pickaway County, Ohio. Bear came to public notice in 1840 through an effective impromptu campaign speech at a Whig rally in Columbus, Ohio. Truly not expecting to be called upon to address the crowd, Bear spoke on that occasion while still covered with soot and clad in his blacksmith clothes ("leather apron and all"). His theatrical attacks on the party of Jackson made him an instant sensation. Whig campaign managers, according to Gunderson, "lured" Bear onto the campaign trail, where the un-schooled orator traversed the nation and became the most frequent Whig speaker in 1840, with a total of 331 addresses. He often spoke with an anvil, hammer, and bellows as props, so that whenever a heckler accused him of being an impostor, he could suspend his speech for a few minutes and prove that he was, indeed, a blacksmith.[39]

REFORM RHETORIC: THE IDIOSYNCRATIC NOBILITY OF COMMON PEOPLE

Gunderson's interest in ordinary people who became extraordinary orators coincided with his interest in the rhetoric of economic and social protest in America, especially agrarian protest and women's rights.[40] As with his studies of election campaign rhetoric, Gunderson's scholarship on reform rhetoric was motivated by his conviction that powerful economic forces were corrupting agents in American democracy. Gunderson's basic political orientation preceded his scholarly career and colored his understanding of American rhetoric. While still an undergraduate in the fall of 1936, he argued vigorously in a public debate that government should take over ownership of all electric utilities. Private util-ities, he charged, were run by "financial overlords" who "exploited" the public, were "motivated solely for selfish profit," and represented the "twin evils of excessive profits and salaries." The youthful Gunderson warned that private utilities did not merely cheat the public out of money. They corrupted regulatory agencies and used persuasion for "the indoctrination of school children."[41]

Such views cast Gunderson as a student radical, even at the University of Wisconsin of the 1930s. His son, Jeff Gunderson, recalled a family story that a group of "frat rats" nearly threw his father "into Lake Mendota for his alleged Socialist leanings."[42] A decade later, when Gunderson pursued his doctoral stud-ies, he found that his mentor, William B. Hesseltine, shared his liberal views. In between writing his many books, Hesseltine regularly contributed polemic articles to *The Progressive* and *The New Leader*.[43]

The political perspective that Gunderson expressed as a college student con-tinued to guide his personal politics (and to influence his scholarly perspective) for decades. Consider his pattern of voting in presidential elections: 1936 Nor-man Thomas (Socialist Party), 1940 Norman Thomas, 1944 Norman Thomas, 1948 Norman Thomas, 1952 Adlai Stevenson, 1956 Adlai Stevenson, 1960 John Kennedy, 1964 Lyndon Johnson, 1968 Dick Gregory (Peace and Freedom Party), and so forth.[44] Historian Martin Ridge remarked that "Gunderson never hesitated to take a liberal position on political and social issues. He was proud of writing progressive history."[45] Ridge added: "He never lost his faith in the human capacity to build a better future."[46]

Gunderson's scholarship on reform rhetoric was rooted in his family tradition as well as the politics of his youth. Gunderson's father was a public school superintendent. Such school administrators occupy community positions that are inherently political, and they often find it safest to express conservative views. In contrast, Gunderson's father was a fervent supporter of Wisconsin Progressive Robert M. LaFollette. In addition, Robert Gunderson's wife, Virginia, was a member of the LaFollette family. She not only shared Gunderson's political heritage and political views but also assisted him with his early archival research—no small matter in the era before the advent of photocopy machines. As Martin Ridge reported, Robert Gunderson lived his entire life as "an unreconstructed Progressive, with a capital 'P' in the Fighting Bob LaFollette tradition."[47]

While Gunderson's studies of campaign rhetoric sought to unmask cynical rhetoric that served the economic interests of the status quo, his studies of reform rhetoric stressed the noble motives and distinctive characters who spoke out against the status quo. Gunderson's first scholarly publication appeared in the *Quarterly Journal of Speech* in 1940—a year before he completed his M.A. degree in history. That article analyzed Populist orators of the 1890s; in it Gunderson argued that historical studies of American public address should be less concerned with famous orators and more concerned with speech making at the grass roots. Gunderson observed that the Populist revolt was part of a long history of American agrarian protest that began with Bacon's Rebellion in colonial Virginia. "Each one of these vigorous protest movements," Gunderson argued, "offers an exciting study to the student of oratory." Instead of faulting the speeches of farm folk as lacking polish, Gunderson celebrated a type of oratory that was "profane, violent, ungrammatical, and ribald," while at the same time being "a sincere and honest brand of public speaking riddled with religious references and Biblical terminology."[48]

Always alert to dramatic language, Gunderson based his conclusions about Populist oratory on colorful profiles of Populists such as "Sage" Ignatius Donnelly (the self-made man of Minnesota who became a writer, a philosopher, and a member of the U.S. Congress), "Bloody Bridles" Waite (Governor Davis H. Waite of Colorado, who paraphrased Biblical prophecies of Armageddon when he threatened violence with blood flowing as high as horses' bridles), and Mary E. Lease of Kansas (best remembered for her injunction that farmers should "raise less corn and more hell"). But Gunderson was uncomfortable making generalizations based on a few stars of Populist oratory, warning that "it is a tendency of historians to immortalize a few of the leaders of this movement and to forget the great group of obscure individuals that harangued crudely garbed sons of the Middle Border at every country crossroads in the nation." He did not slight the oratorical efforts of "Pitchfork" Ben Tillman (South Carolina), "Sockless" Jerry Simpson (Kansas), and the Reverend J. B. Kyle (South Dakota). But "even more deserving of attention," he argued, were "the hosts of nameless cracker-box Ciceros." He reported that each local farm organization included among its officers a "lecturer, whose duty it was not only to speak himself, but to see that other Alliance members had the materials with which to make speeches."[49]

While celebrating the distinctive and colorful style of such "unknown declaimers" in the Populist movement, Gunderson never let the idiosyncrasies of their oratory detract from what he saw as the historic justice of their cause against the abuses of private enterprise. When agrarian audiences gathered to hear a Populist orator, "they were not satisfied with a brief display of political platitudes. They exhausted the grievances of the farmers, and dim kerosene lamps burned until late in the night as rural America denounced its capitalistic enemies." Gunderson saw the Populists' opponents as "privilege-seeking industrialists." He saw the Populist persuaders as heroic: "the battle they waged was a relentless and fearless attempt to overthrow the entrenched and powerful industrial capitalism of a new age."[50] Gunderson had no patience with scholars who defended capitalism in the Gilded Age, dismissing them as "apologists"— as "latter-day neo-Whig historians" whose pro-business arguments were "not unlike praising pirates for redistributing wealth and excusing rapists for promoting fertility."[51]

In his analysis of Populist oratory, Gunderson not only included Mary E. Lease as one of the featured speakers but also noted the widespread participation of women on the Populist podium. Quoting from a contemporary source, he reported that "women who never dreamed of becoming public speakers grew eloquent in their zeal and fervor." Gunderson noted three particularly prominent women Populist orators but saved his greatest praise for those whose speech texts escaped the historical record: "Many an unsung female was making history by rising up to enunciate the oratory of agrarian protest."[52]

Gunderson was teaching speech and studying history at Oberlin College when his first essay on Populist rhetoric was published. In many ways, Oberlin had been the cradle of woman's rights orators of the nineteenth century. Taking advantage of his location, Gunderson researched the rhetorical practice and training of three such women students at Oberlin. Although the college was regarded as a radical institution in the 1830s because it admitted both women and African Americans, Gunderson discovered that the college initially was not so radical as to allow women to speak in public. In a brief essay, Gunderson traced the forty-year struggle for women's speech rights at Oberlin College—a struggle that involved Lucy Stone, a student who would later become one of the leading speakers of the national women's rights movement.

Gunderson's essay documents the discrimination endured by nineteenth-century women even in America's most liberal educational institution. Such prohibitions led women students in 1835 to form the first college women's literary society in America so that they would have a forum for speaking—even if in a sex-segregated setting. A decade later, Lucy Stone, Antoinette Brown (later to become the first American woman to be ordained a minister), and Sallie Holley (who later became an antislavery advocate) lost a battle for women to be allowed to debate in the college's course on Whately's Logic and Rhetoric. In response, the women students formed a secret debating society, which held its meetings "in woods on the outskirts of Oberlin." The women posted sentinels as they in debated in "arboreal seclusion" until cold weather arrived. Then Stone arranged for the secret meetings to continue in the home of an African American family whose child she tutored in reading.[53]

As with his analysis of Populist orators, Gunderson reported not just the oratorical exploits of Lucy Stone but also those of "succeeding Oberlin coeds" who "fought for the right to speak from the academic platform." In 1859 the first woman student was allowed to read aloud her own commencement essay at the graduation ceremony. Up until then, the male students read their own essays aloud, but faculty members (males, of course) would read the essays of the women graduates. Indeed, it was not until 1874 that the Oberlin faculty voted to permit women to present public speeches (as opposed to recitations) to audiences of both men and women.[54]

In the protest rhetoric of the nineteenth century, Gunderson found everyday men and women orators who "believed that they could influence the course of events by persuasion." Acknowledging that some historians doubted the influence of oratory, Gunderson observed that "no one should minimize the rhetorical intensity generated by the combined forces of self-confidence and outrage."[55]

RHETORIC IN THE SERVICE OF PEACE

Gunderson's work reflected a deep concern with peace and war. His family was proud of its pacifist tradition. A favorite family story concerned how Robert Gray Gunderson's father had opposed Wisconsin's war hysteria during World War I. As a public school superintendent, Gunderson's father found himself at a meeting of Wisconsin's school superintendents where all of his fellow superintendents took a voice vote to censor Wisconsin's U.S. Senator Robert M. LaFollette for opposing the entry of the United States in the war. Gunderson's father was the lone dissenting vote.[56] Robert Gray Gunderson grew up in a family that told another story about World War I—a story about how war fever had overwhelmed one Wisconsin community to the extent that the patriotic citizens had seized an elderly woman of German descent, placed her in a small cage, and used a horse to pull the caged woman through the town's dusty streets. It was a story seared into his memory—one he repeated to his students during the Vietnam War.

Robert Gray Gunderson's own military service during World War II fortified his conviction that war was folly. Having risen from the rank of private to captain in the U.S. Army (including a long, cold period in Iceland), Gunderson returned to Oberlin College after the war, where one of his passions was to "make sure ROTC [Reserve Officers' Training Corps] never appeared on campus."[57] When Gunderson pursued his Ph.D. after World War II, he found that his pacifist family tradition fitted well with the views of his mentor at the Uni-

versity of Wisconsin. William B. Hesseltine had been a child of the South. Due
to the early death of his father, he was sentenced to a particularly rigid military
school in Kentucky run by his uncle. There Hesseltine developed what Gunderson called "his life long hatred of militarism and his abhorrence of control
and regimentation." Even during World War II, Gunderson reported, his mentor
had "sturdily maintained his pacifism."[58]

A few years after Gunderson had completed his Ph.D., Bower Aly asked him
to write an analysis of the high school debate topic during the 1952–1953 school
year for publication in the annual discussion and debate manual issued by the
National University Extension Association. The debate topic dealt with the issue
of what form of international organization the United States should support.
Gunderson responded with an essay of over thirty pages, clearly based on his
premise that war was madness. He opened his essay with a description of lem-
mings in Norway rushing headlong to their deaths in the sea. Lest his young
readers failed to grasp his point, he continued in his second paragraph: "Humans,
quite lemming-like, periodically tumble down mountainsides of hysteria into the
fiord of war." Writing in the early years of the Cold War and as the Korean
War continued, Gunderson warned: "Problems of international organization are
not easily solved in a hurry—but frightening advances in warfare and communication may make speedy solutions an essential ingredient for survival."[59]

Gunderson's scholarly writing on the Civil War reflected the same deep concern over the folly of war that he expressed in his chapter on the 1952–1953
high school debate topic. His Civil War scholarship focused on a political convention convened in an effort to forestall the war.[60] The Washington Peace
Conference was called at the invitation of Virginia and was held at the Willard
Hotel in Washington, D.C., during late February and early March 1861—just
days prior to Abraham Lincoln's inauguration as president. Twenty-one states
sent delegates to the conference, but the U.S. Congress declined to act on the
recommendations of the Peace Conference, and the Civil War soon ensued.

After protracted parliamentary maneuvers and debate, the Washington Peace
Conference had proposed a thirteenth amendment to the U.S. Constitution that
would have reinstated the Missouri Compromise of 1820—the federal statute
that had been invalidated in the Supreme Court's Dred Scott decision. In addition, the proposed constitutional amendment would prohibit the national government from abolishing slavery in the South, prohibit any slave trade into the
United States, specify the conditions under which slavery might be abolished in
the District of Columbia, prevent the addition of new states (free or slave)
opposed by a majority of states in either the South or the North, require the
national government to compensate slave owners if legal authorities in the North
did not return escaped slaves under the Fugitive Slave Act, and require unani-
mous consent of the states in order to amend those parts of the U.S. Constitution
that touched upon slavery.

Gunderson's publications about the Washington Peace Conference of 1861
are models of careful historical research, as he drew upon ninety-three manu-

script collections held in the archives of twenty-six different institutions in both the North and the South. He set out to discover the political and rhetorical reasons for the failure of the Peace Conference. Like his mentor, William B. Hesseltine, Gunderson believed that the economic conflict between the North and South (rather than slavery) was the true cause of the Civil War.[61] Indeed, he saw such economic motives as a fundamental cause of any armed conflict.[62] Hence, his basic critique of the Washington Peace Conference was not that it failed to resolve the question of slavery but that the conference "offered no solution for sectional economic conflicts," but merely proposed "constitutional arrangements regarding slavery." Slavery, he believed, was merely "a convenient symbol for rhetorical manipulation."[63] Having set aside the moral issue of slavery, Gunderson argued that rhetorical efforts to avoid America's Civil War failed because of three factors: (1) the inherent disadvantage of moderate rhetoric when addressed to a public caught up in the hysteria of war fever, (2) political inflexibility as leaders debated issues of war and peace, and (3) fatalism about a civil war—the belief that war was inevitable and could not be avoided.

Gunderson found the advocates of moderation not only less organized than the radical "Fireeaters" of the South and the "Black Republicans" of the North but also "far less vocal than strident advocates of extreme positions."[64] While war enthusiasts spoke of men willing to "plunge into blood to the horses' bridles," the moderates at the conference tried to temper the rhetorical climate: "Amendments were appended to amendments and substitutions substituted for substitutions."[65] As historian Hesseltine asked in his foreword to Gunderson's *Old Gentlemen's Convention*: "Could moderation be dramatized . . . so that it could overcome the partisan rhetoric . . . ?"[66] In Gunderson's view, the advocates of war had succeeded in creating "a rising tide of hysteria," which moderates failed to calm.[67]

One problem with the Washington Peace Conference was the age of the delegates, who were often senior political figures drafted out of retirement. For example, former U.S. president John Tyler of Virginia at seventy-one years of age was elected president of the conference.[68] War advocate Horace Greeley, editor of the *New York Tribune*, had no use for the conference. He "damned the gathering as an 'Old Gentlemen's Convention of political fossils, who would not have been again disinterred but for the shock . . . [of] the secession movement.' "[69] Gunderson seemed to portray John C. Wright, an elderly Ohio delegate, as a metaphor for the conference. He was "nearly seventy-seven years of age and almost blind at the time of the Conference," but he made the difficult journey to Washington, was selected as the temporary chairman of the conference, and presided over the organizational sessions of the conference—only to die before the group began its substantive debates.[70]

In Gunderson's view, inflexibility was a key danger to peace rhetoric. Even as the delegates to the Washington Peace Conference gathered at the Willard Hotel, Southern "Minute-Men" and northern "Wide-Awakes" formed militias and began to drill.[71] Among the North's conference delegates, those specifically selected for their opposition to compromise proudly embraced the label of "stiff-backed."[72] Gunderson reported that Michigan viewed "a compromise with the slave oligarchy as a calamity more to be dreaded than civil war itself." Hence, the Michigan legislature refused to send delegates to the Peace Conference, declaring "concession and compromise are not to be entertained or offered to traitors."[73] In New York City, newspaper editor Greeley urged: "Away with such compromise!" "Secession will cure itself. . . . Let [the government] . . . not concede an inch."[74] In the deliberations of the conference itself, northern and Southern extremists used parliamentary tactics to delay any agreement and introduced amendments "designed more to annoy" the delegates of the opposing section, rather "than to solve delicate constitutional problems." Indeed, Gunderson observed, some such proposals seemed to be offered so that their rejection could be used to justify an ensuing war.[75] With studied understatement, Gunderson concluded: "The psychological atmosphere was not congenial to compromise."[76]

Gunderson argued that war rhetoric won over peace rhetoric in 1861 because "the fatalistic sense of inevitability—the concept of the irrepressible conflict—itself hastened the day of mobilization."[77] In fact, northern war advocates took the name of "irrepressibles."[78] Perhaps most vitriolic was Horace Greeley, who proclaimed: "Let this suspense and uncertainty cease! If we are to fight, so be it."[79] Moderates recognized the power of this appeal but seemed helpless to counter it. As the editor of the *Louisville Democrat* wrote in despair: "They must, somehow get a fight, or keep up the idea that one is coming."[80]

Despite his conviction that economic motives drove human behavior—including war—Gunderson still believed that people could deliberate over their choices and could persuade one another to choose peace rather than war. His belief in the human capacity to avoid war was not limited to the rhetoric of the Civil War. In concluding his lengthy analysis of the 1952–1953 high school discussion and debate topic on international relations, Gunderson approvingly quoted from a 1952 speech by Vincent Auriol, then president of France: "We must not agree . . . that war is inevitable; . . . we must not allow ourselves to drift with events, but rather we must anticipate, guide and master them." In his own words, Gunderson counseled those who were growing up during the Cold War: "Above all, perhaps, students should avoid a fatalistic attitude which places human events beyond the control of reason, for a belief in the inevitability of conflict may, in fact, be one of the factors which hastens its outbreak."[81] Just as Gunderson analyzed the 1840 presidential election as a historical parallel to the manipulation of mass media political campaigns that were emerging in the 1950s, he saw the failed rhetoric of peace prior to the Civil War as a parallel to the failure of conciliatory rhetoric in later periods of American history: "In the South, the epithet 'Black Republican' aroused the same revolutionary connotations that 'anarchist,' 'bolshevik,' and 'communist' aroused in succeeding generations, and it was applied with the same lack of discrimination."[82]

In his writings Gunderson did not offer an explanation for the contradiction between his opposition to war and his own military service during World War II. When the draft of the Vietnam War era forced his graduate students to suspend their studies in order to serve in the military or in alternative duties such as the Peace Corps, he would send them off with advice on how to maintain professional academic connections and, when necessary, how to endure military life. Then Gunderson would inquire one more time about how long the student would be away from school. Despite the fact that those interruptions were always shorter than his own military service, he would exclaim with genuine distress: "So long! So long!" Speaking more to himself than anyone else, he would add: "At least we were fighting the god-damned fascists!"

PUBLIC ADDRESS: A REFLECTION OF THE SOCIETY AND THE SPEAKER

Gunderson's scholarship reflected the tension between his interest in American society and his interest in individual speakers. He viewed speeches as a window through which a scholar could discern a society's values, its concerns, and its follies. At the same time, his work reflected a fascination with individual speakers. His numerous studies surveyed an army of less-known speakers whose speeches constituted a kind of grassroots rhetoric. But he was occasionally drawn to the individual speakers—to Daniel Webster, Henry Clay, William Henry Harrison, and Abraham Lincoln.

Reflecting his long involvement with American studies, Gunderson analyzed American political rhetoric to reveal the conflicting values of American society. Yet, the search for social meaning of American oratory could not end with the surface features of such rhetoric. Gunderson's mentor William B. Hesseltine urged scholars to "search for the truth that lays [sic] behind the document" and to keep in mind that "both the written document and the spoken word are used as often to deceive as to inform, to conceal rather than to reveal."[83] Gunderson agreed, remarking that "both rhetorical critic and historian must pry beneath the surface of events to discover the social, psychological, and economic forces motivating behavior."[84] Gunderson did not regard all rhetorical appeals to principle and values as a sham but saw such appeals in competition with economic motives of both speakers and audiences. With regard to persuasion, Gunderson's motto was, "When you've got a man by the pocketbook, his heart and mind will soon follow."[85]

Responding to a paper on American rhetoric by Carroll Arnold,[86] Gunderson proposed that instead of thinking of American public discourse as a matter of "transcendental pragmatism," as Arnold suggested, scholars should focus on the tensions inherent in "the rhetorical balancing of transcendental and pragmatic values" in American public address. In his view, every idealistic appeal had to be investigated to discover its private motive, which he neatly illustrated with examples that swept from the Puritan Cotton Mather, to "repressive champions of liberty" like President Woodrow Wilson and to "the lustful moralism" of

President Jimmy Carter. Still, Gunderson stopped short of dismissing all orators' value appeals as deceit: "The unscrupulous among them exploit our democracy by specializing in a dialogue of contrived ambiguity. Others, like the late Norman Thomas, who refuse to demean themselves by being all things to all people are called successful failures."[87]

Gunderson found the American "rhetoric of success" particularly revealing of American values, because "each generation invents its own heroes and its own distinctive mythology of success." To support his thesis, he cited John Winthrop's "Model of Christian Charity," Russell Conwell's "Gospel of Wealth," and (after still more examples) J. R. Ewing—the appealing personification of greed in the enormously popular 1970s television show *Dallas*. Gunderson argued that studying such public discourse was important because "the right myths . . . conceal, if alas they do not reconcile, clashing objectives in a society."[88] James R. Andrews has succinctly summarized Gunderson's view on the conflicting values reflected in American discourse: "Greed has an edge over ideals—but not so much that our rhetoric can allow us to admit it."[89]

An important subtheme in the rhetoric of American success, Gunderson reported, is "the rhetoric of upward mobility." By the 1980s Gunderson had "a fearful conviction" that recent expressions of that particular myth (especially in the persons of punk rock stars Steve Jones, Sid Vicious, and Johnny Rotten) constituted a "frustrated Nihilism . . . symptomatic of a creeping medievalism in contemporary society."[90] No mere moralistic critic of latter-day rock and roll music, Gunderson was equally appalled by the rhetoric of upward mobility expressed in contemporary self-help books with titles such as *Winning through Intimidation* (1974) and *Winning with Deception and Bluff* (1979)—books, he added, that he had to obtain via interlibrary loan because they had already been stolen from the library of the business school at Indiana University. Gunderson placed the rhetoric of contemporary society within the long history of rhetorical discourse in the British Isles and America. Starting with John Bunyan's *Pilgrim's Progress*, he took only a few pages to travel through the rhetorical discourse of Benjamin Franklin, Henry Ward Beecher, and Horatio Alger as he analyzed the social significance of the rhetoric of a self-help book marketed by the U.S. Chamber of Commerce (*Winning at Confrontation*, 1985) and the lyrics and public statements of the "Sex Pistols."[91]

Gunderson continued his interest in public address as an expression of social values right up to his death. In fact, his final essay submitted for publication contrasted the "sound bytes" of the South and the West—the slogans that local citizens proudly proclaim on automobile bumper stickers, T-shirts, and so forth. Although his final essay draws upon the best scholarly literature on American regionalism (including some of William B. Hesseltine's books), its lifeblood comes from vivid examples of public discourse for which Gunderson's writing had always been known. As a dual resident of "Lapland" (where the South lapped over the Ohio River into southern Indiana) and the far West (southern California), he was confident in summarizing the values of each region. Cars driving through the hills and hollows near Bloomington, Indiana, featured bumper stickers that advised him to "EAT MORE POSSUM," while in his winter home of Pasadena, California, the advice on car bumpers was "SKI NAKED."

Turning to the difficult problem of classifying Texas, Gunderson found the answer in a slogan first used in an antilittering campaign—a slogan that soon became the mantra for the former republic: "DON'T MESS WITH TEXAS." Gunderson had visited Texas several times for meetings of the Southern Historical Society and for visits to Texas A&M University and the University of Texas at Austin, and he had consulted the writings of J. Frank Dobie. He concluded that it would be unwise, not to say dangerous, to treat Texas as a subset of either the South or the West. "No sociologist," he concluded, ". . . would dare to suggest Texas was having anything so narcissistic as a 'mid-life crisis.' It takes a self-confident, hairy-chested chauvinism to maintain the sort of reputation Texas has enjoyed ever since Southerners David Crockett and Jim Bowie arrived" to fight and die at the Alamo. Gunderson used one of Crockett's briefest speeches to capture the regional ethos of the Lone Star State—"In 1835, Davy lost his seat in the Tennessee Congressional delegation to Adam Huntsman, an earthy Valentino with a wooden leg. At a drinking party at the Union Hotel in Memphis, Crockett gave an appropriate farewell: 'Since you have chosen a man with a timber toe to replace me, you may all go to Hell—and I will go to Texas.' "[92]

Despite his interest in aggregates of popular oratory, Gunderson had always been drawn to the study of individuals. Some of his journal articles were biographical in nature—exploring the rhetorical role of one speaker within the context of a broader research project, such as the presidential campaign of 1840 or the Washington Peace Conference of 1861.[93] Other essays consisted of a series of minibiographical studies, as Gunderson profiled the leading speakers in a movement or campaign.[94] Late in his life, even as he published essays on the rhetoric of American society, Gunderson pursued two major biographical projects—one on William Henry Harrison and the other on Abraham Lincoln.

Gunderson hoped to publish a full-fledged biography of William Henry Harrison that would take "Tippecanoe" from his youth in an aristocratic Virginia family to his presidential inauguration and death following the "log-cabin campaign." Although never finished, that project did yield four essays about the man elected in the 1840 presidential campaign—an election that Gunderson described as "a spectacle of slogan and slander" during which Harrison kept "his lips 'hermetically sealed' on the issues" of the day—slavery, the tariff, and the banking system.[95] Gunderson's published essays on Harrison's personal life, his youthful experience leading U.S. soldiers in the trans-Appalachian Indian wars, and the character of the Native American tribes (with whom Harrison negotiated while governor of the Indiana Territory) reflect Gunderson's commitment to careful research into the history of an era.[96] Yet, Gunderson did not view his biography of Harrison as his final scholarly project.

Relatively early in his career, Gunderson established himself as a Lincoln scholar. At first, his interest in Lincoln paralleled his research on the Washington Peace Conference of 1861. Between 1950 and 1963 he published eight journal articles on Lincoln—most of which concerned the crucial period between Lincoln's election in November 1860 and his inauguration as president of the United States in March 1861.[97] Gunderson drew upon some of these essays in writing background material for his book on the *Old Gentlemen's Convention*. But several of Gunderson's Lincoln articles dealt with topics not directly related to the Peace Conference: Lincoln's rhetorical style, the historiography of Lincoln scholarship, and Lincoln's courtroom speaking.[98]

One measure of Gunderson's stature as a Lincoln scholar was an invitation from the Lincoln Fellowship of Wisconsin to deliver its annual Lincoln lecture in 1961. Just five years before, the fellowship's annual lecturer had been the famous historian Richard N. Current, who back in the 1930s had been one of William B. Hesseltine's doctoral students at the University of Wisconsin and a teaching assistant in some of Gunderson's undergraduate classes. With the publication of Gunderson's lecture in 1963, he suspended his Lincoln scholarship. As he noted: "It takes a certain self-confidence, if not to say presumption, to write a book about Lincoln."[99] Three decades later Gunderson found the necessary presumption to write his Lincoln book. In the 1990s he hoped to revise and supplement his earlier writings so as to fashion them into a book-length study of Lincoln's rhetoric.

Gunderson's death in 1996 prevented the completion of his Lincoln book, but his previous Lincoln publications reveal his fascination with a speaker who was both homespun and eloquent.[100] Gunderson's early essays on Lincoln's speaking provide colorful re-creations of speech events in 1861 leading up to his inauguration[101] and hard-eyed analyses of the strategic purposes of those speeches.[102] But Gunderson's most interesting articles on Lincoln discuss how his early life shaped his subsequent rhetoric. Lincoln was known for the remarkable conciseness of his phrasing—most notably in the Gettysburg Address. Gunderson located the origin of that stylistic characteristic in Lincoln's youth: "Writing compositions with a piece of charcoal on the back of a wooden shovel tends to encourage a certain succinctness of style."[103]

Lincoln's reputation for effectively using humorous stories in his informal speeches, Gunderson argued, sprang "inherently from his frontier heritage." Similarly, his reliance on a small number of literary sources reflected his extremely limited frontier education. A self-taught man who avidly read newspapers, Lincoln in his speeches drew upon a few key works, including *Aesop's Fables*, the Bible, and Shakespeare.[104] Indeed, Gunderson reports that in writing his First Inaugural Address, Lincoln borrowed from his law partner William Herndon "the only documents Lincoln needed: Henry Clay's speech on the Compromise of 1850, Webster's Reply to Hayne, Andrew Jackson's Nullification Proclamation, and a copy of the Constitution."[105]

Gunderson concluded that Lincoln's speaking in the courtrooms of rural Illinois proved to be an important influence on his subsequent rhetorical abilities: "In preparing to face frontier juries, the unassuming backwoods pleader had readied himself to influence the behavior of editors, politicians, and diplomats."[106] In particular, Gunderson noted the rhetorical consequences of having to compose legal arguments without easy access to a law library. "The scarcity of law books in the county courthouses," Gunderson observed, "put a premium on a lawyer's memory and ingenuity."[107] Just as Lincoln's courtroom speaking taught him to extrapolate from useful legal principles, his presidential speeches drew conclusions from universal principles. In the opinion of Lincoln's law partner, "Lincoln read less and thought more than any man in America."[108]

Gunderson reveals that with his First Inaugural Address (as with other speeches), Lincoln circulated his initial draft to as many as twenty political allies for comments and suggestions. Not only did his advisers respond with numerous suggestions, but they also kept the content of that speech confidential. Lincoln subsequently "made almost a hundred modifications in the original text," including accepting William H. Steward's "idea but not the phrasing for the moving final paragraph about 'the mystic chords of memory.' " Yet, Gunderson argued, "seldom, if ever, did anyone write a public document for Lincoln." In fact, Gunderson suggests, Lincoln's own ability as a writer and speaker may have been enhanced by the circumstance that Lincoln sometimes "served as a ghost for others"—including a newspaper editor, a governor, and a senator.[109]

In his scholarship, Gunderson moved back and forth between individual orators and political conventions, campaigns, or movements whose rhetoric was created by the individuals. That was the case with his writing on Davy Crockett and Daniel Webster in the "log-cabin" campaign of 1840, on individual delegates to the Washington Peace Conference of 1861, and on Mary E. Lease and David H. "Bloody Bridles" Waite in the Populist revolt of the 1890s. Ultimately, his writing on Lincoln also fit that pattern. In the conclusion of his last essay on Lincoln, Gunderson returned to the people of the prairies from whom Lincoln had sprung. Citing historian Dumas Malone on Lincoln's rhetorical art, Gunderson concluded: "Lincoln's intimate association with the people made him 'a conscious craftsman, an artist in the use of words—spoken words.' "[110]

CONCLUSION: RHETORICAL ANALYSIS AS CIVIC EDUCATION

Despite his deep distrust of Establishment rhetoric, Gunderson was himself a gifted writer and speaker. His historical and rhetorical essays were written as pieces of persuasion. He also presented numerous speeches and had several of them published in *Vital Speeches of the Day*.[111] He was a tireless advocate of the role of rhetorical study in education, promoting the acceptance of speech as an academic field of study within the American academy and arguing that public speaking and debate should be taught in U.S. high schools and colleges.[112] With regard to the contribution that the academic field of speech could make to American education, Gunderson was fond of quoting Harvard University president Nathan M. Pusey on the need "to educate free, independent, and vigorous minds, capable of analyzing events, of exercising judgment, of distinguishing facts from propaganda and truth from half-truth and lies."[113]

In 1950 Gunderson was worried that as speech professors became interested in group dynamics and other social aspects of communication, they would neglect teaching traditional rhetorical skills. He criticized the early research on group dynamics as bad science and attacked the training activities ("T-groups") of the group dynamics movement as personal manipulation masquerading as education. Gunderson's approach to teaching group discussion was rooted in John Dewey's pattern of reflective thinking. He saw informed discussion of significant public issues as an important part of speech teaching. In contrast, he argued that "the inherent artificiality if not actual mockery" of T-group exercises like "role playing" rendered group dynamics "absurd as a method for the discussion and solution of serious public questions."[114]

Gunderson bristled when T-group enthusiasts celebrated their role-playing activities as sufficiently "unrehearsed" and "spontaneous" to overcome the problem of "overintellectual types of discussion." Such T-group activities, Gunderson claimed, were not in the intellectual tradition of rhetoric. If such an approach became popular, he warned, it would be only because it "appeals to those too busy (or too lazy) to participate in discussions which require preparation."[115] Gunderson feared that group dynamics' interest in communication process and technique (as opposed to the substance of the message) would harm education— especially speech education. "In the 19th century," he pointed out, "public demand for competence in personal effectiveness led to excesses which made the word *elocution* synonymous with absurd and fraudulent training. The demand in the 20th century for competence in interpersonal relations may, unless educators take care, lead to similar excesses."[116] Speech scholars such as Franklyn S. Haiman at Northwestern University and psychology researchers such as Herbert C. Kelman at Yale University replied to Gunderson with apologias for group dynamics.[117] But Gunderson's criticisms reached an even wider audience as he responded to his opponents, as he contributed additional essays on group dynamics to education journals and as his original critique was reprinted in abridged forms.[118]

It would be easy to view Gunderson's essays attacking group dynamics as unrelated to his rhetorical studies, but that would be an error. His opposition to group dynamics and his commitment to scholarship on the history of public address sprang from the same passion: Gunderson's conviction that scholars must contribute to a society's civic education. For democracy to work (especially the social democracy in which he so fervently believed), Gunderson insisted that citizens must be able to recognize sham persuasion in politics and also must be able to resist the kind of "engineering of consent" that occurs when the established political and economic powers marshal social science in the service of public relations in order to manipulate public opinion.[119]

Gunderson presented the fullest statement of his pedagogical motive for scholarship on American political rhetoric in a speech initially delivered in 1955. His subtitle stated his message: "Training for an Articulate Democracy." That address was promptly published in *Vital Speeches of the Day* and continued to be reprinted in speech textbooks for the next dozen years.[120] Speaking in the backwash of a period when U.S. senator Joe McCarthy's accusations about communist subversives would have silenced a lesser progressive, Gunderson lamented the lack of vigorous debate on public issues in the United States. American colleges and universities, he concluded, had failed the nation's students, for each year "more people than ever before are graduated but not educated." As a consequence, he noted, when Americans are forced into the "unfamiliar realm of ideas we feel our way timorously like a barefoot boy on a cinder path." One consequence of America's "morass of intellectual timidity" was that its citizens were becoming "docile," "scared," and "uninformed." Such qualities promoted "cynicism" among citizens and "demagoguery" among political opportunists.[121]

Speaking as an educational Jeremiah, Gunderson announced that America had not always been unprepared for participation in democracy. Indeed, he saw nineteenth-century America as a model for articulate and activist citizens: "Foreign travelers invariably testified that nineteenth-century citizens were bold, articulate champions of democracy—convinced of their own stake in the American experiment—and of their own important role in it." Gunderson called upon contemporary Americans to be worthy of their ancestors: "Public officials need the vigorous give-and-take of cross-examination. In a free country, they are our servants, as Davy Crockett and his contemporaries frequently reminded themselves. They are not our masters, nor are they our inquisitors." Reflecting his anger and frustration over McCarthyism, Gunderson concluded: "We are the ones who should be asking the questions."[122]

As both a scholar and a teacher, Gunderson saw himself doing the work of civic education. His many studies on nineteenth-century American public address were part of that educational mission. He celebrated orators who advocated populist revolt and women's rights. He exposed campaign rhetoric as a mask for selfish economic and political motives. He revealed the dangers of inadequate public deliberation in a world threatened by war. Gunderson did not view his historical interests as antiquarian—quite the reverse. He believed that "the rhetorical critic and the historian both have a responsibility to the present."[123] In an essay review of a dozen books on Abraham Lincoln, Gunderson concluded that historians and critics of American rhetoric could "illuminate the future as well as the past."[124]

The pedagogical motive of Gunderson's scholarship is illustrated by how he tried to inform the citizens of Baltimore about the superficiality of much political campaign rhetoric. When Tennessee's U.S. Senator Estes Kefauver presented himself to the citizens of Baltimore in 1952 wearing a coonskin cap as part of his campaign for the Democratic Party's presidential nomination, Gunderson prompted the editor of the *Baltimore Sun* to read Gunderson's recently published historical article on the Baltimore Whig Convention of 1840.[125] The newspaper editor was so struck by the parallels between the two campaign events that he published a summary of Gunderson's essay from *The Maryland Historical Magazine* with the observation that "112 years ago tomorrow" the Whig Party members of Baltimore had anticipated Senator Kefauver's sham appeals as a common man. He added: "And with due respect to the showmanship of the distinguished Senator from Tennessee, the records indicate that they did it as well, if not better."[126]

As we move forward in the twenty-first century, America's political rhetoric reveals a continuing need for scholars like Robert G. Gunderson—scholars capable of being outraged by the abuses of public discourse, scholars whose research on public affairs rhetoric contributes to civic education, and scholars whose compelling style attracts attention both inside and outside the academy. Gunderson's ideal of civic discourse contrasts sharply with the contemporary practice of politicians' using "focus groups" to pretest the themes and phrases for their public speeches just as advertising firms pretest pitches for new consumer products. President Ronald Reagan's pollster Richard Wirthlin market-tested political language prior to nationally televised addresses. President Bill Clinton went so far as to turn to Dick Morris (his morally challenged political consultant) for a private poll on how the public would respond to news of Clinton's affair with a White House intern. With the results of Morris's poll in hand, Clinton went before television cameras on January 26, 1998, to declare: "I did not have sexual relations with that woman."[127]

In the concluding chapter of a book dedicated to Robert G. Gunderson, Robert Hariman invites rhetorical scholars "to the task of making public address in the nineteenth century a resource" for contemporary citizens. Like Gunderson, he notes that "from classical antiquity through the nineteenth century, the study of public address was conducted for the dual purposes of training effective speakers and cultivating civic life."[128] He might have added that in the twentieth century, Robert Gunderson was among those who worked to adapt the classical ideal to the needs of democracy in America. Like Hariman, Gunderson understood that a democracy requires "the ability to discuss public address intelligently."[129]

Certainly one of the qualities of Gunderson's scholarship that is worth emulating is his vivid style. James R. Andrews described it best when he referred to "Gunderson's pungent style." Gunderson's narrative style was particularly compelling. As Andrews has noted, Gunderson "exhibited a style both muscular and clear" in which "relevant facts, interwoven with the public expression of ideas, were cast in compelling narratives."[130] Gunderson was not unaware that some contemporary scholars were "contemptuous of narrative" as lacking in analytical rigor, but he was undaunted. He reminded such critics "that some of the greatest movers and shakers have been story tellers, masters of anecdote and imagery." Although Gunderson wrote that comment during President Ronald

Reagan's second term, he did not have the "Great Communicator" in mind. Instead, he was thinking of earlier narrative stylists: "Christ spoke in parables, Aesop in animal fables, Bunyan in allegory, and Lincoln in folksy western stories." For Gunderson, narration was not "mere" style; it was artful rhetorical proof. He observed that narrative "provided habitation for the most persuasive thought in the western world."[131]

To Gunderson, lack of attention to style was a sign of intellectual indolence— a perspective that he had acquired from his mentor William B. Hesseltine. He passed that view on to his students and to other scholars whose work he reviewed and edited for the *Quarterly Journal of Speech* and the *Journal of American History*. In his own writing and in the writing that he edited, Gunderson declared war "on wordiness, the passive voice and similar linguistic abominations." In particular, Gunderson opposed adverbs and adjectives that slowed the pace of discourse and inadvertently weakened the very noun or verb the writer sought to enhance. His goal was to write so that "one searches in vain for a single blood-sucking qualifier." With a complete innocence of any sexist intent, Gunderson constantly called for flaccid writing to be strengthened with "hairy-chested verbs." From Hesseltine he adopted the commandment: "Thou shalt avoid and abhor all modern jargon."[132] One can only speculate on how dismayed Gunderson would have been with the convoluted writing so characteristic of journal articles published in the late 1990s by communication scholars calling themselves "postmodernists," "cultural critics," "cultural theorists," and so forth.

Gunderson's academic influence reached far beyond Oberlin College and Indiana University. He was a visiting professor at the University of Michigan (1958) and at the University of Hawaii (1964), a visiting scholar at the University Center of Virginia (1973), and frequently a guest scholar at the Huntington Library (1971–1972, 1979, and 1985–1995). Widely sought as a speaker, he presented guest lectures at universities such as Cornell, Ohio State, Pennsylvania State, Virginia, Wisconsin, Kentucky, Michigan, Texas, Louisiana State, Notre Dame, Mississippi State, Western Kentucky, California State at Hayward, and elsewhere.

Ultimately, the enduring influence of Robert G. Gunderson will come from the students and colleagues in both speech communication and history who benefited from his example of detailed historical research and passionate scholarly advocacy. Robert Gunderson resolved the duality of his academic career not by forsaking either speech or history but by using his historical analysis of American public address as his own political rhetoric. Martin Ridge noted: "It would be a mistake to misread either his historical works or those in rhetoric as narrowly restricted to a single field. His studies of rhetoric were excellent history, and his historical analysis often centered on the use of rhetoric."[133] But Gunderson did not just merge history and rhetoric; he used history as rhetoric. Robert Gray Gunderson's legacy is that of historian as civic rhetorician.

NOTES

1. Thomas W. Benson, ed., *Rhetoric and Political Culture in Nineteenth-Century America* (East Lansing: Michigan State University Press, 1997); Kathleen J. Turner, *Doing Rhetorical History: Concepts and Cases* (Tuscaloosa: University of Alabama Press, 1998).

2. James R. Andrews, "Foreword: Contextualizing American Rhetoric," in *Rhetoric and Political Culture*, p. x.

3. Kenneth Cmiel, *Democratic Eloquence: The Fight over Popular Speech in Nineteenth-Century America* (Berkeley: University of California Press, 1990).

4. For example, see Robert G. Gunderson, "Presidential Rally, 1840 Style," *The Gavel* 31 (1948): 8–9; Robert G. Gunderson, "The Dayton Log-Cabin Convention of 1840," *Bulletin of the Historical and Philosophical Society of Ohio* 7 (1949): 202–210; Robert G. Gunderson, "Webster in Linsey-Woolsey," *Quarterly Journal of Speech* 37 (1951): 23–30.

5. Cmiel, *Democratic Eloquence*, p. 11.

6. Ibid., pp. 16, 261–262.

7. Gregory Clark and S. Michael Halloran, "Introduction: Transformations of Public Discourse in Nineteenth-Century America," in *Oratorical Culture in Nineteenth-Century America: Transformation in the Theory and Practice of Rhetoric*, ed. Gregory Clark and S. Michael Halloran (Carbondale: Southern Illinois University Press, 1993), p. 25.

8. Robert Gunderson, et al., "Government Ownership of Electric Utilities: University of Wisconsin Affirmative vs. Ohio State University Negative," *Intercollegiate Debates*, vol. 18, ed. Egbert Ray Nichols (New York: Noble and Noble, 1937), pp. 193–199, 228–230.

9. J. Jeffery Auer, "Remembering Bob Gunderson," National Communication Association, Chicago, 1997, p. 2.

10. See Robert G. Gunderson, "William B. Hesseltine and the Profession of History: A Retrospective—Dutch Uncle to a Profession," *Wisconsin Magazine of History* 66 (1982–1983): 106–110.

11. See William B. Hesseltine and Henry L. Ewbank Jr., "Old Voices in the New South," *Quarterly Journal of Speech* 39 (1953): 451–458; William B. Hesseltine, "Speech and History," *Central States Speech Journal* 12 (1961): 176–181; William B. Hesseltine, "Foreword," in Robert Gray Gunderson, *Old Gentlemen's Convention: The Washington Peace Conference of 1861* (Madison: University of Wisconsin Press, 1961), pp. v–vii; William B. Hesseltine and Larry Gara, "New Governors Speak for War, January 1861," in *Antislavery and Disunion, 1861: Studies in the Rhetoric of Compromise and Conflict*, ed. J. Jeffery Auer (New York: Harper and Row, 1963), pp. 360–377.

12. Correspondence from Henry L. Ewbank Jr. to the author, November 21, 1997. For a discussion of Hesseltine as Gunderson's mentor, see Andrews, "Foreword: Contextualizing American Rhetoric," p. ix.

13. Donald W. Zacharias, "Robert Gray Gunderson: Pioneer in the Historical Study of American Public Address," paper presented to the National Communication Association, Chicago, November 21, 1997, pp. 1–2.

14. Robert Gray Gunderson, *The Log-Cabin Campaign* (Lexington: University of Kentucky Press, 1957); Gunderson, *Old Gentlemen's Convention*; Martin Ridge, "Robert

Gray Gunderson" [obituary], *Organization of American Historians Newsletter* (February 1997): 32.

15. Martin Ridge, "At the Huntington Library," speech at Indiana University's memorial service for Gunderson, January 18, 1997.

16. Douglas L. Wilson, *Honor's Voice: The Transformation of Abraham Lincoln* (New York: Alfred A. Knopf, 1998), pp. 213–215. The *New York Times* selected this volume as "a notable book of the year." Similarly, rhetorical scholar Frederick J. Antczak used Gunderson's book on the 1840 presidential campaign to help develop his argument about the problems occasioned by the rise of the democratic audience in America in his award-winning book, *Thought and Character: The Rhetoric of Democratic Education* (Ames: Iowa State University Press, 1985), pp. 12–24.

17. Michael F. Holt, *The Rise and Fall of the American Whig Party: Jacksonian Politics and the Onset of the Civil War* (New York: Oxford University Press, 1999), p. 999, n. 51. Unlike Gunderson, Holt is sympathetic to the Whigs. He argues that Whig rhetoric was more substantive and less cynical in 1840 than is reflected in the *Log-Cabin Campaign*. He concedes, however, that what he characterizes as issue-based Whig persuasion tended to occur in state and local campaigns rather than in the presidential campaign. Nevertheless, Holt relies heavily on Gunderson's scholarship for material in his chapter on the 1840 campaign (pp. 89–121, p. 999, n. 57, n. 60, p. 1000, n. 66).

18. Ridge, "At the Huntington."

19. On renewed scholarly interest in public address, see Stephen E. Lucas, "The Renaissance of American Public Address: Text and Context in Rhetorical Criticism," *Quarterly Journal of Speech* 74 (1988): 243–262; Michael C. Leff and Fred J. Kauffeld, eds., *Texts in Context: Critical Dialogues on Significant Episodes in American Political Rhetoric* (Davis, CA: Hermagoras Press, 1989); Robert S. Iltis and Stephen H. Browne, "Tradition and Resurgence in Public Address Studies," in *Speech Communication: Essays to Commemorate the 75th Anniversary of the Speech Communication Association*, ed. Gerald M. Phillips and Julia T. Wood (Carbondale: Southern Illinois University Press, 1990), pp. 81–93; Martin J. Medhurst, ed., *Landmark Essays on American Public Address* (Davis, CA: Hermagoras Press, 1993).

20. Books on American public address published by Gunderson's students include Judith L. Anderson, ed., *Outspoken Women: Speeches by American Women Reformers, 1635–1935* (Dubuque, IA: Kendall/Hunt, 1984); Hal Bochin, *Richard Nixon: Rhetorical Strategist* (New York: Greenwood Press, 1990); Bernard J. Brommel, *Eugene V. Debs: Spokesman for Labor and Socialism* (Chicago: Charles H. Kerr, 1978); Carolyn Calloway-Thomas and John Louis Lucaites, eds., *Martin Luther King, Jr., and the Sermonic Power of Public Discourse* (Tuscaloosa: University of Alabama Press, 1993); Arthur F. Fleser, *A Rhetorical Study of the Speaking of Calvin Coolidge* (Lewiston, NY: E. Mellen Press, 1990); Stephen E. Frantzich and John Sullivan, *The C-Span Revolution* (Norman: University of Oklahoma Press, 1996); John C. Hammerback and Richard J. Jensen, *The Rhetorical Career of Cesar Chavez* (College Station: Texas A&M University Press, 1998); John C. Hammerback, Richard J. Jensen, and Jose Angel Gutierrez, *A War of Words: Chicano Protest Rhetoric in the 1960s and 1970s* (Westport, CT: Greenwood Press, 1985); Judith D. Hoover, *Corporate Advocacy: Rhetoric in the Information Age* (Westport, CT: Quorum Books, 1997); Richard J. Jensen, *Clarence Darrow: The Creation of an American Myth* (New York: Greenwood Press, 1992); Richard J. Jensen and

John C. Hammerback, eds., *In Search of Justice: The Indiana Tradition in Speech Communication* (Amsterdam: Rodopi, 1987); Kathleen E. Kendall, ed., *Presidential Campaign Discourse: Strategic Communication Problems* (Albany: State University of New York Press, 1995); Kathleen E. Kendall, *Communication in the Presidential Primaries: Candidates and the Media, 1912–2000* (Westport, CT: Praeger, 2000); Kurt Ritter and James R. Andrews, *The American Ideology: Reflections of the Revolution in American Rhetoric* (Annandale, VA: Bicentennial Monograph, Speech Communication Association, 1978); Kurt Ritter and David Henry, *Ronald Reagan: The Great Communicator* (New York: Greenwood Press, 1992); Lloyd E. Rohler, *Ralph Waldo Emerson: Preacher and Lecturer* (Westport, CT: Greenwood Press, 1995); Lloyd E. Rohler and Roger Cook, eds., *Great Speeches for Criticism and Analysis* (Greenwood, IN: Alistair Press, 1988); C. Brant Short, *Ronald Reagan and the Public Lands: American's Conversation Debate, 1979–1984* (College Station: Texas A&M University Press, 1989); Michael A. Weatherson and Hal Bochin, *Hiram Johnson: A Bio-Bibliography* (New York: Greenwood Press, 1988); Michael A. Weatherson and Hal Bochin, *Hiram Johnson: Political Revivalist* (Lanhan, MD: University Press of America, 1995).

21. Correspondence from C. Brant Short to the author, September 28, 1999.

22. Following his normal practice when preparing a book, Gunderson first wrote a series of journal articles on Harrison; his final essay on Harrison appeared as Robert G. Gunderson, "William Henry Harrison: Apprentice in Arms," *Northwest Ohio Quarterly* 65 (1993): 3–29.

23. Interview with Jeffery R. Gunderson, the younger of Robert Gray Gunderson's two sons, San Francisco, May 15, 1998.

24. For the 1840 presidential campaign as the moment of triumph of popular rhetoric over elevated rhetoric, see Antczak, *Thought and Character*, pp. 11–54. See also Cmiel, *Democratic Eloquence*, p. 12.

25. For the most concise description of the rhetoric of the 1840 campaign, see Robert Gray Gunderson, "Presidential Canvas, Log-Cabin Style," *Today's Speech* 5, No. 2 (1957): 19–20. The most comprehensive treatment, of course, is Gunderson's book *The Log-Cabin Campaign.*

26. Gunderson, "Presidential Rally, 1840 Style," pp. 8–9. This essay recounted the rhetoric of the Whigs' Ohio State Convention in Columbus, Ohio.

27. Robert G. Gunderson, "A Political and Rhetorical Study of the 1840 Presidential Campaign," Ph.D. diss., University of Wisconsin at Madison, 1949.

28. Robert Gray Gunderson, "The Fort Meigs Whig Celebration of 1840," *Northwest Ohio Quarterly* 21 (1949): 69–77; Gunderson, "The Dayton Log-Cabin Convention," pp. 202–210.

29. Gunderson, *The Log-Cabin Campaign.*

30. Hesseltine, "Speech and History," p. 176.

31. Gunderson, *The Log-Cabin Campaign*, pp. 29–40.

32. Gunderson, "Webster in Linsey-Woolsey," pp. 23, 30.

33. Robert G. Gunderson, "The Southern Whigs," in *Oratory in the Old South, 1828–1860*, ed. Waldo W. Braden, J. Jeffery Auer, and Bert E. Bradley (Baton Rouge: Louisiana State University Press, 1970), pp. 112, 114–116, 125.

34. For example, see Robert Gray Gunderson, "The Great Baltimore Whig Convention of 1840," *Maryland Historical Magazine* 47 (1952): 11–18.

35. Robert Gray Gunderson, "Eisenhower on Courage," *Quarterly Journal of Speech* 36 (1952): 401. Ever the historian, Gunderson was careful to note that most newspapers,

including the *New York Times*, subsequently published Eisenhower's prepared text rather than the speech he actually presented in Cleveland (p. 402).

36. Robert G. Gunderson, "Political Phrasemakers in Perspective," *Southern Speech Journal* 26 (1960): 23, 25.

37. Robert Gray Gunderson, "The Magnanimous Mr. Clay," *Southern Speech Journal* 16 (1950): 138.

38. Gunderson, "The Southern Whigs," p. 126.

39. Robert Gray Gunderson, "John W. Bear, 'The Buckeye Blacksmiths,' " *Ohio State Archaeological and Historical Quarterly* 61 (1952): 262–271; Gunderson, *The Log-Cabin Campaign*, pp. 201–208.

40. See Robert G. Gunderson, "The Calamity Howlers," *Quarterly Journal of Speech* 26 (1940): 401–411; Robert G. Gunderson, "Introduction: A Setting for Protest and Reform," *The Rhetoric of Protest and Reform, 1878–1898*, ed. Paul H. Boase (Athens: Ohio University Press, 1980), pp. 1–13; Robert G. Gunderson, "Early Coeds Win the Right to Speak," *The Gavel* 32 (January 1950): 29–30.

41. Gunderson, "Government Ownership of Electric Utilities," pp. 194–196, 228.

42. Jeff Gunderson, "In Memory of His Father," speech at Indiana University's memorial service for Gunderson, January 18, 1997.

43. Gunderson, "William B. Hesseltine and the Profession of History," p. 108.

44. Jeff Gunderson, "In Memory of His Father."

45. Ridge, "Robert Gray Gunderson," p. 32.

46. Ridge, "At the Huntington Library."

47. Jeff Gunderson, "In Memory of His Father"; Ridge, "At the Huntington Library."

48. Gunderson, "The Calamity Howlers," pp. 401–402.

49. Ibid., p. 409.

50. Ibid., pp. 409–411.

51. Gunderson, "Introduction: A Setting for Protest and Reform," pp. 5–6.

52. Gunderson, "The Calamity Howlers," pp. 409–410.

53. Gunderson, "Early Coeds Win the Right to Speak," p. 29.

54. Ibid., p. 30.

55. Gunderson, "Introduction: A Setting for Protest and Reform," p. 9.

56. Correspondence from Jeff Gunderson to the author, March 31, 1998.

57. Jeff Gunderson, "In Memory of His Father."

58. Gunderson, "William B. Hesseltine and the Profession of History," p. 107.

59. Robert G. Gunderson, "International Organization: A Discussion Progression and Debate Analysis," in *International Organization: Twenty-Sixth Discussion and Debate Manual*, vol. 1, ed. Bower Aly (Columbia, MO: Lucas Brothers, 1952), p. 31.

60. See Robert Gray Gunderson, "Letters from the Washington Peace Conference of 1861," *Journal of Southern History* 17 (1951): 382–392; Robert Gray Gunderson, "John C. Wright and 'The Old Gentlemen's Convention,' " *Bulletin of the Historical and Philosophical Society of Ohio* 12 (1954): 109–118; Robert G. Gunderson, "William C. Rives and the 'Old Gentlemen's Convention,' " *Journal of Southern History* 22 (1956): 459–476; Robert G. Gunderson, "The Washington Peace Conference of 1861: Selection of Delegates," *Journal of Southern History* 24 (1958): 347–359; Robert G. Gunderson, "The Old Gentlemen's Convention," *Civil War History* 7 (1961): 5–12; Gunderson, *Old Gentlemen's Convention: The Washington Peace Conference of 1861*; Robert Gray Gunderson, "The Washington Peace Conference of 1861," *Antislavery and Disunion, 1858–*

1861: Studies in the Rhetoric of Compromise and Conflict, ed. J. Jeffery Auer (New York: Harper and Row, 1963), pp. 378–391.

61. Gunderson, "Washington Peace Conference" (1963), p. 385. Gunderson continued to hold this view long after he had completed his studies of Civil War rhetoric. See, for example, Robert G. Gunderson, "The Oxymoron Strain in American Rhetoric," *Central States Speech Journal* 28 (1977): 94.

62. See, for example, Gunderson, "International Organization," pp. 31, 38, 40, 45.

63. Gunderson, *Old Gentlemen's Convention*, pp. 100–101.

64. Ibid., p. 24.

65. Gunderson, "William C. Rives and the 'Old Gentlemen's Convention,' " p. 459; Gunderson, *Old Gentleman's Convention*, p. 64.

66. Hesseltine, "Foreword," p. viii.

67. Gunderson, "William C. Rives and the 'Old Gentlemen's Convention,' " p. 460; Gunderson, "Washington Peace Conference" (1963), p. 378.

68. Gunderson, "The Old Gentlemen's Convention" (1961), pp. 6–9.

69. Gunderson, "William C. Rives and the 'Old Gentlemen's Convention,' " p. 467.

70. Gunderson, "John C. Wright and 'The Old Gentlemen's Convention,' " pp. 113–117.

71. Gunderson, *Old Gentlemen's Convention*, pp. 14–22.

72. Gunderson, "The Washington Peace Conference" (1958), p. 355.

73. Gunderson, *Old Gentlemen's Convention*, pp. 73–74; Gunderson, "Letters from the Washington Peace Conference," p. 383.

74. Gunderson, "Letters from the Washington Peace Conference," p. 384.

75. Gunderson, *Old Gentlemen's Convention*, pp. 81–82.

76. Gunderson, "Old Gentlemen's Convention" (1961), p. 12.

77. Gunderson, *Old Gentlemen's Convention*, p. 102.

78. Gunderson, "Washington Peace Conference" (1958), p. 355.

79. Gunderson, "Old Gentlemen's Convention" (1961), p. 12.

80. Gunderson, "Washington Peace Conference" (1963), p. 391.

81. Gunderson, "International Organization," pp. 62, 32.

82. Gunderson, *Old Gentlemen's Convention*, p. 101.

83. Hesseltine, "Speech and History," p. 176.

84. Robert G. Gunderson, "Reflections on History and Rhetorical Criticism," *Communication Education* 35 (1986): 408.

85. Gunderson, "The Oxymoron Strain in American Rhetoric," p. 92.

86. Carroll Arnold, "Reflections on American Public Discourse," paper presented to the Speech Communication Association, San Francisco, December 29, 1976.

87. Gunderson, "The Oxymoron Strain in American Rhetoric," pp. 92–95.

88. Robert G. Gunderson, "Digging Up Parson Weems: American Concepts of Success from John Winthrop to J. R. Ewing," *Vital Speeches of the Day* (September 1, 1981): 684–687.

89. Andrews, "Foreword: Contextualizing American Rhetoric," p. xi.

90. Robert G. Gunderson, "Making It: The Rhetoric of Upward Mobility from Poor Richard to Punk Rock," *Vital Speeches of the Day* (November 1, 1986): 54.

91. Gunderson, "Making It: The Rhetoric of Upward Mobility," pp. 51–54.

92. Robert G. Gunderson, "Idiosyncrasy: Sound Bytes South and West," *America's Distant Cultures: Regionalism in the South and West*, ed. Judith Hoover (in preparation).

93. See, for example, Gunderson, "Webster in Linsey-Woolsey"; Gunderson, "William C. Rives and the 'Old Gentlemen's Convention.' "

94. Gunderson, "The Calamity Howlers"; Gunderson, "The Southern Whigs."

95. Robert G. Gunderson, "William Henry Harrison," in *Encyclopedia Americana*, international edition (Danbury, CT: Grolier, 1998), vol. 13, pp. 822–823. This essay originally appeared in the edition published in 1970.

96. Robert G. Gunderson, "A Search for Old Tip Himself," *Register of the Kentucky Historical Society* 86 (1988): 330–351; Robert G. Gunderson, "Indian Angst and 'Heathenish Practices': The Indiana Frontier, 1804–1811," in *Selected Papers from the 1989 and 1990 George Rogers Clark Trans-Appalachian Frontier History Conferences*, ed. Robert J. Holden (Vincennes, IN: Eastern National Park and Monument Association and Vincennes University, 1991), pp. 107–119; Gunderson, "William Henry Harrison: Apprentice in Arms," pp. 3–29.

97. Robert Gray Gunderson, "Lincoln in Cincinnati," *Bulletin of the Historical and Philosophical Society of Ohio* 8 (1950): 258–266; Robert Gray Gunderson, "Lincoln and Governor Morgan: A Financial Footnote," *Abraham Lincoln Quarterly* 6 (1951): 431–437; Robert Gray Gunderson, "Presidential Inauguration, 1861," *Bulletin of the Historical and Philosophical Society of Ohio* 11 (1953): 99–106; Robert G. Gunderson, "Reading Lincoln's Mail," *Indiana Magazine of History* 55 (1959): 379–392; Robert G. Gunderson, "Lincoln and the Policy of Eloquent Silence: November 1860 to March 1861," *Quarterly Journal of Speech* 47 (1961): 1–9.

98. Robert G. Gunderson, "Lincoln's Rhetorical Style: A Reflection of His Personality," *Vital Speeches of the Day* 27 (February 15, 1961): 273–275; Robert G. Gunderson, "Another Shelf of Lincoln Books," *Quarterly Journal of Speech* 48 (1962): 308–313; Robert G. Gunderson, " 'Stoutly Argufy': Lincoln's Legal Speaking," *Wisconsin Magazine of History* 46 (1963): 109–117.

99. Gunderson, "Another Shelf of Lincoln Books," p. 308.

100. More recently, Cmiel has noted that Lincoln was able to move back and forth between the old eloquent style and the emerging colloquial style of rhetoric—"at times refined but at other times crude . . . often eloquent but . . . also often folksy" (Cmiel, *Democratic Eloquence*, p. 13). For a study of Lincoln's influence on subsequent American orators, which appeared in one of the books dedicated to Robert G. Gunderson, see Michael C. Leff, "Lincoln among the Nineteenth-Century Orators," in *Rhetoric and Political Culture*, pp. 131–155.

101. Gunderson, "Lincoln in Cincinnati"; Gunderson, "Presidential Inauguration, 1861."

102. Gunderson, "Lincoln and Governor Morgan"; Gunderson, "Lincoln and the Policy of Eloquent Silence."

103. Gunderson, " 'Stoutly Argufy,' " p. 115.

104. Gunderson, "Lincoln's Rhetorical Style," p. 273.

105. Gunderson, "Reading Lincoln's Mail," p. 390.

106. Gunderson, " 'Stoutly Argufy,' " p. 117.

107. Ibid., p. 114.

108. Gunderson, "Lincoln's Rhetorical Style," p. 273.

109. Gunderson, "Reading Lincoln's Mail," pp. 390, 386.

110. Gunderson, " 'Stoutly Argufy,' " p. 117.

111. Gunderson, "Digging Up Parson Weems"; Gunderson, "Making It: The Rhetoric of Upward Mobility"; Gunderson, "Lincoln's Rhetorical Style"; Robert G. Gunderson,

"Davy Crockett's Tongue-Tied Admirers: Training for an Articulate Democracy." *Vital Speeches of the Day* 21 (1 September 1955): 1462–1466.

112. Robert Gunderson, "An Answer to an Oft-Asked Question: Why Have Debating?" *Wisconsin Journal of Education* 71 (1938): 199–200; Robert G. Gunderson, "Teaching Critical Thinking," *Speech Teacher* 10 (1961): 100–104; Robert G. Gunderson, "In Behalf of Rhetoric," *NEA Journal* 52, No. 1 (1963): 12–13; Robert G. Gunderson, "On Teaching Persuasive Speaking," in *Essays on Teaching Speech in High School*, ed. J. Jeffery Auer and Edward B. Jenkinson (Bloomington: Indiana University Press, 1971), pp. 63–80.

113. Gunderson, "In Behalf of Rhetoric," p. 13.

114. Robert Gray Gunderson, "Group Dynamics: Hope or Hoax?" *Quarterly Journal of Speech* 36 (1950): 37.

115. Robert Gray Gunderson, "Dangers in Group Dynamics." *Religious Education* 65 (1951): 343.

116. Robert Gray Gunderson, "This Group-Dynamics Furor," *School and Society* 74 (1951): 100.

117. Franklyn S. Haiman, "Group Dynamics: More Sinned against Than Sinning," *Quarterly Journal of Speech* 36 (1950): 243–245; Herbert C. Kelman, "Group Dynamics: Neither Hope nor Hoax," *Quarterly Journal of Speech* 36 (1950): 371–377.

118. Robert Gray Gunderson, "More Dynamics," *Quarterly Journal of Speech* 36 (1950): 245–246. Abridged versions of Gunderson's "Group Dynamics: Hope or Hoax?" were reprinted as "On 'The Science of Human Relations': Group Dynamics—Hope or Hoax?" *Education Digest* 15, No. 8 (1950): 16–18; and as "Group Dynamics: Hope or Hoax?" in *Planning of Change: Readings in the Applied Behavioral Sciences*, ed. Warren G. Bennis, Kenneth D. Benne, and Robert Chin (New York: Holt, Rinehart, and Winston, 1961), pp. 255–259.

119. Gunderson was particularly galled by the concept of engineering consent, a notion that Edward L. Bernays (one of the "fathers" of modern public relations) had been advancing since the 1940s. For example, see Edward L. Bernays, ed., *The Engineering of Consent* (Norman: University of Oklahoma Press, 1955).

120. Gunderson, "Davy Crockett's Tongue-Tied Admirers: Training for an Articulate Democracy." This address was reprinted and excerpted in the following textbooks: Waldo W. Braden and Mary Louis Gehring, eds., *Speech Practices: A Resource Book for the Student of Public Speaking* (New York: Harper and Brothers, 1958), pp. 83–84; Wilbur E. Gilman, Bower Aly, and Hollis L. White, *Fundamentals of Speaking*, 2d ed. (New York: Macmillan, 1964), pp. 393–402; Jeffery Auer, *Brigance's Speech Communication*, 3d ed. (New York: Appleton-Century-Crofts, 1967), pp. 153–161.

121. Gunderson, "Davy Crockett's Tongue-Tied Admirers," p. 1463.

122. Ibid., p. 1465.

123. Gunderson, "Reflections on History and Rhetorical Criticism," p. 409.

124. Gunderson, "Another Shelf of Lincoln Books," p. 313.

125. Gunderson, "The Great Baltimore Whig Convention of 1840."

126. "Whig Convention, 1840," *Baltimore Sun*, May 3, 1952, p. 10.

127. Bob Woodward, *Shadow: Five Presidents and the Legacy of Watergate* (New York: Simon and Schuster, 1999), pp. 389–391, 394.

128. Robert Hariman, "Afterword: Relocating the Art of Public Address," in *Rhetoric and Political Culture*, pp. 167, 165.

129. Ibid., p. 166.

130. Andrews, "Foreword: Contextualizing American Rhetoric," pp. x–xi.

131. Gunderson, "Reflections on History and Rhetorical Criticism," p. 409; see also Gunderson, "On Teaching Persuasive Speaking," pp. 71–75.

132. Gunderson, "William B. Hesseltine and the Profession of History," pp. 108–109.

133. Ridge, "At the Huntington Library."

BIBLIOGRAPHY

"Government Ownership of Electric Utilities: University of Wisconsin Affirmative vs. Ohio State University Negative." *Intercollegiate Debates*. Vol. 18. Ed. Egbert Ray Nichols. New York: Noble and Noble, 1937. This transcript of a public debate at the University of Wisconsin, Madison, includes two speeches by Robert G. Gunderson.

"An Answer to an Oft-Asked Question: Why Have Debating?" *Wisconsin Journal of Education* 71 (1938): 199–200.

"The Calamity Howlers." *Quarterly Journal of Speech* 26 (1940): 401–411.

"Presidential Rally, 1840 Style." *The Gavel* 31 (1948): 8–9.

"The Fort Meigs Whig Celebration of 1840." *Northwest Ohio Quarterly* 21 (1949): 69–77.

"The Dayton Log-Cabin Convention of 1840." *Bulletin of the Historical and Philosophical Society of Ohio* 7 (1949): 202–210.

"Early Coeds Win the Right to Speak." *The Gavel* 32 (January 1950): 29–30.

"The Magnanimous Mr. Clay." *Southern Speech Journal* 16 (1950): 133–140.

"Lincoln in Cincinnati." *Bulletin of the Historical and Philosophical Society of Ohio* 8 (1950): 258–266.

"Group Dynamics: Hope or Hoax?" *Quarterly Journal of Speech* 36 (1950): 34–38. Abridged versions reprinted as "On 'The Science of Human Relations': Group Dynamics—Hope or Hoax?" *Education Digest* 15, No. 8 (1950): 16–18; and as "Group Dynamics: Hope or Hoax?" In *Planning of Change: Readings in the Applied Behavioral Sciences*. Ed. Warren G. Bennis, Kenneth D. Benne, and Robert Chin. New York: Holt, Rinehart, and Winston, 1961, pp. 255–259.

"More Dynamics." *Quarterly Journal of Speech* 36 (1950): 245–246.

"This Group-Dynamics Furor." *School and Society* 74 (1951): 97–100.

"Dangers in Group Dynamics." *Religious Education* 65 (1951): 342–344.

"Letters from the Washington Peace Conference of 1861." *Journal of Southern History* 17 (1951): 382–392.

"Lincoln and Governor Morgan: A Financial Footnote." *Abraham Lincoln Quarterly* 6 (1951): 431–437.

"Webster in Linsey-Woolsey." *Quarterly Journal of Speech* 37 (1951): 23–30.

"The Great Baltimore Whig Convention of 1840." *Maryland Historical Magazine* 47 (1952): 11–18.

"Thurlow Weed's Network: Whig Party Organization in 1840." *Indiana Magazine of History* 48 (1952): 107–118.

"John W. Bear, 'The Buckeye Blacksmith.' " *Ohio State Archaeological and Historical Quarterly* 61 (1952): 262–271.

"Horace Greeley and the Log-Cabin Campaign." *Bulletin of the Historical and Philosophical Society of Ohio* 10 (1952): 278–290.

"Tippecanoe Belles of 1840." *American Heritage* 4, No. 1 (1952): 3–5.

"International Organization: A Discussion Progression and Debate Analysis." In *International Organization: Twenty-Sixth Discussion and Debate Manual*. Vol. 1. Ed. Bower Aly. Columbia, MO: Lucas Brothers, 1952.

"Eisenhower on Courage." *Quarterly Journal of Speech* 36 (1952): 400–402.

"Presidential Inauguration, 1861." *Bulletin of the Historical and Philosophical Society of Ohio* 11 (1953): 99–106.

"John C. Wright and 'The Old Gentlemen's Convention.' " *Bulletin of the Historical and Philosophical Society of Ohio* 12 (1954): 109–118.

"Davy Crockett's Tongue-Tied Admirers: Training for an Articulate Democracy." *Vital Speeches of the Day* 21 (September 1, 1955): 1462–1466. Reprinted: Wilbur E. Gilman, Bower Aly, and Hollis L. White. *Fundamentals of Speaking*. 2d ed. New York: Macmillan, 1964, pp. 393–402; and J. Jeffery Auer. *Brigance's Speech Communication*, 3d ed. New York: Appleton-Century-Crofts, 1967, pp. 153–161. Excerpted in Waldo W. Braden and Mary Louis Gehring, eds. *Speech Practices: A Resource Book for the Student of Public Speaking*. New York: Harper and Brothers, 1958, pp. 83–84.

"William C. Rives and the 'Old Gentleman's Convention.' " *Journal of Southern History* 22 (1956): 459–476.

"The Late General Crary." *Michigan History* 40 (1956): 344–352.

"Rumpsey, Dumpsey, Colonel Johnson Shot Tecumseh!" *Bulletin of the Historical and Philosophical Society of Ohio* 14 (1956): 301–311.

"Ogle's Omnibus of Lies." *Pennsylvania Magazine of History and Biography* 80 (1956): 443–451.

"Presidential Canvass, Log-Cabin Style." *Today's Speech* 5, No. 2 (1957): 19–20.

"Log-Cabin Canvass, Hoosier Style." *Indiana Magazine of History* 53 (1957): 245–256.

The Log-Cabin Campaign. Lexington: University of Kentucky Press, 1957. Reprinted Westport, CT: Greenwood Press, 1977.

"The Washington Peace Conference of 1861: Selection of Delegates." *Journal of Southern History* 24 (1958): 347–359.

"Reading Lincoln's Mail." *Indiana Magazine of History* 55 (1959): 379–392.

"Political Phrasemakers in Perspective." *Southern Speech Journal* 26 (1960): 22–26.

"Teaching Critical Thinking." *Speech Teacher* 10 (1961): 100–104.

"The Old Gentlemen's Convention." *Civil War History* 7 (1961): 5–12.

Old Gentlemen's Convention: The Washington Peace Conference of 1861. Madison: University of Wisconsin Press, 1961. Reprinted Westport, CT: Greenwood Press, 1981.

"Lincoln and the Policy of Eloquent Silence: November 1860 to March 1861." *Quarterly Journal of Speech* 47 (1961): 1–9.

"Lincoln's Rhetorical Style: A Reflection of His Personality." *Vital Speeches of the Day* 27 (February 15, 1961): 273–275. Reprinted in *The Asian Student* 9 (March 4, 1961): 5–6; in *Perspectives on Public Speaking*. Ed. Nels G. Juleus. New York: American Book Company, 1966, pp. 149–157; and in *An Analysis of Lincoln and Douglas as Public Speakers and Debater*. Ed. Lionel Crocker. Springfield, IL: Charles C. Thomas, 1968, pp. 82–90.

"Another Shelf of Lincoln Books." *Quarterly Journal of Speech* 48 (1962): 308–313.

"In Behalf of Rhetoric." *NEA Journal* 52, No. 1 (January 1963): 12–13.

"The Washington Peace Conference of 1861." In *Antislavery and Disunion, 1858–1861:*

Studies in the Rhetoric of Compromise and Conflict. Ed. J. Jeffery Auer. New York: Harper and Row, 1963.

" 'Stoutly Argufy': Lincoln's Legal Speaking." *Wisconsin Magazine of History* 46 (1963): 109–117. Reprinted under the same title as *Historical Bulletin*, No. 21. Madison: Lincoln Fellowship of Wisconsin, 1963.

"The Southern Whigs." *Oratory in the Old South, 1828–1860.* Ed. Waldo W. Braden, J. Jeffery Auer, and Bert E. Bradley. Baton Rouge: Louisiana State University Press, 1970.

"William Henry Harrison." In *Encyclopedia Americana*, international edition. Vol. 13. Danbury, CT: Grolier, 1998. This essay originally appeared in the edition published in 1970; only the bibliography was updated in subsequent editions.

"On Teaching Persuasive Speaking." In *Essays on Teaching Speech in High School.* Ed. J. Jeffery Auer and Edward B. Jenkinson. Bloomington: Indiana University Press, 1971.

"The Oxymoron Strain in American Rhetoric." *Central States Speech Journal* 28 (1977): 92–95.

"Introduction: A Setting for Protest and Reform." *The Rhetoric of Protest and Reform, 1878–1898.* Ed. Paul H. Boase. Athens: Ohio University Press, 1980.

"Digging Up Parson Weems: American Concepts of Success from John Winthrop to J. R. Ewing." *Vital Speeches of the Day* 47 (September 1, 1981): 684–687.

"William B. Hesseltine and the Profession of History: A Retrospective—Dutch Uncle to a Profession." *Wisconsin Magazine of History* 66 (1982–1983): 106–110.

"Reflections on History and Rhetorical Criticism." *Communication Education* 35 (1986): 408–410.

"Making It: The Rhetoric of Upward Mobility from *Poor Richard* to Punk Rock." *Vital Speeches of the Day* 53 (November 1, 1986): 51–54.

"A Search for Old Tip Himself." *Register of the Kentucky Historical Society* 86 (1988): 330–351.

"Indian Angst and 'Heathenish Practices': The Indiana Frontier, 1804–1811." In *Selected Papers from the 1989 and 1990 George Clark Trans-Appalachian Frontier History Conferences.* Ed. Robert J. Holden. Vincennes, IN: Eastern National Park and Monument Association and Vincennes University, 1991.

"William Henry Harrison: Apprentice in Arms." *Northwest Ohio Quarterly* 65 (1993): 3–29.

"Idiosyncrasy: Sound Bytes South and West." In *America's Distant Cultures: Regionalism in the South and West.* Ed. Judith D. Hoover. In preparation.

Ernest G. Bormann. Photo courtesy of Ernest G. Bormann. Used with permission.

9

Ernest G. Bormann: Roots, Revelations, and Results of Symbolic Convergence Theory

MOYA ANN BALL

Growing up in South Dakota, Ernest G. Bormann saw the Roaring Twenties turn into the decade of depression and experienced dust storms of drought and plagues of grasshoppers. At school he was such an eager student that his teachers regularly asked him to slow down and to refrain from trying to ask and answer all the questions. As a professor emeritus at the University of Minnesota, he has never lost that enthusiasm for learning, that questioning spirit. A remarkable teacher-scholar, playwright, and novelist, he is known best in the communication discipline for developing symbolic convergence theory. Before explaining that theory and its contributions to rhetorical criticism and to the discipline of communication, I provide some background information about Bormann, tracing the historical roots of his work through his life and those who influenced him.[1]

Bormann's natural ability, insatiable reading habits, and questioning mind had early payoffs when he graduated as his high school's valedictorian. By this time, World War II had replaced the depression. Drafted into the Army Specialized Training Program, Bormann was sent to France and Germany just before the end of the war. In Germany he was part of a convoy that stopped at Dachau only hours after an American tank division had liberated its concentration camp. After demobilization, he attended the University of South Dakota, where he was an active undergraduate, writing for the school paper, debating, and playing intramural sports. While there, he disputed with University of Nebraska debating star Ted Sorensen (who became President Kennedy's chief speechwriter) and debated against a Dakota Wesleyan student, George McGovern. Originally, Bormann had planned to go to law school; however, influenced by speech professor Elbert Harrington, he decided to apply to a graduate speech program at the

University of Iowa in Iowa City. Before graduating magna cum laude from the University of South Dakota, though, Bormann was elected to Phi Beta Kappa, and he discovered the topic for his Ph.D. dissertation, the politician from Louisiana, Huey Long.

At the University of Iowa, Ernest Bormann met a charming young graduate student from Virginia, Nancy Curtis, a gifted musician, playwright, and actress. They were married in 1952. In one of his books, he describes her as "fellow traveller, counselor, guide, and encourager as well as consultant, editor, and copyeditor."[2] She was never able to do anything about his lack of musical ability, however, and so to this day he remains the tone-deaf father of a professional opera singer daughter, Ruth. Ironically, Bormann is color-blind, and another daughter, Lisa, is a professional artist. Less ironical is the fact that daughter Ellen has published in the field of small group communication and is managing director of Curtis-Bormann Associates, a communication consulting firm. Daughter Sally has her Ph.D. from the University of Michigan in English language and literature.

At Iowa Bormann shared an apartment with Sam Becker and Owen Peterson, who have remained lifelong friends. At this time, too, Bormann wrote his first play about Huey Long, and Becker starred in its title role. Other intellectual influences were three professors: A. Craig Baird, Orville Hitchcock, and Gustav Bergmann. Under the philosopher Bergmann, Bormann became interested in the philosophy of language, logical positivism, empiricism, and semiotics. After completing his dissertation on the radio addresses of Huey Long, he taught at Eastern Illinois University, Florida State University, and the University of Minnesota.

TEACHING AND RESEARCH

At Eastern Illinois, David Berlo introduced Bormann to the work of R. F. Bales and his associates at Harvard. Using Bales' group coding scheme, interaction process analysis, Bormann began to code the communication of meetings in his small group class. His next stint at Florida State University included helping to develop a program in educational television. At the University of Minnesota, Bormann continued to teach courses in small group communication as well as others, including the history and criticism of public address. At this point in his career, he began to experiment with different ways of doing criticism. He challenged his group seminar students with the possibility of analyzing group dynamics using rhetorical criticism procedures. He challenged his rhetorical criticism students to find new and useful ways to study discourse. In the 1960s he began to study the rhetoric of the abolitionists, the forerunners of Black Power. He wanted to know if there were different kinds of such rhetoric. What was required of successful rhetoric in its historical context? How well did their rhetoric meet the needs of the American people? This research resulted in the book *Forerunners of Black Power: The Rhetoric of Abolition.*[3] Including speeches by women and blacks, it was a forerunner itself in that it featured the works of minority groups and in the way it made the argument that the seeds of the women's movement were sown in the rhetoric of abolition.

In the meantime, in his studies of small groups, Bormann had noticed that not all group laughter could be coded as a tension release. In 1970 R. F. Bales published a book in which he had changed one of his coding categories from "shows tension release" to "dramatizes."[4] Bormann was suddenly taken with what the quantitative data on small groups suggested and how close they were to qualitative studies of rhetoric. In fact, he thought that Bales had finally discovered rhetorical criticism. Excited about the possibility of a rhetorical criticism of small groups and the effect of fantasy sharing, Bormann began to teach a seminar on history and criticism in which he talked at length about the sharing of dramas in groups. At the end of the term, the students were so fired up that they asked if they could meet informally. This group, originally called "the Rhetoric Circle," met at the Bormann's house to talk about research, papers, dissertations, and fantasy theme analysis. Eventually, Bormann christened the group "the Turtle Racers," and the group proceeded to bond with T-shirts. Even a poster was produced that proclaimed, "Behold the turtle, he only makes progress by sticking his neck out."

What else did the Turtle Racers do? According to Bormann, the most important thing that they did was create fantasy theme analysis and symbolic convergence theory. Starting with Bales' notion of a fantasy theme, they added new features and technical terms. They did original research that was published.[5] The original group consisted of a handful of seminar students. Soon other students were added so that over the years there was a constant turnover as some graduated and others enrolled. The Turtle Racers continued until Bormann's sabbatical in Europe in the early 1970s. Later, another group of students nicknamed "the Bullet Train" met at the Bormann's to fathom out how to use symbolic convergence theory to study political campaigns. Later yet, a third group, known informally as "the Chain Gang," used qualitative and quantitative methods to research the possibility of specific rhetorical communities around the world. This last group, of which I was a part, was named informally because Bormann, always a "word man," did not like the negative connotations of a chain gang!

The preceding discussion is important for understanding the roots of Bormann's work. Above all, he is a teacher-scholar who never knew (nor did he want to know) where teaching stopped and research began. In 1961 he published an essay, "An Empirical Approach to Certain Concepts of Logical Proof,"[6] in which he suggests an empirical approach to using and assessing logical proof when teaching argumentation and public speaking. In a book on theory and research, he states, "Research is the most important work of many professors and graduate students. Only teaching challenges or surpasses its importance."[7] He notes, too, how teaching responsibilities are referred to in academe as "loads" and how research is always "our work," to the extent that such attitudes result in "half-hearted and poorly prepared teaching."[8]

Bormann's teaching was never halfhearted. He believed strongly in active learning and experiential teaching. As an instructor for one academic year at the University of South Dakota, before heading to graduate school, he devised a fundamentals course as an experiential class. Students could choose one of three possible simulations to implement: the United Nations General Assembly, the U.S. Congress, or the South Dakota legislature. Other faculty in the department encouraged him to write about the course and submit it for publication. He did and received his first rejection from the *Quarterly Journal of Speech*. The rejection did not discourage him, however, from promoting experiential learning in most of his courses. In his words, "[S]tudents can learn theories best when they can test them against samples of actual discourse."[9] Accordingly, an undergraduate course in small group communication at the University of Minnesota included intensive experience in zero-history, leaderless groups supplemented with theoretical material. An upper-level course, called Group Dynamics Incorporated, simulated an organization with basic divisions, management groups, and chief executive officers.

As a teacher, Bormann stressed the dual needs of creativity and discipline. He and his students were expected to try out new ideas and new ways of doing things with the understanding that creativity seldom strikes without some kind of preparation. Discipline and systematic testing of the results of creativity were required for successful academic work. The dual needs of creativity and discipline are reflected also in the way that he sought to blend the humanities and scientific methodology as well as the rational and nonrational elements of communication. Early in his career, he stated that scholarship was "a way station between the method of the artist and the method of the scientist."[10] Throughout his career, he sought to reconcile the humanist's and the scientist's work, believing that scientific studies and rhetorical studies were different, not antagonistic, approaches to the discovery of knowledge.[11] Later, he said that the conflict between rhetorical theory and communication theory was unproductive and that there was a need to bring social science and humanism into some kind of symbiotic relationship.[12]

Even a cursory knowledge of symbolic convergence theory demonstrates Bormann's efforts to bring about such a symbiotic relationship. Indeed, he states forthrightly, "Fantasy Theme Analysis bridges the gap between humanism and social science research."[13] Several studies incorporate this approach. Investigators start with a rhetorical criticism of selected artifacts and look for traces of fantasy themes, which are then organized into fantasy types, which then make up a composite drama called a rhetorical vision. Key aspects of that vision are developed into items for a Q-sort. After the Q-sort has been administered to a sample of subjects, the results are used to compile a large sample survey.[14] Thus, increasingly, Bormann and his students attempted to blend humanistic and social scientific studies.

Additionally, Bormann had recognized a need to account for what he perceived to be the more nonrational elements of persuasion. He had read Ernest Cassirer and thought that he provided the rhetorical critic with an approach to the relationship between discursive material and fantasy themes, especially with his idea that "myth, art, language, and science appear as symbols; not in the sense of mere figures which refer to some given reality by means of suggestion and allegorical renderings, but in the sense of forces each of which produces and posits a world of its own."[15] Therefore, the mind expresses itself in different forms, discursive logic and creative imagination. Fantasies, of course, represented an expression of creative imagination. Years later, though, Bormann suggested that "shared fantasies account for irrational and non-rational aspects of persuasion but they provide the grounds for rational elements as well and a base for debate and discussion."[16]

Bormann, then, thought that teaching and research were inseparable, that there was a need to reconcile humanistic and social scientific studies as well as rational and nonrational elements of communication. But there were other hallmarks of scholarship that he was to stress in the classroom and in his work. He noted that historians search for structure in materials examined and that the structures found are as much a function of the viewpoints and talents of the researchers as they are of the events under study. Thus, scholars as much invent the structure as find it.[17] Bormann's search for structure is evidenced from the beginning of his scholarship. His dissertation on Huey Long,[18] his essay on William Henry Milburn,[19] his work on the evangelists of the Anti-Slavery movement,[20] and his examination of Abraham Lincoln's rhetorical use of calamity[21] culminate in his full-blown account of a unifying structure that moves from the abolitionists through the Civil War to the twentieth century.[22] His work *The Force of Fantasy* is the most comprehensive view of his theory of symbolic convergence. Also, the theory is the structure used to examine power and authority in organizations,[23] political cartoons in presidential campaigns,[24] media coverage of the Iranian hostage release and Reagan's inaugural,[25] the social realities of voters,[26] and the demise of the Cold War rhetorical vision.[27]

Finally, his teaching and research were rooted in a search for historical context and authenticity. Believing strongly that the past enriches the present and provides direction and purpose for the future, he stressed also the need to keep the historical record straight.[28] Indeed, he states that there is an "ethical imperative to keep an authentic record,"[29] reminding his readers that the Nazis rewrote the German past and that the Soviet Union modified its record, too.[30] Consequently, he thought that in order to understand the rhetoric of racial justice, it was necessary to know the history of the nineteenth-century antislavery campaign. As early as 1971, he warned against any movement to decontextualize scholarship, saying: "We are in the midst of several great rhetorical campaigns for change, and to be buffeted by the bombardment of television images, print-media messages, and public address without knowledge of the first great reform rhetorics in our history is to fail to understand the full relevance of today's rhetorical battles."[31] History and criticism, therefore, are closely related and work to supplement and enrich one another in the study of rhetoric and other forms of communication.[32]

His accentuation of authenticity may be seen as well in his articles on ghostwriting. In the late 1950s and early 1960s Bormann became increasingly concerned about the mushrooming of bureaucracy with its accompanying growth of committee work, believing that such developments encouraged what we would call today "talking heads" in which candidates spoke for parties, and presidents for corporations.[33] He was concerned about the apparent deception inherent in ghostwriting. He believed that ghostwriters could fool people into thinking that a poor political candidate was a good one[34] and that "if an audience is to know a candidate through what he speaks and writes, then he must be honest with them and present himself as he really is."[35] Considering that so many of the professionals in our discipline are speechwriters, Bormann's concerns seem like a platonic cry against sophistry, destined to make a few enemies. Also, of course, with today's mass media demands, the need for speechwriters is particularly practical. Yet, Bormann has a point: such rampant use of speechwriters—the White House has an army of them—encourages the election of politicians who may have more delivery skill than substance.

PHILOSOPHICAL AND THEORETICAL ASSUMPTIONS OF SYMBOLIC CONVERGENCE THEORY

Before explaining symbolic convergence theory and its accompanying critical method of fantasy theme analysis, it would be helpful to discuss the theory's philosophical and theoretical assumptions. First of all, Bormann had studied under Gustav Bergmann, a member of a school of philosophers who analyzed the language of the natural sciences. As a graduate student, Bormann was interested in the philosophy of rhetoric. "If we had a theory of rhetoric, what was the nature of its language? If we had a theory of communication, what was the nature of its language?"[36] Also, much of Bormann's work seems to rest on the assumptions of symbolic interactionism, which grew out of the work of George Herbert Mead at the University of Chicago. In fact, an early piece of Bormann's, coauthored with George Shapiro, refers to Mead's concept of the "looking-glass self."[37] The central concern of symbolic interaction is the study of symbols as data for understanding meaning. According to Bormann, "[R]hetoric . . . relates primarily to the study of words and how they work to shape meaning for individuals, groups, and nations."[38] Going even further and sounding somewhat like Kenneth Burke, he suggests that rhetorical analysts assume that when there is a discrepancy between the word and the thing, the most important cultural artifact for understanding the event "may not be the thing but the word."[39] Put differently, words are reality; they reflect, reinforce, and structure our world. According to Bormann, "[S]ymbolic change may be more significant and prior to and influential in technological changes."[40]

Like Kenneth Burke, there is a strong dramatistic bent to Bormann's work. One of his favorite quotes is from the poet Robert Frost, who wrote, "Society can never think things out; it has to see them acted out by actors."[41] When groups of people share fantasies, they are acting out, with dramatic language, their hopes, their fears, their joys, their values. There are some similarities to Jungian theory, too. In 1995 Bormann saw the possibility of archetypal fantasies.[42] For Carl Jung, the idea of a "collective unconscious" relates to his observation that the unconscious is not just individual; it is a storehouse of cultures that generates "mythic heroes for the primitive and still generates similar and individual fantasies for the civilized."[43] Thus, the existence of this collective unconscious establishes certain archetypes. Jungian critics use a psychoanalytic approach in which the conscious and the unconscious interact, and so, in this respect, the approach resembles somewhat the social interaction underpinnings of Bormann's theory. A psychoanalytic approach is seen also in R. F. Bales' work at Harvard University, which has a decidedly Freudian basis. Bormann, however, maintains that this general psychiatric perspective is "unsatisfactory," believing that one could "accept the importance of the chaining out of dramas to the group's culture without the Freudian explanation."[44]

Putting aside for now the similarities between Bormann's work and Burke's, Jung's, and Freud's, it may well be that the roots of symbolic convergence theory go back even further to Giambattisto Vico and the eighteenth century. Vico, known as the "Father of Cultural History," wrote that myths were not tales that were spun but stories told in language that was immediate and natural.[45] Seeming to capture the essence and power of fantasy sharing, Vico believed that stories are "the language in which a culture both states and achieves its existence," that "images become social reality," and that "such images are not static but enter into a dialectic with the society that created them, giving rise to conseqent actions, and being themselves enlarged or revised."[46] Here, Vico can be seen as a forerunner to Bormann's notion of the way that fantasies can chain out through groups to society at large, a phenomenon that is at the heart of symbolic convergence theory.

SYMBOLIC CONVERGENCE THEORY

As mentioned previously, Bormann's theory was sparked by work done by R. F. Bales at Harvard University. Beginning in the 1950s, Bales had investigated small group dynamics. Eventually, he discovered the dynamic process of group fantasy in which there was a noticeable period in group work when members became excited and used dramatic communication.[47] It was Bormann, however, who saw theoretical and practical possibilities in Bales' discovery. Bormann, who in his work with hundreds of case studies at the University of Minnesota, began to map out a theory of communication that accounted for the way in which messages are transmitted from small groups, to public speeches, to mass media, and, eventually, to the larger public.[48] Bormann, with his rhetorical background, realized that meanings and motives are in such messages and that when fantasy chaining results in a composite drama, a rhetorical vision, that vision contains motivations for action. Symbolic convergence theory, therefore, can be used in a predictive way.

In some respects, the terminology of symbolic convergence theory has been controversial and confusing. An understanding of the bases of the taxonomy may clear up any misunderstanding. The word "fantasy" has its etymological root in the Greek word *phantastikos*, which means that which is able to present or show to the mind, to make visible.[49] Thus, when fantasy themes—the story lines or content of the dramatic communication—are shared, certain assumptions, beliefs, attitudes, and values are made visible to the minds of the communicators. In many respects, this process resembles empathic communication or "a meeting of the minds."[50] As group members share stories that are vivid, the group seems to come to life, with members contributing their own versions of the narratives. Consequently, there is a fantasy "chaining" effect in which one fantasy theme chains out to another in a rhetorically powerful way. Unlike Kenneth Burke's work, Bormann's represents a social theory. It does not have its roots in literary criticism; it has its roots in communication processes and in small group interaction. It is a speaker, message, and audience theory, and so its terminology helps to distinguish it from metaphorical analysis, Burkeian analysis, and so on. There are other reasons for the terminology. As shown in the section on fantasy theme analysis, the terminology allows critics to trace the dramatic communication through multiple levels with a language that can be immediately recognized by others.

One of the clearest explanations of symbolic convergence theory is given by Bormann in a publication of *The Jensen Lectures*.[51] He explains how dramatizing elements in group communication consist of any comment or statement that tells a narrative about real or fictitious people, imaginary characters, or personifications of concepts, groups, or countries. The action is set in a time or place other than the here and now of the group. Such dramatizations are fantasy themes if a majority of group members participate. The members sympathize with the central elements in the narrative. They may dislike or like the characters and events involved. In such episodes, the tempo of the conversation quickens, and members become more involved in the conversation, interrupting one another, laughing, grimacing, and showing emotions. As Bormann suggests, a record of a meeting in which such dramas are shared "would contain the fossilized remains of the communication process. These traces would be in the form of fantasy themes."[52] The content of the narratives of the themes could then be clustered to form stock scenarios or "fantasy types." For instance, in my work on the Vietnam decision-making process in the Kennedy and Johnson administrations, I discovered that the presidents and their advisers repeatedly referred to one another as members of various sports teams—football, basketball, boxing, and so on—to the extent that one of their stock scenarios or fantasy types was "war as a game." Because motives, attitudes, values, and beliefs are embedded in the fantasy themes and types, it was possible to extrapolate my findings to suggest that when war was a game, it was more likely that the players would negate opportunities for negotiation: games are usually played out until there is a clear winner or loser. Sports events in the group's culture were also analogous to its decison-making process. Members shared fantasies in which they were likened to a basketball team without formal rules, dropping balls, failing to pick them up, and failing to make the basket. The fantasies, in fact, represented an accurate picture of a process that was often disorganized and that seemed to have little direction or firm leadership.[53]

Bormann goes on to suggest that "when sufficient fantasies have been shared and the members develop enough fantasy types they may begin to shape them into a unified system which portrays a broad and consistent view of much or a portion of their social and material reality. The result is a rhetorical vision."[54] A rhetorical vision is a composite drama constructed from fantasy themes and types that have recurred in the history of a group and may have chained out into a larger public through written works, media, and other public formats. Rhetorical visions contain key characters, personae, heroes, and villains and typical plotlines that can be alluded to in various contexts, sparking a response. Rhetorical visions help to define rhetorical communities. When individuals move toward a sense of community, there is a need to create a common identity. Bormann and others have shown how new communities and rhetorical movements go through the stages of consciousness-creating, consciousness-raising, and consciousness-sustaining communication.[55] Rhetorical visions are solidified when groups go through such stages. Essentially, a rhetorical vision provides a particular worldview for the group, a specific social reality in which are embedded attitudes, values, and beliefs that become an impetus for action.

Obviously, some groups or communities share some fantasies and not others. Bormann explains this phenomenon by saying that (1) there is a predisposition to share some fantasies and not others. This tendency is brought into the group setting. (I would suggest that this predisposition is related also to the ways in which some groups polarize toward riskier or conservative decisions.)[56] (2) As groups meet, they simply share common concerns that are revealed in their sharing of fantasies. (3) Group members who are good storytellers or rhetorically skillful may accidentally or purposely create a group consciousness.[57]

More than anyone else (other than Bormann), John Cragan and Donald Shields have applied and developed symbolic convergence theory. For instance, they have applied fantasy theme analysis to fire chief's management styles,[58] corporate interventions,[59] foreign policy communication,[60] and market research and advertising.[61] Constantly developing the theory, they have listed some of its assumptions as:

1. Meaning, emotions, and motives for action are in the manifest content of messages.
2. Reality is created symbolically.

3. Fantasy theme chaining creates symbolic convergence that is dramatic in form.

4. Fantasy theme analysis is a basic method to capture symbolic reality.

5. Fantasy themes occur in, and chain out from, all discourse.

6. At least three master analogues compete—righteous, social, and pragmatic.[62]

(The last assumption means that competitive symbolic interpretations of rhetorical communities that are caught up in specific rhetorical visions reflect what they call a "master analogue" or a deep structure that tends to be either righteous, social, or pragmatic. So, a vision based on a righteous analogue would stress the right way of doing things, a vision linked to a social analogue would stress human relations, and a pragmatic analogue would stress expediency, utility, and so on.)[63]

In 1994 Bormann, Cragan, and Shields further spelled out the basic presuppositions undergirding the theory. The four presuppositions are as follows: (1) The building of the theory represents a grounded approach. As such, key concepts emerged from hundreds of case studies rather than being derived from previous writings such as those of Bales and Freud. Communication events were observed in diverse contexts so that concept definitions were the outcomes of research, not its prerequisites. (2) An empirically based study of the sharing of imagination can provide an account of the relationship between the rational and the irrational. The theory represents a movement to recover the importance of imaginative language in all communication contexts. (3) The audience should be an important part of the rhetorical paradigm. "The concepts of rhetorical community and consciousness as related to consciousness creating, raising, and sustaining is a major finding of subsequent research. . . . This linking of the audience to the messages is the key to the extensive applications" of the theory to practice. (4) It is possible to make generalizations based on results of previous studies.[64]

Before explaining the method of fantasy theme analysis in more detail, it is necessary to complete this section with a short discussion of how Bormann perceives symbolic convergence theory to be what he terms a "general theory of communication." In 1996 he wrote that special and general theories are crucial to understanding his work.[65] Accordingly, he divides the general field of communication theory into those components. Special theories of speech communication are those that are artistic, restricted to people who have learned standard usages, rules, and examples of specific styles.[66] As an example, he writes about the Oneida Community in the nineteenth century, which developed a rule-governed communication practice of "mutual criticism."[67] Special theories of communication, therefore, represent ideal models to be used in specific contexts, at specific times. They are rules of thumb for conversing, discussing, speaking, arguing, debating, persuading, and so on.

On the other hand, general theories are transcultural and transhistorical. They are not bound to specific times, communities, or cultures and so can be traced across cultures and across time. This scheme is then used to set up symbolic convergence theory as a general theory of communication, a general theory that explains how special theories come into being, develop, and function.[68] Again, I think that the influence of the likes of Gustav Bergmann can be detected because, repeatedly, Bormann talks about symbolic convergence theory in the context of scientific theories such as those of Newton and Darwin. At first glance, such associations seem somewhat pretentious, but, on reflection, they do make some sense. For instance, when Bormann likens symbolic convergence theory to Newton's theory of gravity, he is simply suggesting that people will share fantasies in various communication contexts and that this phenomenon will happen regardless of time of day, setting, and composition of groups even as the laws of gravity cover the earth and the sun as well as the apple falling to the earth.[69] Similarly, when he says that symbolic convergence theory can be compared to Darwin's theory of evolution, he means that, as such, it demonstrates a plausible pattern of communication, "a coherent and plausible accounting" of communication.[70] This accounting of communication is a large part of fantasy theme analysis.

RHETORICAL CRITICISM AND FANTASY THEME ANALYSIS

A key book on the history of rhetorical theory suggests that Bormann's model of rhetorical criticism has been the theme of countless convention programs, colloquia, term papers, and theses since the publication of his germinal essay in 1972.[71] For Bormann, rhetorical criticism is an "avenue to knowledge," a "liberal and humanizing art" used to "illuminate the human condition."[72] The rhetorical critic asks such questions as, How does communication function to divide individual from individual, group from group, and community from community? How does communication function to create a sense of community, integrating individuals and groups into large, cooperative units? How does communication function to interpret reality for symbol-using human beings? How does it function to provide for social change and continuity?[73]

Fantasy theme analysis is a way to answer such questions. It is what Bormann refers to as "metacriticism" in that it seeks to provide explanations of human symbol-using that transcend particular times, places, and styles.[74] As metacriticism, it views the entire process of communication, practices, and special theories as objects of analysis. Moreover, the "fossilized remains" of shared group fantasies can be found in the texts of oral and written communities.[75]

Fantasy theme analysis can be used to diagnose communication malfunctions[76] as well as communication successes. Certainly, it is a dramatistic viewpoint, but it differs from other approaches in that its focus is on communication interaction, and so it bridges the gap between rhetoric and audience consciousness. This function is one of its major contributions to rhetorical criticism and reflects a crucial part of Bormann's approach to researching communication in that, consistently, he never forgot the role of the audience in the communication context. As far back as 1961, he tested the hypothesis that speakers behaved more confidently if they believed that their audience perceived them to be confident.[77] He never forgot that communication, even rhetorical communication, was a process and that it was always addressed to someone else.

Bormann's original advice on how to do fantasy theme analysis still holds today.[78] First, a critic must choose an aspect of communication, a decision-making group, a rhetorical controversy, a social group, a support group, a rhetorical community, a policy-making unit, a political campaign, a social movement, or the like that is intellectually intriguing, about which there are questions to be answered. Next, the critic collects evidence in the form of audiotapes or videotapes of group meetings, memoranda, group transcripts, letters, speeches, recollections of participants, interviews, or whatever records are available. Examining such documents, the critic looks for evidence of shared narratives, dramatic communication, imagery, figures of speech, and the like that are clues to periods of fantasy sharing.

Having identified the content of different fantasies, those patterns that have recurred over time, the critic can then cluster the fantasy themes under umbrella-like headings called fantasy types. (E.g., in a recent small group class that I taught, one group spent a great deal of time sharing fantasies. The fantasy themes had content relating to topics such as being kids and watching television programs that had been banned by their parents and to stories of how they had managed to circumvent certain systems. The students eventually identified one of their key fantasy types as being "it's fun to break rules." Consequently, verifying that a group's fantasies become motivations for action, this particular group ignored the rules for their formal class presentation.) In some respects, therefore, fantasy themes can be seen as the species of fantasy events, and fantasy types are a kind of genus, the broad category.

Once various fantasy themes and types have been identified, the critic can then begin to compile the composite drama, the rhetorical vision. In that vision there will be heroes and villains, key personae, characterizations, attitudes about work, praising and blaming, valorization of some emotions and not others, scenic backdrops or settings that are privileged over others, behavior that is praised and behavior that is censored, insiders and outsiders, and a multitude of beliefs and values that, ultimately, become warrants for argument and action. As Bormann writes, "[W]hen a critic begins instead with the approach that each rhetorical vision contains as part of its substance the motive that will impel the people caught up in it, then he can anticipate the behavior of the converts." He continues that "to view motives as embedded in the rhetorical vision rather than hidden in the skulls and viscera of people makes it possible to check the critic's insights by going directly to the rhetoric rather than relying on inferences about psychological entities unavailable for analysis."[79] Fantasy themes and fantasy types are, ultimately, the building blocks of a group's culture, propelling its members to some attitudes and actions and not others.

APPLICATIONS OF FANTASY THEME ANALYSIS

As a young scholar, Bormann saw the need for both basic and applied research.[80] A book coauthored with William Howell presented a "practical, nonacademic treatment of communication," noting that outside academe there was a demand for "plain talk."[81] In an article on the promise and paradox of small group research, he observed that some small group work had exhibited sophisticated methodology but with "barren results," having no practical or theoretical significance.[82] A limited survey of Bormann's, his students', and others' applications of fantasy theme analysis shows that that practical bent has not been lost.

Some researchers have traced the sharing of fantasy themes through media, either electronic or print.[83] Some have looked at how different sources of fantasy chaining have provided evidence of the way that messages can be spread, can chain, throughout the public sector.[84] Other scholars have empirically verified given symbolic realities, rhetorical visions by having subjects respond to Q-sorts and then using factor analytic, construct validity procedures for testing the theory's elements.[85] Another group of researchers found that voters came to share political fantasies in media, as reflected in their responses to Q-sort statements, and that, moreover, their voting behavior followed the predicted patterns expressed in the study.[86] Scholars have used symbolic convergence theory to investigate interpersonal, small group, organizational, political, mass, intercultural, and marketing communication.[87] Thus, with its explanatory and predictive power, fantasy theme analysis has the potential to help family communication and drug and alcohol abuse counseling, as well as being a basis for market analysis and public opinion polling.[88]

CRITICISM OF SYMBOLIC CONVERGENCE THEORY AND FANTASY THEME ANALYSIS

When I was preparing to defend my dissertation in 1988, Professor Bormann included in his advice for me the warning that I should accept, even welcome criticism because only mediocre work had no response. He was speaking from experience because his work has had a parade of detractors. In fact, his most vocal critic, G. P. Mohrmann, became the focus of what we used to call in graduate school "the Bormann-Mohrmann controversy," said with an appreciation for its Gorgias-like assonance. Among Mohrmann's multiple criticisms of Bormann's work were accusations that he was taking Bales where he was not intended to go; that the taxonomy of symbolic convergence theory was confusing and led to formulaic writing; that to believe fantasies were social reality and that this reality compelled people to act was "to live in a world of *ipse dixit*," and that those who practiced fantasy theme analysis were caught up in "a dangerous thing."[89] To read such warnings by Mohrmann was to have the distinct impression that, at least for Mohrmann, those who practiced fantasy theme analysis were members of a strange cult, fantasy fanatics, and potential rhetorical terrorists. Bormann, though, would be the first to say that criticism and argument are essential paths to knowledge. Even so, I have a hunch that some of the criticism was not always in the spirit of inquiry, not always entirely constructive.

Robert Craig agreed with Mohrmann that Bormann was speculative and added that he tended to make too neat a distinction between special and general theories and that he exhibited "unrestricted moral relativism."[90] Actually, Craig makes a lot of sense to me when he singles out Bormann's use of Aristotle's *Rhetorica* as a special theory written for fourth-century Greeks and, therefore, limited to that particular culture.[91] Bormann's dismissal of the classicist may seem sweeping when considering that Aristotle's theory of persuasion, especially the coordinated use of the three artistic proofs, remains effective today because, like symbolic convergence theory, it transcends time and culture. Bormann, however, explains his position by suggesting that people can choose either to use or not to use Aristotelian rhetorical theories. On the other hand, symbolic convergence theory happens without any conscious choice. The criticism regarding the confusion surrounding his terms has some validity, too. For instance, critics using fantasy theme analysis and even authors of textbooks on criticism routinely confuse fantasy themes with fantasy types. The confusion would be lowered, I think, if Bormann replaced fantasy theme with fantasy content. Otherwise, authors will continue to assume that a "theme" is a recurring motif and use it as a "type."

Not all criticism of Bormann's theory has been constructive, though, and so in an effort to dispel some of the misconceptions, Bormann, Cragan, and Shields wrote an in-depth essay, published in *Communication Theory*, that systematically deals with some of the theory's detractors.[92] It is not necessary to repeat their arguments in this context, but I do want to point out that the authors of this essay pay tribute to criticism that has been constructive, that has encouraged the development of the theory, and that has encouraged researchers to be less vague about concepts used and how they are applied. On the other hand, they regret that some editors have been so biased against the theory that they insisted on essays being stripped of the theory's technical language before they could be published. I confess that I was one of the authors who eventually caved in to the pressure to be published. I can only say that even when the technical terms are treated lightly, the basics, the premises of the theory remain.

I have a hunch, as well, that the major critics of the theory are rhetoricians who have never taught small group communication. As an undergraduate student, I became fascinated with symbolic convergence theory when, in a group in a small group communication class, I became aware of distinct periods of fantasy sharing that, on analysis, reflected key characteristics of the group as well as its decisions. Then, as a graduate student and, later, as a professor, I taught numerous kinds of groups in similar classes. Journals written by group members, audiotapes, and videotapes have confirmed that groups often participate in periods of fantasy sharing and that a group's language shapes their specific culture, steering them to certain behaviors and decision making and not others. Subsequently, I remain convinced that some critics of symbolic convergence theory would write from a more enlightened position had they studied and taught small group communication.

FUTURE DIRECTIONS OF SYMBOLIC CONVERGENCE THEORY

When it was not so fashionable to do so, Bormann studied the public address of women and other minorities, suggesting that the women's movement grew out of the abolition movement.[93] Similarly, in 1972 he began one of his books with a section on the impact of technology on the spoken word.[94] Almost three decades later, it is clear that media have an enormous impact on the electorate and on voting patterns. This trend was not so evident in 1973, when Bormann wrote: "[It is an] awesome power of the electronic media to provide in the form of breaking news, the dramatizations that cause fantasies to chain through large sections of the American electorate . . . [providing] attitude reinforcement or change that results in voting behavior which elects a president and a vice-president."[95] Although not dealing with a presidential election, media coverage of Princess Diana's death in 1997 is a prime example of how fantasies surrounding an event chain into the public at large and then ricochet back to media representatives in a dramatizing cycle that exaggerates the original event out of all proportion. Also, even the labeling of communication specialists in the White House as "spin doctors" captures some of the phenomenon of fantasy chaining. Bormann's theory, therefore, has applications that are especially contemporary. In fact, it would seem to me that the theory would be particularly useful for examining communication on the Internet, especially that of specific network groups and chat rooms.

Actually, for several years now, Bormann has been fascinated with the possibilities of artificial intelligence and artificial imagination. For some time, he has worked on a project to develop artificial imagination in computer systems, studying how fantasy sharing might enable computers to communicate in ways that simulate human communication that is imaginative.[96] In other words, how can computers be programmed so that they will be predisposed to share dramatic communication? Thus, it may well be that symbolic convergence theory will become even more important to understanding a global village that is connected by computer networks, media satellites, and future technologies.

CONCLUSION

Ernest G. Bormann is a remarkable teacher-scholar whose symbolic convergence theory has contributed greatly to our understanding of communication in its social setting. He has forced students and practitioners of communication to consider the dynamism involved in the sharing of fantasies. Fantasy sharing occurs among friends, families, colleagues, committees, high-level policy-making groups, media, and so on. It is a theory particularly applicable to the mass-mediated world of the late twentieth and early twenty-first centuries. It is a theory for all seasons.

Ernest G. Bormann is a scholar for all seasons, too. When asked what he was up to these days, he wrote:

I am working on my yard.

I am working on my house.

I am playing golf.

I am writing fiction.

I am trying to sell or have fiction produced.

I am doing some professional writing (a book in Japanese to be co-written with Asako Uehara, a chapter on Huey Long in a book on the rhetoric of the New Deal).

I am responding to queries about SCT [symbolic convergence theory] from students around the country.

I am travelling.

I am teaching (three months in Japan, sitting on Final Dissertation Committees at the University of Minnesota).

I am sitting in my rocking chair on my front porch watching the world go by.

I am doing some reading.

I am taking it easy.[97]

I doubt that Ernest G. Bormann has ever "taken it easy." His life still reflects that eagerness for learning, that enthusiasm about the quest for knowledge that is the mark of a remarkable teacher-scholar.

NOTES

1. Information related to Professor Bormann's personal life, career, and teaching is based on conversations and correspondence with him.

2. Ernest G. Bormann, *The Force of Fantasy: Restoring the American Dream* (Carbondale: Southern Illinois University Press, 1985).

3. Ernest G. Bormann, *Forerunners of Black Power: The Rhetoric of Abolition* (Englewood Cliffs, NJ: Prentice-Hall, 1971), ix.

4. Robert F. Bales, *Personality and Interpersonal Relations* (New York: Holt, Rinehart, and Winston, 1970).

5. Such publications include Charles R. Bantz, "Television News: Reality and Research," *Western Speech* 39 (1975): 13–130; James W. Chesebro, John F. Cragan, and Patricia W. McCullough, "The Small Group Technique of the Radical Revolutionary: A Synthetic Study of Consciousness Raising," *Communication Monographs* 40 (1973): 136–146; Carl Wayne Hensley, "Rhetorical Vision and the Persuasion of a Historical Movement: The Disciples of Christ in Nineteenth Century American Culture," *Quarterly*

Journal of Speech 61 (1975): 250–264; Virginia Kidd, "Happily Ever After and Other Relationship Styles: Advice on Interpersonal Relationships in Popular Magazines, 1951–1973," *Quarterly Journal of Speech* 61 (1975): 31–39.

6. Ernest G. Bormann, "An Empirical Approach to Certain Concepts of Logical Proof," *Central States Speech Journal* 12 (1961): 85–91.

7. Ernest G. Bormann, *Theory and Research in the Communication Arts* (New York: Holt, Rinehart, and Winston, 1965), 6.

8. Ibid., 418.

9. Bormann, *Forerunners of Black Power*, Preface.

10. Ibid., 33.

11. Ernest G. Bormann, "Generalizing about Significant Forms: Science and Humanism Compared and Contrasted," in Karlyn Kohrs Campbell and Kathleen Hall Jamieson, eds., *Form and Genre: Shaping Rhetorical Action* (Falls Church, VA: Speech Communication Association, 1978), 51.

12. Ernest G. Bormann, *Communication Theory* (New York: Holt, Rinehart, and Winston, 1980), 15.

13. Ernest G. Bormann, *The Rhetoric of Western Thought*, quoted by James L. Golden, Goodwin F. Berquist, William E. Coleman, eds., 5th ed. (Dubuque, IA: Kendall/Hunt, 1992), 363.

14. See Ernest G. Bormann, Jolene Koester, and Janet Bennett, "Political Cartoons and Salient Rhetorical Fantasies: An Empirical Analysis of the '76 Presidential Campaign," *Communication Monographs* 45 (1978): 317–329; David L. Rarick, Mary B. Duncan, David G. Lee, and Laurinda W. Porter, "The Carter Persona: An Empirical Analysis of the Rhetorical Visions of Campaign '76," *Quarterly Journal of Speech* 63 (1977): 258–273.

15. Ernest G. Bormann, "Fantasy and Rhetorical Vision: The Rhetorical Criticism of Social Reality," *Quarterly Journal of Speech* 58 (1972): 405.

16. Ernest G. Bormann, John F. Cragan, and Donald C. Shields, "In Defense of Symbolic Convergence Theory: A Look at the Theory and Its Criticisms after Two Decades," *Communication Theory* 4 (1994): 265.

17. Bormann, *Theory and Research in the Communication Arts*, 208–209.

18. Ernest G. Bormann, "A Rhetorical Analysis of the National Radio Broadcasts of Senator Huey P. Long," Ph.D. diss., University of Iowa, 1953.

19. Ernest G. Bormann, "The Rhetorical Theory of William Henry Milburn," *Speech Monographs* 36 (1969): 28–37.

20. See Bormann, *Forerunners of Black Power*.

21. Ernest G. Bormann, "Fetching Good Out of Evil: A Rhetorical Use of Calamity," *Quarterly Journal of Speech* 63 (1977): 130–139.

22. Bormann, *The Force of Fantasy*.

23. Ernest G. Bormann, Jerie Pratt, and Linda Putnam, "Power, Authority, and Sex: Male Responses to Female Leadership," *Communication Monographs* 45 (1978): 119–155.

24. Bormann, Koester, and Bennett, "Political Cartoons and Salient Rhetorical Fantasies."

25. Ernest G. Bormann, "A Fantasy Theme Analysis of the Television Coverage of the Hostage Release and the Reagan Inaugural," *Quarterly Journal of Speech* 68 (1982): 133–145.

26. Ernest G. Bormann, Becky Swanson Kroll, Kathleen Watters, and Douglas

McFarland, "Rhetorical Visions of Committed Voters: Fantasy Theme Analysis of a Large Sample Survey," *Critical Studies in Mass Communication* 1 (1984): 287–310.

27. Ernest G. Bormann, John F. Cragan, and Donald C. Shields, "An Expansion of the Rhetorical Vision Component of the Symbolic Convergence Theory: The Cold War Paradigm Case," *Communication Monographs* 63 (1996): 1–28.

28. Bormann, *Theory and Research in the Communication Arts*, 42.

29. Bormann, *Communication Theory*, 203.

30. Bormann, *Theory and Research in the Communication Arts*, 43.

31. Bormann, *Forerunners of Black Power*, 24.

32. Bormann, *Communication Theory*, 205.

33. See Ernest G. Bormann, "Ghostwriting Agencies," *Today's Speech* 4 (1956): 20–23; Ernest G. Bormann, "Ghostwriting and the Rhetorical Critic," *Quarterly Journal of Speech* 46 (1960): 284–288; Ernest G. Bormann, "Ethics of Ghostwritten Speeches," *Quarterly Journal of Speech* 47 (1961): 262–267.

34. Ernest G. Bormann and Nancy Bormann, *Speech Communication: A Comprehensive Approach* (New York: Harper and Row, 1972), 14.

35. Bormann, "Ethics of Ghostwritten Speeches."

36. Ernest G. Bormann, "On Communication as a Practical Discipline," in Brenda Dervin, Lawrence Grossberg, Barbara J. O'Keefe, and Ellen Wartella, eds., *Rethinking Communication: Volume I, Paradigm Issues* (Newbury Park, CA: Sage, 1989), 135.

37. Ernest G. Bormann and George L. Shapiro, "Perceived Confidence as a Function of Self-Image," *Central States Speech Journal* 13 (1962): 253–256.

38. Bormann, *Forerunners of Black Power*, 19.

39. Ibid., 17, 18.

40. Ernest G. Bormann, "The Symbolic Convergence Theory of Communication and the Creation, Raising, and Sustaining of Public Consciousness," in John I. Sisco, ed., *The Jensen Lectures: Contemporary Communication Studies* (Tampa: University of South Florida Press, 1983), 71.

41. See Bormann, *The Force of Fantasy*, 9.

42. Ibid.

43. Stanley Edgar Hyman, *The Armed Vision* (New York: Vintage Books, 1955), 132.

44. Ernest G. Bormann, "Fantasy and Rhetorical Vision: Ten Years Later," *Quarterly Journal of Speech* 68 (1982): 288–305.

45. Michael Mooney, *Vico: In the Tradition of Rhetoric* (Davis, CA: Hermagoras Press, 1994), 240.

46. Ibid., 241.

47. Bormann, "Fantasy and Rhetorical Vision: The Rhetorical Criticism of Social Reality," *Quarterly Journal of Speech* 58 (1972): 396, 397.

48. Ibid., 398.

49. Ernest G. Bormann, "Symbolic Convergence Theory of Communication: Implications for Teachers and Consultants," *Journal of Applied Communication Research* 10 (1982): 50–61.

50. Ibid., 51.

51. Bormann, *The Jensen Lectures*.

52. Ibid., 74.

53. Moya Ann Ball, *Vietnam-on-the-Potomac* (New York: Praeger, 1992), 189.

54. Bormann, *The Jensen Lectures*, 75.

55. See Cheseboro, Cragan, and McCullough, "The Small Group Technique of the

Radical Revolutionary"; Bormann, Cragan, and Shields, "An Expansion of the Rhetorical Vision Component of the Symbolic Convergence Theory."

56. For a discussion of group polarization, see S. Alderton and L. Frey, "Effects of Reactions to Arguments on Group Outcome: The Case of Group Polarization," *Central States Speech Journal* 34 (1983): 88–95.

57. Ernest G. Bormann, "Symbolic Convergence Theory and Communication in Group Decision Making," in Randy Y. Hirokowa and Marshall Scott Poole, eds., *Communication and Group Decision Making* (Thousand Oaks, CA: Sage, 1996), 98.

58. John F. Cragan, Michael Cuffe, L. Pairitz, and L. H. Jackson, "What Management Style Suits You?" *Fire Chief Magazine* (1985): 24–30.

59. John F. Cragan and Donald C. Shields, "The Use of Symbolic Convergence Theory in Corporate Strategic Planning: A Case Study," *Journal of Applied Communication Research*, 20 (1992): 199–218.

60. John F. Cragan and Donald C. Shields, "Foreign Policy Communication Dramas: How Mediated Rhetoric Played Out in Peoria in Campaign '76," *Quarterly Journal of Speech* 63 (1977): 274–289.

61. John F. Cragan and Donald C. Shields, "Communication Based Market Segmentation Study: Illustrative Excerpts," in John F. Cragan and Donald C. Shields, eds., *Applied Communication Research: A Dramatistic Approach* (Prospect Heights, IL: Waveland Press, 1981).

62. Cragan and Shields, "The Use of Symbolic Convergence Theory in Corporate Strategic Planning," 200.

63. Bormann, Cragan, and Shields, "An Expansion of the Rhetorical Vision Component," 4.

64. Bormann, Cragan, and Shields, "In Defense of Symbolic Convergence Theory," 263–269.

65. Bormann, "Symbolic Convergence Theory and Communication in Group Decision Making," 81.

66. Bormann, *Communication Theory.*

67. Bormann in Golden et al., *Rhetoric of Western Thought*, 373.

68. Bormann, "Symbolic Convergence Theory and Communication," Golden et al., 372.

69. Bormann, *Theory and Research in the Communication Arts*, 97.

70. Ibid., 101–102.

71. Golden et al., *Rhetoric of Western Thought*, 363.

72. Bormann and Bormann, *Speech Communication: A Comprehensive Approach*, 354.

73. Ibid.

74. Bormann, "Generalizing about Significant Forms," 185.

75. Bormann, "Symbolic Convergence Theory of Communication: Implications for Teachers and Consultants," 51.

76. Ibid., 54.

77. Ernest G. Bormann, "An Empirical Approach to Certain Concepts of Logical Proof," *Central States Speech Journal* (1961).

78. Bormann, "Fantasy and Rhetorical Vision: The Rhetorical Criticism," 401–402.

79. Ibid., 407.

80. Bormann, *Theory and Research in the Communication Arts*, 41.

81. Ernest G. Bormann, William S. Howell, Ralph Nicholas, and George I. Shapiro,

Interpersonal Communication in the Modern Organization (Englewood Cliffs, NJ: Prentice-Hall, 1969), Preface.

82. Ernest G. Bormann, "The Paradox and Promise of Small Group Research," *Speech Monographs* 37 (1970): 211.

83. Bantz, "Television News,"; Kidd, "Happily Ever After."

84. Sonja K. Foss, "Equal Rights Amendment Controversy: Two Worlds in Conflict," *Quarterly Journal of Speech* 65 (1979): 275–288; Dan Nimmo and J. Combs, "Fantasies and Melodramas in Television Network News: The Case of Three Mile Island," *Western Journal of Speech Communication* 46 (1982): 45–55.

85. See Donald C. Shields, "Fire-Fighters' Self-Image, Projected-Image, and Public-Image," *Fire Command* 41 (1974): 26–28; Thomas G. Endres, "Rhetorical Visions of Unmarried Mothers," *Communication Quarterly* 37 (1989): 134–150.

86. See David L. Rarick, Mary B. Duncan, David G. Lee, and Laurinda W. Porter, "The Carter Persona: An Empirical Analysis of the Rhetorical Visions of Campaign '76," *Quarterly Journal of Speech* 63 (1977).

87. For an excellent summary of such research, see Bormann, Cragan, and Shields, "In Defense of Symbolic Convergence Theory."

88. Bormann, "Symbolic Convergence Theory of Communication: Implications for Teachers and Consultants," 59.

89. G. P. Mohrmann, "An Essay on Fantasy Theme Criticism," *Quarterly Journal of Speech* 68 (1982): 109–132.

90. Robert T. Craig, "Communication as a Practical Discipline," in Brenda Dervin, Lawrence Grossberg; Barbara J. O'Keefe, and Ellen Wartella; eds., *Rethinking Communication: Volume I, Paradigm Issues* (Thousand Oaks, CA: Sage, 1989), 116.

91. Golden et al., 363.

92. Bormann, Cragan, and Shields, "In Defense of Symbolic Convergence Theory."

93. Bormann, *Forerunners of Black Power.*

94. Bormann and Bormann, *Speech Communication: A Comprehensive Approach.*

95. Ernest G. Bormann, "The Eagleton Affair: A Fantasy Theme Analysis," *Quarterly Journal of Speech*, 59 (1973): 43.

96. See Ernest G. Bormann, "Artificial Imagination," *Halcyon: A Journal of the Humanities* 15 (1993): 87–102.

97. Ernest G. Bormann, correspondence with author, June 1998.

BIBLIOGRAPHY

Alberton, S., and L. Frey. "Effects of Reactions to Arguments on Group Outcome: The Case of Group Polarization." *Central States Speech Journal* 34 (1983): 88–95.

Bales, Robert F. *Personality and Interpersonal Relations.* New York: Holt, Rinehart, and Winston, 1970.

Ball, Moya Ann. *Vietnam-on-the-Potomac.* New York: Praeger, 1992.

Bantz, Charles R. "Television News: Reality and Research." *Western Speech* 39 (1975): 13–130.

Bormann, Ernest G. "Symbolic Convergence Theory and Communication in Group Decision Making." In Randy Y. Hirokowa and Marshall Scott Poole, eds., *Communication and Group Decision Making.* Thousand Oaks, CA: Sage, 1996.

———. "Artificial Imagination." *Halcyon: A Journal of the Humanities* 15 (1993): 87–102.

———. "On Communication as a Practical Discipline." In *Rethinking Communication: Volume I, Paradigm Issues*, eds. Brenda Dervin, Lawrence Grossberg, Barbara J. O'Keefe, and Ellen Wartella. Newbury Park, CA: Sage, 1989.

———. *The Force of Fantasy: Restoring the American Dream*. Carbondale: Southern Illinois University Press, 1985.

———."The Symbolic Convergence Theory of Communication and the Creation, Raising, and Sustaining of Public Consciousness." In John I. Sisco, ed., *The Jensen Lectures: Contemporary Communication Studies*. Tampa: The University of South Florida, Press 1983, 71–90.

———. "Fantasy and Rhetorical Vision: Ten Years Later." *Quarterly Journal of Speech* 68 (1982): 288–305.

———. "A Fantasy Theme Analysis of the Television Coverage of the Hostage Release and the Reagan Inaugural." *Quarterly Journal of Speech* 68 (1982): 133–145.

———. "Symbolic Convergence Theory of Communication: Implications for Teachers and Consultants." *Journal of Applied Communication Research* 10 (1982): 50–61.

———. *Communication Theory*. New York: Holt, Rinehart, and Winston, 1980.

———."Generalizing about Significant Forms: Science and Humanism Compared and Contrasted." In Karlyn Kohrs Campbell and Kathleen Hall Jamieson, eds., *Form and Genre: Shaping Rhetorical Action*. Falls Church, VA: Speech Communication Association, 1978.

———. "Fetching Good Out of Evil: A Rhetorical Use of Calamity." *Quarterly Journal of Speech* 63 (1977): 130–139.

———. "The Eagleton Affair: A Fantasy Theme Analysis." *Quarterly Journal of Speech* 59 (1973): 143–159.

———. "Fantasy and Rhetorical Vision: The Rhetorical Criticism of Social Reality." *Quarterly Journal of Speech* 58 (1972): 396–407.

———. *Forerunners of Black Power: The Rhetoric of Abolition*. Englewood Cliffs, NJ: Prentice-Hall, 1971.

———. "The Paradox and Promise of Small Group Research." *Speech Monographs* 37 (1970): 211.

———. "The Rhetorical Theory of William Henry Milburn." *Speech Monographs* 36 (1969): 28–37.

———. *Theory and Research in the Communication Arts*. New York: Holt, Rinehart, and Winston, 1965.

———. "An Empirical Approach to Certain Concepts of Logical Proof." *Central States Speech Journal* 12 (1961): 85–91.

———. "Ethics of Ghostwritten Speeches." *Quarterly Journal of Speech* 47 (1961): 262–267.

———. "Ghostwriting and the Rhetorical Critic." *Quarterly Journal of Speech* 46 (1960): 284–288.

———. "Ghostwriting Agencies." *Today's Speech* 4 (1956): 20–23.

———. "A Rhetorical Analysis of the National Radio Broadcasts of Senator Huey P. Long." Ph.D. diss., University of Iowa, 1953.

Bormann, Ernest G., and Nancy Bormann. *Speech Communication: A Comprehensive Approach*. New York: Harper and Row, 1972.

Bormann, Ernest G., John F. Cragan, and Donald C. Shields, "An Expansion of the Rhetorical Vision Component of the Symbolic Convergence Theory: The Cold War Paradigm Case." *Communication Monographs* 63 (1996): 1–28.

———. "In Defense of Symbolic Convergence Theory: A Look at the Theory and Its Criticisms after Two Decades." *Communication Theory* 4 (1994): 259–294.

Bormann, Ernest G., William S. Howell, Ralph Nichols, and George I. Shapiro. *Interpersonal Communication in the Modern Organization.* Englewood Cliffs, NJ: Prentice-Hall, 1969.

Bormann, Ernest G., Jolene Koester, and Janet Bennet. "Political Cartoons and Salient Rhetorical Fantasies: An Empirical Analysis of the '76 Presidential Campaign." *Communication Monographs* 45 (1978): 317–329.

Bormann, Ernest G., Becky Swanson Kroll, Kathleen Watters, and Douglas McFarland. "Rhetorical Visions of Committed Voters: Fantasy Theme Analysis of a Large Sample Survey." *Critical Studies in Mass Communication* 1 (1984): 287–310.

Bormann, Ernest G., Jerie Pratt, and Linda Putnam. "Power, Authority, and Sex: Male Responses to Female Leadership." *Communication Monographs* 45 (1978): 119–155.

Bormann, Ernest G., and George L. Shapiro. "Perceived Confidence as a Function of Self-Image." *Central States Speech Journal* 13 (1962): 253–256.

Cheseboro, James W., John F. Cragan, and Patricia W. McCullough. "The Small Group Technique of the Radical Revolutionary: A Synthetic Study of Consciousness Raising." *Communication Monographs* 40 (1973): 136–146.

Cragan, John F., Michael Cuffe, L. Pairitz, and L. H. Jackson. "What Management Style Suits You?" *Fire Chief Magazine* (1985): 24–30.

Cragan, John F., and Donald C. Shields. "The Use of Symbolic Convergence Theory in Corporate Strategic Planning: A Case Study." *Journal of Applied Communication Research* 20 (1992): 199–218.

———. "Communication Based Market Segmentation Study: Illustrative Experts." In John F. Cragan and Donald C. Shields, eds., *Applied Communication Research: A Dramatistic Approach.* Prospect Heights, IL: Waveland Press, 1981.

———. "Foreign Policy Communication Dramas: How Mediated Rhetoric Played Out in Peoria in Campaign '76." *Quarterly Journal of Speech* 63 (1977): 274–289.

Craig, Robert T. "Communication as a Practical Discipline." In Brenda Dervin, Lawrence Grossberg, Barbara J. O'Keefe, and Ellen Wartella, eds., *Rethinking Communication: Volume I, Paradigm Issues.* Thousand Oaks, CA: Sage, 1989.

Endres, Thomas G. "Rhetorical Visions of Unmarried Mothers." *Communication Quarterly* 37 (1989): 134–150.

Foss, Sonja J. "Equal Rights Amendment Controversy: Two Worlds in Conflict." *Quarterly Journal of Speech* 65 (1979): 275–288.

Hensley, Carl Wayne. "Rhetorical Vision and the Persuasion of a Historical Movement: The Disciples of Christ in Nineteenth Century American Culture." *Quarterly Journal of Speech* 61 (1975): 250–264.

Hyman, Stanley Edgar. *The Armed Vision.* New York: Vintage Books, 1955.

Kidd, Virginia. "Happily Ever After and Other Relational Styles: Advice on Interpersonal Relationships in Popular Magazines, 1951–1973." *Quarterly Journal of Speech* 61 (1975): 31–39.

Mohrmann, G. P. "An Essay on Fantasy Theme Criticism." *Quarterly Journal of Speech* 68 (1982): 109–132.

Mooney, Michael. *Vico: In the Tradition of Rhetoric*. Davis, CA: Hermagoras Press, 1994.

Nimmo, Dan, and J. Combs. "Fantasies and Melodramas in Television Network News: The Case of Three Mile Island." *Western Journal of Speech Communication* 46 (1982): 45–55.

Rarick, David L., Mary B. Duncan, David G. Lee, and Laurinda W. Porter. "The Carter Persona: An Empirical Analysis of the Rhetorical Visions of Campaign '76." *Quarterly Journal of Speech* 63 (1977): 258–273.

Shields, Donald C. "Fire-Fighters' Self-Image, Projected-Image, and Public-Image." *Fire Command* 41 (1974): 26–28.

Edwin Black. Photo courtesy of Edwin Black. Used with permission.

10

Edwin Black on the Powers of the Rhetorical Critic

FRED J. KAUFFELD

Professor Edwin Black was born on October 26, 1929. In 1951 he completed undergraduate studies at the University of Houston, where he majored in philosophy and represented the university in intercollegiate debate. He studied rhetoric and public address at Cornell University, earning a master's degree in 1956 and a Ph.D. in 1962. His dissertation was directed by Herbert A. Wichelns. Black began his teaching career at Washington University in Saint Louis, where he served from 1956 to 1961. He served on the faculty of the University of Pittsburgh from 1961 to 1967. From 1967 until his retirement in 1994, he taught at the University of Wisconsin, Madison.

INTRODUCTION

The body of Edwin Black's work as a rhetorical critic is composed of a set of essays. Characteristically, his publications are relatively short compositions unified by a central subject, reflecting the author's point of view and providing a trial of the conjecture of approach under discussion.[1] The essay nicely serves Black. It fits his view that "critical method is too personally expressive to be systematized,"[2] and it accommodates his belief that a humane understanding of persuasive discourse can best emerge from critical interpretation of "a body of rhetorical transactions that had actually occurred."[3]

Black's essays have a well-deserved reputation as seminal contributions to rhetorical criticism. His groundbreaking book *Rhetorical Criticism: A Study in Method* is often admired for liberating rhetorical criticism from a narrow and ossified set of practices. His critical studies on the second persona and the sentimental style have enriched the conceptual apparatus available to rhetorical critics. The latter essay (Black, "The Sentimental Style") stands as a model of generic criticism. His reflections on the "mutability of rhetoric" have profoundly enlarged the frame for the history of rhetorical art. He has illuminated ways in which rhetorically established conventions undergird the formation of ideologies, and he has deepened our understanding and appreciation of rhetors as diverse as Lincoln and Nixon. In essay after essay, Edwin Black has demonstrated what an insightful rhetorical critic can do to illuminate rhetorical discourses and to enlarge understanding of the potentials of rhetorical criticism.

However, Black's reliance on the essay somewhat obscures his enduring contribution to our understanding of rhetorical criticism and its possibilities. The essay's economy imposes on Black's work the fragmented appearance of unconnected studies, whereas careful, consecutive reading reveals deep continuity, unity, and development both in Black's reflections on rhetorical criticism and in his work as a rhetorical critic.[4] In this chapter I elicit the coherence and development of Black's teachings about rhetorical criticism. This effort requires that we draw out the underlying logic of our critic's position. It will, I believe, enable us to better comprehend the continuing interest of studies that we might otherwise too hastily regard as "fully absorbed into the disciplinary consciousness" and may even help us to better comprehend the ongoing work of this important critic.[5]

In what does this unity consist? It is composed of an analysis of the inherent capacities of the critic and of a diagnosis of where those powers can and should be fully exercised in critical studies of persuasive discourse. Black's fundamental contribution to our understanding of rhetorical criticism has three closely related parts: first, he delineates the fundamental powers of the critic; second, he argues that a narrowly instrumental focus on persuasive discourse, as exemplified by neo-Aristotelian criticism, stultifies exercise of the critic's proper capacities; and, third, he demonstrates that study of the developmental power of persuasive discourse (e.g., the capacity of rhetorical discourse to shape its own conventions) affords opportunity for full and productive exercise of the critic's intrinsic possibilities.

BLACK ON THE INHERENT CAPABILITIES OF THE CRITIC

Black's conception of rhetorical criticism and its potentials flows from his analysis of the basic powers of critics. Where others focus on critical methods or methodologies, on how critics should do their work, Black's discussion of rhetorical criticism is premised on an analysis of what critics per se are capable of doing. This important point is not immediately obvious. Black's earliest and most extensive discussion in *Rhetorical Criticism: A Study in Method* seems, as the title of the book indicates, to focus on critical method, not the critic. Nevertheless, while the surface of that work is organized around a discussion of the generic functions of criticism and while the author's terminology includes frequent reference to "methods," *Rhetorical Criticism* says remarkably little about *how* rhetorical critics are to penetrate a text or to fit a text into its context. The sort of exposition of critical method that Kenneth Burke provides in The *Philosophy of Literary Form* under the rubric "cluster analysis" is almost entirely absent from Black's book.[6] Insofar as questions of method enter that discussion, they do so in order to show something about what critics can do or to identify where the critic's inherent powers ought be exercised. Black's subsequent reflections on rhetorical criticism focus quite explicitly on questions about the critic's capabilities and manifest a marked aversion to discussions of critical method.[7]

Black recognizes two capacities as essential to the critical process: critics' personal capacity to respond to the work of art and their ability to publicly instruct the larger cultural community that they address. Critics' personal response to the object of their criticism is perceptual, affective, and intuitive.[8] Through their public educational efforts, critics enable their audience to understand, appreciate, and evaluate works of art. As educators critics can provide arguments for their conclusions and for the works that they evaluate.[9] In his early *Rhetorical Criticism*, Black regards the critic's personal response as an indispensable *preliminary* to criticism proper, which he takes to be an essentially public activity.[10] This initial view is based on the idea that critics' report of their personal experience of a work does not provide their audience with reason to accept what the critics apprehend in that experience as the optimal interpretation of that work. Black subsequently comes to hold that reflexive statements, based on, and expressive of, the critic's personal experience of the critical object, can be framed so as to warrant claims upon the critic's own audience.[11] This possibility connects the critics' own experience of the work with the public argument that they provide for their interpretation and so warrants inclusion of the critics' intuitive apprehension of the work within the scope of criticism proper.[12]

In Black's view, the most basic power of competent critics is their intuitive, perceptual, and affective capacity to respond appropriately to the object of their study. A critically interesting object, Black holds, "is so constructed that that there is a normative reaction to it"—an ideal response that, in a sense, re-creates what the artist achieved in constructing the critical object.[13] In "an undistracted and unmediated confrontation . . . with the work," a competent critic can closely approximate that ideal response.[14] As we will see, Black's account of the competent critic's personal capacity to engage the object of his or her criticism matures over the course of his studies, but it does not change fundamentally. Quoting Theodore Green with approval, *Rhetorical Criticism* holds that the critic can have "an immediate artistic experience in the presence of the work of art itself," in which the critic apprehends "the content which its author actually expressed in it" and "feels" what the critic would judge.[15] Somewhat later, in "A Note on Theory and Practice in Rhetorical Criticism," Black endorses emic criticism, premised fundamentally on the critic's unmediated perception of the work, over and against etic approaches, which regard the object of criticism through the lens of some theory or prior conceptual framework.   '

Here is an approach to criticism in which, as a prerequisite to the interpretation of an object, the critic will undertake to see the object on its own terms—to see it with the utmost sympathy and compassionate understanding. This sympathetic explication is, of course, only a phase in the process of critical engagement. The emic critic may, and probably will, proceed from sympathy to distance, from the suspension of judgment to the rendering of judgment. But at some moment—probably early—in his or her engagement with an object, the emic critic will aspire to so sympathetic an account that the critic's audience will understand that object as, in some sense, *inevitable*.[16]

An etic approach, by comparison, would apprehend the critical object not simply on its own terms but a prioristically through the conceptual lens of some rhetorical theory. Both the chapter in *Rhetorical Criticism* on "Rhetoric and General Criticism" and Black's "Note on Theory and Practice in Rhetorical Criticism" attribute to the critic the capacity to directly engage the work of art and to intuitively apprehend and affectively experience what the artist has managed to express in the work.[17]

It is important to notice that Black does not endorse naive apprehension of the critics' object of study. To be sure, he describes critics' personal engagement with the work as "unmediated," and he holds that at their best, critics try "to become, for a time, a pure perceiver, an undistorting slate on which an object or an event external to him can leave a faithful impression of itself, omitting nothing."[18] Nonetheless, Black does not hold that in their personal apprehension of a work critics are to nullify their sensibilities. They ought to strive to be an undistorting, but not a blank, slate. Competent critics, in Black's view, are trained and sensitive instruments. Their experience with, and study of, the kind of artifacts that interest them have given them a discerning eye and ear; they have "that vague quality, *taste*"—a "set of scruples that refine the critic's perception."[19] The crucial requirement is that, at that phase in the critical process in which critics personally apprehend the work and strive to re-create in their own experience what the artist has managed to express, at this key moment, emic critics rely only on concepts that they have assimilated to their ways of perceiving. Discussing this point, Black writes,

Because only the critic is the instrument of criticism, the critic's relationship to other instruments will profoundly affect the value of critical inquiry. And in criticism, every instrument has to be assimilated to the critic, to have become an integral part of the critic's mode of perception. A critic who is influenced by, for example, the Burkean pentad and who, in consequence of that influence, comes to see some things in a characteristically dramatistic way—that critic is still able to function in his own person as the critical instrument, and so the possibility of significant disclosure remains open to him. But the would-be critic who has not internalized the pentad, who undertakes to "use" it as a mathematician would use a formula—such a critic is certain (yes, *certain!*) to produce work that is sterile.[20]

Notice that this observation concerns critics' powers; insofar as the apprehension of the work relies only on concepts that they have fully assimilated to their mode of perception, they can engage the critical object in their own right with the possibility of apprehending aspects of the object that do not fit their pre-conceptions. However, insofar as critics' personal encounter with the critical object is trammeled by some cognitively managed method or methodology, their discoveries will be limited to whatever fits that conceptual frame.[21]

The critic's capacity to personally experience what the artist has managed to achieve in the work, in Black's view, is fundamental to honest and productive criticism. The need for re-creative personal engagement with the work is partly a matter of the requisites for valid evaluation of the work. Critics are in a position to fairly judge a work of art only when they themselves fully apprehend what the artist managed to express in that work.[22] "Only then," writes Black, "will the emic critic be in a position to judge the object, for only then would the critic have fully disclosed what it is that is the subject of judgment."[23] Of equal importance for Black, critics' personal engagement with the work is nec-essary to rescue their studies from potential circularity. If critics do not engage the work emically, if they read the work only through the conceptual screen of some theory or preestablished methodology, their criticism will find just what their theory or methodology ordained beforehand. Their study will be circular. "A problem of applying any pre-existing theory to the interpretation of a rhe-torical transaction is that the critic is disposed to find exactly what he or she expected to find. The epistemological constraints imposed by a theoretical ori-entation inhibit the critic from seeing new things, from making new discoveries. Such criticism tends much more to be a confirmation than an inquiry. It is, in the strictest sense, a *prejudice*."[24] As we have seen, Black is uncompromising and certain on this point.

The priority that Black assigns to the critic's unmediated experience of the critical object helps to explain a curious aspect of Black's remarks about criti-cism, rhetorical criticism in particular. When Black writes criticism, he is meth-odologically pristine. The arguments that he provides for his conclusions exhibit a self-conscious awareness of evidentiary and inferential requirements. Yet Black's own remarks about criticism repeatedly express disdain for discussion of critical methods.[25] This aversion to discussion of critical methodology in the work of a critic so conscious of the need for argumentatively adequate criticism can be explained, in part, by critics' belief that they must, at some point, engage the object of their criticism free from the direction of consciously held method or methodology. At that point in their work, even an unassimilated theory of reading or of interpretation would narrow and distort their intuitive apprehension of the work. Black's aversion to methodological discussion involves two further points. First, when it comes to the argument that critics make for their interpre-

tation of the critical object, they may need to draw on a great variety of sources
and kinds of argument in order to open their audience to that object's structure
and function. In general, it can be said that the critics' argument for their interpretation and evaluation of the work at hand must be grounded in the properties of that critical object, though their argument need not be limited to those
properties. Beyond this important point, Black recognizes only a few abstract
principles as *generally* applicable to critical interpretation and evaluation. Second, what warrants confidence in critics' conclusion is not the supposition that
they have followed this or that methodology but, rather, the insight that their
criticism affords insight into the object of criticism. This brings our discussion
to the public face of the critical process.

Critics' capacity to educate the audience for their critique presupposes prior
personal engagement with the critical object and is based on critics' ability to
argue for their interpretation and evaluation of that object. In both his early and
more mature views of criticism, Black regards critics, first, as analogous to
instruments that perceive the critical object and, then, as educators who having
thereupon formed an interpretation and evaluation of that object, proceed by
reason and argument to direct their audience's attention to a similar perception
and evaluation. As Black explains in *Rhetorical Criticism*, "The critic . . . oc-
cupies the office of mediator, receiving from one source and conveying to another. The critic proceeds in part by translating the object of his criticism into
the terms of his audience and in part by educating his audience to the terms of
the object of criticism."[26] Looking back on his early *Rhetorical Criticism,* Black
elaborates, "A critique represents a particular mind at work on an object: apprehending it, examining it, coming to understand it, placing it into history. A
function of such writing is to bring its reader to corroborate an interpretive
process—not necessarily the same one that the critic has experienced but in any
case one that will finally bring the reader to the interpretation that the critique
proposes."[27] Except in very rare cases, critics' ability to educate is not simply
a matter of reporting their personal experience of the critical object. Critics are
able to instruct their audience because they can provide an argument for their
interpretation and evaluation of the critical object; by these means they can, at
least in principle, put their public in a position to "verify for itself that the
critical object can be apprehended as the critic proposes without offending reason, and should further find reason to believe that the critic's way of apprehending the object yields moral understanding of it."[28]

Critics' capacity to educate depends, in part, on their ability to situate the
critical object historically. Here critics' preliminary tasks consist in the authentication of artifacts, situating them in their temporal context and ascertaining the
expressive intent of their creators.[29] "The authentication of texts (and other artifacts) and their interpretation in light of biographical, social, and ideological
evidence," Black observes, "proceeds along lines prescribed by scholarly
traditions."[30] Establishing the historical context for work may pose difficulties,
and care should be taken not to conceive context too narrowly.[31] Determining

the expressive intent of a work can be difficult. However, Black maintains "that in the great majority of cases the aims and purposes of the communicator will be expressed, through conventional tokens, in his discourse."[32] So the speaker's expressive purpose can usually be inferred from the discourse itself, and aspects of context serve as a guide. In principle, the critic's work as a historian can put the critic and his or her readers in a position from which it is possible to commence interpretation of the critical object.

In Black's view, critics' paramount capacity is their ability to interpret the work, enabling readers to apprehend what the artist has achieved in creating the critical object. In this connection critics' analysis of the work will be part formal and part functional. Formally, they can offer a characterization of the work in terms of how its structure resolves a problem or difficulty facing the artist—how its structure enables the artist to express something. Functionally, they can identify how that structure enables a certain response to the work. Presumably, the response that critics identify for their readers is the normatively ideal response apprehended by critics in their own engagement with the work.[33] The burden of critics' argument is to defend their "reading" of the work over and against alternative readings as the interpretation that optimally accounts for characteristics of the work in formal and in corresponding functional terms.[34] Thus, their interpretation stands as an argument for the work.[35] It identifies the artist's achievement and places the critics' readers in a position to appreciate that achievement.

Growing out of interpretation but extending beyond, critics have the capacity to judge the works of art that they study.[36] At the outset of his essay on "The Second Persona," Black articulates his view of the importance of judgment in criticism.

[T]here is something acutely unsatisfying about criticism that stops short of appraisal. It is not so much that we crave magistracy as that we require order, and the judicial phase of criticism is a way of bringing order to our history. . . . It is through moral judgments that we sort out our past, that we coax the networks and the continuities out of what has come before, that we disclose the precursive patterns that may in turn present themselves to us as potentialities, and thus extend our very freedom.[37]

The exercise of judgment, in short, is essential to the contribution that criticism makes to the humane "understanding of man himself."[38]

Ideally, as the critical process unfolds, critics' personal engagement with the work and the interpretation that they are consequently able to communicate to their audience put them in a good position to publicly and fairly evaluate the critical object in terms of its form and its function. Formally, critics have a view of the work's inherent structure, of its constituents and their relationship to one another.[39] Functionally, they have experienced the response that structure serves to illicit. It is a basic tenet of Black's view of critics' powers that where emically oriented critics attain the normative response that the work is constructed to elicit, they both apprehend the formal structure of the work and experience the response that the work is designed to elicit. In principle, their interpretation of the work puts their audience in a position to similarly apprehend the structure of the work and to respond appropriately. Thus, in Black's view, the bases for judgments of form and evaluation of function are intimately related; accordingly, he remarks that there "is a point beyond which the distinction between the formalistic and the pragmatic judgments is a quibble."[40] Judgments of form and judgments regarding function are, however, distinguishable.

Critics are able to render formal judgments of the work independently of its effects because they have access to touchstones as a basis for comparison and because they have developed tasteful expectations about the potentials of the art that they serve. It is important to note that Black accepts a sharp limitation on critics' capacity for formal evaluation. They will not be able to provide an exhaustive, generic definition for the evaluative terms that they use to appraise a critical object. They will not, for example, be able to provide a strict definition for "rhetorically good." But they can use evaluative language meaningfully because they can define their terms by example. They can justify their "appraisals of specific discourses by recourse to generally accepted touchstones of rhetorical excellence—Demosthenes, Cicero, Edmund Burke, for example—and can show the relative merit of a discourse by comparing it to these touchstones."[41] Moreover, properly trained critics' selection of the touchstones for use in evaluation will be guided by their expectations about what can be achieved in the art that they serve. Their familiarity with examples of past artistic excellence will have sharpened their perceptions and elevated their expectations. Their experience, in short, will have endowed them with a cultivated taste, and that capability will enable critics to teach their audience to make appropriate demands of the critical object.[42]

We should notice at this point that Black's view of critics' capacity to evaluate a work's form supposes that critics' intuitive apprehension of the work's structure will provide them with an intimation of the work's value. To be sure, full exercise of critical judgment involves inferences beyond critics' immediate perception of the work. Black does not believe that critics should *evaluate* an object emically.[43] Nevertheless, critics' taste—their assimilated experience of past instances of artistic excellence—sharpens their perceptions of the critical object. As a result, emic critics sense the value of the critical object in their unmediated apprehension of what the artist has contrived to express. Accordingly, Black observes, "Beyond perception is appraisal; beyond seeing the thing is attaching a value to it. These two acts—perception and evaluation—distinguishable as they are in theory, are generally experienced as inseparable phases of the same process. That process is criticism."[44] Critics' re-creative experience of the work shades off into their judgment of the work.[45] Thus, while the critics may not be able to provide generic definitions for their evaluative vocabulary, their judgments are linked to the object both by comparison to past examples of excellence and by their immediate intuition of the work's quality.[46]

When regarding the work functionally, critics have a capacity to provide both pragmatic and moral judgments. For the benefit of rhetorical critics habituated to a highly restricted exercise of critical judgment, Black stresses that critics can pass a wide range of pragmatic judgments. Critics can evaluate the work in terms of the normative response that the work would elicit and in terms of the actual response that it evokes from particular audiences—even those remote in time from the production of work. Critics can further evaluate the way the techniques employed in the work would shape an appetite for subsequent works and so condition the conventions of an art. Critics may also evaluate the effects of the work on the artist and on other artists. They can, in short, assess all the differences that the critical object "has made in the world and will make, and how the differences are made and why."[47] As many of these judgments will reflect how the critical object shapes or would shape its audience, critics will often be led to moral appraisal of the work.

THE PROPER SCOPE OF RHETORICAL CRITICISM

For Black the scope of rhetorical criticism, the objects to which rhetorical critics properly direct their attention and the interest that they take in them, is determined by two considerations: (1) rhetorical critics' inherited focus on persuasive discourse and (2) the demands that humane interest in such discourse imposes on critics.

Black's view of the proper object of rhetorical criticism evolves somewhat over the course of his studies, but throughout he maintains that the rhetorical critic is to focus on persuasive discourse. Maturation occurs in the terms that Black uses to define and identify *persuasive discourse*. His early *Rhetorical Criticism* conceives persuasive discourse in terms of the rhetor's intent: "Rhetorical discourses are those discourses, spoken or written, which aim to influence men."[48] In this connection Black defends his identification of the rhetorical with persuasive discourse on grounds of tradition and current practice. "Essays in rhetorical criticism," he writes, "focus on persuasive speakers or discourses, and the weight of rhetorical tradition too falls in that direction."[49] Some years later, in *Rhetorical Questions*, Black identifies the object of rhetorical criticism in structural and functional terms. Now the objects subject to rhetorical criticism are distinguished structurally as discourses that exhibit incongruities of the sort that occur "when public discourse is made to serve private motives."[50] In such cases, Black maintains, "there is a perceptible disparity between form and substance; . . . language is used to convey more than the literal sense of a claim and literal report of the evidence warranting it."[51] In terms of function, rhetorical discourse is to be found at work in contexts where the central claims of a discourse, the propositions or pieties that it advances, "must be affirmed against the countervailing prospect of the decay or neglect or discredit of those claims."[52] This shift from intentional concepts to structural and functional terms reflects, as we later see, a refinement in Black's view of the critic's capacity to respond normatively to a work. Since a discourse may function persuasively even though it was not deliberately designed to work in that way, the movement from a conception of the rhetorical in intentional terms to a conception in structural and functional terms somewhat broadens the scope of rhetorical criticism. But across this evolution in Black's views, the proper object of rhetorical criticism remains persuasive discourse.[53] Strictly informative discourse falls outside the scope of the rhetorical.[54] By tradition and training the rhetorical critic is prepared to deal competently only with persuasive discourse.[55]

While Black adopts a traditional view of the object for rhetorical criticism, he takes an explicitly modern view of the scope of the rhetorical critic's interests. Commenting on the critics of classical antiquity, Black observes, "They assumed the mission of elevating intuitive acts of creation to the status of viable method. Their aim was to formulate technical principles that artists could use: to make creativity systematic. They wrote primarily, not for the critic himself, or for the auditor, but for the artist."[56] Modern critics address a larger audience. Their critiques speak not just to the artist but to all who share a humane interest in the object of critical study. Where the ancient critic was concerned to formulate technical principles of art, the modern critic, "like other humanistic studies, seeks to understand men by studying men's acts and creations. If the critic has a motive beyond understanding . . . that motive is to enhance the quality of human life."[57] Accordingly, Black assigns to contemporary rhetorical critics a considerably broader interest in persuasive discourse than was typical of their classical counterparts.

To comprehend the scope of the interests that in Black's view ought to engage the rhetorical critic, it is useful to distinguish between, on the one hand, a focus on the instrumental design of persuasive discourses and, on the other, a concern for their developmental powers. It is natural to regard persuasive discourse *instrumentally* (i.e., as discourse [apparently] calculated to influence the attitudes and beliefs of particular audiences to which it is primarily addressed). However, an instrumental orientation does not exhaust the interest that a critic may take in how persuasive discourses function. Significant persuasive discourses may have consequences that ramify beyond the results that they are apparently designed to produce: the style of a discourse may engender an appetite for similar discourses; the discourse itself may contribute to an ongoing dialogue that unfolds into an indefinite future; the discourse may become a hallowed statement, oft repeated and formative of the very fabric of the polity; the discourse may become a model for subsequent discourses of that kind or serve as an exemplary modification of inherited patterns of rhetorical practice.[58] Thus, a discourse may shape rhetorical conventions, contribute to the formation of rhetorical genres, promote traditions of rhetorical practice, feed an ideology, and so on. It is useful to think of these and other larger functions of the discourse as *developmental*: they all involve the gradual bringing into being, elaboration, stabilization, or reinforcement of patterns of attitude and belief, of discursive practices and conventions, of systems of interpretation, and so on. To be sure, a discourse's instrumental design and its developmental powers may overlap and intertwine in complicated ways. Some developmental functions may be intended by rhetors and achieved through their design, and it may happen that the production of functions that initially were accidental or otherwise unintended comes to be understood and sought for instrumentally. Nor is it the case that the instrumental design of a discourse is always pursued as a deliberate matter by the rhetor. Persuasive strategies become established practices that may be employed more or less mindlessly by rhetors who only dimly comprehend the calculations underlying their attempts to persuade. A rhetorical critic can, in one and the same study, attend both to a discourse's instrumental design and also to its developmental powers. But it can also be, and has all too often been, the case that the critic regards the discourse only as an instrument designed to move some relatively well specified auditors toward acceptance of attitudes, beliefs, policies, doctrines, and so on advocated by the would-be persuader, while neglecting the discourse's larger potential to initiate, elaborate, reinforce social, psychological, or artistic patterns.

Black holds that humane interests in rhetorical phenomena require attention not just to the instrumental design of persuasive discourses but also to their developmental powers. Rhetorical phenomena, he argues, are radically mutable: just as there have been "radical discontinuities in the history of consciousness," so, too, "the ways in which auditors experience rhetorical communication have altered over time."[59] Rhetorical phenomena change, Black observes, as the techniques used in significant persuasive discourse shape the sensibilities, appetites, and expectation of audiences with respect to subsequent discourse and so mold rhetorical conventions.[60] With respect to these developmental powers of persuasive discourse, rhetorical criticism can, in Black's view, make its deepest contribution to humane understanding, for, he maintains, it seems entirely probable that as the techniques employed in persuasive discourse, at least in the modern era, shape audience appetites and sensibilities, they mold the very structure of the audience's consciousness, and that is to say that the techniques used in persuasive discourses have a formative impact on their audiences' humanity.[61]

This insight that humane interests call the rhetorical critic to attend to the developmental potentials of persuasive discourses is a major and fundamental theme in Black's reflections on rhetorical criticism and in his work as a practicing critic. As we see in the discussion that follows, it undergirds his critique of rhetorical criticism as he found it in the middle of the twentieth century. While Black is not averse to critical interest in rhetoric's instrumental nature, he warns against narrowly focusing on persuasive discourse as means designed to influence the audience immediately addressed. Through a critique of the critical practices that he identifies as neo-Aristotelianism, Black argues that a narrow focus on the instrumental nature of rhetorical discourse severely impairs exercise of the powers inherent in the critic's office and, consequently, leaves the critic unable to address the developmental potentials of persuasive discourses. Interest in the developmental powers of persuasive discourse is apparent through much of Black's work as a practicing critic. It is reflected in his attention to the sensiblities cultivated by forms of rhetorical discourse, to the rhetorical genres that thereupon emerge and, ultimately, to the ideologies and forms of consciousness fed by those persuasive structures. This deep connection between the developmental power of persuasive discourses and the formation of human consciousness commits the rhetorical critic, in Black's view, to moral evaluation.[62]

THE CRITIQUE OF NEO-ARISTOTELIANISM'S NARROW INSTRUMENTAL FOCUS

Perhaps Professor Black's best-known service to rhetorical criticism is his critique of the orientation that dominated rhetorical criticism at the outset of his career. He baptized that critical approach "neo-Aristotelianism," because it relied heavily on "techniques of criticism derived from Aristotle's *Rhetoric*."[63] Tracing the origins of this school to a misreading of the program for rhetorical criticism set out by Herbert Wichelns in "The Literary Criticism of Oratory," Black documents the influence that it exercised over rhetorical criticism at midcentury.

It is generally agreed that Black's critique of neo-Aristotelian criticism is both devastating and liberating. Thomas Benson summarizes the impact of Black's critique in these terms:

Until the early 1960's, perhaps the most influential book for students of criticism was Lester Thonssen and A. Craig Baird's *Speech Criticism*, published in 1948. But in 1965, Edwin Black published his *Rhetorical Criticism: A Study in Method*. Black's book, originally a dissertation directed by Herbert Wichelns at Cornell, directly attacked the methods, assumptions, and results of what he called the neo-Aristotelian critics, whose mission had been defined by Wichelns in 1925, exemplified by the Brigance and Hochmuth studies in American public address, and described as method by Thonssen and Baird. Black voiced many of the dissatisfactions that had been gathering with the field. Implicitly, his title shifted the center of studies from speech to rhetoric, and hinted at new directions.[64]

Dilip Gaonkar's estimate is more opinioned. "Neo-Aristotelianism eventually collapsed under the weight of its own massive failure. But the privilege of writing its obituary belonged to Edwin Black who, in his influential book *Rhetorical Criticism*, offered a brilliant diagnosis of how its critical failure stemmed from a flawed conceptual apparatus."[65]

Black provides a clear and succinct characterization of neo-Aristotelian rhetorical criticism. Considered in general terms, neo-Aristotelianism has the following features. First, it regards persuasive discourses as instruments designed to affect an immediate audience: on the whole, "the new-Aristotelian critics tend . . . to comprehend the rhetorical discourse as tactically designed to achieve certain results with a specific audience on a specific occasion,"[66] and they are preoccupied with judging the discourse in terms of whether it achieved the immediate results intended by its source. Second, in their analysis, interpretation, and evaluation of persuasive discourse, neo-Aristotelians rely on the lexicon of rhetorical art developed in classical antiquity. "The primary and identifying ideas of neo-Aristotelianism that we can find recurring in the critical essays of this school are the classification of rhetorical discourses into forensic, deliberative, and epideictic; the classification of 'proof' or 'means of persuasion' into logical, pathetic, and ethical; the assessment of discourse in the categories of invention, arrangement, delivery, and style; and the evaluation of rhetorical discourse in terms of its effects on its immediate audience."[67] Third, neo-Aristotelian critics "ignore the impact of the discourse on rhetorical conventions, its capacity for disposing an audience to expect certain ways of arguing and certain kinds of justification in later discourses that they encounter," and "the neo-Aristotelian critics do not account for the influence of the discourse on its author."[68] In short, neo-Aristotelians narrowly focus on the persuasive discourse as an instrument designed by the would-be persuader to influence the specific audience immediately at hand; they rely on a lexicon of art inherited from classical antiquity, and they ignore the larger contexts in which persuasive discourses function and the developmental impact that such discourses may have.

A narrowly instrumental focus, as instanced by neo-Aristotelian criticism, has a strong and inherent appeal as an approach to critical study of persuasive discourse. In the first place, it fits the nature of much persuasive communication. A good deal of the persuasive discourse that publicly addresses individual and community decisions of political and economic importance is calculated to influence the attitudes, beliefs, and commitment of particular audiences in specific situations. It is only natural to interpret and evaluate such discourse in terms of its immediate instrumental value. Second, whatever the limitations of the conceptualization of rhetorical art provided by classical sources, the ancient treatises do provide a convenient lexicon that seems on its face to characterize the instrumental character of persuasive discourse.[69] Finally, it is not obvious how rhetorical critics can engage persuasive discourse on terms other than those dictated by its instrumental nature. The appeal of a narrowly instrumental focus on persuasive discourse is general, as is the force of Black's critique of neo-Aristotelianism.

The crucial defect of orthodox neo-Aristotelianism is that its restrictive interest in the instrumental value of persuasive discourse does not sanction rhetorical critics' personal engagement with their critical object. Black, it will be recalled, regards an unmediated personal response on the part of critics, which approximates the normatively ideal response appropriate to the critical object, as indispensable to productive criticism. Neo-Aristotelianism attenuates critics' attention and directs them to concentrate on the immediate audience's response to the work. As the critics are not in their own right members of that audience, this restricted focus makes their response to the work irrelevant. Black, quoting T. S. Eliot, explains in *Rhetorical Criticism*, "Rather than seek an interpretation of the discourse that realizes all that is in it and that aims 'to see the object as it really is,' the neo-Aristotelian critic attempts to make an estimate of the historically factual effects of the discourse on its relatively immediate audience. The critic's own sensitivity may or may not disclose anything."[70] Later in the same work, he elaborates this important point: "The neo-Aristotelian critic is preoccupied with the immediate audience of the discourse; in a sense, his eye is where that audience's eyes are: on the issues of the discourse, on its doctrines, on the ideas to which the audience is asked to assent. And insofar as his focus is thus, then his own responses to the discourse will have no place in the critical performance."[71] In short, a restricted concern with the instrumental value of the discourse deflects critics' attention from their proper critical object and renders their intuitive response to that discourse irrelevant. This orientation, which precludes a normatively proper re-creative response on the critics' part, renders them unprepared to exercise other powers inherent in their public office.

Neo-Aristotelian critics are able to situate the persuasive discourse historically and to provide their audience with an account of its context and expressive intent. However, even here, in the exercise of powers that are principally those of the historian, the neo-Aristotelian critic is inclined to a restricted view of the discourse's context and so is apt to underestimate the complexity and reach of the expressive intent that may animate the persuasive discourse. Neo-Aristotelian critics habitually identify the discourse's context as the situation that prompts the speakers to address their immediate audience and to restrict their conception of the speakers' communicative purpose to an intention to affect the beliefs, attitudes, commitments, and so on of that audience. In *Rhetorical Criticism,* Black offers two examples that support this complaint. The first is provided by critical studies of Lincoln's First Inaugural Address. The narrow instrumentalist is inclined to situate this address singularly in the context of events leading directly to the Civil War and to overlook Lincoln's preoccupation with his discourse as a longer-run "force in American culture."[72] For his second example, Black provides a critique of John Jay Chapman's Coatesville Address. Delivered in 1912 to an audience of three, the Coatsville Address would be of little significance to a critic who focused narrowly on its effectiveness in persuading its meager immediate audience. But this discourse, Black argues, is properly situated "as joining the dialogue participated in by Jefferson, Tocqueville, Lincoln, Melville, Henry Adams, Samuel Clemens, Santayana, and Faulkner—a dialogue on the moral discussion of the American."[73] Seen in this light, the proper context for the address includes contemporary America. A narrow focus on persuasive discourse as an instrument for affecting some immediate audience blinds the critic to the larger historical context. This is particularly unfortunate because the fragmentary nature of persuasive discourse makes proper historical situation of the work of great importance to rhetorical criticism.[74]

Neo-Aristotelian critics' tightly circumscribed focus has still graver consequences for their ability to interpret the persuasive work. Given the powers inherent in their office as critics, rhetorical critics should be able to (1) provide an interpretation of the discourse that enables their audience to apprehend what the rhetors have managed to express in the work and (2) offer the critics' audience an argument grounded in the work and supporting the critics' reading. However, the neo-Aristotelians' critical orientation impairs their capacity to perform these tasks.

In the place of a sensitive reading of the discourse, neo-Aristotelian critics' attention is drawn away from their proper critical object and directed to what the critics can learn about the immediate audience's understanding of the discourse. As noted earlier, the critic's own apprehension and response to the discourse are, from the standpoint of neo-Aristotelianism, irrelevant to interpreting the discourse. The neo-Aristotelian's narrowly instrumental view focuses on "rhetorical discourse as an arrangement of tactics adapted to the relatively immediate audience."[75] The interpretation of the discourse relevant to this critical interest is that audience's understanding of the work. Critics with this orientation would support their interpretation by reference to data about the audience's response and not primarily by reference to the discourse itself. Their attention is driven from the work, to external data about the response of the audience specifically addressed. The closest that a neo-Aristotelian critic can come to an interpretation grounded in the work, Black argues, would be to attempt to reconstruct "the interaction between the work and its immediate audience."[76] "This reconstruction involves the critic's thinking and feeling himself into the thoughts and feelings of the rhetor's immediate audience, so that he can empathize with that audience and attempt to gauge their reactions to the discourse. In this procedure, the critic's own reactions to the discourse play a decidedly subordinate role. He apprehends the discourse, insofar as he is able, via the minds of others. The success of the reconstruction turns on the suppression of the critic's own responses."[77] Black denies that the critic can reasonably expect to succeed in so reconstructing discourses from the past. "No matter how vividly the critic may make the past live in his pages, no matter with what incorruptible verisimilitude he may present it to us, it is still the past. The voices we hear speak from the grave."[78]

Finally, neo-Aristotelian critics have an acutely limited capacity to prepare their audience to appreciate the value of persuasive discourses. They are left with no basis on which they can argue for any reading other than actual reception of the work by its immediate audience. "A literary critic," Black observes, "may argue for a poem so convincingly, illuminating its merits and the skill of its execution, that the poem comes to be accepted as fine literature and may even pass into the category of accepted touchstones of literature where the burden of critical proof passes to the poem's detractors."[79] A narrowly instrumental focus does not enable rhetorical critics to argue for the discourse that they interpret; this critical orientation "does not yield a sanction for saying that one should have been persuaded by a speech."[80] In fact, narrow instrumentalists are so bound to the immediate audience's response as basis for their critical orientation that, were they to successfully argue for a contemporary persuasive message, thereby affecting the reception of that discourse by its immediate audience, they would, on their own premises, be guilty of distorting the basis for evaluation of the discourse.

In summary, a narrowly instrumental reading of persuasive messages leaves the critic without personal basis for apprehending what the rhetor has managed to express in the discourse. Accordingly, critics have very limited capacity to appreciate discourses that do not conform to their theoretical preconceptions. At their best, they can try to reconstruct the immediate audience's response to the work, but such a reading does not enable their readers to re-create and experience the work for themselves. In the end, a narrowly instrumental focus on persuasive discourse leaves the critic without grounds for arguing for the work as an artistic achievement in any terms other than the work's success in securing understanding on the part of its immediate audience.

Nor have the neo-Aristotelians a vigorous capacity to evaluate rhetorical discourses. They are, one would presume, prepared to do that work. They have carefully studied the history of their art and are familiar with its past achievements, so one would suppose that they are in a position to intuitively recognize the quality of the techniques used by the rhetors in the discourses that they study, and they have at hand notable examples of rhetorically good discourses that they can use as touchstones to argue for their evaluation of the particular discourses that they deem worth judging. But their narrowly instrumental focus so hamstrings their efforts that they are unable to exercise their critical abilities in significant judgments.

Here, too, the neo-Aristotelian critics are impaired by the supposition that their own response to the work is irrelevant. Educated observers of persuasive discourse, they themselves might clearly apprehend the power of what the rhetor has managed to express, and they may intuitively recognize the good quality of the techniques that the rhetor has employed. But these intuitions are not to color their judgment. Insofar as they evaluate the discourse in terms of its power to evoke a response, they are preoccupied with the response of the audience immediately addressed. If they are concerned with the quality of the rhetorical means employed in the discourse, and they may well be, they have no auditors other than the rhetor's immediate audience, whose response might be considered pertinent to their judgment.

The priority that a narrow, instrumentalist perspective assigns to the immediate audience's response forces the rhetorical critic to accept a false opposition between formalistic judgments and pragmatic ones. Among Black's most important insights into the internal logic of neo-Aristotelian criticism is his observation that the neo-Aristotelian critics' restricted view of persuasive discourse compels them to choose between a starkly pragmatic judgment of the discourse's immediate effectiveness and an impossible formalism divorced from consideration of rhetorical function. The neo-Aristotelian critics in the first half of this century, Black observes, fall into two schools concerning the evaluation of persuasive discourse. A pragmatic school, following what Black regards as a mis-reading of Professor Herbert Wichelns' essay on rhetorical criticism, holds that the effect of the discourse on an immediate and specific audience is "the prime criterion of rhetorical criticism."[81] A formalist school, represented by Wayland Maxfield Parrish, holds that the rhetorical critic should judge the quality of the discourse as a "self-contained unit" without regard for its effect on any particular audience.[82] Examining this division among neo-Aristotelian critics, Black advances two objections.

First, the opposition between pragmatists and formalists involves a false dichotomy forced on neo-Aristotelians by their narrow preoccupation with the immediate audience.

There is a point beyond which the distinction between the formalistic and the pragmatic judgments is a quibble. That point is defined by the critic's very conception of *effect*. When the effects of a discourse are understood by the critic to be only those that discourse has on the beliefs of its immediate audience, then the distinction between the formalist judgment and the pragmatic judgment is a substantial one. It is substantial because the pragmatic judgment limits the critic's view to the circumscribed transaction between a rhetor and an audience isolated in time, while the formalistic judgment tends to ignore the specific audience entirely, having invoked what is assumed to be timeless standards. When, however, the conception of *effect* comprehends more than the immediate audience, the judgment rendered comes increasingly to resemble the judgment of formalism.[83]

The argument implicit in this passage is worth unpacking. Neo-Aristotelian formalists start from the supposition that evaluation of a persuasive discourse solely in terms of its effect on the immediate audience is an unsatisfactory basis for estimating the quality of the discourse. But working from the narrowly instrumental focus that they share with their pragmatic cousin, neo-Aristotelian formalists do not (and perhaps cannot) conceive any other audience whose responses to the discourse might be relevant to their judgment; accordingly, neo-Aristotelian formalists elect to evaluate the persuasive discourse's quality independently of the discourse's effect on *any* audience. Thus, neo-Aristotelian critics are forced to choose between a position that evaluates the discourse pragmatically in terms of its effect on some immediate audience or a position that judges the discourse formally independently of the response on any audience. Black holds that this choice, if it can be called one, is falsely imposed on the neo-Aristotelian critics by their narrowly instrumental focus. Were rhetorical critics able to conceptualize an ideal auditor capable of a normative response to the discourse, they could comprehend judgments of form and function not as alternatives but as interrelated.

We now come to Black's second complaint. Should the neo-Aristotelian critics elect to evaluate persuasive discourse formally, attempting to apply standards that are independent of the discourse's effect on any particular audience, they will have adopted a stance that cannot be consistently maintained. The conceptions of quality that neo-Aristotelians offer as divorced from consideration of effect, Black argues, turn out on closer inspection to be based on pragmatic calculations. Thus, where neo-Aristotelian formalists claim to evaluate persuasive discourses using standards that are "different from and more important than effect," the criteria that they apply are fundamentally pragmatic.

According to Black, neo-Aristotelian formalists base their conceptions of rhetorical quality on tradition and on a property called "persuasiveness." The standards derived from both sources, Black maintains, reduce to pragmatic considerations. To make this point, Black first considers the warrants provided by Plato, Aristotle, Cicero, and Quintilian for the principle that persuasive discourses ought to be clearly organized. His review of these classical sources argues that classical recommendations regarding the organization of speeches are based on ideas about how the parts of a speech function to affect its audience.[84] Classical principles of disposition, on this showing, turn out to be pragmatic, not strictly formalistic, standards. What is true of organization, Black suggests, is probably also true of other neo-Aristotelian principles of judgment. Accordingly, he concludes, "When the neo-Aristotelian critic appraises the quality of a discourse in terms of criteria derived from the Aristotelian tradition, the ultimate justification of these criteria is effect."[85]

The second notion of formal standards to which Parrish appeals, but does not explicate, suggests that rhetorical discourses are to be evaluated in terms of whether they possess elements of a quality that Parrish calls "persuasiveness."[86] In an extended analysis of senses of the term "persuasive," Black argues that we have no ordinary conception of a discourse as *persuasive* that is not based on some idea of the discourse's effect.[87]

Finally, the narrowly instrumental critics are hamstrung by their inability to evaluate the rhetor's ends and objectives. Because they are committed to considering the discourse as an instrument calculated to affect an immediate audience, the neo-Aristotelian critic is to take the rhetor's objectives as given.

Let us be reminded once again of the focus of neo-Aristotelianism. It is on the discourse as an instrument serving the objectives of the rhetor. These objectives are taken by the neo-Aristotelian critic as they are given by the rhetor. They are not themselves the objects of appraisal. Rather, they are the stable underpinnings of the methodology. If the neo-Aristotelian critic would assess the later discourses of John C. Calhoun, and Calhoun's principal objective in these later discourses is to justify the institution of slavery, then this objective is accepted by the neo-Aristotelian as a standard from which the discourses can be assessed. The objective itself is not evaluated, not even in its rhetorical aspects.[88]

A narrow focus on the instrumental character of persuasive discourses leaves the critic without grounds on which to evaluate the ends that those instruments are used to implement. "A critical methodology," Black writes of neo-Aristotelian criticism, "that induces its practitioners to efface themselves and yield an essential aspect of judicial criticism to other hands has abdicated some of its responsibility."[89]

In summary, Black argued that the neo-Aristotelians' narrow focus on the instrumental value of persuasive discourse grievously impairs their capacity to exercise the powers that inhere in their office as critics. He felt that they must disregard their own intuitive apprehension of, and felt response to, the discourses that they study, no matter how sensitive their reading and cultivated their rhetorical taste. They are inclined to take a highly restricted view of a discourse's context and so are prone to a limited view of the rhetor's expressive intent. At best, they can try to interpret a discourse through the eyes and ears of its immediate audience, but they have only marginal access to that perspective. They are left without a coherent basis for evaluating a discourse other than its effect on the audience immediately addressed.

A critic so impaired, Black argues, has a very limited capacity to speak to substantial, humane interests in rhetorical discourse. Black observes, as a matter of fact, "The neo-Aristotelians ignore the impact of the discourse on rhetorical conventions, its capacity for disposing an audience to expect certain ways of arguing and certain kinds of justifications in later discourses that they encounter, even on different subjects."[90] His analysis of neo-Aristotelianism shows this neglect of the developmental powers of persuasive discourse to be a product of the limitations of that school's narrowly instrumental focus. The neo-Aristotelian simply is ill-prepared to study potentials of rhetoric which Black deems to be of paramount humane interest.

Inherent in the neo-Aristotelians' narrow focus on the instrumental value of rhetoric lurks the strong possibility that the critic will arbitrarily impose prior theoretical concepts on emergent forms of discourse, instead of comprehending their development. If rhetorical critics are to entertain the prospect that rhetorical phenomena are radically mutable, they must be able to recognize and respond to forms of discourse which, from the perspective of inherited rhetorical theories, appear novel. This, Black argues, neo-Aristotelian critics are poorly positioned to do. Their critical orientation, it will be recalled, renders their own direct and immediate apprehension of the discourse irrelevant to their interpretation. Insofar as they might aspire to an experience of the discourse relevant to their highly restricted view of its instrumental nature, they must undertake to reconstruct the discourse through the eyes and ears of its immediate audience, a task which Black holds to be futile. Thus the neo-Aristotelian critic has little choice but to approach the discourse from an etic perspective and to interpret the discourse through the lens of inherited theoretical concepts. This focus limits their capacity to recognize and attend to aspects of the discourse which do not fit their preconceptions; consequently, they are apt to miss those features which would engender in audiences an appetite for new, theoretically unanticipated possibilities. By working in a fashion which tempts circular confirmation of inherited rhetorical theories, the neo-Aristotelian critic runs the risk of overlooking the mutability of rhetorical phenomena and neglecting the developmental powers of persuasive discourse.[91]

Black argues in some detail that the neo-Aristotelians' orientation not only tempts, but actually leads, rhetorical critics to seriously misconstrue significant modern and contemporary discourse and, consequently, to neglect the contribution which persuasive discourse makes to the formation of ideology, social identity, and the structure of consciousness. In their critical practice, neo-Aristotelian critics habitually rely upon a lexicon borrowed from classical theories of rhetoric. This application of classical conceptions of rhetoric to modern and contemporary discourse is, Black argues, a doubtful enterprise:

We can hardly expect the principles of rhetoric formulated two thousand years ago to be uniformly germane today. The nature of political institutions and the modes of communication have drastically changed in twenty centuries. It would be naive to suppose that there would not be concomitant changes in the character of rhetorical discourse, particularly when we know that more subtle modulations in society are echoed in rhetorical discourse. The world changes, and the uses of language with it.[92]

Nevertheless, the neo-Aristotelian proceeds as though the kinds of persuasive discourse practiced in modern societies were limited to those developed in classical antiquity and as though the range of persuasive techniques employed by contemporary rhetors were limited to the persuasive art found in the rather more tribal communities of Greek antiquity. Moreover, Black argues, insofar as neo-Aristotelian critics rely specifically on Aristotle's conception of rhetoric, they adopt a "restricted view of human behavior" which neglects discourses "which function in ways not dreamed of in Aristotle's Rhetoric."[93] Committed to a critical orientation that allows "the critic little room for interpretive originality," neo-Aristotelian critics are poorly prepared to help their audience comprehend the emergence of novel forms of modern and contemporary persuasive discourse.[94]

Black's indictment of neo-Aristotelian criticism is directed to his perception of a methodology specific to a body of rhetorical critics working in the first half of the twentieth century. Critics, of course, may take a narrowly instrumental view of persuasive discourse without adopting a specifically Aristotelian point of view. However, Black's analysis penetrates so deeply into the logic of the neo-Aristotelian position as to raise serious and general questions as to whether a narrow focus on persuasive discourse as an instrument calculated to effect a specific immediate audience can serve as adequate orientation for rhetorical critics. From Black's account we learn that the narrowly instrumental critic has a severely limited capacity to explore the development powers of persuasive discourse and, so, is unable to speak to important humane interests in rhetorical discourse.

BLACK'S POSITIVE CONTRIBUTIONS TO
DEVELOPMENTAL STUDIES OF PERSUASIVE DISCOURSE

Professor Black has not only sustained a highly influential critique of neo-Aristotelian criticism but also contributed positively to our understanding of rhetorical criticism and to its practice. He has identified a focus for rhetorical criticism that affords the critic opportunity for full exercise of the interpretive powers that critics inherently possess, and in his own critical practice, he has shown that by exercising those powers, rhetorical critics can contribute to a humane appreciation of persuasive discourse.

It is not enough to diagnose the infirmity of neo-Aristotelianism; one must also show that the full complement of a critic's powers can be exercised by the rhetorical critic. To the critic with a narrowly instrumental focus, the liabilities that Black identifies in neo-Aristotelian criticism seem to be dictated by the pragmatic nature of persuasive discourse itself. Responding to this objection, Black argues that the limitations of neo-Aristotelianism are a consequence not of the nature of rhetorical discourse but of the neo-Aristotelian's myopic critical perspective. If critics take a larger view of the instrumental potentials of rhetorical discourse and attend to the developmental powers of persuasive communication, they find ample latitude for exercise of their interpretive capacities. Black's defense of this claim is the core of his positive contribution to our understanding of rhetorical criticism.

At issue is whether the instrumental design of persuasive discourse imposes blinders on rhetorical critics, which need not be worn by their counterparts in the fine arts. As a rule, aesthetic objects have an appeal that transcends the immediate context of their production, so critics in the fine arts can respond directly and profoundly to works that originate at great cultural distances from the critics. Persuasive discourse, the neo-Aristotelian maintains, is characteristically addressed to particular audiences that do not number the critic among their members. The situations to which persuasive discourse responds are often historically remote, and, from the critic's point of view, the issues addressed may be archaic and without vitality. Neo-Aristotelian critics are inclined to suppose that these pragmatic aspects of persuasive discourse preclude the possibility of significant response from persons outside the immediate audience. These critics may be inclined to doubt whether they have the power to personally and intuitively respond in critically relevant ways to historically removed rhetorical objects.

Black denies that the pragmatic, situated nature of persuasive discourse precludes the possibility that rhetorical critics can directly and intuitively engage such discourse in ways that yield insights relevant to interpretation and evaluation of their critical object. His response is complex and evolves over the course of several essays from a position initially articulated in *Rhetorical Criticism.*

Black's first argument for the possibility of personal critical engagement with persuasive discourses focuses on the alleged contrast between aesthetic objects

and the more pragmatically oriented objects of interest to rhetorical critics. Some
critics have tried to articulate a "categorical opposition of fine art and rhetorical
activity" by contrasting poetry and rhetoric.[95] Responding to this line of thought,
Black denies that there is a sharp distinction between imaginative literature and
rhetoric. No sooner is such a distinction drawn than it must be qualified to the
"vanishing point."[96] There are rhetorical elements in poetry and poetic passages
in rhetorical discourse. Moreover, Black observes,

> We have discourses that fall exactly between the "realms" of imaginative literature and
> rhetoric . . . and these discourses solicit the attention of the critic as imperatively as any
> other. The Gettysburg Address is one such; Chapman's Coatesville Address . . . is an-
> other. One may also think of *The Grapes of Wrath*, or *Crime and Punishment*, or *Gul-
> liver's Travels*, or the *Annals* of Tacitus, or the *Symposium of Plato*, of the whole
> literature of social protest, of the genres of parody and satire, of countless sermons and
> epideictic discourses, even of such examples of "pure" poetry as *Paradise Lost* with its
> rhetorical object of justifying "the ways of God to man."[97]

It follows that, although many persuasive discourses that fall in the range between rhetoric and poetic may have originated in contexts quite remote from
rhetorical critics, they can still personally and directly apprehend their force.
Lincoln's Gettysburg Address, for example, and much of his other public discourse are designed to speak not just to his immediate audience but to subsequent generations as well. It is part of the power of Lincoln's discourse that it
still speaks to us.[98] Other persuasive discourses, such as Chapmann's Coatesville
Address, contribute to ongoing debates that stretch over centuries and continue
to the present.[99] In these cases the issues addressed continue to have vitality for
critics, and they may regard themselves as part of the rhetor's audience. So, the
idea that, unlike fine literature and other aesthetic objects, rhetorical discourse
cannot reach beyond its context of production is not true for a wide range of
persuasive discourses. Where it does, the rhetorical critic can aspire to a full
and sensitive personal reading.

This first answer, however, does not adequately resolve the challenges that
the pragmatic nature of persuasive discourse poses for rhetorical critics. While
they may hope to personally and intuitively engage persuasive discourses that
fall in the range between rhetoric and poetic, still, as Black recognizes, many
critically interesting persuasive discourses fall clearly into the rhetorical, con-
textually bound end of this spectrum. Here one encounters discourses designed
to affect the commitments of audiences often remote from the critic in time and
place and addressed to issues that the critic can no longer find vital and immediate. It is generally true, Black admits, "that the work of rhetoric is fragmentary outside its environment; it functions only in a particular world."[100] On
the face of the matter the doctrinally archaic, situation-bound nature of such
discourse seems to pose an insuperable difficulty for any critic's effort to intu-

itively apprehend and personally experience what the rhetor has managed to express.

No matter how vividly the critic may make the past live in his pages, no matter with what incorruptible verisimilitude he may present it to us, it is still the past. The voices we hear speak from the grave. We do not have the power of choice with Clay's compromise on the Wilmot Proviso. *Our* assent is not being solicited; *our* convictions cannot be engaged. The doctrines embodied in Clay's speech are historical archaisms, and the modern audience cannot stand in the same relation to them as to the humblest aesthetic object.[101]

What, if any, basis for response does doctrinally dead discourse afford the critic? "What responses can a contemporary critic have to a rhetoric discourse of the past? How can the critic respond to, say, Clay's speech of 1850 when, as we have argued, that speech is doctrinally archaic? Is it even possible for any critic, for any contemporary, to experience a reaction to a substantively dead discourse?"[102] On Black's account of rhetorical criticism, this question must be regarded as crucial to the possibility of full and productive exercise of the critic's capacities in studies of persuasive discourse.

We come now to Black's second argument for the possibility of direct critical engagement with persuasive discourses. In response to the challenge that substantively dead discourse poses for the rhetorical critic, *Rhetorical Criticism* argues that, even where a persuasive discourse is ideologically archaic, the critic may still have an immediate response to the rhetorical techniques employed in that discourse. In a passage that foreshadows much of Black's own work as a critic, he explains:

The critic who believes that some techniques of argument can have an effect independent of the substance of argument is able to experience an immediate response to the discourse. If, in other words, a critic were to see any rhetorical discourse as working to make certain techniques conventional, to shape an audience's expectations for discourses that they will later hear or read, to mold an audience's sensibilities to language, then that critic would be in a position to respond with immediacy, even to a doctrinal archaism. He will be able to do so because, we shall assume, rhetorical techniques do not become archaic in the way that doctrines and issues become archaic; a rhetorical technique will almost always stand as a live possibility at any point in history.[103]

By focusing on, and responding to, the persuasive techniques in a work, rhetorical critics can personally engage and be affected by the work in those ways that Black regards as an indispensable first step in the critical process; they can re-create in their own experience the impact of the work's technique.

In his work as a practicing critic, Black recognizes some limits to a critic's capacity to respond to culturally remote persuasive techniques. Soon after affirming that "a rhetorical technique will almost always stand as a live possibility at any point in history," Black's study of Daniel Webster as an exemplar of the

sentimental style brings our critic up to the limits of our capacity to respond to
Webster's style. Focusing on Webster's epideictic discourse, specifically, the
Bunker Hill address, Black encounters a discourse that is not only doctrinally
but also stylistically archaic. "Webster," Black observes, "is excessively didactic."

He over instructs. Permitting no chance response, he prohibits spontaneity. To be the
people he wants us to be, to honor the claims he makes on his auditors, we must totally
surrender ourselves to his speech; we must feel only what he wants us to feel. And since
we cannot bring ourselves to so total a surrender, we stand to some extent outside the
speech. We understand what it asks. Hence, we understand that we are not its auditors,
we are merely spectators. We are standing apart from a rhetorical transaction, observing
it. This orientation enlists our spectatorial responses.[104]

Contrary to Black's earlier optimism, Webster's discourse presents our critic a
style from the past that he (and we) can engage only as a spectator and not as
participant. So, the view that rhetorical critics can respond as ideal auditors to
the persuasive techniques in doctrinally archaic discourses must admit of limitations; at best, "a rhetorical technique will *almost always* stand as a live possibility at any point in history" (emphasis added). But even in the case of
Webster, the critic's efforts to personally engage the discourse bear fruit. As a
sympathetic observer Black is able (1) to identify, and to enable his reader to
recognize, the response that Webster demands of his auditor, (2) to understand
how Webster's style could function to produce that response, and also (3) to
recognize the limits of the critic's own capacity to respond to Webster's address.
Thus, Black's interpretation of Webster's style shows that, even when confronting an archaic rhetorical technique, the emic critic's attempt to respond sensi-
tively to a discourse, though inhibited, can nevertheless yield significant insight
into the discourse's structure and functions.
    Still there is a crucial difficulty in Black's initial conception of the rhetorical
critic's capacity to respond to culturally remote persuasive techniques, a difficulty that Black does not resolve until later in his studies. The difficulty lies in
how critics are to situate themselves and their reader so as to apprehend the
discourse in its own terms "with the utmost sympathy and compassionate understanding." Critics aspire to experience the discourse's techniques as ideal
auditors. But in what capacity are they and their reader to attend to the discourse? According to Black, it will be recalled, a major limitation of neo-
Aristotelian criticism is its inability to conceive any audience for persuasive
discourse other than the historical audience to which the discourse was immediately addressed. Consequently, the neo-Aristotelian critic does not aspire to
the experience of an audience or auditor whose response to a persuasive discourse approximates the normatively ideal response that the discourse solicits.
But Black's critic faces a similar challenge, and most ask, who is the auditor
capable of responding fully to the discourse at hand? Out of the myriad of

capacities that the critic might bring to bear in apprehending the discourse's persuasive techniques, which configure into an ideal auditor for that discourse?

This difficulty is not resolved by the insight that critics have a capacity to respond emically to the persuasive techniques employed in a discourse. The capacity to respond is a situated capacity. The ideal auditor for a discourse may have an identity, may exercise capacities, and may have response potentials that are within the conceptual and experiential range of rhetorical critics and their readers; however, if critics and readers are to aspire to the ideal normative response to the discourse's techniques, critics must know and be able to convey to their readers in just what capacities the discourse's techniques ideally solicit a response. Accordingly, critics need a conception of the ideal audience for the discourse at hand, and that conception must approximate the position that they attain in their personal engagement with the text, it must support an interpretation of the techniques employed in the discourse, and it must enable them to argue for the interpretation of the discourse by reference to evidence from the text. This problem of how to conceptualize the ideal auditor for a rhetorical discourse is not explicitly addressed in *Rhetorical Criticism*, and Black's earliest critical essays deal with the problem in ways that are less than entirely satisfactory.

Black's initial attempts to position his own reader as the discourse's ideal audience invite the reader to interpret the rhetorical discourse from the perspective of the audience as envisioned and addressed by the rhetor. This solution requires that the critic make inferences about the rhetor's expressive intention based on the text of the discourse, and then, given this specification of the rhetor's communicative purpose, the critic's reader is invited to infer the response ideally expected. For example, Black's interpretation of the Coatesville Address proceeds, first, by positing four possible responses to the vicious lynching that formed the subject of the speech: "[T]here would conceivably be those who would perceive the event as a righteous act of vengeful justice; there would be those who would perceive it as a hideous expression of mob violence; there would be those who would perceive it, clinically, as the concrete illustration of an abstract sociopathic idea; there would be those who would refuse to perceive the event at all, who would dismiss it and put it out of mind."[105] Black then proceeds to identify the function of the address on the basis of a conjecture about Chapman's intentions in relation to these four possible responses: "Of these four reactions, we can infer that Chapman regarded the first and last of them as wrong, and the second and third of them as requiring emendation. The function of his speech was to provide this emendation—to shape the appropriate reaction to the event."[106] Black's readers, then, are to rely on Chapman's intentions in determining the ideal audience for the Coatesville Address and the function of that address for this audience. This would be a defensible procedure, for, as Black argues, "in the great majority of cases the aims and purposes of the communicator will be expressed, through convention tokens, in his discourse."[107] So the speaker's expressive purpose can usually be inferred from the discourse itself, and in the unusual case aspects of context will serve as a guide.

However, while an estimate of the speaker's intentions and expressive purpose would be relevant to the critic's identification of what the speaker has managed to express in a persuasive discourse, it could not satisfactorily serve as the sole or arbitrating desideratum for the critic's interpretation of the form and function of the techniques employed in the discourse. Speakers' expressive achievements may or may not coincide with their intentions. Sometimes achievements exceed all expectations; sometimes speakers' achievements may be other than their intentions; one can achieve a quite unexpected and unplanned result. Indeed, as Black observes in *Rhetorical Questions*, the expressive power of a work may reflect the artist's subconscious struggles.[108] A rhetorical discourse may engender appetites and sensibilities quite different and divergent from the rhetor's strategic calculations. Critical practices that rely primarily on speaker intentions to identify the perspective from which the critic argues for his or her interpretation of the work would, to put the matter simply, drive the critic's work in the direction of instrumental interpretations, sometimes at the expense of understanding the work's developmental potentials.

Subsequently, Black's study of "The Second Persona" provides a more satisfactory solution to the problem of how the critics are to position themselves and their readers in relationship to the work for purposes of interpretation. There Black extends Wayne Booth's observation that the structure of a work implies certain characteristics of its author, which may, in turn, be deduced from features of the work. Black identifies this implied author/speaker as the first persona in rhetorical transactions, and he observes "that there is a second persona also implied by a discourse, and that persona is its implied auditor."[109] There are two parts to Black's conception of the second persona. First, this persona is inferable from the discourse. The concept of an implied auditor, Black writes, "does not focus on a relationship between a discourse and an actual auditor. It focuses instead on the discourse alone, and extracts from it the audience it implies."[110] The nature of the implied auditor is typically inferable from stylistic tokens in the text of the discourse. Second, the implied auditor identifies a "vector of influence."[111] The critic can apprehend in the response that a discourse would elicit from its implied auditor "a model of what the rhetor would have real auditors become."[112] The implied auditor, then, is a hypothetical auditor whose response to the discourse corresponds exactly to the response that, according to Black, the critic ought to approximate in his or her preliminary re-creation of the work. The concept of a second persona, in short, provides Black's critics with a vehicle for translating his or her personal intuitive response to a work into a publicly accessible audience perspective that can be identified and defended directly by reference to the linguistic indicators found in the text.

The concept of a second persona rounds out Black's view that by focusing on the persuasive techniques in a discourse, the rhetorical critics find space for full exercise of their interpretive powers. Black is now able to work free of exclusive reliance on the rhetor's persuasive intent as a guide for the critic's orientation to the text. Instead, the critic can deduce, from the discourse itself, the orientation that the discourse's ideal auditor would adopt in responding to the discourse's style and other persuasive techniques. Moreover, the critics can situate their reader as the discourse's implied auditor and can guide their reader to the normative response that presumably the critics have attained in their own engagement with the discourse.

Our attention now turns to Black's own work as a rhetorical critic. Two observations are in order. First, Black's own practices as a working critic exercise the interpretive powers that he holds to be inherent in criticism generically considered. Second, drawing on those capacities, Black has been able to address the developmental powers of persuasive discourse, which he considers crucial to humane appreciation of persuasive discourse.

It is important to speak cautiously about Black's *practices* as a working critic. In reflecting on Black's critical studies, it would be a mistake to speak of his "methods" or his "methodology." He repudiates the idea that insightful criticism can be reduced to methods, much less methodologies. His own practices as a working rhetorical critic are too flexible and variable to qualify as regular and systematic procedures, nor does Black rest his claims on the grounds that he arrived at them by use of this or that method. But it is possible and useful to see in Black's work as a critic certain practices—habitual and polished ways in which he interprets and evaluates rhetorical discourses. As a working critic, Black exercises the powers that his analysis attributes to critics per se, bringing those powers to bear on just those aspects of persuasive discourses that his reflections on rhetorical criticism mark out as available and suitable for serious study. We can, then, better understand and appreciate Black's teachings about rhetorical criticism as we see them embodied in his critical practices.

According to Black's analysis of the powers of critics, they should be able to directly engage the work of apprehending the interstices of its form and function, and their interpretation should give the critics' readers access to the work from the vantage point of the work's implied auditor, enabling readers to apprehend the structure at least of the techniques employed in the work and to sense their function. Black's critique of Lincoln's Gettysburg Address, a pyrotechnical display of rhetorical criticism, nicely illustrates critical practices that realize the promises of Black's analysis of the critic's inherent powers. We may presume that our emic critic has attained, in his own right, an intuitive and affectionate experience of the discourse that, to his satisfaction, approximates that of an ideal audience. We may also presume that this experience informs the interpretation of the discourse that he presents to us, his readers. However, our critic does not appeal to that experience per se in the course of his critique; there are no first-person-singular references in this essay, though there are critically important first-person-plural references. Personally and as an individual, the critic intrudes in this essay only to the extent that its tone implicates an authoritative reading on the part of the critic. Instead of appealing directly to his prior experience of Lincoln's Address, the critic invites us to jointly engage the discourse with him, therein guiding our attention and response. The essay speaks to a question about the function of the discourse: "How does the Gettysburg Address function rhetorically?"[113] In order to answer this question Black deduces from evidence in the text the audience implied by Lincoln's Address, the address' second persona. That audience, Black concludes, "transcribes a movement through the speech from unspecified universal . . . to national . . . to local . . . back to national again."[114] This section of the essay provides a detached analysis of the structure of the discourse; no explicit reference is made to the critic or his readers. The next section of the essay, subtitled "The Movement of the Address," carefully connects Black's analysis of the overall structure of the address, first, to an account of the functions of that structure and, then, to a characterization of the response that those functions would elicit from the implied audience. This discussion of function and response is initiated by a shift in the relationship between the critic and his reader. Having identified a position from which both the critic and reader can engage the text, Black directly addresses his readers using the first person plural, thus merging both the critic's orientation and his reader's orientation with the orientation attributed to the implied auditor. The reader is now to regard the discourse as addressed to an ideal audience that includes both critic and reader. The overall structure of the address, Black argues, pivots on the first sentence in the address' third paragraph. Paragraphs 1 and 2 lead the audience on historical and moral grounds to conclude that "it is altogether right and proper" that the audience gather on this spot to dedicate a portion of the battlefield "as a final resting place for those who here gave their lives that that nation might live." Following this conclusion, "a normal extrapolation" would lead to an utterance performatively dedicating the cemetery. Lincoln violates this expectation with the line opening paragraph 3, "But, in a larger sense, we can not dedicate—we can not consecrate—we can not hallow—this ground." Black describes this sentence as the beginning of a process of rejection. Writing in the first person plural, he says, "Our past has led us to the point of declaring this burial ground sacred; but yet, we demur. Why? Because we have neither the right nor the duty. A moral intervention prevents the fulfillment of conventional form; a customary itinerary has been deflected. Our right has been superseded by those who have died. Our duty is elsewhere; it is to take up the task left unfinished by the dead."[115] The critic offers a description of the structure of the address that includes us, his readers, among the address' audience and that has already begun to shade into a description of function; the structure has effected a rejection: our attention has been redirected, and our expectation of fulfillment has been denied. Black parallels this discussion of function with an account of the corresponding affective experience of the audience. Black invites us to consider this movement in terms of what, following Berenson, he calls "respirational values." "We can appreciate that the speech is temporarily arrested at the point of maximum contraction. The narrowing of the location from continent . . . to nation . . . to battlefield . . . to portion of that field . . . to resting place . . . finally pivots with 'but' even to a rejection of our capacity to affect 'this ground.' Then, . . . a movement recommences, and an expansion continues to the end."[116] Thus, Black argues, the "structure of the Gettysburg Address imposes a corresponding form on the experience of its auditor. That experience is composed of initial tension, followed by tightening, followed by progressive exhilaration."[117] "We are," he writes, "coiled by the Address, and then sprung. The structure of the Gettysburg organizes the auditor's energy,"[118] until, at the end, in a moment of dedicatory release and with experience of soaring elevation, "we here highly resolve that these dead shall not have died in vain—that this nation, under God, shall have a new birth of freedom—and that government of the people, by the people, for the people, shall not perish from the earth."[119] Carefully detailing this structure and its functions, Black provides a highly nuanced and compelling interpretation of Lincoln's enduring address.

Black's reading of the Gettysburg Address fairly represents how our critic argues for his interpretation of a discourse.[120] Here and elsewhere Black tries to enable his reader to apprehend both the structure and function of the techniques employed in a discourse. Relying on evidence from the text, Black situates his reader in a position approximate to that of the ideal auditor implied by Lincoln's Address. From that vantage point, Black prompts his reader to attend to salient features of the discourse and invites his reader to at least recognize the response that those features invite from the discourse's ideal auditor. Thus, our critic provides the reader with an argument for his interpretation of the discourse that is designed to communicate to the reader what Black presumably experienced in his own unmediated engagement with the work. It is apparent, and ought not be surprising, that Black's critical practice reflects his mastery of the very powers that his analysis identifies as inherent in the critic's office.

We should also notice that these critical practices enable Black to work autonomously as an emic critic. His interpretation of a discourse typically draws on a wide variety of corroborating sources and on a wealth of data external to his critical object, and his discussion of the functions of a discourse typically extrapolates speculatively to identify functions well beyond the response that Black claims, the discourse immediately invites.[121] His account of the sentimental style, for example, makes reference to six nineteenth-century oratorical instances of the sentimental style, Alex de Tocqueville's *Democracy in America*, various historians of the period, Freud, Matthew Arnold, Walter Benjamin, Hanna Arendt, biographies of Oscar Wilde, and anthologies of English and American melodramas.[122] These resources are needed to arrive at the far-reaching general conclusion that the sentimental style functions "to subordinate all values to aesthetic values. As such, it is the fallible sign of an evasion of moral responsibility."[123] But this larger interpretation (and judgment) is anchored by the emic reading, discussed earlier, of a key passage in Webster's Bunker Hill Address.[124] Similarly Black's study of the "Idioms of Social Identity" ranges over texts from the period of the American Civil War, to Nazi Germany, and to the civil rights crisis of the mid-1960s. His conclusions in the study are supported by an extended conceptual comparison of the terms used to articulate a social identity on the basis of heredity as contrasted with the language used to base a social identity on convictions. Ultimately, the essay offers a general characterization of the rhetorical components of American social identity. These extended reflections start from a critical interpretation of key passages in then-President Lyndon Johnson's civil rights speech of March 15, 1965.[125] Confronting a discourse that is part of a long and ongoing national dialogue, Black situates his reader historically and directs his reader's attention to how Johnson's language powerfully aligns national values with the cause of justice for "American Negroes" and against racism and Southern sectionalism.[126] The emic character of the reading is most apparent in Black's comments on Johnson's portrait of the poverty-stricken Mexican American children whom he, as a Southerner, taught in his first job out of college. The auditor, Black directs, must "be moved by such a depiction or reject it."[127] The reader is to apprehend Johnson's text as a historically situated second persona and to, at least, recognize the response that its stylistic techniques would elicit from its ideal auditor. In these and other essays, Black exercises critical autonomy in that he claims an evidentiary basis for his argument that is available to his reader independently of any prior theory or conceptual framework. Having situated his reader in a position approximating that of an ideal auditor, Black rests his case on what he can bring his reader to apprehend of the structure and function of the particular rhetorical discourse to which he directs the reader's attention.

The autonomy that Black exercises as an emic critic affords him a consistent basis on which to investigate the developmental powers of persuasive discourse and so to address what he regards as deeply humane interests in rhetorical discourse. It will be recalled that, in Black's view, exploration of the developmental powers of persuasive discourse requires that the critic be open to novelty in rhetorical techniques and to discontinuities in the sensibilities and appetites that those techniques inculcate in audiences. Critical practices must be guided by the prospect that rhetorical phenomena are radically mutable. In order to satisfy this requirement, Black argues, the critic must be able to engage and interpret rhetorical discourses emically, refusing to impose on the discourse a preexisting theory or conceptual framework. As noted earlier, part of Black's critique of neo-Aristotelian criticism holds that this approach to criticism distorts modern and contemporary persuasive discourse by forcing it into the largely antiquated categories of classical rhetorical theories. His positive contribution to our understanding of rhetorical criticism includes an analysis of the possibilities for emic interpretation of the techniques used in persuasive discourses. His critical practice exploits those possibilities, directing his readers' attention to the key rhetorical transactions independent of prior theoretical orientation or conceptual framework. It is a measure of Black's autonomy as a working critic that the success of his enterprise depends ultimately on what he enables his reader to directly apprehend about the structure and functions of particular persuasive discourses.

It remains to be noted that working autonomously as an emic critic, Black has produced a remarkably coherent body of studies that explore just those developmental powers of persuasive discourse that Black takes to be of paramount humane interest. Much of Black's work as a critic is guided by an overarching conjecture about the developmental power of persuasive discourse. Particular rhetorical discourses, according to this hypothesis, contribute to the development of rhetorical genres by reinforcing, modifying, and/or engendering their auditors' appetites for discourses with similar appeal. The sensibilities of both speakers and audiences are shaped by the discourses that they respectively produce and experience. In modern and contemporary Western societies, where social identities are founded on the basis of shared convictions, a person's rhetorical sensibilities, Black argues, dispose that individual toward a corresponding ideology.[128] Rhetorically developed sensibilities, in this view, are key determinants of an individual's consciousness, constituting a matrix of cognitive and perceptual proclivities that undergirds that person's ideology and commits that individual to a "durable social unit . . . to whose laws a public submits and with whose fortunes they have bound their lives."[129] The task for rhetorical critics, in Black's view, is to interpret specific transactions—persuasive discourses, sets of discourses, campaigns, or persuasive movements—that, taken together, have the aggregated shape of rhetorical genres and that can reveal the formation of human consciousness and the pull of ideologies.[130]

Professor Black's work as a practicing critic engages specific rhetorical artifacts and uses them to disclose development of rhetorical genres and corresponding ideological proclivities. The richness and variety of these studies defy ready summary; a brief sampling will have to suffice. In studies of discourses marked by the sentimental style, Black attempts to delineate a rhetoric genre that functions to subordinate "moral to aesthetic consideration" and so to promote "psychic comfort and subcutaneous harmony through the refusal to apprehend the jarring, the unwholesome, the corrupt."[131] In his essay on "The Second Persona," Black analyzes the metaphor "the cancer of communism," characteristically deployed by the Cold War rhetoric of the Radical Right, as a stylistic token that tightly fits the form of consciousness underlying rightist ideology.[132] Critical study of "Idioms of Social Identity" investigates the language in which race, nation, and section are rhetorically configured in the transformations of social identity that Americans underwent in 1860 and 1965 and Germans in 1932 and that continue to shake Eastern Europe.[133] Black has attempted to map secrecy and disclosure as basic oppositional and complementary rhetorical forms that correspond to two distinct publics.

One public, convinced that concealment is bad, is disposed to embrace an associative plexus of values and to accede to arguments that are warranted by those values. The values include disclosure, openness, sharing, being equal, being unacquisitive. And the other public, convinced that some knowledge can be dangerous, is disposed with equal commitment toward a plexus of values that includes privacy, private property, hierarchy, capital accumulation, individuality. These groups differ in their politics, in their sexual attitudes, in their views of science and of art, probably even in what they eat and drink and wear on their backs. . . . At a deeper, less mutable level, these publics are distinct from one another in the rhetorical forms to which they respond.[134]

Examining "The Aesthetics of Rhetoric, American Style," Black contrasts two aesthetic sensibilities informing American rhetorical discourse, one structural and the other textural, and associates with each a corresponding regulatory principle governing the public sphere. A structural aesthetic, represented by the rhetoric of Nixon and Johnson, works "to banish unacceptable material from the public sphere either through explicit legal prohibition or, more subtly, through the operation of social pressures." A textural aesthetic, represented by Martin Luther King, proceeds inwardly and works "to focus perception itself so selectively that unacceptable material [is] simply excluded from consciousness."[135] In close examination of a *New York Times* editorial commenting on mob actions following a 1977 power outage and in an extended study of Nixon's rhetoric, Black undertakes to analyze discourses as symptoms of their author's ideological proclivities.[136] These essays cohere as the work of an active critical intelligence animated by a continuing interest in developmental powers of persuasive discourse.

CONCLUSION

At the outset of *Rhetorical Questions*, Professor Black modestly and elegantly describes his *Kampf* as an "effort to confront rhetorical phenomena with real questions, to elicit information rather than confirmation from them, to elude the role of interrogative *Schnorrer* that the asker of rhetorical questions plays."[137] I have showed that Black's reflections on rhetorical criticism and his work as a practicing critic are unified by a more specific struggle. Black has endeavored to understand the full interpretive and evaluative powers of the critic, to clear the field of restricting conceptions that inhibit exercise of those powers in rhetorical criticism, to identify a focus for rhetorical critics that enables the critic to bring those powers to bear in studies of the developmental powers of persuasive discourses. My objectives in this study have been modest and interpretive. It is part of the merit of Professor Black's work that it stands ultimately on the insights into rhetorical discourses that he is able to elicit from his readers. Evaluation of Black's contribution to our understanding of rhetorical criticism and to its practice, then, requires a very different chapter from the one that I have undertaken.

NOTES

1. Even Black's first book, *Rhetorical Criticism: A Study in Method*, is a set of closely related essays. His essay on the second persona explicitly tests a conjecture (113). The same is true of Black's essay "The Mutability of Rhetoric" (173), and "Ideological Justification" is similarly identified as an exploration of critical technique in Black's Introduction to *Rhetorical Questions: Studies of Public Discourse* (19).

2. Edwin Black, "Author's Foreword," *Rhetorical Criticism: A Study in Method, 2nd ed.* (Madison: The University of Wisconsin Press, 1978), p. x.

3. Edwin Black, *Rhetorical Questions: Studies of Public Discourse* (Chicago: University of Chicago Press, 1992).

4. There is scarcely a central theme or problem in any of Black's essays that is not foreshadowed by discussion in a previous essay. The need for moral evaluation of rhetorical artistry, for example, is raised in his early essay on Plato, difficulties attendant to such judgments are addressed in his later essay on the second persona, and the resolution to those problems informs Black's subsequent criticism (Black, "Plato's View," 374; Black, "Second Persona," 109–113). The title of his last book's penultimate essay, "The Mutability of Rhetoric," is a phrase drawn from a discussion of that topic that occurred in his first book.

5. Dilip Gaonkar, in "The Idea of Rhetoric in the Rhetoric of Science" (Albany: State University of New York Press, 1997), suggests that Black's critique of neo-Aristotelianism has been fully digested by rhetorical critics, and on the next page of the same essay Gaonkar puzzles that they have neglected an explicit consequence of Black's argument, namely, that if Black's account of the mutability of rhetoric is correct, and if his complaints about the dearth of critical concepts appropriate to modern and contemporary rhetorical criticism are sound, then critics need to rethink the use of concepts from classical rhetoric in interpretation and evaluation of modern persuasive discourse (31–32). Were Black's teaching fully integrated into the discipline, this problem about the lexicon of rhetorical art would be near the top of the common agenda of rhetorical critics.

6. Kenneth Burke, *The Philosophy of Literary Form: Studies in Symbolic Action* (Baton Rouge: Louisiana State University Press, 1941).

7. In the Author's Foreword to the second edition of *Rhetorical Criticism*, which appeared some thirteen years after the original edition, Black observes, "Behind the composition of *Rhetorical Criticism: A Study in Method* was an idea that was too dimly understood by its author to possess the book as firmly as it would if the book were to be written now. That idea is that critical method is too personally expressive to be systematized" (x). The conceptual point that corresponds to this observation is that Black consistently focuses on critics' powers—their capabilities—and not primarily on their methods. A passage representative of Black's attitude toward critical methods and methodology can be found in the Introduction to *Rhetorical Questions* (18).

8. Edwin Black, "A Note on Theory and Practice in Rhetorical Criticism," *Western Journal of Speech Communication* 44 (1980) 331–336. Also, Edwin Black, *Rhetorical Criticism: A Study in Method* (New York: The Macmillan Company, 1965), pp. 43, 48.

9. Black, "Note," p. 6.

10. Black, "Rhetorical Criticism," pp. 43–44.

11. Black, "Author's Foreword," p. xiii.

12. Black briefly discusses the claim that critics' reflexive statements may make on their readers in the Author's Foreword to the second edition of *Rhetorical Criticism* (xiii). Leff has discussed this development in Black's thought (343).

13. Black, *Rhetorical Criticism*, p. 44.

14. Ibid., p. 48.

15. Ibid.

16. Black, "A Note on Theory and Practice in Rhetorical Criticism," p. 334.

17. In the Author's Foreword to the second printing of *Rhetorical Criticism*, a brief note roughly contemporaneous with Black's "Note on Theory and Practice," our critic parethetically observes, "When I wrote *Rhetorical Criticism: A Study in Method*, I was much too sure of the distinction between statements about the world and statements about oneself. I attributed public significance to the former, but not to the latter. I was wrong. I now understand better that even reflexive statements make claims on their auditors and that our private experience cannot be divorced from our social history. Therefore, my present conception of criticism would put more emphasis than this book did on the personal requisites for the tasks of criticism and on the scruples that refine the critic's perception" (xiii). Black's observation that he has come to believe that our private experience cannot be divorced from our social history seems to imply some refinement in his early conception of re-creative criticism as originating in a moment of pure perception. But Black does not abandon the view that critics can, in a personal moment of apprehension, perceive what the artist has managed to express in the critical object. That doctrine is present both in *Rhetorical Criticism* and in his later "Note on Theory and Practice."

18. Black, *Rhetorical Criticism*, p. 4.

19. Black, "Author's Foreword," p. xiii; Ibid., pp. 67–68.

20. Ibid., p. xii.

21. For a critical response to Black's conception of emic criticism, see Michael Leff's "Interpretation and the Art of the Rhetorical Critic" (1980).

22. Ibid., pp. 43, 48.

23. Black, "A Note," p. 334.

24. Ibid., pp. 333–334.

25. Black, *Rhetorical Questions*, pp. 17–18, 98.

26. Black, *Rhetorical Criticism*, p. 6.

27. Black, "Author's Foreword," p. xiv.

28. Ibid., pp. xii–xiii.

29. Black, *Rhetorical Criticism*, pp. 37–42.

30. Ibid., p. 37.

31. Ibid., p. 39.

32. Ibid., p. 17.

33. Ibid., p. 44.

34. Ibid., p. 55.

35. Ibid., p. 49.

36. Ibid., pp. 4–5, 37.

37. Edwin Black, "The Second Persona," *Quarterly Journal of Speech* 56.2 (1970) 109–119.

38. Black, *Rhetorical Criticism*, p. 9.

39. Ibid., p. 62; Black, *Rhetorical Questions*, p. 98.

40. Ibid., pp. 67–68, 73.

41. Ibid., p. 67.

42. Ibid., p. 68.

43. Black, "A Note," p. 334.

44.. Black, *Rhetorical Criticism*, p. 5.

45. Ibid., p. 55.

46. In *Rhetorical Criticism*, Black suggests that his conception of evaluative terms is common in ethics and aesthetics (67). The philosopher G. E. Moore's intuitivist position in ethics is strikingly similar in important respects to Black's conception of formal evaluation. C. D. Broad observes in "Certain Features in Moore's Ethical Doctrines" (LaSalle: Open Court, 1942), "It is a fundamental doctrine of Moore's ethical theory that the good, in its most fundamental sense, is a name for a characteristic which is simple and non-natural. He compares it in the first respect, and contrasts it in the second, with the word yellow" (57). Like Moore, Black holds that good in the sense of intrinsically good refers to a characteristic strictly defined but can be intuitively apprehended.

47. Black, *Rhetorical Criticism*, p. 74.

48. Ibid., p. 15.

49. Ibid., p. 14.

50. Black, *Rhetorical Questions*, p. 3.

51. Ibid., p. 10.

52. Ibid., p. 14.

53. Ibid., p. 2.

54. Ibid., p. 10; Black, *Rhetorical Criticism*, pp. 12–15.

55. Ibid., p. 11.

56. Black, *Rhetorical Criticism*, p. 2.

57. Ibid., p. 9.

58. For a discussion of the development of traditions of rhetorical performance, see James Jasinski's "The Forms and Limits of Prudence in Henry Clay's (1850) Defense of the Compromise Measures" (1995). Black's own studies do not give much attention to the development of traditions of performance; his studies pivot around the development of audience sensibilities, but an interest in traditions of rhetorical performance would fall within the very broad scope of developmental possibilities to which Black would direct the rhetorical critic's attention.

59. Ibid., p. 125; Black, *Rhetorical Questions*, pp. 172–173.

60. Ibid., p. 35.

61. Black, *Rhetorical Questions*, p. 112.

62. Edwin Black, "Plato's View of Rhetoric," *Quarterly Journal of Speech* 44 (1958) 361–374; Black, "Second Persona," pp. 109–113, 119.

63. Black, *Rhetorical Criticism*, p. 27.

64. Thomas W. Benson, "History, Criticism, and Theory in the Study of American Rhetoric," *American Rhetoric: Context and Criticism*. Thomas W. Benson, ed. (Carbondale: Southern Illinois University Press, 1989), 1–18.

65. Dilip Gaonkar, "The Idea of Rhetoric in the Rhetoric of Science," *Rhetorical Hermeneutics: Invention and Interpretation in the Age of Science*. Alan Gross and William Keith, eds. (Albany: State University of New York Press, 1997) 25–88; Stephen E. Lucas, "The Renaissance of American Public Address: Text and Context in Rhetorical Criticism," *Quarterly Journal of Speech* 74.2 (1988) 241–260.

66. Black, *Rhetorical Criticism*, p. 39.

67. Ibid., p. 67.

68. Ibid., p. 35.

69. A narrowly instrumental view of persuasive discourse need not depend on classical sources for its theoretical framework. This type of critical approach needs a larger analysis of the social/political/economic functions of persuasive discourse, which might be drawn from Dewey or Marx or some more ad hoc account, and it needs a lexicon for discussing the techniques that would-be persuaders employ. But that lexicon might come from sources other than classical rhetorical traditions. The producers of advertising and of marketing strategies interpret and analyze their message strategies using terminology partly developed in the course of their own self-understanding and partly borrowed from social psychology; for example, see Belch and Belch's *Advertising and Promotion: An Integrated Marketing Communications Respective* (Boston: Irwin/McGraw-Hill, 1998). It is fair to say that much analysis of contemporary advertising, though not neo-Aristotelian, shares with that school of rhetorical criticism a narrowly instrumental view of persuasive discourses (see J. Michael Sproule's *Propaganda and Democracy: The American Experience of Media and Mass Persuasion*. Cambridge: Cambridge University Press, 1997).

70. Black, *Rhetorical Criticism*, p. 70.

71. Ibid., p. 57.

72. Ibid., p. 40.

73. Ibid., pp. 33–34.

74. Ibid., p. 39.

75. Ibid., p. 49.

76. Ibid., p. 54.

77. Ibid., p. 56.

78. Ibid., p. 52.

79. Ibid., p. 49.

80. Ibid., p. 44.

81. Black, *Rhetorical Criticism*, p. 61; Black, *Rhetorical Questions*, p. 17.

82. Black, *Rhetorical Criticism*, pp. 61–62.

83. Ibid., pp. 73–74.

84. Ibid., pp. 68–72.

85. Black supplements his historical consideration of disposition with analytical reflection on what constitutes good organization in prose composition. His conclusion is that available concepts of good organization are pragmatic at base (Black, *Rhetorical Criticism*, pp. 72–73). This particularly interesting argument nicely illustrates Black's general view of the unity of form and function.

86. Black, *Rhetorical Criticism*, p. 63.

87. Elsewhere I have to identified an ordinary sense of persuasive test that seems to have escaped Black's analysis. "Persuasive" in this formally interesting sense refers to the quality of the discourse independent of whether the discourse tends psychologically to persuade the auditor. Using this sense, we say that a discourse is persuasive and mean that, in view of the quality of its argumentation, the discourse deserves consideration, even though we are not at present persuaded by it (see Fred J. Kauffeld's "The Persuasive Force of Arguments on Behalf of Proposals." Amsterdam: International Centre for the Study of Argumentation, 1995).

88. Ibid., p. 77.

89. Ibid., p. 89.

90. Ibid., p. 35.

91. Black, "A Note," p. 333.

92. Black, *Rhetorical Criticism*, p. 124.

93. Ibid., p. 131.

94. Black, *Rhetorical Questions*, p. 17.

95. Black, *Rhetorical Criticism*, p. 46.

96. Ibid., p. 47.

97. Ibid.

98. Edwin Black, "Gettysburg and Silence," *Quarterly Journal of Speech* 80.1 (1994) 21–36; Black, *Rhetorical Criticism*, pp. 40–41.

99. Black, *Rhetorical Criticism*, pp. 33–34.

100. Ibid., p. 39.

101. Ibid., p. 52.

102. Ibid., p. 56

103. Ibid., pp. 56–57.

104. Edwin Black, "The Sentimental Style as Escapism, or the Devil with Dan'l Webster," *Form and Genre: Shaping Rhetorical Action*. Karlyn Kohrs Campbell and Kathleen Hall Jamieson, eds. (Falls Church, VA: Speech Communication Association, 1976) 75–86. Revised and republished in *Rhetorical Questions*, 97–112.

105. Ibid., p. 35.

106. Ibid., p. 85.

107. Ibid., p. 17.

108. Black, *Rhetorical Questions*, pp. 12–13.

109. Black, "Second Persona," p. 112.

110. Ibid., p. 112.

111. Ibid., p. 113.

112. Ibid.

113. Black, "Gettysburg," p. 22.

114. Ibid., p. 24

115. Ibid.

116. Ibid.

117. Ibid., p. 26.

118. Ibid., p. 27.

119. Ibid., p. 21.

120. Black's interpretation of the Gettysburg Address treats the discourse as a whole; often Black's criticism discusses only a portion of the discourse, as in comments on Webster's Bunker Hill Address in his study of the sentimental style (Black, *Rhetorical Questions*, pp. 100–101).

121. Black's critical practice is informed by the observation that much rhetorical discourse is highly conventional. In *Rhetorical Questions*, he observes, "Inasmuch as originality is not prized among rhetors as it is among litterateurs, there is an almost complacent conventionality in rhetorical practice, one that would be appalling to connoisseurs of literature. The rhetorical critic is driven by the nature of the critical object to comparative judgments and generic understandings" (8). One would expect, then, that Black's critical practice would be marked by extensive reference to other persuasive discourses that corroborate his reading of the particular rhetorical discourse upon which his interpretation focuses.

122. Black, *Rhetorical Questions*, pp. 195–196.

123. Ibid., p. 109.

124. Black, "Sentimental Style," pp. 27–28.
125. Black, *Rhetorical Questions*, pp. 24–29.
126. Ibid.
127. Ibid, p. 27.
128. Black, "Second Persona," pp. 112–113.
129. Black, *Rhetorical Questions*, p. 22.
130. Ibid., p. 130.
131. Ibid., pp. 105–106.
132. Black, "Second Persona," pp. 113–119.
133. Black, *Rhetorical Questions*, p. 21.
134. Ibid., p. 72.
135. Ibid., p. 3–4.
136. Ibid., p. 19; Edwin Black, "Richard Nixon and the Privacy of Public Discourse," *Rhetoric and Public Affairs* 2 (1999) 1–29.
137. Black, *Rhetorical Questions*, pp. 1–2.

BIBLIOGRAPHY

Belch, George E., and Michael A. Belch. *Advertising and Promotion: An Integrated Marketing Communications Perspective*. 4th ed. Boston: Irwin/McGraw-Hill, 1998.
Benson, Thomas W. "History, Criticism, and Theory in the Study of American Rhetoric." In *American Rhetoric: Context and Criticism*. Ed. Thomas W. Benson. Carbondale: Southern Illinois University Press, 1989, 1–18.
Black, Edwin. "The Aesthetics of Rhetoric, American Style." *Rhetoric and Political Culture in Nineteenth-Century America*. Ed. Thomas W. Benson. East Lansing: Michigan State University Press, 1997, 1–14.
Black, Edwin. "Author's Foreword." In *Rhetorical Criticism: A Study in Method*. 2d ed. Madison: University of Wisconsin Press, 1978, ix–xv.
Black, Edwin. "Gettysburg and Silence." *Quarterly Journal of Speech* 80.1 (1994): 21–36.
Black, Edwin. "Ideological Justifications." *Quarterly Journal of Speech* 70.2 (1984): 144–150. Republished in *Rhetorical Questions*, 135–146.
Black, Edwin. "The Mutability of Rhetoric." In *Rhetoric in Transition*. Ed. Eugene E. White. University Park: Pennsylvania State University Press, 1980, 71–88. Revised and republished in *Rhetorical Questions*, 171–186.
Black, Edwin. "A Note on Theory and Practice in Rhetorical Criticism." *Western Journal of Speech Communication* 44 (1980): 331–336.
Black, Edwin "On Objectivity and Politics in Criticism." *The American Communication Journal* 4.1 (2000). http:///www.acjournal.org/
Black, Edwin. "Plato's View of Rhetoric." *Quarterly Journal of Speech* 44.4 (1958): 361–374.
Black, Edwin. *Rhetorical Criticism: A Study in Method*. New York: Macmillan, 1965.
Black, Edwin. *Rhetorical Questions: Studies of Public Discourse*. Chicago: University of Chicago Press, 1992.
Black, Edwin. "Richard Nixon and the Privacy of Public Discourse." *Rhetoric and Public Affairs* 2 (1999): 1–29.

Black, Edwin. "The Second Persona." *Quarterly Journal of Speech* 56.2 (1970): 109–
119.
Black, Edwin. "The Sentimental Style as Escapism, or the Devil with Dan'l Webster."
In *Form and Genre: Shaping Rhetorical Action.* Ed. Karlyn Kohrs Campbell and
Cathleen Hall Jamieson. Falls Church, VA: Speech Communication Association,
1976, 75–86. Revised and republished in *Rhetorical Questions*, 97–112.
Broad, C. D. "Certain Features in Moore's Ethical Doctrines." *The Philosophy of G. E.
Moore.* Ed. Paul Arthur Schilpp. La Salle: Open Court, 1942, 43–67.
Burke, Kenneth. *The Philosophy of Literary Form: Studies in Symbolic Action.* Baton
Rouge: Louisiana State University Press, 1941.
Gaonkar, Dilip. "The Idea of Rhetoric in the Rhetoric of Science." In *Rhetorical Her-
meneutics: Invention and Interpretation in the Age of Science.* Ed. Alan Gross
and William Keith. Albany: State University of New York Press, 1997, 25–88.
Jasinski, James. "The Forms and Limits of Prudence in Henry Clay's (1850) Defense of
the Compromise Measures." *Quarterly Journal of Speech* 81.4 (1995): 454–478.
Kauffeld, Fred J. "The Persuasive Force of Arguments on Behalf of Proposals." In *Anal-
ysis and Evaluation: Proceedings of the Third ISSA Conference on Argumentation.* Vol. 2. Ed. Frans H. van Eemeren et al. Amsterdam: International Centre
for the Study of Argumentation, 1995, 79–90.
Leff, Michael. "Interpretation and the Art of the Rhetorical Critic." *Western Journal of
Speech Communication* 44 (1980): 347–348.
Lucas, Stephen E. "The Renaissance of American Public Address: Text and Context in
Rhetorical Criticism." *Quarterly Journal of Speech* 74.2 (1988): 241–260.
Sproule, J. Michael. *Propaganda and Democracy: The American Experience of Media
and Mass Persuasion.* Cambridge: Cambridge University Press, 1997.

Lloyd F. Bitzer. Photo courtesy of the National Communication Association. Used with permission.

11

Lloyd F. Bitzer: Rhetorical Situation, Public Knowledge, and Audience Dynamics

MARILYN J. YOUNG

Few contributions to rhetorical theory have generated as much controversy over such a sustained period as has Lloyd Bitzer's conception of the rhetorical situation: "a complex of persons, events, objects, and relations presenting an actual or potential exigence which can be completely or partially removed if discourse, introduced into the situation, can so constrain human decision or action as to bring about the significant modification of the exigence."[1] Bitzer elaborated, claiming, "In any rhetorical situation there will be at least one controlling exigence which functions as the organizing principle: it specifies the audience to be addressed and the change to be effected."[2]

The original essay appeared in the inaugural issue of *Philosophy and Rhetoric* in 1968 and immediately became the target of criticism.[3] Bitzer's "sin" was publishing his essay at the dawn of the postmodern era, as the emphasis in critical assessment of rhetoric was shifting from the rhetor to the audience, though many of his critics relied on classical concepts to refute his ideas. In 1980 Bitzer responded to these critics, publishing (in Eugene White's *Rhetoric in Transition*) modifications to his original conception. These modifications took into account many of the analyses that had been offered early on, though it is not at all clear that Bitzer placated his critics. He certainly did not succeed in gaining their favor: in two recent essays Benoit[4] recommended overlaying Burke onto Bitzer's construct, while Smith and Lybarger[5] suggested expanding the notions of exigence, audience, and constraints still further to incorporate greater multiplicity.

Despite the attempts to discredit "The Rhetorical Situation," Lloyd Bitzer is one of the most respected rhetorical scholars of the latter half of the twentieth century. After receiving his Ph.D. in 1962 from the University of Iowa, Bitzer spent most of his career at the University of Wisconsin, Madison; his work helped to make the Department of Communication Arts one of the premier centers for the study of rhetoric and public address. Professor Bitzer is currently professor emeritus and still lives in the Madison area.

In this chapter I suggest that much of what critics have complained about is accounted for by Bitzer if one examines the body of his work, particularly the previously overlooked essay on public knowledge. In the process of this analysis, I examine the criticisms that have been offered to date and suggest that they are, for the most part, off the mark.[6] At the conclusion of the chapter, I offer a comprehensive bibliography of essays devoted to Bitzer's ideas.[7]

What is most interesting about early commentary on the rhetorical situation is that it did not seek to expand Bitzer's ideas but to refute them, to demonstrate that they had no place in the constellation of current rhetorical theory. Only later did scholars, perhaps realizing the immediate place that Bitzer's concepts had assumed in the critical lexicon, begin to view his ideas as modifiable through the critical process, much as are the ideas and theories of other scholars.[8]

EARLY COMMENTARY

The first essay addressing Bitzer's theory appeared in *Philosophy and Rhetoric* in 1970, just two years after publication of "The Rhetorical Situation." K. E. Wilkerson places Bitzer's theory in the context of a system of evaluating theories.[9] Wilkerson's underlying assumption is that if a new theory of rhetoric is needed, "that is because traditional theory is unsatisfactory in specifiable ways."[10] He goes on to argue that those problems within existing theory constitute the "requirements for a replacement theory."[11] In this calculus, theory building becomes a zero-sum game, with each new theory replacing the one that went before. Such a narrow view of rhetorical theory denies the value of a pluralistic view of rhetorical discourse. Human communication is not a scientific endeavor, and our understanding of the myriad ways in which rhetors persuade and audiences are persuaded cannot profitably be delimited by constraints on theory-building.

In the course of his essay, Wilkinson develops three criteria (which he calls "desiderata") for an evaluation of rhetorical theories. First, "*a theory of rhetoric should establish natural boundaries for the area of human activity it would comprehend.*"[12] Second, "*a theory of rhetoric should specify a set of phenomena which can be readily observed and which provides the central focus for rhetorical inquiry.*"[13] Third, "*its hierarchical alignment with a general theory of human communication and with theories of specific communication processes is desirable.*"[14] Wilkinson then tests Bitzer's theory against these desiderata and finds it wanting in all three instances. In the first case, the theory arbitrarily excludes too much persuasive and informative discourse; in the second, the notion of situation is seen as both too vague and too complex to specify which phenomena are described by the theory; and in the third instance, Bitzer does not situate his own theory within a hierarchy of theories but appears to align it with history. Wilkinson fails to find distinctive outlines of a discipline or a distinct view of the human condition in Bitzer's discussion of the rhetorical situation.

The difficulty with Wilkinson's discussion, astute though it is, is that it expects too much of a single theory of rhetoric; it fails to consider the endless creativity of both rhetors and audiences in responding to rhetorical situations and thus assumes that a single theory can cover the broad spectrum of human communication activity. Bitzer's theory is not assessed on its own terms, as an explanation of how rhetorical discourse exists within one set of parameters.

In the same issue of *Philosophy and Rhetoric*, Richard L. Larson discusses Bitzer's idea in terms of the classification of discourse.[15] Like many critics of Bitzer's ideas, Larson focuses on the exclusivity of Bitzer's definition of rhetoric—that "the designation 'rhetorical' be reserved exclusively for discourse generated in circumstances" that have the characteristics that Bitzer identifies: the existence of an exigence that an audience can remedy when so persuaded by discourse.[16] There can be no question that Bitzer's definition narrows the conception of rhetoric, and Larson spends considerable time demonstrating the intricate difficulties of adhering to such a restrictive notion. For example, Larson asks about the classification of discourse that was rhetorical (according to Bitzer's definition) when it was constructed but that is unable to modify the exigence.[17] Larson also notes that Bitzer's explanation leaves the reader in doubt as to the disposition of discourse that is a failure, that is, discourse that fails to achieve its intended purpose of moving the audience to remedy the situation. With this uncertainty in mind, one might ask whether President Clinton's August 17, 1998, address to the American people "apologizing" for his conduct in the Lewinsky affair would be considered rhetorical under Bitzer's definition. If it is not rhetorical, can it then become the object of scholarly (rhetorical) criticism?

At the same time that he points out the narrowness of Bitzer's construction of rhetoric, Larson also (perhaps unwittingly) points out ways in which Bitzer broadened our notions of rhetoric. Thus, when he describes the ways in which functional speech can be rhetorical, Larson foreshadows some of the research in conversation and discourse analysis; in so doing, he is enlarging considerably that which had been previously considered worthy of rhetorical analysis.[18] Likewise, Larson argues that scholarly publications are also rhetorical, even the "scientific" ones that Bitzer specifically excludes from his calculus. Again, Larson foreshadows an amplification of the province of rhetorical analysis, as the field generally acknowledges the rhetorical nature of scholarship, including its own; indeed, the rhetorical properties of scientific discourse have become a rewarding line of inquiry for several scholars in our field. Thus, as Larson points out, while Bitzer has narrowed the scope of *speeches* that are considered rhetorical, he has widened the possibilities for *categories* of discourse that can be considered rhetorical.[19]

In 1970 Walter Fisher published "A Motive View of Communication," an essay that laid the foundation for his seminal work in narrativity a decade later.[20] While not a critique of Bitzer's work, Fisher's analysis relies on, and expands, the assumptions found in "The Rhetorical Situation."[21] Fisher's focus, as indicated in his title, is on "motive," which, he argues, is as much the ground for rhetorical communication as is "situation." He views motive and situation as two of the essentials in rhetorical communication; indeed, it appears that Fisher's conception of motive subsumes Bitzer's situational construct: "Rhetorical communication is as much grounded in motives as it is in situation, given that motives are names which essentialize the interrelations of communicator, communication, audience(s), time, and place."[22] Nevertheless, it is not entirely clear that Fisher has fully realized Bitzer's ideas regarding situation, for Bitzer explicitly argues that his notion of situation goes beyond the setting to encompass the totality of the interaction between the exigence, the rhetor, and the audience; motive would seem a logical component of this calculus.[23]

Nevertheless, Fisher goes on to argue that rhetorical situations can be characterized in terms of motive; he outlines four such situations/motives: affirmation, reaffirmation, purification, and subversion. In so doing, he supports the "assumption that there are recurrent rhetorical situations throughout history" and succeeds in bonding Burke to Bitzer.[24] However, Fisher's ideas, while affirming the place of the rhetorical situation in the critical lexicon, seem more closely aligned with Brockreide than with Bitzer in his discussion of audiences, time, and place rather than context and exigence.[25]

In his 1971 study of Muskie's address to the nation on the eve of the 1970 midterm elections, Robert Wayne Norton argues that the rhetorical situation *is* the message.[26] Importantly, Norton interprets the notion of the rhetorical situation in a way that has become the norm: as an active participant in the rhetorical transaction. However, it is not at all clear that this was Bitzer's intent, for he describes the rhetorical situation as determinative, as the arbiter of that which is rhetorical. Undoubtedly, Norton's situation meets that definition also; in his essay he argues that the situation was predictable and yet dynamic: predictable in that the nation, which was especially divided in these waning days of protest, looked to its leaders for unity and hope; dynamic in that the Republican Party, in the person of President Richard Nixon, chose to defy that expectation and preach the politics of division. Since Nixon's address preceded Muskie's, a vacuum was created into which Muskie could step with his statesmanlike message of healing. This historical instance fulfills Bitzer's definition of the rhetorical situation in that the apparent exigence—the impending elections—is one that can be ameliorated by the audience, the electorate. Yet the dynamism exposed by Norton's analysis is inconsistent with the preordained nature of the situation as described by Bitzer. As Norton offers neither a justification for modifying Bitzer's theory in this way nor an interpretation of the theory that supports a situation such as he describes, one can only conclude that Muskie's speech represents either a situational anomaly or a shortcoming of Bitzer's theory—unless, of course, support for this interpretation can be found in Bitzer's explication of situation.

Perhaps that support can be located in the notion not of situation but of exigence. I argue that it is not the situation that is dynamic in the case of the Muskie speech, but rather the exigence that is altered by Nixon's gaffe.

Exigence is the focus of the 1972 essay by Arthur B. Miller that appeared in *Philosophy and Rhetoric*.[27] Miller points out the need for the rhetor to understand the exigence in crafting a response (speech). If the rhetor fails to understand fully the exigence, the response will be a failure. Miller also points out that the nature of an exigence is not a static, objective thing that can easily be identified but rather something that depends on the perceptions of both rhetor and audience. The rhetor must understand the way that the audience perceives the exigence before addressing common ground; intrinsic to this process is the rhetor's understanding of how the three interrelate: speaker perception of the exigence/audience perception of the exigence/speaker in relation to audience and self-perceptions of the exigence. As Miller notes, "[R]hetors not only perceive and judge exigences but *themselves* in relation to those exigences"[28] as they seek to find shared ground with the audience. Thus, in Miller's analysis, the exigence takes on something of a dynamic quality as the role of perception is revealed. The difficulty in reconciling this with Bitzer's explication is that it opens the door to modifying the perception of the exigence through rhetoric, rather than modifying the exigence itself.[29] This would seem to fly in the face of Bitzer's notion of exigence, which is a controlling factor—an organizing principle—specifying both the audience to be addressed and the exigence to be changed.[30] Thus, while one cannot deny the role of perception in identifying a condition as an exigence, Bitzer obviously entertains the idea of something that is clearly identifiable. Miller's essay, while instructive, does not explain how Bitzer's ideas can be expanded to accommodate Miller's argument.

Nor does Pomeroy offer much in the way of constructive interpretation and expansion of Bitzer's theory, though his essay in the *Georgia Speech Communication Journal* challenges many of Bitzer's postulates.[31] Pomeroy focuses on the relationship among exigence, situation, and discourse, questioning the ambiguity in Bitzer's discussion. Specifically, he asks about when we know whether a "situation is truly rhetorical." First, he notes, "[W]ithin the context of Bitzer's theory it is always possible to argue that any rhetorical exigence which did *not* produce rhetorical discourse was not truly rhetorical in the first place."[32] He further notes, "[W]ithin the context of Bitzer's theory it is impossible to argue conclusively that any exigence . . . which *did* produce some kind of discourse (fitting or otherwise) was really nonrhetorical."[33] Pomeroy raises some significant questions in this discussion, but he leaves them there, rather than offering any concrete extensions of the theory.

In the third and final discussion section of the essay, Pomeroy describes what he considers to be the major conceptual and methodological inconsistency in Bitzer's theory: "[T]he *conceptual* dependency runs one way and the *method-*

ological dependency another."[34] "The existence of rhetorical discourse [depends] on the presence of a rhetorical situation—or, more accurately, on the presence of a 'controlling' rhetorical exigence that prescribes the audience and constraints within the situation."[35] However, "the only reliable sign of the existence of a rhetorical situation is the presence of a rhetorical discourse—or, more accurately, on the presence within that discourse of a quality, 'fitness of response,' which marks it as rhetorical and indicates the nature of the exigence it is responding to as rhetorical."[36] This brings us to what is perhaps the major problem with the theory as Pomeroy describes it: "At some points in Bitzer's theory . . . his discussion of the quality 'fitness of response' sounds descriptive, suggesting that it functions as a defining quality of any rhetorical discourse. At other points, however, his discussion sounds normative, suggesting that 'fitness of response' functions as a standard or norm for effective rhetorical discourse."[37]

Again, however, Pomeroy does not offer an extension of the theory. In fact, at one point he indicates that he expects Bitzer to do that, since Bitzer has indicated that the theory is incomplete. He does suggest the imposition of the concept of "rhetorical sanction," without explaining how this interacts with, and improves on, Bitzer's notion of the "fitting response."

The highlight of this essay, setting it apart from the others that appeared in this time frame, is Part 4, an exchange with Bitzer. Yet, ultimately, the exchange is unsatisfying, settling nothing—offering no new information—about the relationships among exigence, situation, and discourse.

Richard Vatz wrote what is probably the best-known critique of Bitzer in his 1973 essay, "The Myth of the Rhetorical Situation."[38] Vatz argues that, in explicating his theory of situation, Bitzer has not accounted for the creativity of the rhetor. In making his argument, Vatz provides some of the grounding for the role of perception that was missing from Miller's essay a year earlier. Nevertheless, in presenting his thesis, Vatz sells short Bitzer's conception of the rhetorical situation by labeling it a myth. Yet none of Vatz's analysis denies the existence of a rhetorical situation. Arguing that situations are created by rhetors, Vatz claims that "events become meaningful only through their linguistic depiction . . . meaning is not discovered in situations, but *created* by rhetors."[39] Without disagreeing with Vatz's basic premise, I argue that this is not at variance with Bitzer's notions, nor does it deny the basic elements that constitute the situation.

The issue is one of perception: the rhetor's perception of the situation and the audience's perception of the situation. When they converge, by Bitzer's analysis, persuasion occurs. This is, in many ways, quite similar to Burke's notion of identification and consubstantiation. Yet, to return to Bitzer, what happens when only the rhetor perceives the situation in a particular way? I suggest that in this situation the exigence shifts slightly, and the rhetor, to be successful, must persuade the audience to accept that view of the situation.

Nevertheless, it is not true, as Vatz suggests, that situations become meaningful *only* "through their linguistic depiction." Some events do have intrinsic meaning and demand a "fitting response" and even, to some extent, dictate what that response must be. For example, the Japanese attack on Pearl Harbor, December 7, 1941, had intrinsic meaning at a fundamental level; it is unrealistic to argue that Roosevelt had any option other than to request a declaration of war or that he could request such a declaration in terms other than those that depicted the Japanese as evil incarnate. While there may be variations in the specific depiction or words chosen, and while there could be numerous reactions in the aftermath, the situation itself is a fundamental exigence that bears no other interpretation or action. Indeed, this is the basis for genre criticism.

Similarly, the assassination of John F. Kennedy was an event with a fundamental, intrinsic meaning that demanded an appropriate response. Had Lyndon Johnson not understood this, his presidency could have been forever marred. While there could be variations in the details of the response, the basic moves were virtually dictated by the situation. Vatz attempts to account for this by arguing that the "communication of the event was of such consensual symbolism that expectations were easily predictable and stable"—and, therefore, rhetorically uninteresting. However, Bitzer is not claiming that he is describing what makes events interesting rhetorically; he is exploring what makes them rhetorical. Certainly, not everything surrounding the assassination as a rhetorical event is situationally determined; but the core of the event is such that everyone knows instinctively what is "fitting" and what is not. What is intriguing about this is that few people could probably articulate the attributes of a "fitting response" in advance of a situation such as the assassination of a president; yet, as was the case in 1941, all who participated, directly or vicariously, knew immediately whether each action was appropriate, required, "fitting."

In his discussion of the Kennedy assassination and its treatment by Bitzer, Vatz makes two claims that are insupportable. First he notes that "one cannot maintain that reports of anything are indistinguishable from the thing itself,"[40] an observation that obviates his own notion of the rhetorical construction of reality. In an absolute, objective sense, Vatz is correct. Nevertheless, his whole point is that history and even reality are not objective, and, in some circumstances—insofar as the individual auditor is concerned—the report is indistinguishable from the thing itself. Thus were we all glued to our television sets in November 1963, watching over and over first the film of the motorcade and then the funeral and then the film of the funeral as though we were experiencing it for the first time. This inability to distinguish is the visual power of television, which enables us to relive over and over the events that traumatize us and to experience them anew.

The second insupportable claim is that, at the time of the Kennedy assassination, "rhetoric created fears and threat perception."[41] While there may not have been any objective threat to the nation from the assassination, people did not know that, and fears were spontaneous and real, albeit misplaced. It was this exigence to which the vice president responded by the actions that he took in the hours following the assassination, not by the rotunda speeches on which Vatz focuses.

In "Generic Constraints and the Rhetorical Situation," Jamieson explores the relationship between the recurring situations described by Bitzer and the notion of rhetorical genre.[42] Essentially, Jamieson establishes the link between situation and genre; indeed, insofar as genres represent the collective wisdom of rhetors and audiences through time, Jamieson's construction melds with Bitzer's notion of the rhetorical situation buttressed by his concept of public knowledge.[43] It is not clear, however, that Jamieson understood this connection at the time that she wrote her essay, for she writes of Bitzer: "I do not wish to deny Bitzer's contention that rhetorical forms are prompted by comparable responses to comparable situations. What I do wish to suggest is that perception of the proper response to an unprecedented rhetorical situation grows *not merely from the situation* but also from antecedent rhetorical forms."[44]

I think Bitzer would agree with this; certainly, his theory envisions it. He is careful to note that his concept of the rhetorical situation includes more than the setting and context of the discourse. Rather, the rhetorical situation includes all of this and more, and, surely, part of the situation calling forth rhetorical discourse is the recurring nature of certain circumstances—the very genres that Jamieson discusses. What Jamieson reveals are the relationship between emerging genre theory—the idea that rhetorical situations recur over time—and Bitzer's insistence that the totality of the situation calls rhetoric into existence.

Scott Consigny proposes a system of topics to resolve the differences between Bitzer and Vatz, but in so doing, he takes a particularly narrow view of the rhetorical situation.[45] By simplifying Bitzer's concept of the situation, Consigny suggests that Bitzer and Vatz are in antinomy, that rhetorical situations are fraught with confusion and incoherence. His analysis begins to go awry when he extends Bitzer's comment that "rhetorical discourse comes into existence as a response to a situation in the same sense that an answer comes into existence in response to a question or a solution in response to a problem."[46] "Presumably," Consigny writes, "the 'exigence' is similar in kind to such well-formed problems and questions as 'what is the square root of seventy-two?' and 'what is the chemical analysis of a given organic compound?' "[47] Why presumably? Bitzer writes that the situation controls the response "in the same sense that the question controls the answer and the problem controls the solution."[48] In other words, the situation obtains the elements from which the rhetorical response must be drawn.

This is not to discount the role of invention, which is Vatz's complaint against Bitzer, for the rhetor still must find the fitting response—or persuade the audience that the response is fitting. Just as one must discover "the available means of persuasion," one must locate the elements of the fitting response. So, while Consigny is not incorrect in his description of the rhetor's task, he, like so many others, has not considered the full power of Bitzer's conception and its ability to subsume the complaints of its detractors.

To take the issue one step further, I argue that Consigny mischaracterizes rhetorical situations when he continuously refers to them as "novel." Certainly, in the way that Bitzer conceives it, there are few truly "novel" rhetorical situations—though each will have unique elements. If one considers the rhetorical moments of our history, few of them are, in fact, wholly unique. As Jamieson points out, Washington faced a unique situation in his delivery of the first inaugural address. Nevertheless, he correctly read the situation and set the parameters for future inaugural addresses, establishing in a few words a genre of discourse.[49] Yet even Washington was not entirely free of the discursive traditions that were such an intrinsic part of the public life of the new nation, and no president since has been free of the precedent set by the first president. So, while presidents may well encounter incoherent rhetorical situations when dealing with matters of public policy, the inaugural address is not among them; the form of the inaugural comes in an unbroken line from Washington to Clinton and would likely address issues such as policy toward Latin America only in the most general terms.[50] Even Lyndon Johnson's rhetorical situation in the aftermath of the Kennedy assassination was not entirely unique. Thus, Consigny's example belies his argument.

Consigny's notion of the incoherent situation loses some of its power when one attempts to imagine a rhetorical situation into which a rhetor is thrown without considerable prior knowledge. Similarly, his proposal that we look to a system of topics to resolve the antinomy does not displace the theory of the rhetorical situation, for topics—*topoi*—are the precursors of an understanding of situation and of a comprehension of the nature of genres of discourse. Consigny fails to comprehend that the very determinacy of the rhetorical situation engulfs its critics.

In one of the first essays to apply the rhetorical situation as an analytic framework, Rubin and Rubin "explore the operation of discourse in the Weight Watchers movement."[51] Their interest is focused on the "constituent elements of an ongoing, rhetorical situation in order to understand why Weight Watchers is a successful organization" and "how the discourse of the organization functions to effect changes in the lives of its members." To this end, the authors describe Weight Watchers meetings and programs by following the taxonomy of constituent elements laid out by Bitzer. They stray from this formula only when discussing the rhetorical forms used by the organization, overlaying Gronbeck's notion of rhetorical timing onto Bitzer's concept of the "fitting response." In their conclusion, Rubin and Rubin suggest that exigence may be a more complex phenomenon than Bitzer first suggested. In the case of Weight Watchers, the exigence is never completely or even partially removed. Rather, at some point, the exigence is modified to become "maintenance of the goal weight," resulting in altered constraints and a reformed message. Members who have not reached the appropriate state of exigency about their weight or who cannot follow the stages of the program will find the Weight Watchers' messages ineffective. Thus, Rubin and Rubin illustrate the utility of the constituents of a situational analysis. However, this essay does not make any significant theoretical contribution to our understanding of rhetorical situations; rather, it demonstrates that the theory can be effectively applied to everyday life situations as well as to situations of great public moment. The only difference is that many everyday situations have a recurring character, in that they may affect small groups of people sequentially or simultaneously over an extended period. On the other hand, they may be affecting individuals—who may come together as groups to address the problem—either sequentially, or simultaneously, or cyclically (in other words, the problem may recur in specified individuals and have to be addressed again). Thus, by broadening our understanding of the notion of "exigence," Rubin and Rubin demonstrate the accessibility of situational analysis as a critical tool.

In a different vein, Gerald D. Baxter and Bart F. Kennedy compared Bitzer's theory to the philosophy of organism introduced by Alfred North Whitehead.[52] It is difficult to discern the purpose of this exercise or what it adds to our understanding of rhetorical situations. The most interesting observation in the essay occurs about two-thirds of the way through, when the authors claim that "the rhetor is *not* antecedent to the audience response."[53] "In fact, the rhetor emerges in response to the truths, motives, and the need for community of an audience. More specifically, the audience 'produces' a rhetor for the expression of its prehensions."[54]

In keeping with Whitehead's theory of organism, this view of the rhetorical situation is organic, and the elements described by Bitzer are seen as part of an organic process of concrescence. It is not at all clear what the analysis of Richard Nixon's 1969 Vietnamization address adds. In the first place, the authors do not develop their analysis enough to test their view of either Bitzer or Whitehead. Further, the analysis appears to have an internal contradiction. They write: "In effect, the nation needed to be purged of its feelings about the Vietnam War. Mr. Nixon was called upon to *further* the diversity of the nation. There was to be no ullage of concrescence. The multiple feelings about the war were demanding transformation from an aggregate into a synthesis. Mr. Nixon became the tool to effectuate the further progression of that process."[55] Unless the Hegelian elements of thesis, antithesis, and synthesis are here, this paragraph contradicts itself, and we are left in the dark as to how the organic view of the rhetorical situation actually functions.

In fairness, one should note that the authors claim that 69 percent of Americans "studied in a Gallup poll taken shortly after the speech did not feel that the Administration was telling the people all they should know about the war" and that this "indicates that Mr. Nixon's speech was a tool of transmutation towards the creation of a 'society.' "[56] One assumes that the unifying element was the distrust of government inspired by Nixon, but since the Vietnam War is still a divisive element in society, it is not apparent that a concrescence ever occurred, particularly if one agrees with the authors that the exigence was society's need not to resolve the war but to purge its *feelings* about the war.

However, Baxter and Kennedy do not discuss the concept of exigence as elaborated by Bitzer; rather, they subsume it into the notion of the rhetorical situation as they define it: audience, subject, occasion, speech, and rhetor. Presumably, exigence is covered by subject and occasion and, to some degree, speech. Yet the exigence is key to Bitzer's theory, for the exigence creates the need for rhetoric and must be wholly or partially removed.

Finally, although the organic view espoused by Baxter and Kennedy presents the rhetorical situation as a dynamic process—in contrast to the somewhat static progression envisioned by Bitzer—I argue that this is not at all incompatible with Bitzer's ideas, and to the extent that it vitalizes the theory, the authors have made a contribution, however minor, to our understanding.

In contrast, Hunsaker and Smith build on the critics of Bitzer's work who came before them, refining and broadening Bitzer's ideas in the process.[57] Hunsaker and Smith focus on exigence and audience in relation to issues; they discuss the ways in which the situation and the rhetor grow out of both exigence and audience to constitute and constrain the rhetorical situation. In so doing, they are able to address the complaints of Vatz and Consigny, while also fleshing out the work of Miller. Thus, their work advances our understanding of the rhetorical situation by focusing on the role of the audience in the creation, development, and resolution of issues. Issues, according to Hunsaker and Smith, grow out of audience perceptions of the exigence; Bitzer, while mentioning audience as an element of the rhetorical situation, does not, in this essay, account for variations in the audience. Hunsaker and Smith identify two such variations: the situational audience (which witnesses the rhetorical situation) and the actual audience (the audience addressed by the rhetor). These are not necessarily the same, for the actual audience may not have witnessed the situation directly and may not find the issues addressed by the rhetor to be salient. Thus, Hunsaker and Smith reconcile the role of invention with the situational construct, as the rhetor convinces the audience of the importance of the issues.

By considering perceptions, then, this essay involves the audience more in the process, thereby expanding the notion of the rhetorical situation. Similarly, Patton seeks to expand our understanding of Bitzer's theory in his 1979 essay.[58] Patton divides criticism of the situational theory into three categories and discusses each in turn. His initial concern is with the critics who object to the determinism in Bitzer's construction of the exigence. Through his analysis, Patton demonstrates that these objections are misguided, closer to fatalism than determinism.[59]

The second section of Patton's essay discusses the "Explanatory Functions of Exigences and Constraints," noting that exigences, while necessary conditions for rhetorical discourse, are not in themselves sufficient conditions. Underlying this argument is the assumption that "rhetoric is essentially historically"; that is, it has to be related to a set of historically observable events or experiences in order to make sense. In this way exigence addresses the causal concept "why?"[60]

In the third section, Patton turns to the question of "Unavoidability, Perception, and Purposeful Response." Like Smith and Hunsaker, Patton reaffirms the importance of perception in identifying and defining the rhetorical situation. Patton extends the earlier discussion by adding the role of constraints to the perceptual matrix. In the intermix of perception, exigence, and constraints, creativity and invention enter the calculus of rhetorical discourse. Thus, Patton advances our understanding of the situational theory by demonstrating that it is not inimical to invention and creativity on the part of the rhetor. Indeed, it is through invention and creativity that the rhetorical situation—including exigences and constraints—is appropriately addressed, producing the "fitting response" that every rhetor seeks. Similarly, the relationship between rhetorical situation and discourse is not one of inevitability; rather, the situation, if perceived, constitutes the necessary condition for discourse to emerge, but Bitzer does not claim that such emergence is inevitable.

In his essay on "Point of View in Rhetorical Situations," David Kaufer does not make a direct connection to Bitzer's theory but nevertheless provides an interesting perspective on the development of our understanding of the rhetorical situation.[61] Kaufer examines constructions of rhetorical situations during the classical and Romantic periods and relates them to contemporary concerns. His conclusion, though somewhat circular, is instructive:

[R]hetorical inquiry can neither be divorced from various empirical (i.e., historical cultural) assumptions of social interaction nor restricted by a priori conceptions of rhetorical function. Whether one conceives of the essential function of rhetoric as instrumental, expressive, relational, or negotiative depends in part upon how one interprets the general role of language in defining social situations. Yet the perceptions one entertains of these functions themselves depend on . . . assumptions concerning the dominant perspective from which a situation is to be defined.[62]

Thus, Kaufer, too, extends our understanding of situational analysis by giving a historical and linguistic perspective to the construction and perception of rhetorical situations. In that sense, Kaufer's essay blends well with Patton's.

THE MIDDLE YEARS

In 1980 the *Quarterly Journal of Speech* (*QJS*) devoted its "Forum" section to a discussion of Patton's essay.[63] This entry is particularly valuable, for it features an exchange between Patton and Phillip K. Tompkins, followed by a response from Lloyd Bitzer. Tompkins takes Patton to task for creating a "straw man" when he characterizes Consigny's criticism as attributing "fatalism" to Bitzer's theory. Tompkins also argues that Patton defines "determinism" out of Bitzer's original essay, making it "immune to the label."[64] Tompkins then turns to Bitzer's exposition of the rhetorical situation, arguing that the theory is flawed "by an admixture of the descriptive and the idealistic."[65] He seeks to resolve the conflict between positions taken by Vatz and Consigny by asserting that "[b]oth are talking about rhetoric" and follows this with his own formulation: "Rhetorical discourse shapes, and is shaped by, rhetorical situations; by imputing causal status either to discourse or situation, in whatever degree of force, one may be simply bracketing a sequence of events in an arbitrary manner."[66]

Not surprisingly, Patton takes issue with Tompkins on both fronts: his characterization of Patton's own essay and his understanding of Bitzer's. The most important point that Patton makes is that "Bitzer explicitly allowed for the process of exigence perception and the creative activity of rhetors in shaping responses. The efforts to explain more fully the processes of perception and creativity in relation to exigences, . . . were extensions of undeveloped but nonetheless intrinsic elements of the situational approach."[67] Indeed, this would seem to be the standard approach to theory development, even in the sciences and certainly in rhetoric, where theories are more explanatory than predictive and where theory-building is an intrinsic goal of the critical process. All rhetorical theories are dynamic, as each application to an artifact allows the critic to discover new aspects that modify and extend the theory. In the demand that Bitzer's presentation of situational theory be complete, his critics employ an expectation that is unrealistic and, perhaps worse, one that would stultify the process of criticism.

In his commentary, Bitzer argues that Tompkins's position is internally inconsistent, for he "responds to a rhetorical situation he regards as real or genuine, and yet he has doubts about the reality of situations."[68] More importantly, he supports Patton's interpretation of "the rhetorical situation" in terms of fatalism or determinism, the link between rhetoric and situational exigences and constraints, and the role of creativity in the crafting of a "fitting response." He notes that "we cannot predict the details and nuances of the discourses of creative rhetors, who often perceive elements we do not see and whose artistry produces works having parts or aspects we could not have anticipated."[69]

This exchange seems to function as a watershed for commentary on Bitzer's theory of the rhetorical situation. From this point, the heuristic value of the theory seems to be assumed, and it is absorbed into, and referred to in, the theoretical and critical literature. For example, Cox seeks to expand our understanding of both situations and constraints when he argues that actors' "interpretations of the meaning of a situation 'constitute' the essential constraints upon actor's decisions."[70] Cox's essay goes well beyond consideration of the rhetorical situation, positing a theory of behavior, but it illustrates the ways in which Bitzer's theory assumed its place in the literature of the field.

In contrast, Brinton's discussion of situation—published approximately the same time as Cox's—indicates that debate about the theory had not yet been laid to rest.[71] In the first part of his essay, Brinton takes on Bitzer's critics, noting that they have emphasized a causal reading of the theory of situation.

Not surprisingly—and correctly, I believe—Brinton points out that the causal nature of the situation vis-à-vis the rhetorical act is not emphasized by Bitzer; rather, Bitzer characterizes the definitional aspects of the relationship: an "*act is a genuinely rhetorical act* only if it occurs in the context of, in response to, a *genuinely rhetorical situation*."[72]

Brinton also sees a normative function for Bitzer's theory, based on the notion of exigence: "A given situation *prescribes* a given response (or sort of response)."[73] In this vein, the situational theory becomes a proposal for evaluating rhetorical discourse.

From this point, Brinton concentrates on the reasons that rhetorical theory ought to be normative before returning to the question of whether the "constituents of the rhetorical situation are objective matters of fact." Again, his discussion centers around the notion of exigence. Bitzer makes clear that the true exigence is an objective, factual defect in the world that can be modified through rhetoric. This notion is central to Bitzer's theory, since the rhetorical act is grounded in the rhetorical situation. In developing his analysis, Brinton incorporates the modifications presented by Bitzer the previous year—specifically, the notion of "interest"—and argues that "exigence is objective in the sense that it is composed of phenomena, some of which may be subjective, but all of which are objectively phenomena."[74] This is probably the most significant contribution that Brinton makes to the development of situational theory, for it entails the concept of definition from the perspective of the rhetor: "As rhetors, Brutus and Mark Antony may confront the same factual circumstances, but each speaks to and attempts to modify (through his hearers) a different exigence." The difference in exigence is accounted for by the rhetor's interest; the factual component is the same for both.

Interestingly, in 1981 *QJS* devoted part of another "Forum" to an exchange among Tompkins, Patton, and Bitzer, this time featuring Vatz as well.[75] Unfortunately, this edition does not add much to our understanding of situational theory, as each of the respondents focuses primarily on reiterating his position and refuting that of the others. The exchange concentrates on the question of objective versus perceived situational characteristics, thus replicating much of the discussion that has gone before. For his part, Bitzer does emphasize that he recognizes the complexity of situations and the role that perception and interest play in the understanding and articulation of situational properties. Nevertheless, he again illustrates his arguments with the simple examples that have confounded his critics and led to much of the misunderstanding of his theory.

Halford Ross Ryan, writing in 1982, again demonstrates that the language of situational theory has become safely ensconced in the lexicon of rhetorical criticism and renews hope that the controversy over Bitzer's ideas has abated.[76] Ryan's focus is generic criticism, and his reference to situational theory is the role that exigence plays in the foundation of genre theory: the speaker's perception of an exigence that he seeks to modify through accusatory or apologetic discourse serves as the motive. In tying the discourse in question to Bitzer's theory, Ryan relies on the explication of motive suggested by Fisher in the 1970 essay discussed earlier in this essay.

Similarly, Carolyn Miller centers her essay on notions of genre, examining the theory of the rhetorical situation only as it serves to point the way to genre theory through Bitzer's observation that situations recur.[77] Like so many others, Miller's concern is with Bitzer's notion of exigence as "the focus of situation."[78] She notes that "Bitzer's use of demand-response language has made it possible to conceive of exigence as an external cause of discourse and situation as deterministic."[79] Because her concern is with genre theory and because the deterministic aspects of Bitzer's view of exigence present problems for genre theory, Miller argues for a reconceptualization of exigence that incorporates the process of definition: "Exigence must be located in the social world, neither in a private perception nor in material circumstance. . . . Exigence is a form of social knowledge."[80] In this, she moves closer to the Burkean notion of situation, exigence as social motive.[81]

In her explanation, Miller dismisses Brinton's essay, placing it in the same category as Bitzer's and Patton's, emphasizing the "ontological status of situations as real, objective, historical events."[82] In doing so, she ignores Brinton's discussion of interest and its role in modifying the objective exigence. While Brinton does not go as far as Miller in moving the concept of exigence toward social knowledge, he does provide a means for softening the hard-edged objectivity of exigences advocated by Patton and, originally, by Bitzer. Of course, one must keep in mind that Miller's true concern is with genre theory, and her suggested modification of the concept of exigence is to make it more compatible with rhetorical practice in the service of genre analysis.

Branham and Pearce take a somewhat different approach, focusing not on situations that recur but those that are modified by the text offered in response: "We are particularly intrigued by those texts which change the context in which they occur to one in which they might 'fit.' "[83] This essay does not dwell on the rhetorical situation as Bitzer describes it but rather assumes the significance of that construct as it frames an oppositional notion of the reflexive relationship of text and context. Thus, Branham and Pearce illustrate the position that Bitzer's ideas have assumed in the constellation of rhetorical theory.

Building on the work of Branham and Pearce, Young and Launer analyze governmental response to the Soviet downing of KAL 007 as an instance in which the rhetorical situation is in flux, altered in reflexive turn by the rhetoric emanating from the White House and the Kremlin and confounded by the revelations of the investigative press.[84] Young and Launer visualize the multiple narratives that surround a crisis as indicative of an unstable context as public understanding of an unexpected event attempts to coalesce. The flow of information—some confirmed, some speculative—that surrounds a crisis produces alterations in public knowledge that may become permanent, thus modifying the dynamic relationship among public knowledge, exigence, the rhetorical situation, and a "fitting response." Like Branham and Pearce, Young and Launer

accept the salience of Bitzer's ideas for the understanding of situationally bound
rhetorical texts. They suggest two subtle modifications to the theory of situations, however. First, they argue that all parties in an administration should be
included in the definition of the rhetor; this is not to say that an administration
necessarily speaks with one voice but, rather, to point out that, in a crisis, the
complete "text" often emerges over time, with segments assigned to, or appro-
priated by, various functionaries. Second, they suggest that public knowledge
constitutes the boundaries of a rhetorical situation and serves as the authorizing
agency in determining whether a response is "fitting"; during a crisis, public
knowledge is in flux, potentially modified by new information that may affect
perception of the event(s). As public understanding is altered, the rhetorical
situation changes.[85]

RECENT EXTENSIONS OF THE THEORY

Barbara Biesecker took the discussion of situational theory to another level
in her 1989 essay, "Rethinking the Rhetorical Situation from within the Thematic of *Differance*."[86] One of the recognized shortcomings of Bitzer's conceptualization of situation is the lack of consideration for the audience. This gap in
the theory becomes increasingly problematic as the locus of concern for theorists
and critics shifts from the rhetor and the text to the audience. Biesecker attempts
to address this theoretic lacuna by focusing on the thematic of *differance* as part
of the postmodern perspective on situation. One reason for the general lack of
attention to audience in past theories of rhetoric is the assumption that audiences
are reasonably homogeneous and serve as receptive vessels for the invention
and presentation of the rhetor. Postmodern thought has shattered this illusion of
homogeneity, a realization that is reinforced by modern cultural awareness. In
Biesecker's construction, the audience becomes part of the situational dynamic,
both acted upon and acting upon the discourse. "Once we take the identity of
audiences as an effect-structure, we become obliged to read every 'fixed' identity
as the provisional and practical outcome of a symbolic engagement between
speaker and audience."

From within the thematic of *differance*, we would see the rhetorical situation neither as
an event that merely induces audiences to act one way or another nor as an incident that,
in representing the interests of a particular collectivity, merely wrestles the probable
within the realm of the actualizable. Rather, we would see the rhetorical situation as an
event that makes possible the production of identities and social relations. That is to say,
if rhetorical events are analyzed from within the thematic of *differance*, it becomes possible to read discursive practices neither as rhetorics directed to preconstituted and known
audiences nor as rhetorics "in search of" objectively identifiable but yet undiscovered
audiences. *Differance* obliges us to read rhetorical discourses as processes entailing the
discursive production of audiences, and enables us to decipher rhetorical events as sites
that make visible the historically articulated emergence of the category "audience."[87]

After a hiatus of some four years, situational theory returned to the academic literature in an essay by Mary Garrett and Xiaosui Xiao in 1993.[88] Like several others, Garrett and Xiao seek to expand situational theory, in this case by applying it to nineteenth-century Chinese political discourse. Examining the rhetoric surrounding the Opium Wars, Garrett and Xiao suggest three alterations in our understanding of the rhetorical situation: "1) seeing the audience rather than [the] speaker as the pivotal element, as [an] active entity which is crucial in determining exigence, constraints, and the 'fittingness' of the rhetor's response; 2) recognizing the powerful influence of a culture's discourse tradition in shaping both speaker and audience perceptions of the same elements; and 3) placing much greater stress on the interactive, organic nature of the rhetorical situation."[89]

This discussion is consistent with the increasing emphasis on the audience in rhetorical theory and blends nicely with Biesecker's exposition of *differance*. What is most significant about this treatment of the rhetorical situation is its stress on the importance of culture in determining the definition of exigence. Of course, a recognition of the role of cultural factors leads inexorably to inclusion of the audience as an active part of the situational matrix. Garrett and Xiao find that one of the primary functions of culture is in the instantiation of appropriate *topoi*, or lines of reasoning, thus rehabilitating, at least in part, Consigny's argument from 1974. Of course, the "discourse tradition," as Garrett and Xiao term it, serves also as a constraint or limiting factor on the rhetor's use of invention. In this way, Garrett and Xiao bring together the seemingly incommensurate positions argued by Consigny and Vatz.

Their primary departure from standard treatments of situational theory, however, is in the centrality of the audience. Bitzer acknowledges the existence of the audience, but only as a facilitator: that which can effect positive modification of the exigence. This passive/active role is accepted by Vatz; indeed, his focus on the speaker's power of invention renders the audience virtually invisible. By locating the source of invention *and* constraint in the audience, Garrett and Xiao reinvigorate the notion of audience, making it a central player in a "dynamic tension." Thus, this essay moves us beyond arguments over the facticity and determinism of the exigency to a more organic notion of the rhetorical act.

Benoit in his 1994 essay argues that by failing to assimilate the criticisms of Bitzer's model into our "understanding of the nature of rhetoric," the field has allowed the situational perspective to "shape our conception of rhetoric" and to influence our understanding of rhetorical invention.[90] Benoit's recommendation, as noted in the introduction to the present discussion, is that critics and theorists should overlay Kenneth Burke's notion of scene and purpose onto Bitzer's ideas of exigence and constraints.

Benoit believes that Burke's notion of ratios is a superior vehicle for understanding the genesis of rhetorical action because it allows consideration of all the significant components: act, scene, agent, agency, or purpose. Furthermore, as the relationships can be reversed, there are as many as twenty possible combinations from which to examine discourse. In contrast, Bitzer accounts only for situation (which Benoit equates to "scene"); Bitzer's harshest critic, Vatz, also presents a flawed analysis with his emphasis on the agent. Benoit's position is that neither emphasis is sufficient to explore all discourse.

This is certainly the case, as no single theory can stand up under the burden of accounting for the endless variation in human discourse. To expect it to do so is unrealistic. Thus, while Benoit is correct in his particular concern, it is difficult to see how adding the Burkean schema to Bitzer's theory improves the situation. Burke's theories are certainly sufficient to stand alone and are not enhanced by the addition of Bitzer's ideas. The addition of Vatz's insistence on invention as the key to rhetorical action does not result in a synthesis. Indeed, Benoit does not appear to extend Bitzer's conception; rather (despite his claim to the contrary), he seeks to replace it with Burke's. His complaint seems to be that rhetorical scholars have not listened to Bitzer's critics, that situational language is too firmly ensconced in the critical lexicon, and that Burke, not Bitzer, provides the superior framework for viewing rhetorical action.

Yet, there must be a reason that so many scholars have essentially ignored the arguments against situational theory. Burke's ideas have been around longer than Bitzer's; Burke himself is revered as a philosopher, theorist, and critic. Nevertheless, the terminology of the pentad has not entered the critical lexicon as has the vocabulary of the rhetorical situation. Perhaps we have not fully appreciated the dynamism of Bitzer's notions; it would appear that the audience of rhetorical critics and theorists has "authorized" the critical frame introduced by Bitzer while simultaneously embracing other perspectives as appropriate.

Smith and Lybarger also reject Benoit's claims, arguing instead that the situational model should be reconstructed by infusing the notion of exigence with a greater understanding of perception and institutional forces.[91] In this, they echo some of the commentary that has preceded them. "Our project reconstructs Bitzer's notion of exigence and offers it as the primary locus of critical inquiry because it transcends, . . . as we shall show, speaker's purpose, audience, perception and scene."[92]

The authors spend some time discussing responses to Bitzer's theory and describe Bitzer's own attempts to refine it. While they see the work of prior critics as loosening "the determinism inherent in Bitzer's model" and Bitzer's own refinements as moving the model "toward postmodern conceptions," nevertheless, they write, Bitzer "retained the linear causality of his 1968 theory."[93] What is most significant to Smith and Lybarger, however, is that Bitzer, in his refinements, opened the door to a more complex view of perception and situation, particularly through his addition of interest to the complex of situation. After noting the revision that Bitzer offered in 1980 (pragmatic influences that determine the degree of an audience's felt interest and factors that predict the response of the audience to an exigence), Smith and Lybarger test the revised model against the antidrug speeches of President George Bush.[94]

Following their examination of exigences, audiences, and constraints, Smith and Lybarger conclude that the model has strengths in organizing critical assessments; "on the other hand, it was necessary to reconstruct Bitzer's model so that it could be used to deal with questions of perception and postmodern fragmentation of public discourse and audience."[95] They continue: "While we retain Bitzer's superstructure from 1968 in terms of exigence, audience, and constraints, and incorporate his notions of 'factual condition,' 'audience response,' and 'felt interest' from 1980, our postmodern reconstruction of Bitzer's model looks very different than what he intended and what has traditionally been used for situational criticism. Exigences are not always objective and publicly available; they may be created by the rhetor."[96]

As a result of their analysis, Smith and Lybarger recommend a number of modifications to Bitzer's theory. They eliminate the notion of the "controlling exigence"; reorient the model to account for multiple exigences, multiple audiences, and the plethora of constraints imposed on, or derived from, any situation; open the model to close readings, reconstructions of texts, and ideological critiques; and finally, facilitate ideological criticism by turning some of the model's major questions around.[97] "By serving as an organizing meta-approach which generates questions that push critics toward more complete criticism, the revised model facilitates a multiperspectival approach. It allows critics to talk across theories while encouraging more complete and enduring criticism in the postmodern age."[98]

This essay is one of the most useful in assessing situational theory and its evolution. By reviewing previous commentary as part of a dynamic process, Smith and Lybarger emphasize the process of theory development from initial offering, through criticism and commentary, to modification and expansion. Rhetorical theories are not born whole, to be accepted or rejected, but must grow out of a continuous process of testing and modification to reflect changes in discursive practice and advances in our understanding of the rhetorical act.

The difficulty that plagues much of the comment on, and criticism of, Bitzer's theory is its apparent insistence that the theory stand or fall as Bitzer presented it. The strength of Smith and Hunsaker's treatment is that they not only assess the theory in its own right and in combination with previous commentary but also take the further step of testing the results of that commentary against a recent discursive campaign. Finding the recent formulation wanting, Smith and Lybarger then offer further modifications that will adapt the theory to the rhetorical situation that they discover.

Thus, Bitzer's theory proves to be more malleable and more resilient than many may have believed. Its strength appears twofold. First, the substance of the ideas rang true in such a way that the basic concepts were accepted into the rhetorical lexicon almost without hesitation. The quibbles were over features of those concepts, such as the nature of exigence, whether it was determinative, the role of invention, and so on. The actual existence of exigence was not challenged, nor was the overarching concept of a rhetorical situation.

So the question that remains is the degree to which one who offers a theoretical construct "owns" that construct and the extent to which the theory, once placed into the public domain, becomes the property of those who inhabit the particular domain of which it is a part. Early critics seem to have wanted Bitzer to improve on, or embellish, his theory when that should have been the responsibility of critics, who, in testing the theory against actual discursive and rhetorical practice, would bolster, modify, extend, and thereby improve the situational theory and its ability to grant us insight into human communication.

Yet, some of the early critics did that, and Smith and Hunsaker's generous reading of others shows how even those who sought to discredit the theory provided useful considerations for future iterations to take into account. Surely, in his insistence on the primacy of invention, Vatz forced us to consider the creativity of the rhetor in addressing situational exigences and constraints. Many false starts were made, such as suggestions that we substitute *topoi* for exigences; nevertheless, we have gradually come to a greater understanding of the role of situation and its power as an explanatory construct.

RHETORIC AND PUBLIC KNOWLEDGE

Finally, while it is curious that Bitzer seemed to have so much difficulty articulating his theory in terms of real discursive practice in real rhetorical situations, one aspect of his work has been overlooked to date.[99] In 1978 Don Burks published a collection that included the text of a lecture that Bitzer had delivered at Purdue University.[100] In "Rhetoric and Public Knowledge," delivered after the 1968 publication of the theory of situation and before the 1980 publication of the "modifications," Bitzer explicates his understanding of the role of the public in rhetorical practice.

By "the public" Bitzer does not mean the audience, although the audience for rhetorical discourse may overlap with the public. Rather, Bitzer has in mind something more akin to Perelman's notion of the "universal audience."[101] Bitzer is speaking of those who "authorized" the sentiments in the Declaration of Independence, that is, those who understood and assented to the arguments embedded in that document.[102] "A public is a community of persons who share conceptions, principles, interests, and values, and who are significantly interdependent. This community may be characterized further by institutions such as offices, schools, laws, tribunals; by a duration sufficient to the development of these institutions; by a commitment to the well-being of members; and by a power of authorization through which some truths and values are accredited."[103]

Public knowledge, in Bitzer's construction, "may be regarded as a fund of truths, principles, and values which could only characterize a public," while a public that possesses this knowledge "is made competent to accredit new truth and value and to authorize decision and action."[104] In this scheme, rhetoric "generates truths and values previously unknown to a public, gives voice to interests and principles whose locus is a public, serves as an instrument with which to test public truths and values and to select and justify public means and ends."[105]

Read as part of the theory of situation, Bitzer's ideas on the public, public knowledge, and the role of rhetoric shed additional light on the working of that theory. It tells us where notions of exigence come from in Bitzer's formulation. Exigences are not simply created by the rhetor but are recognized and authorized by the public. Thus, the fears of critics such as Vatz are allayed, for it isn't the mechanistic process of event followed by response that he and others describe. Rather, the public, through what Bitzer terms its "wisdom," acknowledges the existence of an exigence that demands a response.

Nor does this reading vitiate the notion of invention. The rhetor who perceives an exigence can still urge it on the public, but only the public will determine whether it is a true exigence with a fitting response. Countless numbers of politicians have urged problems and solutions on the public to no avail. Perhaps the Clinton impeachment is a case in point, where congressional Republicans attempted to convince the public—and, hence, enough Democrats—that the president's behavior constituted a sufficient exigence to remove him from office; the public rejected that notion. Of course, there is always the possibility of the charlatan or the evil ruler; a study of Hitler's Germany reveals that possibility. Even in this case the generative exigence was real; Germany's economy was in shambles following the peace treaties enforced after World War I. The historical public was led astray; the broader public, created by the exigence of the war and the discovery of the Holocaust, condemned Hitler's "solution."

This reading of the *komplekt*, the "set," of Bitzer's work also reveals the broader role of concepts such as "fitting response" and "interest." It accounts for perception. It even elevates the notion of *differance* espoused by Biesecker, for Bitzer acknowledges the existence of multiple publics, as well as the fluidity of publics that are created and pass out of existence. Finally, a comprehensive reading of Bitzer discloses the source of his own perception that exigences are real, existing in the phenomenological world or material world. In our post-modern world, we acknowledge that perceptions often create realities, though they may exist only for us. By extension, if the public perceives an exigence, that exigence assumes a reality that subsumes individual perception into a sort of mass fantasy (à la Bormann), and it becomes real in the sense that it must be responded to.

Jim A. Kuypers in his 1997 book, *Presidential Crisis Rhetoric and the Press in the Post–Cold War World*, provides some insight into how a blend of situation and public knowledge might work as a critical construct.[106]

In his analysis of three crises facing the Clinton administration (North Korea, Bosnia, and Haiti), Kuypers argues that the end of the Cold War has altered the rhetorical situation significantly. During the Cold War years, the metanarrative that formed the heart of U.S. foreign policy provided the situational boundaries within which presidential rhetoric operated. In the absence of that lens, presidential crisis discourse is significantly altered, as the chief executive searches for a new theme to inform U.S. actions abroad. "Crisis rhetoric is about the creation of stable contextual frames through which to view the event and justify any action taken in response to the event. As an interanimation of text and context occur, the situational elements combine either to effect a stable frame or to modify a frame in some way. As a frame stabilizes, the president will find increased freedom to pursue his present course of action and increased limits on courses for new action."[107] As Kuypers notes, the Cold War metanarrative was part of the public consciousness, the public knowledge of this country and its people. The demise of the Cold War has altered that knowledge, changing the rhetorical situation and creating a perceptual vacuum that leaves political leaders searching for new inventional resources in which to ground foreign policy initiatives. Without the unifying theme of the Cold War, the context and, therefore, public perception are unstable, making it more difficult for the president to engage foreign policy exigences with a "fitting response" that is perceived as such.

In sum, then, only by viewing the whole, rather than focusing on its parts, can one apprehend the flexible, yet comprehensive nature of Bitzer's theory of situation and appreciate its resilience and its explanatory power, for if the public does not acknowledge or cannot be led to acknowledge the existence, in a particular instance, of an exigence-situation-response pattern, one can surely question whether rhetorical discourse has occurred.

NOTES

1. Lloyd F. Bitzer, "The Rhetorical Situation," *Philosophy and Rhetoric* 1 (1968), 1–14. This definition can be found on page 6.

2. Ibid., p. 7.

3. See, for example, K. E. Wilkerson, "On Evaluating Theories of Rhetoric," *Philosophy and Rhetoric* 3 (1970), 82–96; Richard E. Vatz, "The Myth of the Rhetorical Situation," *Philosophy and Rhetoric* 6 (1973), 154–161.

4. William L. Benoit, "The Genesis of Rhetorical Action," *The Southern Communication Journal* 59:4 (Summer 1994), 342–355.

5. Craig R. Smith and Scott Lybarger, "Bitzer's Model Revisited," *Communication Quarterly* 44:2 (1996), 197–213.

6. In fairness, it should be noted that not all commentaries were negative and that those that were positive or neutral are also reviewed in this essay. Interestingly, Bitzer generally fared better with philosophers who commented on his ideas than he did with rhetoricians.

7. This bibliography is certainly not exhaustive, however. In doing the research for the present chapter, I became even more aware of the extent to which Bitzer's terminology and his ideas have permeated the lexicon of criticism. It is impossible to include every essay or dissertation that used Bitzer's theoretical concepts as a foundation for the author's own ideas. Nevertheless, this bibliography should prove useful to someone interested in the body of Bitzer's work. Credit for the early work on this bibliography

should go to Dr. Carl Cates of Valdosta State University, who, as a doctoral student at Florida State University, compiled a bibliography of work by and about Bitzer for a seminar.

8. Walter Fisher's ideas on a narrative paradigm for rhetorical discourse were similarly the target of refutation when they were first published. Like Bitzer's, Fisher's ideas have become part of the lexicon of criticism and theory; however, unlike Bitzer's, Fisher's theoretical progeny have modified and extended his initial ideas.

9. Wilkerson, "On Evaluating Theories of Rhetoric."

10. Ibid., p. 82.

11. Ibid.

12. Ibid., p. 83.

13. Ibid., p. 84.

14. Ibid.

15. Richard L. Larson, "Lloyd Bitzer's 'Rhetorical Situation' and the Classification of Discourse: Problems and Implications," *Philosophy and Rhetoric* 3 (1970), 165–168.

16. Ibid., p. 165.

17. Ibid., p. 166.

18. Ibid.

19. This essay is not entirely critical of Bitzer's ideas; Larson points out that "Bitzer's article, . . . calls attention to what seemingly unrelated instances of discourse have in common, and helps differentiate rhetorical from non-rhetorical discourse more deftly than we have done before" (p. 168).

20. Walter R. Fisher, "A Motive View of Communication," *Quarterly Journal of Speech* 56 (1970), 131–139.

21. See Ibid., footnote 1, p. 131.

22. Ibid., p. 132.

23. Cf. Bitzer, "The Rhetorical Situation," p. 58.

24. Fisher, p. 132.

25. See Ibid., p. 139 and note 8.

26. Robert Wayne Norton, "The Rhetorical Situation Is the Message: Muskie's Election Eve Television Broadcast," *Central States Speech Journal* 22 (1971), 171–178. Norton notes that he is using " 'message' . . . in the same spirit that Marshall McLuhan employs it. 'Message' is defined as the change of scale or pace or pattern that introduces itself into human affairs" (p. 171).

27. Arthur B. Miller, "Rhetorical Exigence," *Philosophy and Rhetoric* 5 (1972), 111–118.

28. Ibid., p. 116.

29. Of course, some exigences cannot themselves be modified, and the best that one can hope for is the modification of perceptions of the exigence. In this vein, deciding that unemployment could not be eliminated, economists developed the notion of "hardcore" unemployed, so that full employment no longer meant that everyone was employed but that all those who were actively seeking work had a job.

30. Bitzer, "The Rhetorical Situation," p. 6.

31. Ralph J. Pomeroy, "Fitness of Response in Bitzer's Concept of Rhetorical Discourse," *Georgia Speech Communication Journal* 4:1 (1972), 42–71.

32. Ibid., p. 46.

33. Ibid., p. 47.

34. Ibid., p. 51.

35. Ibid.

36. Ibid., p. 52.

37. Ibid.

38. Vatz.

39. Ibid., p. 157.

40. Ibid., p. 160.

41. Ibid.

42. Kathleen Hall Jamieson, "Generic Constraints and the Rhetorical Situation," *Philosophy and Rhetoric* 6:3 (1973), 162–170.

43. Although Bitzer's discussion of public knowledge was not published until 1978, it clearly informs his understanding of the rhetorical situation.

44. Jamieson, p. 163.

45. Scott Consigny, "Rhetoric and Its Situations," *Philosophy and Rhetoric* 7:3 (1974), 175–186.

46. Bitzer, "The Rhetorical Situation," p. 5.

47. Consigny, p. 177.

48. Bitzer, "The Rhetorical Situation," p. 5.

49. Jamieson, pp. 163–164.

50. One might well argue that President Bill Clinton found himself in a unique and incoherent rhetorical situation during the scandal-plagued months of 1998. Without the tradition of rhetorical form to rely on, he stumbled and regained his composure only when he reframed the situation in terms of the duties of his office. One can only hope that Clinton has not established a new genre of presidential discourse.

51. Alan M. Rubin and Rebecca Boring Rubin, "An Examination of the Constituent Elements in a Presently-Occurring Rhetorical Situation," *Central States Speech Journal* 26 (1975), 133–141.

52. Gerald D. Baxter and Bart F. Kennedy, "Concrescence and the Rhetorical Situation," *Philosophy and Rhetoric* 8:3 (1975), 159–164.

53. Ibid., p. 162.

54. Ibid.

55. Ibid.

56. Ibid., p. 163.

57. David M. Hunsaker and Craig R. Smith, "The Nature of Issues: A Constructive Approach to Situational Rhetoric," *Western Journal of Speech Communication* 40 (1976), 144–156.

58. John H. Patton, "Causation and Creativity in Rhetorical Situations: Distinctions and Implications," *Quarterly Journal of Speech* 65 (1979), 36–55.

59. To the contrary, as I note earlier, what Bitzer seeks to do is note the infinite variety of human responses to rhetorical situations that share a structural or procedural commonality (described as the relationships among exigence, rhetor, audience, and fitting response), but nothing more.

60. Patton, p. 44.

61. David S. Kaufer, "Point of View in Rhetorical Situations: Classical and Romantic Contrasts and Contemporary Implications," *Quarterly Journal of Speech* 65 (1979), 171–186.

62. Ibid., p. 186.

63. "The Forum," *Quarterly Journal of Speech* 66 (1980) 85–95.

64. Tompkins, p. 85.

65. Tompkins, p. 86.

66. *QJS* [Tompkins], p. 87.

67. *QJS* [Patton], p. 89.

68. *QJS* [Bitzer], p. 90.

69. *QJS* [Bitzer], p. 93.

70. J. Robert Cox, "Argument and the 'Definition of the Situation,' " *Central States Speech Journal* 32 (1981), 133–141.

71. Alan Brinton, "Situation in the Theory of Rhetoric," *Philosophy and Rhetoric* 14:4 (1981), 234–248.

72. Ibid., p. 235.

73. Ibid., p. 236.

74. Ibid., p. 244.

75. "The Forum," *Quarterly Journal of Speech* 67 (1981), 93–101.

76. Halford Ross Ryan, "*Kategorica* and *Apologia*: On Their Rhetorical Criticism as a Speech Set," *Quarterly Journal of Speech* 68 (1982), 254–261.

77. Carolyn R. Miller, "Genre as Social Action," *Quarterly Journal of Speech* 70 (1984), 151–167.

78. Ibid., p. 155.

79. Ibid., p. 156.

80. Ibid., p. 161.

81. Kenneth Burke, *Permanence and Change* (Indianapolis: Bobbs-Merrill, 1965).

82. Miller, p. 160.

83. Robert J. Branham and W. Barnett Pearce, "Between Text and Context: Toward a Rhetoric of Contextual Reconstruction," *Quarterly Journal of Speech* 71 (1985), 19–36.

84. Marilyn J. Young and Michael K. Launer, *Flights of Fancy, Flight of Doom: KAL 007 and Soviet–American Rhetoric* (Lanham, MD: University Press of America, 1988). See also Marilyn J. Young and Michael K. Launer, "KAL 007 and the Superpowers: An International Argument," *Quarterly Journal of Speech* 74 (August 1988), 271–295.

85. Young and Launer, *Flights of Fancy*, pp. 20–22.

86. Barbara Biesecker, "Rethinking the Rhetorical Situation from within the Thematic of *Differance*," *Philosophy and Rhetoric* 22 (1989), 110–130. Reprinted in John L. Lucaites, Celest Michelle Condit, and Jolly Caudill, *Readings in Rhetorical Theory*, (New York: Guilford Press, 1999).

87. Biesecker, p. 243.

88. Mary Garrett and Xiaosui Xiao, " 'The Rhetorical Situation' Revisited," *Rhetoric Society Quarterly* 23:2 (1993), 30–40.

89. Ibid., pp. 30–31.

90. Benoit, p. 343.

91. Smith and Lybarger, pp. 197–213.

92. Ibid., p. 198.

93. Ibid., pp. 200–201.

94. Ibid., p. 202.

95. Ibid., p. 209.

96. Ibid.

97. Ibid., p. 210.

98. Ibid.

99. For example, critics such as Tompkins and Vatz objected that Bitzer's examples were "trivial." There is some truth to that claim, and Bitzer's inferred refusal to frame his ideas in terms of contemporary examples—or even historical ones beyond the Kennedy eulogies—was frustrating. While it is true that examples such as the "moon is made of cheese" illustrate the point, they do little to reveal how the concepts that Bitzer is discussing will work when applied to complex-rhetorical situations such as those found in the political arena. Perhaps he, too, thought that it was the responsibility of critics to refine his ideas by applying them to real-world examples.

100. Lloyd Bitzer, "Rhetoric and Public Knowledge," in Don Burks (ed.), *Rhetoric, Philosophy, and Literature: An Exploration* (West Lafayette, IN: Purdue University Press, 1978), 67–94.

101. Chaim Perelman and L. Olbrechts-Tyteca, *The New Rhetoric: A Treatise on Argumentation*, John Wilkinson and Purcell Weaver, trans. (Notre Dame, IN: University of Notre Dame Press, 1969), 31–35.

102. Bitzer, "Public Knowledge," pp. 86–87.

103. Ibid., p. 68.

104. Ibid.

105. Ibid.

106. Jim A. Kuypers, *Presidential Crisis Rhetoric and the Press in the Post–Cold War World* (Westport, CT: Praeger, 1997).

107. Ibid., p. 195.

BIBLIOGRAPHY

Baxter, Gerald D., and Bart F. Kennedy. "Concrescence and the Rhetorical Situation." *Philosophy and Rhetoric* 8:3 (1975), 159–164.

Benoit, William L. "The Genesis of Rhetorical Action." *The Southern Communication Journal* 59:4 (Summer 1994), 342–355.

Biesecker, Barbara. "Rethinking the Rhetorical Situation from within the Thematic of *Differance.*" *Philosophy and Rhetoric* 22 (1989), 110–130. Reprinted in Lucaites, Condit, and Caudill, *Readings in Rhetorical Theory*, 1998.

Bitzer, Lloyd F. "Political Rhetoric." In Dan D. Nimmo and Keith R. Sanders (eds.), *Handbook of Political Communication*. Beverly Hills, CA: Sage, 1981, 225–248.

Bitzer, Lloyd F. "Functional Communication: A Situational Perspective." In Eugene E. White (ed.), *Rhetoric in Transition: Studies in the Nature and Uses of Rhetoric*. University Park: Pennsylvania State University Press, 1980, 21–38.

Bitzer, Lloyd F. "Rhetoric and Public Knowledge." In Don Burks (ed.), *Rhetoric, Philosophy, and Literature: An Exploration*. West Lafayette: Purdue University Press, 1978, 67–94.

Bitzer, Lloyd F. "The Rhetorical Situation." *Philosophy and Rhetoric* 1 (1968), 1–14.

Branham, Robert J., and W. Barnett Pearce. "Between Text and Context: Toward a Rhetoric of Contextual Reconstruction." *Quarterly Journal of Speech* 71 (1985), 19–36.

Brinton, Alan. "Situation in the Theory of Rhetoric." *Philosophy and Rhetoric* 14:4 (1981), 234–248.

Consigny, Scott. "Rhetoric and Its Situations." *Philosophy and Rhetoric* 7:3 (1974), 175–186.

Cox, J. Robert. "Argument and the 'Definition of the Situation.'" *Central States Speech Journal* 32 (1981), 133–141.

Fisher, Walter R. "A Motive View of Communication." *Quarterly Journal of Speech* 56 (1970), 131–139.

"The Forum." *Quarterly Journal of Speech* 67 (1981), 93–101.

"The Forum." *Quarterly Journal of Speech* 66 (1980), 85–95.

Garrett, Mary, and Xiaosui Xiao. "'The Rhetorical Situation' Revisited." *Rhetoric Society Quarterly* 23:2 (1993), 30–40.

Hunsaker, David M., and Craig R. Smith. "The Nature of Issues: A Constructive Approach to Situational Rhetoric." *Western Journal of Speech Communication* 40 (1976), 144–156.

Jamieson, Kathleen Hall. "Generic Constraints and the Rhetorical Situation." *Philosophy and Rhetoric* 6:3 (1973), 162–170.

Kaufer, David S. "Point of View in Rhetorical Situations: Classical and Romantic Contrasts and Contemporary Implications." *Quarterly Journal of Speech* 65 (1979), 171–186.

Kuypers, Jim A. *Presidential Crisis Rhetoric and the Press in the Post–Cold War World.* Westport, CT: Praeger, 1997.

Kuypers, Jim A., Marilyn J. Young, and Michael K. Launer. "Of Mighty Mice and Meek Men: Contextual Reconstruction of the Iranian Airbus Shootdown." *Southern Communication Journal* 59:4 (1994), 294–306.

Larson, Richard L. "Lloyd Bitzer's 'Rhetorical Situation' and the Classification of Discourse: Problems and Implications." *Philosophy and Rhetoric* 3 (1970), 165–168.

Miller, Arthur B. "Rhetorical Exigence." *Philosophy and Rhetoric* 5 (1972), 111–118.

Miller, Carolyn R. "Genre as Social Action." *Quarterly Journal of Speech* 70 (1984), 151–167.

Norton, Robert Wayne. "The Rhetorical Situation Is the Message: Muskie's Election Eve Television Broadcast." *Central States Speech Journal* 22 (1971), 171–178.

Patton, John H. "Causation and Creativity in Rhetorical Situations: Distinctions and Implications." *Quarterly Journal of Speech* 65 (1979), 36–55.

Pomeroy, Ralph J. "Fitness of Response in Bitzer's Concept of Rhetorical Discourse." *Georgia Speech Communication Journal* 4:1 (1972), 42–71.

Rubin, Alan M., and Rebecca Boring Rubin. "An Examination of the Constituent Elements in a Presently-Occurring Rhetorical Situation." *Central States Speech Journal* 26 (1975), 133–141.

Ryan, Halford Ross. "*Kategorica* and *Apologia*: On Their Rhetorical Criticism as a Speech Set." *Quarterly Journal of Speech* 68 (1982), 254–261.

Smith, Craig R., and Scott Lybarger. "Bitzer's Model Revisited." *Communication Quarterly* 44:2 (1996), 197–213.

Vatz, Richard E. "The Myth of the Rhetorical Situation." *Philosophy and Rhetoric* 6 (1973), 154–161.

Wilkerson, K. E. "On Evaluating Theories of Rhetoric." *Philosophy and Rhetoric* 3 (1970), 82–96.

Young, Marilyn J., and Michael K. Launer. *Flights of Fancy, Flight of Doom: KAL 007 and Soviet–American Rhetoric.* Lanham, MD: University Press of America, 1988.

Index

"Second Persona, the," 265, 267 n.4, 268–
    269 nn.37, 62
Shaw, George Bernard, 7, 34–35, 65
    n.11, 145
Skinner, B.F., 128, 131
Smith, Bromley, xviii
Sophists, 10–11
The South, myths of, 146–153
Speech Monographs, 56, 62, 103, 105,
    167
St. Augustine, xviii, 19, 87
Swarthmore College, 19, 24, 26 n.6

Talon, Omer, 109
Tapia, John, xix, 103
"Time Marches On," 50, 65 n.38
Tompkins, Phillip K., 286–288, 300 n.99
Topoi, 112, 165, 283, 294
Trueblood, Thomas C., 33, 38–39, 43, 64
    n.5

University Radio Committee, 47, 52
Utterback, William E., xv, 10–12

Vatz, Richard E., 280–282, 285, 287–
    288, 292, 294, 295, 300 n.99

Wallace, Karl R., 26 n.9, 56, 94 n.2, 118
    n.3, 139 n.7

Wander, Phillip, xvii
Weaver, Andrew T., 49, 57, 66 n.39
Weaver, Richard, 153
Webster, Daniel, 37, 80, 85–86, 96–97
    n.33, 98 n.67, 182, 191, 257–258, 263,
    271 n.104
Wells, H.G., 35, 65 n.11
White, Eugene, 134, 275
Wichelns, Herbert A., x, xii, xv, 10–13,
    15–16, 19, 24, 26 n.2, 28 n.50, 48, 58,
    75, 78, 82, 95 n.10, 97 n.50, 105, 130–
    131, 235, 246, 251
Wilkerson, K.E., 276–277
Willis, Edgar E., 55–56, 66 n.52
Wilson, Woodrow, 37, 88, 191
Winans, James Albert, xv, xviii, 5, 10,
    12, 14, 17–18, 26 n.12, 42, 44, 57, 95–
    97 nn.10, 14, 50, 105–107, 131
Windt, Theodore Otto, Jr., 26 n.10, 73,
    94–95 nn.2, 5
Wisconsin, University of, 61, 126, 177–
    178, 188, 235, 276
Woolbert, Charles Henry, xv, 6–9, 12,
    14, 17, 21, 26, 27 nn.16, 27, 97 n.58,
    131

Yancey, William, 49
Yeager, Willard Hayes, 48, 65 n.20
Young, Marilyn J., 275, 299 n.84, 301
"Young turks," 10

About the Editors and Contributors

MOYA ANN BALL is Associate Professor of Speech Communication at Trinity University, San Antonio. As well as chapters and articles, she has authored one book, *Vietnam-on-the-Potomac*. Her research focuses on the Vietnam decision-making activities of Presidents Kennedy, Johnson, and Nixon and their advisers.

THOMAS W. BENSON is the Edwin Erle Sparks Professor of Rhetoric at Penn State University. He is the author or editor of ten books and over 100 journal articles, chapters, and reviews. He is former editor of *Communication Quarterly* and *Quarterly Journal of Speech*. His primary research interest is rhetorical criticism.

HENRY L. EWBANK, JR. is a distinguished and prolific scholar whose publications span four decades. His most recent work has dealt with the courtesy manuals of the early American Republic. A longtime member of the faculties of Purdue and Arizona, he is a professor emeritus and an independent scholar living in the Catalina Mountains in Arizona.

FRED J. KAUFFELD is Professor of Communication Arts at Edgewood College in Madison, Wisconsin. He has edited and written essays dealing with rhetorical criticism, rhetorical theory, and argumentation.

ANDREW KING is Professor and Chair of the Department of Communication Studies at Louisiana State University. He has authored two previous books—*Power and Communication* and *Postmodern Political Communication*. He is the former editor of the *Quarterly Journal of Speech* and the *Southern Communi-*

cation Journal. Professor King's academic interests lie in the areas of communication and power, and medieval and Renaissance rhetorical theory.

JIM A. KUYPERS is Senior Lecturer and Director of the Office of Speech at Dartmouth College. He has authored *Presidential Crisis Rhetoric and the Press in a Post–Cold War World* and *Media Manipulation of Controversial Issues* (forthcoming). He is a former editor for the *American Communication Journal.* His research interests include political communication, metacriticism, and the moral/poetic use of language.

JOHN H. PATTON is Associate Professor of Communication and a Fellow of Newcomb College, Tulane University, New Orleans. He has authored twenty articles in communication and interdisciplinary journals and has contributed chapters to several volumes on public address. His research interests focus on the rhetoric of civil rights, the rhetoric of the American presidency with an emphasis on the Carter administration, and rhetoric and performance in Caribbean cultures.

KURT RITTER is Professor of Speech Communication at Texas A&M University. He is the author of two books and twenty book chapters and articles on American political rhetoric. His research interests include political speechwriting, political campaign speeches and debates, and presidential rhetoric.

JOHN E. TAPIA is Professor at Missouri Western State College. He has authored four books. His research interests include the relationship between culture and rhetorical theory and practice. Currently, he is working on a book tentatively entitled *The Thirty-Six-Hour President.*

THEODORE OTTO WINDT, JR. is professor emeritus at the University of Pittsburgh. He is the author of numerous articles dealing with presidential rhetoric, political communication, rhetoric of cynicism, and the history of the Cornell School of Rhetoric. His books include *Presidents and Protestors: Political Rhetoric in the 60s, Cold War as Rhetoric: 1945–1950, Presidential Rhetoric: 1961–Present,* and *Rhetoric as a Human Adventure: A Short Biography of Everett Lee Hunt.*

MARILYN J. YOUNG is Professor of Communication at Florida State University. She has authored two books, *Flights of Fancy, Flight of Doom: KAL 007 and Soviet-American Rhetoric* and *Coaching Debate.* Her research interests are in argumentation, rhetorical theory and criticism, and political (particularly international) rhetoric, especially the development of political language and argument in newly emerging democracies.